CHALLENGING THE STATUS QUO

Studies in Critical Social Sciences Book Series

Haymarket Books is proud to be working with Brill Academic Publishers (www.brill.nl) to republish the *Studies in Critical Social Sciences* book series in paperback editions. This peer-reviewed book series offers insights into our current reality by exploring the content and consequences of power relationships under capitalism, and by considering the spaces of opposition and resistance to these changes that have been defining our new age. Our full catalog of *SCSS* volumes can be viewed at https://www.haymarketbooks .org/series_collections/4-studies-in-critical-social-sciences.

CHALLENGING THE STATUS QUO

Diversity, Democracy, and Equality in the 21st Century

EDITED BY
DAVID G. EMBRICK
SHARON M. COLLINS
MICHELLE S. DODSON

Haymarket Books
Chicago, IL

First published in 2018 by Brill Academic Publishers, The Netherlands.
© 2018 Koninklijke Brill NV, Leiden, The Netherlands

Published in paperback in 2019 by
Haymarket Books
P.O. Box 180165
Chicago, IL 60618
773-583-7884
www.haymarketbooks.org

ISBN: 978-1-64259-065-4

Distributed to the trade in the US through Consortium Book Sales and
Distribution (www.cbsd.com) and internationally through Ingram Publisher
Services International (www.ingramcontent.com).

This book was published with the generous support of Lannan Foundation and
Wallace Action Fund.

Special discounts are available for bulk purchases by organizations and
institutions. Please call 773-583-7884 or email info@haymarketbooks.org for
more information.

Cover design by Jamie Kerry and Ragina Johnson.

Printed in United States.

10 9 8 7 6 5 4 3 2 1

Library of Congress Cataloging-in-Publication Data is available.

We dedicate this book to all of the young scholars of diversity who will take the field to the next level and beyond.

∵

Contents

PART 7
Meanings, Discourse, and Identity

Acknowledgments

This tome of 18 chapters could not have been possible without the support of David Fasenfest, who received us with endless patience, and followed up with a ton of gentle prodding. He never minced his words, yet at the same time, he let us know that what we had was something that needed to be published and put out there. For that, and much more, we are ever grateful. I started out my academic career, many moons ago, hoping that I could one day meet and even work with one of my idols, Sharon M. Collins. Here we are, many years later, and I call myself fortunate to call Sharon my friend—we have shared ideas, collaborated and published on a number of projects, and we have even found time here and there to talk smack about people. It has been a great journey. Michelle S. Dodson stepped in when we needed additional help on this project and we appreciate all her hard work on this book. Finally, we could not have done any of this without our many colleagues who contributed chapters for this book—they stuck with us through thick and thin and we appreciate them so much.

David G. Embrick

I gratefully acknowledge our series editor David Fasenfest for his valuable support as we developed this project and for spurring us on. I also want to acknowledge my co-editor David G. Embrick for his energy, sharp intellect, and vision, which guided this volume from start to finish. I thank our authors without whom this project could not exist. Finally, I want to acknowledge the family of scholars who devote their research to the sociology of diversity and inequality. I hope this project will contribute to new insights in the evolution of the field.

Sharon M. Collins

Working on this book has been a privilege. I am forever grateful to Dr. Embrick and Dr. Collins for inviting me to be a contributing editor. I have truly enjoyed being able to work with each contributing author. The work that they have created for this volume is insightful. As for my own contribution, I would also like to thank Dr. Barbara Risman and Dr. R Stephen Warner for their invaluable feedback and guidance.

Michelle S. Dodson

Map and Tables

Map

Tables

Notes on Contributors

Sharla Alegria
is an Assistant Professor of Sociology at the University of California, Merced. She studies persistent inequalities where individuals and organizations reject discrimination. Her research has received funding from the National Science Foundation and the Anita Borg Institute. Her work has appeared in edited volumes and academic journals including *Ethnic and Racial Studies,* the *International Journal of Gender, Science, and Technology*, and *Proceedings of the National Academy of Science.*

Joyce M. Bell
holds a Ph.D. in sociology from the University of Minnesota and a BA in Spanish and sociology from the University of St. Thomas. She is an Upward Bound & McNair Scholars alumna and is a past recipient of both the Minnesota and National TRIO Achievers Awards. Bell has also been awarded fellowships from Harvard University's Radcliffe Institute for Advanced Study, the National Humanities Center, the University of Connecticut Humanities Institute, and the University of Pittsburgh Humanities Center. She is the 2016 recipient of the American Sociological Association Section on Racial & Ethnic Minorities Distinguished Early Career Award.

Ellen Berrey
is Assistant Professor of Sociology at the University of Toronto and an affiliated scholar of the American Bar Foundation. Her work examines the crossroads of culture, racism, law, organizations, and inequality. Her research interests include the symbolic politics of diversity, college admissions, university and corporate diversity policies, employment discrimination law, political activism, and social entrepreneurship. She is the author of *The Enigma of Diversity: The Language of Race and the Limits of Racial Justice* (University of Chicago Press, 2015), which demonstrates that the organizational push for diversity has watered down the more radical fight for African American equality and liberation. The Enigma of Diversity was awarded the 2016 Herbert Jacob book prize of the Law and Society Association as well as book awards from the Sociology of Law and Sociology of Culture sections of the American Sociological Association. Her second book, with Robert Nelson and Laura Beth Nielsen, *Rights on Trial: How Workplace Discrimination Law Perpetuates Inequality* (University of Chicago Press, 2017), shows how anti-discrimination litigation reinscribes the very hierarchies that civil rights laws were created to dismantle. Her research

also has been published in *American Behavioral Scientist, Annual Review of Law and Social Science, City & Community, Contexts, Critical Sociology, Du Bois Review, Law & Society Review, Sociological Science,* and *Theory & Society.* For more, visit: ellenberrey.com and rightsontrial.com.

Enobong Hannah Branch

is the Associate Chancellor for Equity & Inclusion and the Chief Diversity Officer for UMass-Amherst. She provides strategic leadership for campus diversity efforts to promote an institutional culture that values and supports diversity, equity, and inclusion. Dr. Branch is also an Associate Professor of Sociology with research interests in race, racism, and inequality; intersectional theory; work and occupations; and diversity in science. Her book *Opportunity Denied: Limiting Black Women to Devalued Work* (Rutgers University Press, 2011) provides an overview of the historical evolution of Black women's work and the social-economic structures that have located them in particular and devalued places in the U.S. labor market. She is the editor of *Pathways, Potholes, and the Persistence of Women in Science: Reconsidering the Pipeline* (Lexington Books, 2016) which outlines the inadequacy of the pipeline metaphor in understanding the challenges of entry and persistence in science and offers an alternative model that better articulates the ideas of agency, constraint, and variability along the path to scientific careers for women. Dr. Branch is also the founding editor of the Rutgers University Press Book Series, *Inequality at Work: Perspectives on Race, Gender, Class and Labor.* She is author of several articles published in the *International Journal of Gender, Science, and Technology; The Sociological Quarterly; Sociological Perspectives; Social Science History; Journal of Black Studies; and Race, Gender, & Class.* Her current stream of research funded by the National Science Foundation, investigates rising employment insecurity in the post-industrial era through the lens of racial and gender inequality.

Meghan A. Burke

is Associate Professor of Sociology at Illinois Wesleyan University, where her areas of specialty are social theory and race. Dr. Burke is the author of two books, one about race and whiteness in racially diverse Chicago neighborhoods, and one about the race, gender, and class dynamics in the Tea Party. She recently guest edited a special issue of *Sociological Perspectives* on "New Frontiers in the Study of Colorblind Racism," for which she also earned an American Sociological Association Fund for the Advancement of the Discipline grant. Her third book, on colorblind racism, is forthcoming from Polity Press. Dr. Burke has published articles in *The Sociological Quarterly, Sociological Perspectives, Critical Sociology,* and *Teaching Sociology,* among others, and in 2016 earned the Midwest Sociological Society Early Career Scholarship Award. On her campus, Meghan co-developed and directs the Engaging Diversity pre-orientation program, a 3-day intensive program for incoming white students to deeply consider white privilege and antiracism so that they can work as partners for social and racial justice. This program has been featured in *The Chronicle* and *Inside Higher Ed.* Dr. Burke was also named 2013 Professor of the Year and 2016 Advisor of the Year by IWU students, and among Nerd Wallet's 40 under 40: Professors Who Inspire.

Sharon M. Collins

is Associate Professor Emerita of Sociology. Dr. Collins works as an independent consultant on issues of diversity and expert witness on workplace discrimination. She has published numerous articles on workforce discrimination, diversity and affirmative action have earned her national recognition in her field. Her book, *Black Corporate Executives,* was published by Temple University Press (1997). She has been featured in *Black Enterprise* magazine, *The Chicago Tribune, U.S. News and World Report, Newsweek* magazine, as well as by the British Broadcasting Corporation, and WGN television. She has spoken widely on the issue of affirmative action and workforce diversity at various organizations, including Russell Reynolds Associates, the American Bar Association, Stanford University Law School, University of Michigan, The Winthrop-King Institute on French and U.S. Anti-Discrimination Policy, Northwestern University Kellogg School of Management, the Harvard Business School, and the National Black MBA Association.

Tiffany Davis

is an Associate Professor of Sociology at Chicago State University and she received her Ph.D. in Sociology from the University of Minnesota. Her current research deals with issues of race, class and higher education. Her work has two primary foci in this area. First, she explores the best teaching practices for students who attend Minority Serving Institutions (MSI), as much existing research focuses on pedagogical practices as they apply to students attending mainstream universities. Second, she is currently working to extend the literature on racial attitudes through her research on African Americans' perspectives of race and race relations in which she explores some of the patterns that exist by social location. Much of her previous work focuses on the racialization of first-generation Mexican migrants and how their experiences with racism and discrimination in the U.S. cause them to re-conceptualize how they view themselves in "American" racial terms and in relation to other racial groups.

Michele C. Deramo

is Assistant Provost for Diversity Education in the Office for Inclusion and Diversity at Virginia Tech. Her scholarly interests include diaspora studies, auto-ethnography and arts-based methodologies, and critical feminist pedagogy. She is currently working on a series of images that re-appropriate Italian folk charm through a feminist lens.

Michelle S. Dodson

is a Ph.D. student at Loyola University Chicago. Her focus is in the sociology of religion with an emphasis on multiracial congregations. She is also the Assistant Pastor at New Community Covenant Church- Bronzeville. Michelle has been dedicated to the work of racial justice for nearly two decades and has helped to plant two intentionally multiracial churches in Chicago.

David G. Embrick

holds a joint position as Associate Professor in the Sociology Department and African Studies Institute at the University of Connecticut. Prior to UConn, he spent a decade at Loyola University Chicago as faculty in the Sociology Department. He received his Ph.D. from Texas A&M University in 2006. He is a former American Sociological Association Minority Fellow; Past-President of the Southwestern Sociological Association; past Vice President of the Society for the Study of Social Problems; and current President of the Association for Humanist Sociology. In addition, Dr. Embrick serves as the Founding Co-Editor of *Sociology of Race and Ethnicity;* Founding Book Series Editor of *Sociology of Diversity*, with Bristol University Press; and Founding Book Series Co-Editor of *Sociology of Race and Ethnicity*, with University of Georgia Press.

Edward Orozco Flores

is an Associate Professor of Sociology at the University of California Merced. He is author of *God's Gangs: Barrio Ministry, Masculinity, and Gang Recovery* (New York University Press, 2013).

Emma González-Lesser

received her B.A. in Women's and Gender Studies from Simmons College and her M.A. in Sociology from the University of Connecticut. She is currently pursuing her Ph.D. in Sociology at the University of Connecticut, with a focus on race and ethnicity. Her specific research interest lies in the constructions of Jewishness within the black/white racial schema in the United States. Her work appears in *Sociological Inquiry*, as well as in multiple encyclopedia articles, and she has often presented her research and organized panels at the Eastern Sociological Society's annual meetings. She is the managing editor for *Humanity and Society*, and guest editor of a special issue for the same journal. She has received grants from El Instituto at the University of Connecticut, and a pre-doctoral fellowship from the Sociology department at the University of Connecticut.

Bianca Gonzalez-Sobrino

is a Ph.D. candidate in Sociology at the University of Connecticut and the Jackie McLean fellow at the University of Hartford. Her work focuses on (1) the construction of racial threat, (2) racial identity formation, and (3) the Puerto Rican diaspora. Her work has appeared in *Critical Sociology, Sociology Compass*, and *Sociology of Sport Journal*. She also is co-guest editing a special issue on the mechanisms of racialization beyond the Black/White binary for the journal *Ethnic and Racial Studies*. She is currently working on her dissertation, which looks at how Puerto Ricans in Hartford understand racial threat, and how they interact with other racial groups living in the city. The project uses ethnographic, interview, and content analysis data to explore micro-level processes of racial threat.

Matthew W. Hughey

is Associate Professor of Sociology at the University of Connecticut. Professor Hughey's research concentrates on (1) white racial identity; (2) racialized organizations; (3) mass media; (4) political engagements; (5) science and technology, and; (6) public advocacy with racism and discrimination. He has published over eighty scholarly articles and seven books, some of which include *The White Savior Film: Content, Critics, and Consumption* (Temple University Press, 2014), which received the 2016 Outstanding Publication Award from the Southwest Sociological Association and *White Bound: Nationalists, Antiracists, and the Shared Meanings of Race* (Stanford University Press, 2012), which was co-winner of the Eduardo Bonilla-Silva Outstanding Book Award from the Society for the Study of Social Problems in 2014. He has been honored with the 2014 Distinguished Early Career Award from the American Sociological Association's Section on Racial and Ethnic Minorities and the 2016 Mentoring Excellence Award from the Society for the Study of Symbolic Interaction. Professor Hughey has also served as visiting fellow and/or professor at the Center for the Study of Ethnicity and Race at Columbia University (New York, USA), The University of the Free State (South Africa), Warwick University (England), and Trinity College-Dublin (Ireland). He is also currently a Research Associate for the Centre for Critical Studies in Higher Education Transformation at Nelson Mandela Metropolitan University (South Africa).

Paul R. Ketchum

is an Assistant Professor in the College of Professional and Continuing Studies at the University of Oklahoma. His career examining the impact of systemic racial bias on juveniles began as a practitioner working as a co-department chair and academic decathlon coach at Los Angeles Unified School District. This led to later work as a residential treatment center program director at Los Hermanos Residential Treatment Center as well as work within the Texas Juvenile Detention system and the Texas Prison system. These experiences led him to his doctoral studies in Race and Ethnic Relations and Criminology at Texas A&M University. Today, Dr. Ketchum teaches courses in Race, Minority, and Ethnic Groups, Race and Crime, Juvenile and Criminal Justice, Social Problems, and Sociology at the University of Oklahoma. For the past six years, he has conducted mixed methodology, grant funded, research for the Oklahoma Office of Juvenile Affairs studying disproportionate minority contact (DMC) in the state.

Megan Klein

is a Ph.D. candidate in Sociology at Loyola University Chicago. She also holds a M.A. in Anthropology from the University of Illinois at Chicago, a M.A. in Spanish from Loyola University Chicago, and undergraduate degrees in Spanish and Management from the University of Iowa. She is an Assistant Professor of Sociology and Anthropology at Oakton Community College. Her dissertation research which examines how lived experience shapes the meaning of integration is supported by grants from the Illinois State Historical Society and the Black Metropolis Research Consortium at the University of Chicago. She was awarded Loyola University's Presidential Medallion in 2016.

Michael Kreiter

is a Sociology Ph.D. student at Kent State University, where he was also awarded a Master's degree in 2017. He graduated from Boise State University in 2014, earning degrees in both Multi-Ethnic Studies and Sociology. He has a forthcoming, coauthored publication in *Issues in Race & Society* that qualitatively looks at how suicide has been presented in Ebony magazine over the last five decades. He is currently completing work on two projects related to race and criminal justice in the United States. The first project examines ecological factors that partially explain the overrepresentation of African Americans among those killed by police. The second project is a study of authorship for books in the nascent genre of children's literature written about an incarcerated parent.

His dissertation work is in the field of cultural sociology, in which he studies the cultural reproduction of inequality through content analysis of speculative fiction novels and through ethnographic study of fandom conventions.

Marie des Neiges Léonard

is a sociologist and a race scholar. She has published numerous essays pertaining to the question of race in France, particularly race as a social category and its notable absence in the French census. The author has also published essays related to the significance of race and racism to explain the development of the 2005 riots. Such scholarship already focused on the question of race as a socially constructed category central to the debates in France demonstrates the natural progression of the author's expertise and research.

Wendy Leo Moore

is an Associate Professor in the Department of Sociology at Texas A&M University. A sociologist and lawyer, her work focuses on the provocative intersections of race, the law, and legal institutions. She received her Ph.D. in Sociology from the University of Minnesota (2005) and her J.D. from the University of Minnesota Law School (2000). Dr. Moore is the author of the award-winning book *Reproducing Racism; White Space, Elite Law Schools and Racial Inequality* (Rowman & Littlefield Publishers, 2007), which analyzed the intersections of educational and legal institutional contexts and explicated a theory of white institutional space. She has published a wide range of articles that explore this and other areas concerning racism and law, and is currently working on her second book tentatively entitled *The Legal Alchemy of White Domination*, an examination of the parallel discursive tactics utilized by the U.S. Supreme Court to stall progress toward racial equity in the post-Civil War era and the post-Civil Rights era.

Shan Mukhtar

is Assistant Director of the English as a Second Language Program at Emory University. Dr. Mukhtar earned her M.A. and Ph.D. in Race and Ethnic Studies from Emory University in 2014, where she was Imagining America Fellow, Laney Diversity Fellow, and received the Bobby Paul Mentoring Award for her work in undergraduate education. Her interdisciplinary research on diversity formation draws from sociological, American Studies, and educational studies, with a focus on diversity discourse in higher education in the post-civil rights era. Recent publications include "Looking Ahead: Envisioning the Next Generation of Civic Work" (*Diversity & Democracy*, Volume 18, No. 1, Winter 2015) with B. Kliewer, and the forthcoming "From Olympic Dreams to College

Dorms: Atlanta's Universities and the Formation of a New South Global Imaginary," in *Race and Place in Two Cities*, R. Jackson, ed. Dr. Mukhtar's current research examines the relationship between community-engaged pedagogy and the development of critical, multilingual literacies among English language learners.

Antonia Randolph
is an Assistant Professor of Sociology in the Department of Behavioral Sciences at Winston-Salem State University. Her research and teaching interests include diversity discourse in education, multicultural capital, non-normative black masculinity, and the production of misogyny in hip-hop culture. Her book *The Wrong Kind of Different: Challenging the Meaning of Diversity in American Classrooms* (Teachers College Press, 2012) examined the hierarchies elementary school teachers constructed among students of color. She has also published in *Sociology of Race and Ethnicity*, *The Journal of Contemporary Ethnography*, and *The Feminist Wire*. Her current book project, *That's My Heart*, examines portrayals of intimate relationships and of black inner-life in hip-hop culture.

Victor Erik Ray
is an assistant professor of Sociology at the University of Tennessee Knoxville. His academic work examines race and gender discrimination in organizations and has been published in the *Ethnic and Racial Studies, Annals of the American Academy of Political and Social Science, The Journal of Marriage and Family* and *Contexts*. His commentary has appeared at *Newsweek, Boston Review, Gawker,* and *Inside Higher Ed.*

Arthur Scarritt
is Professor and Chair of the Department of Sociology at Boise State University. He studies how people challenge and reproduce the multiple forms of inequality that make up their daily lives. His book, *Racial Spoils from Native Soils: How Neoliberalism Steals Indigenous Lands in Highland Peru* (Lexington Books, 2015), investigates the history, structure, and culture of anti-indigenous racism in Peru. This ethnography details the lived experiences of how the economic development infrastructure systemically deepens racial oppression. And it explains how neoliberal reforms seize even the most marginal indigenous lands in order to create new feudal-like forms of indigenous dependence and precarity. His ongoing work, from which the contribution in this current volume comes, investigates how intersecting forms of oppression make (particularly white) college students embrace a model of higher education based on steeply rising tuition and declining educational returns. But this research also reveals

counter hegemonic student practices that challenge our truly dangerous state of higher education.

Laurie Cooper Stoll

is Associate Professor of Sociology and the founding Director of the Institute for Social Justice at the University of Wisconsin-La Crosse. Her research focuses on social inequalities in institutions, particularly education. She is the author of *Race and Gender in the Classroom: Teachers, Privilege, and Enduring Social Inequalities* (Lexington Books, 2013), which explores the paradoxes of education, race, and gender, as she follows eighteen teachers carrying out their roles as educators in an era of "post-racial" and "post-gender" politics. *Race and Gender in the Classroom* was awarded the 2015 American Sociological Association Section on Race, Gender, and Class Distinguished Contribution to Scholarship Book Award. Dr. Cooper Stoll has published articles in peer-reviewed journals such as *Race, Ethnicity and Education, Violence Against Women, Journal of Latinos and Education, Computers in Human Behavior, Qualitative Sociology, Research in Social Movements, Conflict, and Change,* and *Review of Religious Research.* She also recently contributed a chapter to the book *Intersectionality in Education Research,* edited by D.J. Davis, R.J. Brunn-Bevel and J.L. Olive (Stylus Publishing, 2015).

PART 1

Introduction

∵

Diversity: Good for Maintaining the Status Quo, Not So Much for Real Progressive Change

David G. Embrick

1 Introduction

What is Diversity? Depending on who you ask, it is an opportunity (Herring 2009), an emotion (Bell and Hartmann 2007), an enigma (Berrey 2015), a regime (Thomas 2017), a bargain (Warikoo 2016), an excuse to shut down progressive programs (Collins 2011), and even a pervasive ideology that informs our understanding of how society works to some degree (Embrick 2011, 2010, 2008). In general, however, diversity is a curious concept. It is ubiquitous yet ambiguous. The term diversity has become so common in our society that we are shocked when we do not find it embedded in some form or fashion in our institutions. Equally, we are shocked when folks seem to not be "down with the problem" and express worry or discontent with the concept of diversity. Walter B. Michaels (2006:12) noted that diversity "has become virtually a sacred concept in American life today;" no one is really against it, yet folks tend to have different degrees of enthusiasm toward the concept. Yet, diversity is a term that excels in its lack of specificity; it embraces a laundry list of possible interpretations that make it completely useless for adequately (if at all) dealing with current and existing issues of inequality (Embrick 2011). Bell and Hartmann, in their 2005 American Sociological Review article, contend that while the term evokes feelings of happiness—what they have labeled as "happy talk,"—it is also a confusing idea. Ellen Berrey (2015) concludes that the language of diversity limits racial progress; it reaffirms the status quo in many ways. Natasha K. Warikoo, in her 2016 book, *Diversity Bargain*, argues that in many elite institutions of higher education, diversity has become a bargaining chip for many white students who are ambivalent about diversity and only support diversity programs so long as it benefits them. On a more macro-level scale, Embrick (2011) suggests that more than just language, ideas, and policies, diversity has become a central ideology in how we understand life in America. More than colorblind racism or genderblind sexism, diversity ideology allows many of us, on the one hand, to acknowledge that we still have work to do before we can get to the promised land of equality, equity, and equal opportunity. On the other hand, diversity ideology allows us the freedom to be at ease when we tell ourselves that we are not bigots or sexists because at least we admit that racism, sexism, and other inequalities still exist. We just need more time to right the wrongs. Today, few words generate uplifting feelings like the word diversity. We use the word all of the time, in our personal and collective commitment to embrace diversity. But what exactly does diversity mean? More importantly, how do social science and other scholars examine diversity as it relates to our institutions and our lives within the context of these institutions. In this edited book, we showcase 18 chapters that represent new and innovative research in 6 institutional areas of interest. Our contributors highlight new ideas and cutting-edge research in what we believe is fast becoming an area of scholarship to look out for in the near future: the sociology of diversity (and inclusion).

2   Why this Book: The Need for Unpacking Diversity

When we (David G. Embrick and Sharon S. Collins) first began our collaborative journey in 2008, we realized that while there was a trend in how diversity was being used, social science research still lagged behind understanding what was really going on with the diversity phenomenon. Our initial attempts to showcase the best of what sociologists had to offer in this area led to us guest editing a special issue in volume 37 of *Critical Sociology*. Since that time, we have witnessed a regime change in US politics that has all but perfected the ability to take us back to the Jim Crow era with its crass and overt racism, sexism, classism, and homophobia, all the while espousing deep admiration for both diversity and inclusion. Indeed, the past couple of years in US history has been a time of devastation, depression, escapism, and mass consumption. Police violence toward brown and black bodies continue to increase despite the many voices that protest; victims include, among many, Alton Sterling who was killed by Baton Rouge, Louisiana police officers for selling CDs outside of a local convenience store, and Philando Castile who was killed by a St. Anthony Minnesota police officer for having a broken taillight and for obeying a request from the officer to show his license and registration. Globally, the killing spree in Nice, France, the social unrest in Istanbul, Turkey, and the attacks in Dhaka, Bangladesh, mark just a handful of not so distant events of which we should all be concerned. Alarmingly, as these horrific events unfolded, Poke'mon Go was released worldwide and within a matter of a few days manages to increase Nintendo's market value by over US$9 billion. Some see a correlation between violence and gaming, the latter fueled by a desire to escape, even momentarily, from real-world stresses. Perhaps it is not so much a means to escape, as it is a way to deny our responsibilities to be socially and politically responsible citizens. Through it all, though, was the idea that diversity, in some form or fashion, might be one solution to the many problems that ail our societies. The fact that diversity also saw a backlash from certain segments of the population (namely, though not exclusively, right-wing populists and Nazi extremists, for example), only adds to the confusion regarding how this concept has been used, and what it actually means to be "diverse" or have more "diversity."

2.1   The Meaningless Meanings of Diversity and Inclusion

Ask a group of people to define the word diversity and you are likely to get multiple interpretations. What does it mean to be diverse or to achieve diversity? Does it mean we should accept the racial and ethnic differences of others? Does it mean we should be tolerant of class differences? Perhaps it refers to gender, sexual orientation, age, culture, religion, political affiliation, disability, phenotype, or any number of other so-called differences between people who live in our society? Increasingly, diversity has come to refer to all of the aforementioned ways that people identify themselves or from which people are identified by others.

Since I began studying diversity over a decade and a half ago, the number of categories that has been included, in various ways, under the broad umbrella of diversity has expanded dramatically. Now, in addition to race, class, and gender, for example, we might hear folks talking about clothing and hair styles, pet ownership, personality types, and ideas and perspectives, to name just a few. Such broad defining of diversity has led many organizations to claim their commitment to diversity through diversity workshops that teach tolerance or through the creation of support groups that celebrate peoples' differences in marital status, for example. In addition to the celebration of difference that is attached to the word diversity is the underlying perception of equality that is often associated with the term. That is, the term diversity elicits the assumption that not only are many institutions interested in the differences between people, but, that somehow, institutions that are interested in promoting diversity are also interested in issues of justice and equality. However, in reality, rarely do we find variety or equality in our U.S. institutions, both at the lower and middle strata, but especially at the upper administrative levels.

2.2   Diversity, Inclusiveness, and Pulling the "We Are All in this Together" Card

Diversity by itself has no substance. It is an empty shell. Over the past few decades, the broadening of the term diversity has helped to minimize or erase specific issues of oppression and inequality that have long plagued our society, in favor of a "we are all in this together" approach. This idea of togetherness in spite of our oppressive history and our current state of hostilities toward women, non-heterosexuals, and brown and black folks does little more than shut down important conversations about real change for the greater good of society. We see colleges and universities doing this all the time as they respond to persistent racial issues on their campuses by ignoring the issues of "race" and "racism" in favor of a we are all in this together approach. Responses to anything other than the enchanting chants of inclusion bring backlash that questions one's motive for even bringing up the dreaded word race.

We see this in other areas, as well—for example, the All Lives Matter countermovement, that has become increasingly popular among whites, although we see other racial and ethnic groups participate also to a lesser degree. There is a seemingly alarming parallel between diversity and the All Lives Matter movement. Proponents of All Lives Matter are quick to argue that the Black Lives Matter movement is inherently racist because it is only concerned with blacks in the United States. All Lives Matter, in contrast, proposes to be more democratic and socially responsible because it is concerned with the lives of all people, not just blacks. The logic of All Lives Matter lies in its promotion as a diverse and inclusive group that does not discriminate against anyone. Herein lies the rub: There is no dispute that "all lives" matter, just as there is no dispute that we should strive to be a "diverse" and "inclusive" society. The reality is that in the United States, the treatment of blacks by police, educators, politicians, businesses, and society, in general, provides data that conclude some lives do matter more than others. When a white male terrorist murders a group of black churchgoers and is treated to a fast-food meal by police, yet a black male is killed by police for supposedly driving with a broken taillight, there should be no question that race still matters in America. Listening to All Lives Matter, however, one is led to believe either that race no longer matters (i.e., color-blind racism) or that race matters, but it is not just about being black or brown—white people suffer too.

Similarly, diversity ideology and diversity language allow us to minimize or shut down important conversations about racism, sexism, homophobia, or class. The lack of specificity allows us to pretend that we are concerned about equality, even as we continue to maintain the status quo. As diversity comes to represent more of the differences between people in society, less attention is paid to historical and persistent racial, ethnic, and gender discrimination in organizations, for example. For women and minorities, progressive steps to insure racial and gender justice have seemingly plummeted since the Civil Rights triumphs of the sixties. Thus, although there has been an increase in the rise of individual and organizational philosophy espousing diversity, there is also overwhelming data that suggest minorities and women are still unable to obtain opportunities or to achieve success at the same rates as their white male counterparts.

What, then, is the solution if diversity is not? I have argued elsewhere that we should stop using the term diversity (and its cousin term inclusion) in favor of specific issues that need to be addressed. Instead of suggesting that everything matters or that we should be concerned with more than just race matters or class matters, we need to keep our eyes on the prize by acknowledging and addressing issues of oppression that continue to hold ourselves and our organizations hostage. Being specific to one or two issues does not mean that we care less about other forms of inequality. In fact, I contend that it means we care more as we are able in the end to concentrate on making "real" changes. Like the All Lives Matter countermovement, diversity and inclusion are great for lip service about ending oppression and they certainly make us feel good about ourselves and the organizations in which we belong, but they do little but help to maintain the status quo.

3 What's in Your Wallet?

The chapters in this volume showcase the latest ideas and scholarship in the area of diversity and inclusion. Our contributors offer critical analyses on many aspects of diversity as it pertains to institutional policies, practices, discourse, and beliefs. Our edited collection is broken down into 18 chapters over 6 sections that cover: policies and politics; pedagogy and higher education; STEM; communities; complex organizations; and discourse and identity. Collectively, these chapters contribute to answering three main questions: (1) what, ultimately, does diversity mean; (2) what are the various mechanisms by which institutions understand and use diversity; and (3) and why is it important for us to rethink diversity?

The first set of chapters begin with Section 2: Policies, Politics, Practice, and Law. In this section, contributors examine how certain policies contribute to meaningless change or reaffirmation of status quo inequality in various institutions. The first two chapters by Sharon Collins and Ellen Berrey, respectively, provides the impetus for distinguishing between diversity (and inclusion) and affirmative action. Both note that one difference between the two can be found in their goal and rationale, as well as the historical context in which each of the terms emerged. The diversity umbrella is often more broad and more ambiguous. In Chapter 3, specifically, Berrey interrogates diversity in terms of its contributions to the conditions of inequality and exclusion on college campuses. In Chapter 4, Bell and Moore examine the role that the diversity rationale, and its concomitant abstract liberalistic frame, plays in shaping race-based higher education law and policy concerning racial equity. Kreiter and Scarritt, in Chapter 5, question how campus diversity engages with the neoliberalization of the university, i.e., creating a paradox of cutting resources to students while claiming to invest in multiculturalism.

Section 3 highlights two chapters on pedagogy and higher education. Chapter 6 by Davis, Moore, and Bell detail three experiences of educators who try to better understand how we, as scholars, can better teach about the socially constructed nature of race in meaningful ways. In Chapter 7, Shan interrogates the dual process by which "social, economic, and political forces" determine how diversity is institutionalized in higher education.

Chapters 8 and 9 are covered in the 4th Section. In Chapter 8, Leonard provides a critical overview of the different perspectives (from individual to structural level) that explain gender disparities in STEM disciplines. In Chapter 9, Branch contends that, absent external pressure, full participation of all U.S. workers in STEM work fades as a national priority—that the U.S., ultimately, is not concerned with long-term commitment to diversity.

The three chapters in the next section (by Dodson, Stoll and Klein, and Burke) examine diversity and communities in two ways: how white residents in "integrated" communities either use various colorblind racial frames similar to their white counterparts who live in segregated communities, or how liberals and progressives reproduces racism in their efforts to denounce it; and the specific factors that predict Black participation in churches.

Section 6, titled: Diversity and Complex Organizations, consists of three chapters. Contributors in this section examine, in detail, how the lack of racial diversity matters in the juvenile justice system (Chapter 13 by Paul R. Ketchum); the role of punitive empathy in terms of diversity in the military, particularly the racial and other mechanisms that suppress reports of discrimination in that institution (Chapter 14 by Victor E. Ray); and how anti-incarceration may extend racial inequalities from the for-profit sector to the non-profit sector (Chapter 15 by Edward Orozco Flores).

Our final Section—Meanings, Discourse, and Identity—concludes with three chapters that examine (1) on demand diversity—i.e., racial diversity and inequality in popular Netflix television serious (Chapter 16 by Gonzalez-Sobrino, Hughey, and Lesser); (2) how teachers create a market for diversity when they treat students of color as thought their racial and/or ethnic minority status was valuable and reward those students for that value (Chapter 17 by Randolph); and (3) the spectacle of volunteerism—i.e., specific programs that target African nations as sites for global learning and recipients of Western globalization (Chapter 18 by Deramo).

As noted previously, the contributors in this edited book represent some of the cutting-edge scholarship currently being done in the area of sociology of diversity. Our approach has been to assemble the latest research that contributes to better examining and understanding the concepts of diversity (and inclusion), specifically three main questions: (1) what, ultimately, does diversity mean; (2) what are the various mechanisms by which institutions understand and use diversity; and (3) and why is it important for us to rethink diversity? We hope you find the chapters as stimulating and though-provoking as we have.

References

Bell, Joyce, and Douglas Hartmann. 2007. "Diversity in Everyday Discourse: The Cultural Ambiguities and Consequences of 'Happy Talk.'" *American Sociological Review*, 72: 895–914.

Berrey, Ellen. 2015. *The Enigma of Diversity: The Language of Race and the Limits of Racial Justice*. Chicago, IL: University of Chicago Press.

Collins, Sharon M. 2011. "From Affirmative Action to Diversity: Erasing Inequality From Organizational Responsibility." *Critical Sociology*, 37 (5): 517–520.

Embrick, David G. 2011. "Diversity Ideology in the Business World: A New Oppression for a New Age." *Critical Sociology* 37: 541–556.

Embrick, David G. 2008. "The Diversity Ideology: Keeping Major Transnational Corporations White and Male in an Era of Globalization." In Globalization and America: Race, Human Rights & Inequality, edited by Angela Hattery, David G. Embrick, and Earl Smith. Lanham, MD: Rowman and Littlefield.

Embrick, David G., and Mitchell F. Rice. 2010. "Understanding Diversity Ideology in the United States: Historical and Contemporary Perspectives." In Diversity and Public Administration: Theory, Issues, and Perspectives (2nd ed.), edited by Mitchell F. Rice. Armonk, NY: M.E. Sharpe.

Herring, Cedric. 2009. "Does Diversity Pay?: Race, Gender, and the Business Case for Diversity." *American Sociological Review*, Vol. 74: 208–224.

Michaels, Walter B. 2006. *The Trouble With Diversity: How We Learned to Love Identity and Ignore Inequality*. New York, NY: Metropolitan.

Thomas, James M. 2017. "Diversity Regimes and Racial Inequality: A Case Study of Diversity University." *Social Currents*, online before print. DOI: 10.1177/2329496517725335.

Warikoo, Natasha K. 2016. *The Diversity Bargain: And Other Dilemmas of Race, Admissions, and Meritocracy at Elite Universities*. Chicago, IL: University of Chicago Press.

PART 2

Policy, Politics, and Practice

∴

CHAPTER 2

Diversity and Affirmative Action: A Closer Look at Concepts and Goals

Sharon M. Collins

1   Introduction

To most people affirmative action is a synonym for the entire range of recruitment and training programs that proactively increase the proportion of minorities and women who are underrepresented in high-paying jobs and in higher education. The term often refers to both voluntary and involuntary programs. This is because over time the term has been decoupled from the administrative apparatus that gave it power to achieve equal opportunity for all Americans. In retrospect we see that affirmative action is a formal national policy that emerged from legislative actions and judicial decisions and it is defined and enforced on that basis. In the context of employment, which is the subject of this paper, affirmative action is administered by the US Department of Labor and is a set of employer obligations tied to financial incentives. Their primary obligation is to assure equal job opportunity as stipulated in Executive Orders 10925 and 11246 to take affirmative action to safeguard nondiscrimination. These Executive Orders were issued first by President Kennedy and then by President Johnson to remedy the cumulative economic disadvantage faced by African Americans.

Administrative oversight of affirmative action requirements is the responsibility of the Department of Labor's Office of Federal Contract Compliance Programs (OFCCP). The mission of the OFCCP is to enforce employment obligations applicable to private enterprise as a condition of doing business with the federal government. For example, financial institutions that are federally insured, that operate as a fund depository, or act as an issuing agent of federal bonds are required by the federal government to have affirmative action programs. The construction industry relies heavily on federally guaranteed mortgages and other federally funded projects and is a second example of job settings that are covered. Aside from the financial and constructions industries, a large proportion of major manufacturers and retailers have federal (and also state and city) contracts to provide goods and services. Affirmative action requirements also exist for government contractors at the state and local level.

The potential to achieve fair employment in the US under the policy of affirmative action is expansive.

In theory, these programs could dramatically alter the workforce composition and the racial and gender bias that is entrenched in the occupational hierarchy.

For instance, Affirmative action requires organizations to eliminate unfair barriers to getting a job such to stop the use of unrelated job tests to make hiring decisions. Concrete hiring goals and new outreach efforts may also be required in order to expand the applicant pool to underrepresented minorities. An example of this would be making recruitment visits to predominately non-white college settings (i.e., HBCUs), and placing job ads in ethnic in addition to white media outlets. In the post-employment phase, affirmative action may include developing mentoring and job training programs all designed to increase minority retention and promotion. Not all employers are covered by federal affirmative action policy and uncovered employers typically do not implement these programs unless they are required by the court to do so.

A common misconception is that affirmative action addresses discrimination based on age or disability. However, discrimination falling within these categories is prohibited by the Age Discrimination in Employment Act (ADEA), the Americans With Disabilities Act (ADA), and the Rehabilitation Act. Further, Title VII does not address discrimination against lesbian, gay, bisexual, and transgender (LGBT) people, although attempts to amend Title VII or to enact new anti-discrimination legislation date back to 1975.

In education, affirmative action opens colleges and university admissions to qualified underrepresented minority groups who have been historically excluded from competition in the absence of the program. The effects of affirmative action in education and jobs are intertwined. Job gains among minorities are made possible by affirmative action programs that expanded admissions in colleges, law schools, business schools, medical schools, and elsewhere. The discussion in this article focuses on the history and effects of affirmative action (and diversity) in the workplace, not affirmative action in education.

2   The Backdrop

Affirmative action was the first federal policy to directly confront the reality that the US ideal of equal opportunity for all is deceptive and insufficient to address racial (and later gendered) economic differences. Indeed, the imbalance between the economic position of disadvantaged minorities and the rest of the nation derived primarily from their unequal positions in the labor market. One way to view the federal policy of affirmative action in employment (and education) is to see it as product of a new awareness in the US that race matters. In the forefront of the national consciousness was the recognition that social groups have differential power and that access to the American dream based on egalitarianism, individualism, and meritocracy is a substantively flawed ideal. In response to what the US Department of Labor termed the "Negro revolution" the initial aim of affirmative action policies was to "even the playing field" for African Americans.

Given the entrenched nature of race-based job discrimination and the escalation of black civil protest it is not surprising that between the 1940s and 1960s the passive (and inadequate) policy of equal employment opportunity evolved into a more aggressive strategy known as affirmative action. With varying degrees of effectiveness, since at least the 1940s executive orders have been issued and federal legislation enacted to prohibit discrimination based on race, gender and national origin. The first executive order issued by President Roosevelt was a direct response to A. Phillip Randolph's threat to bring 250,000 African Americans to march on Washington in order to force the President to enact civil rights legislation. In 1941 President Roosevelt issued Executive Order 8802 declaring an end to discrimination in the federal civil service and creating the Fair Employment Practices Committee (FEPC). The Order banned racial discrimination in any defense industry receiving federal contracts and pronounced, "there shall be no discrimination in the employment of workers in defense industries or government because of race, creed, color, or national origin." The order also empowered the FEPC to investigate complaints and take action against alleged job discrimination.

Throughout the 1940 and the 1950s Blacks' demands civil rights intensified as did federal efforts to address job discrimination and other forms of institutionalized discrimination. For example, extending the reach of the government beyond federal contractors in the defense industry, President Truman issued two executive orders to establish fair employment practices in all federal government agencies and to abolish discrimination in the armed forces. President Truman also established fair employment compliance procedures for government contractors. In the 1950s, President Eisenhower introduced The Civil Rights Act of 1957. The Act was largely voting rights legislation and in support of the Supreme Court decision in *Brown v Board of Education*, which ruled the "separate but equal" doctrine was unconstitutional. Although the Act was largely ineffective it symbolized greater federal willingness to write civil rights legislation and create enforcement mechanisms. This and previous Acts paved the way for more civil rights legislation, including the Civil Rights Act of 1964 (and also the Voting Rights Act of 1965, and the Housing Act of 1968.)

In 1961, Executive Order No.10925 directed government contractors to take "affirmative action to ensure that applicants are employed, and that employees are treated during employment, without regard to their race, creed, color, or national origin." The Executive Order also established the President's Committee on Equal Employment Opportunity, which is now known as the Equal Employment Opportunity Commission (EEOC.)

In 1965 nonviolent resistance-which had been the hallmark of the Black Civil Rights Movement—morphed into urban riots. President Lyndon Baines Johnson solidified the federal government's enforcement of antidiscrimination policy in employment and issued Executive Order 11246. Under this Executive Order the concept of "affirmative action" was used to guide the policy of the federal government. This Executive Order was essentially the same as that issued by President Kennedy in 1961 and required government contractors and subcontractors to take "affirmative action" to insure that applicants and employees were not discriminated against. In sum, over the course of the three decades, affirmative action evolved when federal employment polices relying on "good faith" efforts and "equal opportunity" proved to be ineffectual.

3   Affirmative Action Policy Enforcement

When Title VII was debated in Congress the evidence was clear that meaningful enforcement of fair employment laws would require direct governmental intervention.

Moreover, change would require virtually all major employers to be covered by the law. Based on companies' past poor performance, the premise of the law was that employers left to their own devises were unlikely to remove employment barriers to African Americans. On the contrary, they would staunchly maintain those very barriers to equal opportunity that in the 1960s jeopardized the well-being of the entire nation. Title VII therefore was endowed with a regulatory sphere that includes a vast array of employment settings and almost every area in which the federal government has responsibilities. As originally written Title VII applies to three categories of employers: (1) companies with 100 or more employees, (2) federal contractors with 50 or more employees, and (3) federal contractors or sub-contractors selling goods or services worth at least $50,000. The order currently in force requires firms with 15 or more employees that sell products to the federal government to establish and implement detailed plans for hiring women and under-represented minorities.

Title VII established the Equal Employment Opportunity Commission (EEOC) as the law's administrative agency. Initially, the Commission's effectiveness as an instrument for equal employment was constrained by a lack of enforcement power. This is because, responding to corporate interests, members of Congress limited the Commission's role to investigation, persuasion, and conciliation. However, Congress later granted the Commission the power to initiate litigation. This power made available to individual workers the ability to file job discrimination complaints and the private right to bring suit for job discrimination. Important here is that these rights made legal prohibitions against job discrimination enforceable for the first time in history (Hill 1977). Indeed, written affirmative action plans could be required by a court as a remedy for discrimination, although the EEOC does not monitor them.

In 1963, the Illinois Fair Employment Practices Commission assigned damages to the Motorola Corporation and ordered it stop using a biased test and to either stop testing or develop a test that was non-discriminatory (Hill 1977). Although the monetary award for damages was eventually rescinded, the ruling was considered an important precedent for lawsuits that followed (Hill 1977). In *Hall v Werthan Bag Corp.*[1] the district court upheld the right to bring class action suits. In *Quarles v Phillip Morris, Inc.*[2] the court ruled that Phillip Morris' assignment of black employees to departments with limited advancement potential was discriminatory. The court further required the company to adopt an affirmative action plan for interdepartmental transfer and promotion to eliminate this disadvantage.

Greggs v Duke[3] is a hallmark case in civil litigation charging job discrimination. The backdrop is this: Prior to July 1964, the Duke Power Company—as did most employers—had a longstanding policy of segregating black workers from white workers. This policy tracked each black worker into all-black labor classifications, which paid less than the all-white labor classifications. When Title VII made this practice illegal, Duke Power used tests as a biased surrogate to keep occupational segregation in place. Black applicants who wanted to work in formerly all-white classifications were required to pass two aptitude tests and prove that they had a high school diploma. Neither of these requirements measured an employee's ability to learn or perform the jobs.

Willie Griggs was the plaintiff who filed a class action lawsuit on his own behalf and on behalf of other black workers. Willie Griggs argued that the new rules constituted illegal discrimination because they had the effect of making

---

1   251 F. Supp. 184, 186 M.D. Tenn 1966.
2   279 F. Supp. 505 E.D. Va. 1968.
3   Griggs v. Duke Power Co., 401 U.S. 424 1977.

the vast majority of blacks ineligible for the better paying (white-only) jobs. The Supreme Court ruled in his favor and, in doing so, broadened the definition of discrimination under Title VII. A new theory emerged to acknowledge that Intentional discrimination mattered *and* that disproportionate impact—intentional or not—was a form of discrimination, and mattered as well. In this case, a seemingly neutral practice resulted in harsher treatment of members of a protected class (African Americans) and was deemed to be illegal discrimination under the law.

Discrimination lawsuits such as these may have made the EEOC the most publically recognized enforcement agency, but the Office of Federal Contract Compliance Programs (OFCCP) was arguably the more powerful of the two instruments of affirmative action, at least until the decade of 1980s. Initially, affirmative action put racial preference remedies and additional accountability measures in place. Employers were required to create hiring goals and timetables, which opponents of affirmative action quickly and erroneously termed "quotas."

The OFCCP enforces requirements that federal contractors identify, hire, and promote minorities and women in numbers roughly proportional to their availability in the labor market. The underlying premise of this requirement is that if employers acted in a non-discriminatory fashion, their work force would at some point reflect the composition of the populace that surrounded their establishments. Hiring criteria to guide the employment efforts of government contractors became the concrete standards and procedures that underpin the concept of affirmative action. The OFCCP is vested with the authority to withhold or withdraw federal funds from federal contractors if employers failed to meet or demonstrate a good faith effort in meeting these goals. The OFCCP is also vested with the power to award back pay.

The mandates of the OFCC played a key role in the transformation of the concept of affirmative action into a specific and accountable private sector employment practice. The OFCC issued Order No. 4 that obligated contractors to make detailed and extensive efforts to increase the employment of underrepresented minorities. Revised Order No. 4 added goals and timetables for women and specified in detail how contractors should analyze the utilization of minorities and women in order to comply with hiring standards. Under Revised Order No. 4, federal contractors also are obligated to submit a written "affirmative action plan" with numerical goals. As well, they were required to create timetables for achieving these goals for hiring and promoting women, blacks, and other designated minorities. However, systems of accountability have been persistently challenged as an affront to US individualism and merit—particularly the emphasis on achieving numerical results (Silberman 1977; Abram 1983; Roberts and Stratton 1995).

In 1967, the Office of Federal Contract Compliance (OFCC) began to impose affirmative action standards involving numerical goals at certain designated federal projects, such as during the construction of the Bay Area Rapid Transit system in the bay area of San Francisco, California (United States Commission on Civil Rights 1969). In 1969, the OFCC for the first time commenced proceedings to debar five contractors for noncompliance (United States Commission on Civil Rights 1969). These proceedings, however, were the exception. Enforcement actions were virtually nonexistent. The ultimate sanction of debarment was used less than 30 times (Leonard 1990).

Despite weak enforcement, private employers developed practices to satisfy their affirmative action compliance obligations. Hiring goals were rarely adhered to but companies that promised to increase black employment did increase it (Leonard 1990).

Employers' responses to federal mandates were adjudicated and the scope of affirmative action today is now accepted as a standardized set of practices (Edelman 1990; Dobbin et al. 1993). Among contemporary mid-and large sized employers, one would be hard pressed to find any that do not have EEO/AA offices or officers, do not have formal policy statements mirroring the language of EEO laws prohibiting discrimination, or lack mechanisms to create an EEO workplace (such as targeted recruitment procedures and training) (Duster and Wellman 1999).

4   Affirmative Action and Personnel Recruitment

The effect of affirmative action on corporate recruitment practices is an important component of its relative effectiveness. It is well documented that employers rely on the social networks of their current employees to fill job openings, and job-seekers use their networks to get a job (Holzer 1987, Kirschenman and Neckerman 1991, Braddock and McPartland 1987, Granovetter 1995, Reskin and McBrier 2000). The ability to get a job depends on who you know—social networks—as much as on what you know, that is, human capital (Lin 2001; Holtzer 1987; Topa 2001). Associating with "your own" and trying to help them is human nature, but whites are more likely to hold better-paying white collar and professional jobs that have the potential for advancement.

The American Values Survey (AVS 2013) finds that networks tend to be segregated by race and a large majority of whites (estimated at 75 percent) have entirely white social networks (also see Shrum et al. 1988; DiTomaso 2013). Racial segregation and segregated networks converge to recreate job applicant pools consisting of the same race and sex as existing employees. From a broad perspective, social reproduction in the job recruitment phase of employment underpins sex and race job segregation. Social reproduction and opportunity hording exclude women and minorities from better paying blue collar and white collar jobs with promotion ladders (Reskin and McBrier 2000; DiTomaso 2013). Affirmative action interrupted the cycle of exclusion associated with closed networks and in-group preference to narrow race and gender based employment gaps.

After the mid-1960s, companies consciously altered the recruitment process to expand the candidate pool, particularly for jobs in the professions and in management. By 1963 the New York Times reported, "Personnel officers are taking a new look at their recruiting methods and seeking advice from Negro leaders on how to find and attract the best-qualified Negroes" (Stetson, 1963, p. 1 as cited in Dobbin and Kalev 2013). The Bureau of National Affairs 1967 survey found 31 percent of leading employers created new recruitment systems for blacks between 1965 and 1967; more than half advertised through black civil rights organizations like the NAACP and the Urban League (Bureau of National Affairs, 1967, p. 1 as cited in Dobbin and Kalev 2013). General Electric was among the first high-tech companies to create support programs to increase their applicant pool of engineers. General Electric also began a summer job-training program for minorities, and funded minority scholarships at colleges and universities. Similarly, Continental Bank in Chicago set up an Inroads program to provide summer jobs for black college students to familiarize them with the banking industry. A black Northwestern student sponsored by the program became a first black in the bank's bond department.

Systematic recruitment at HBCUs took place for the first time in history. In 1965, Lockheed brought busloads of black college students from Tuskegee Institute in Alabama on recruitment visits (Mattison, 1965, pp. 151–152 as cited in Dobbin and Kalev 2013). The Chicago office of Arthur Andersen & Co., a Big 8 accounting firm in 1965 also began recruiting at HBCUs. The Chicago office of Touche Ross started recruiting at HBCUs in 1967 (Chicago Reporter 1975). IBM's programs for qualified employees from diverse of backgrounds is one illustration of the positive impact of affirmative recruitment and training. Results show a 170 percent increase in the share of minority executives at IBM—from 117 to 316 minority executives between 1996 and 2001 (Civil Rights Fact Sheet 2015).

Table 2.1 is based on a survey of HBCUs conducted by the labor economist Richard Freeman (1976:35). The table shows dramatically how corporate recruitment policies toward African Americans were transformed. Large employers very likely have affirmative action obligations and they shifted their recruitment to meet these obligations over the decade of the 1960s. In 1960 virtually no major white corporation made recruitment visits to historically black institutions. The lack of recruitment meant that college educated blacks were excluded from entering the private sector pipeline into entry level jobs

TABLE 2.1   Recruitment visits of representatives of corporations to predominantly black colleges and universities

College	Number of representatives of corporations interviewing job candidates		
	1960	1965	1970
Atlanta University	0	160	510
Howard	a	100	619
Clark	0	40	350
Alabama A&M	0	0	100
Alabama State	0	7	30
Hampton	20	247	575
Jackson State	a	a	280
Johnson C. Smith	0	25	175
Morehouse	a	a	300
Miles	0	12	54
Norfolk State	5	100	250
North Carolina A&T	6	80	517
Prairie View	a	a	350
Southern	0	25	600
Southern, New Orleans	0	5	75
Texas Southern	0	69	175
Tuskegee	50	85	404
Virginia State	0	25	325
Winston-Salem	a	a	25
Virginia University	5	25	150
Xavier	0	44	185
Average per school	4	50	297

a   Not available

Source: Survey and interviews conducted for *Black Elite* study in 1970. Richard Freeman 1976: 11

in management and the professions. But in 1965 about 50 visits by white corporations to black college campuses took place. By 1970, the average black college received campus visits from about 300 recruiters from various firms. Corporations shunned these college campuses before the 1960s but used them as a valuable resource for the recruitment of blacks by 1970.

5   Effects on Employment

In 1961, eight of the largest government contractors signed the "Plans for Progress", which called on employers to make voluntary efforts to extend equal employment opportunities to all Americans, regardless of race, ethnicity, or religion. More than 60,000 jobs were covered by that voluntary agreement. However, by the time Congress enacted Title VII of the 1964 Civil Rights Act protests by African Americans made the laissez-faire approach to employment equality unsustainable. The meaningful enforcement of Title VII of the Act would require a more activist federal intervention in hiring (Hill 1977). Even outside a legal framework Presidents Roosevelt, Kennedy and Johnson fully recognized the government's tremendous leverage over private sector employment because of contracting relationships. The United States Commission on Civil Rights (1969) estimated that federal contractors (businesses that that sell products and services to government agencies) employed one third of the nation's labor force and that a sizable proportion of the largest industrial employers were federal contractors. Thus, large segments of corporate America are financially linked to governmental agencies as a source of profitability. It is this part of the employment sector that came under scrutiny as described above. Facing the potential of huge financial penalties the corporate world almost overnight found ways to open job opportunities to created a new echelon of skilled and college educated blacks (Collins 1997), followed by women and other minorities. Thus, although affirmative action was not a full corrective to racial and gendered biases in corporate cultures and structures, it proved to be an effective way to get around them.

Affirmative action was under siege quickly for being politically unpopular, but for also for being ineffective as a policy for reducing levels of occupational inequality for targeted groups. However, minimizing the policy's role in the upward mobility of women and minorities—particularly the mobility of African Americans—is inconsistent with research. We know that affirmative action significantly improved several aspects of the labor market for college-educated blacks in the post-1960 period (Heckman and Payner 1989; Leonard 1982, 1984, 1990; Collins 1997). Moreover, gender and racial segregation declined after the

1970s when employers first adopted antidiscrimination programs (King 1993; Tomaskovic-Devey and Stainback 2007).

One case on point is the jump in the minority percent of officials and managers employed by Philip Morris. No minorities were employed in these jobs in 1969. In 1972, minorities filled 5.7 percent of these jobs. In 1985, 15.4 percent of the company's officials and managers were minorities. Apparently, the threat to withdraw contracts for non-compliance—coupled with the setting of hiring goals during compliance negotiations—were strong enough factors to alter private-sector employment practices (Leonard 1985). Heidrick and Struggles' 1979 survey of Fortune 500 companies found that 45 percent of survey respondents underwent compliance reviews and were threatened with contract ineligibility based on compliance issues (also see Braddock and McFarland 1987). Freeman (1985) finds that contractors that were reviewed did a significantly better job hiring protected groups than did non-reviewed contractors.

Using various enforcement mechanisms—such as compliance reviews and goal setting—affirmative action had the power to restructure personnel policies and interrupt systematic hiring bias. Comparative research during the 1970s on the impact of contract compliance in the white private sector found that government contractors increased the employment of black males significantly more than did non-government contractors (Ashenfelter and Heckman 1976; Heckman and Wolpin 1976). Ashenfelter and Heckman (1976) found that in the short run government contractors raised the employment of blacks relative to white males 3.3 percent more than non-governmental contractors. In the long run this effect was estimated to be 12.9 percent. Research on companies before the contracting compliance program was fully developed noted that government contracts are awarded to less-discriminatory firms (Heckman and Wolpin 1976) and that segregated white contractors are more likely to integrate than segregated white non-contractors (Ashenfelter and Heckman 1976).

Subsequent studies also find that federal contract compliance programs improved employment opportunities for African Americans and women (Citizen's Commission on Civil Rights 1984; Heckman and Payner 1989; Leonard 1982, 1985; Herring and Collins 1995). In their study of the South Carolina textile industry, Heckman and Payner (1989) isolated the specific effects of antidiscrimination laws from other programs and economic events that occurred at the same time and to reveal similar benefits. Leonard (1982) used establishment-level EEO-1 reports on more than sixteen million employees for 1974 and 1980 and establishment-level affirmative action compliance review reports for the period 1973 to 1981 to compare a matched sample of contractors with non-contractors. He found blacks' share of employment with government contractors grew significantly more than at non-contractor establishments. He also found that federal contract compliance programs substantially improved the employment opportunities for black men in particular. Black women were the last to benefit from federal affirmative action legislation (Leonard 1989). He also showed that affirmative action supported the post-civil rights elaboration of the black middle class by increasing the demand for black men in higher-paying occupations, i.e., white-collar jobs, relatively more than in blue-collar, operative, and laborer occupations. Herring and Collins (1995) analyzed the 1990 General Social Survey and a 1992 survey of Chicago adults and also found that affirmative action was associated with higher occupational prestige for African-Americans, and that its incremental effects on the income for racial minorities were substantial. Research conducted by the Citizens' Commission on Civil-Rights (1984) shows that women made greater gains in employment at companies doing business with the federal government, and therefore subject to federal affirmative action requirements, relative to other companies. Women's share of employment rose 15.2 percent at federal contractors, and only 2.2 percent elsewhere. The study also shows that federal contractors employed women at higher levels and in better paying jobs than other firms.

Legal scholar Derrick Bell's theory of interest convergence explains how affirmative action arose during the civil rights era as a response to the racial protests and converged with other interests that were differently motivated. Recent studies show that the effects of affirmative action and its organizational supports are most beneficial for white women, followed by back women. Black men benefit least (Kalev et al. 2006). Still, women of color lag far behind in employment (and education) and long-standing barriers to women remain pervasive (Federal Glass Ceiling Commission 1995). White men constitute a minority of the total work force (46%) but remain dominant in the top jobs in virtually every field (Federal Glass Ceiling Commission 1995).

In sum, affirmative action provided a protective umbrella under which minorities and women could achieve unprecedented access to higher paying professional and managerial jobs, although racial and gender gaps in occupational status and pay remain. Indeed, affirmative action requirements had the power to change entire industries. In 1978, the Labor Department's Office of Federal Contract Compliance (OFCCP) reviewed the employment practices of the five largest banks in Cleveland. Three years later, the percentage of women officials and managers at these institutions had risen more than 20 percent. When OFCCP first looked at the coal mining industry in 1973, there were no women coal miners. By 1980, 8.7 percent were women (Citizens' Commission on Civil Rights 1984).

Research on the impact of affirmative action finds that the program's effectiveness is linked to several conditions. The policy is most effective when the labor market is expanding (Leonard 1976–85), when companies assign responsibility for compliance to a manager (Kalev et al. 2006), when organizational sanctions associated with hiring are in place (Freeman 1976), when hiring goals are promised (Freeman 1976), and when corporate leadership is supportive. Most of these conditions have fluctuated over time and, except for the initial phases of implementation, rarely exist in the same historical period (Collins 1997).

6   Challenges to Affirmative Action

The Civil Rights Act of 1964 had to overcome the longest obstruction in Senate history (see Hill 1977). The federal government's ability to exercise the full power of the law to overcome institutionalized job discrimination against minorities and women was short-lived. As outlined in earlier sections of this chapter, between 1965 and 1973 major employers made strides to improve in the employment prospects of women and racial minorities, initially African American men. Yet, as federal efforts crystalized into patterns of labor market mobility for women and nonwhite workers resistance to the program crystalized as well in charges of "quotas" and "reverse (anti-white) discrimination." These terms were pointedly used against anti-bias remedies. Opponents of affirmative action continue to use these pejoratives in the present.

Legal challenges to affirmative action in employment were mounted during the 1970s but—relative to the drawbacks to affirmative action in education—the results seem more ambiguous. In 1979 a white employee of Kaiser Aluminum named Brian Weber brought an unsuccessful lawsuit alleging the company's affirmative action efforts to increase the proportion of blacks in a company training program violated Title VII. Weber argued that the race-conscious hiring should be prohibited or applied evenly, to blacks as well as to whites. The Supreme Court held that Kaiser's affirmative action was legal and permissible under the law and did not violate the legislative intent of Title VII, even if some qualified whites were disadvantaged. Soon after this ruling, the Supreme Court[4] made a very different determination. In this case, the Court ruled that white employees could not be laid off in favor of black employees with less seniority. The "last hired and first fired" effects of past discrimination against black candidates for firefighter jobs were not judged as legitimate shields against disproportionate black layoffs. By 1986, the Supreme

---

4   Firefighters Local Union No. 1784 v. Stotts, 467 U.S 561.

Court ruled that the school board's policy of protecting minority teachers by laying-off non-minority teachers regardless of seniority was unconstitutional, citing the burden imposed on innocent parties.[5]

In the 1980s, the Reagan Administration promoted a major reversal in equal employment opportunity and affirmative action policies. The Administration took the position that it "oppose[d] court-ordered and court-sanctioned racial preferences for non-victims of discrimination". The Administration also argued against the use of preferential treatment and "quotas." Seeking to end affirmative action as it had evolved since the Johnson administration, the core administrative components the program were challenged or gutted by the Reagan Administration through conservative court appointments, political hiring and firing decisions, and through proposed new rules and cuts to the budget and staff of antidiscrimination enforcement agencies (Leonard 1984, duRivage, 1985, Belz, 1991). For example, by appointing Clarence Thomas to head the EEOC Reagan effectively curtailed EEO enforcement (Blumrosen 1993 and Skrentny 1996 as cited in Dobbin and Kalev 2013). The Reagan administration also proposed—but failed—to close the OFFCP. The Reagan administration took aim—but failed—to dismantle several key responsibilities of federal contractors including the requirement for federal contractors to have written affirmative action plans. The Reagan administration also proposed—but failed—to end goals and timetables requirements for private sector contractors. Between 1981 and 1983 the budget of the OFCC was cut by 24 percent; the staff was cut by 34 percent during these same years (Leonard 1984; Malonis and Cengage, 2000). The number of compliance reviews actually increased but the manpower to conduct investigations and rule on these reviews was severely diminished (Leonard 1987). These acts and others signaled that the days of strong affirmative action enforcement would soon be over (also see Edelman 1992: 1541).

In a similar vein, US Supreme Court appointments and decisions also signaled a strong retreat from the endorsement of the principle of race-based remedies to overcome discrimination (Wilson et al., 1991). Although the court twice upheld affirmative action policies during the decade, the majority of decisions indicated that use of remedial policies to combat racial discrimination was on eroding ground. By the 1980s, the courts had so narrowly defined discrimination that the onus was on the victims of racial bias to prove the intent of employers and institutions that had exhibited racism in their policies and practices. Thus, by 1989 the Supreme Court held that plaintiffs would have to

---

5   *Wygant v. Jackson Board of Education.*

go beyond demonstrating disproportionate impact to prove discrimination—
an important standard used to dismantle seemingly neutral employment
practices that disadvantaged minorities and women. Rather, plaintiffs must
show either discriminatory "intent" or that numerical imbalance results from a
discriminatory practice that is not a "business necessity."[6] The labor economist
Jonathan Leonard (1987) wrote an article with a prescient title foreseeing the
future of affirmative action in the US, entitled, *"Affirmative action in the 1980s:
With a Whimper not a Bang."*

Between 1989 and 1993 affirmative action policies continued to be shaped
during the Bush Administration. In 1990, President George H.W. Bush vetoed
a new version of the Civil Rights Act on the grounds that it would require employers to establish quotas. Proponents of the legislation argued that it simply
restored the legal framework of the workplace to what it had been prior to a
series of Supreme Court decisions in the late 1980s. The Civil Rights Act of 1990
passed with severe penalties for those employers who discriminate and shifted
the burden of proof from employee to employer. Bush also nominated Clarence Thomas for the Supreme Court of the United States to replace Thurgood
Marshall, who had announced his retirement. Chief Justice Thomas' decisions
aligned him within the most conservative justices on the Court. President
George W. Bush like his father and predecessor also opposed "quotas" and "racial preferences".

Racial and gender inequality remains entrenched in corporations despite
corrective interventions—from antidiscrimination training to major federal
legislation—spanning the last 50 years. Yet, contemporary Supreme Court
decisions revised and curtailed affirmative action while the administrative
apparatus was cut-back (Also, see discussions of affirmative university admissions programs in other sections of this book, in particular Berrey). The
decisions under Chief Justice John Roberts' high court are conservative and
reflect a "post-racial" or "color-blind" perspective that discounts the continuing
presence of institutionalized bias in the US. The prevailing view of the Court is
summed up by Roberts' summary in the 2007:[7] "The way to stop discrimination
on the basis of race is to stop discriminating on the basis of race."

---

6   This discussion draws heavily from the on-line source: The Beginning of the End; http://
    www.understandingrace.org/history/gov/begin_end_affirm.html.
7   *Parents Involved v. Seattle School District; Jefferson County Board of Education* (127 S. Ct. 2738).

7   The Problem of Diversity

As affirmative action initiatives weakened new trends in human resource management called "managing diversity" and "diversity and inclusion" gained popularity. By the 1990s affirmative action had shifted to the wings of regulatory, corporate, and ideological environments while "diversity" took center stage. Diversity became the organizing concept used by large employers in the private sector for human resource management (US Glass Ceiling Commission 1995; Hirschman et al. 2002; Kelly and Dobbin 1998). A 1995 survey of the 50 largest US industrial firms found that 70 percent had a formal diversity management program, which typically including training, and an additional 8 percent were developing one (Lynch 1997: 7). In 1998 the Survey of Diversity Programs conducted by the Society for Human Resource Management (SHRM) found that 75 percent of Fortune 5007 companies had programs promoting diversity; 60 percent of those with programs had staff exclusively dedicated to diversity. Along the same lines, a survey of Fortune 1000 companies in 2001 found that almost 75 percent of respondents had a diversity manager (Kelly and Dobbin, 1998). In 2008 just 23 percent of 176 companies reporting in a survey conducted in conjunction with the online source HR.com indicated they have no diversity strategy at all; just 11 percent of 89 companies with more than 10,000 workers in that survey indicated they had no diversity strategy.

Diversity is frequently confused for affirmative action in the public sphere and even among scholars. Both policies are designed to heighten organizational inclusiveness but "diversifying" an organization is not the same as taking affirmative action to overcome the cumulative effects of hiring discrimination. The difference between affirmative action and diversity is found in their goals and rationale and in the historical context in which each strategy emerged. Affirmative action and diversity are artifacts of different socio-political circumstances and represent separate points on a continuum.

Affirmative action is a race-conscious corrective policy squarely aimed at barriers faced by African Americans, and later refocused on women, Hispanics, and other minorities. Federal regulations mandated and enforced this policy while case law defined it. Diversity stands in contrast as a voluntary agenda companies developed due to (real or perceived) business necessities associated with changes in the labor and consumer markets. This means the targets of diversity expands well beyond those of affirmative action to include nativity, religion, and sexual orientation. Diversity also includes different perspectives (which often are part-and-parcel of the organizational inclusion of nontraditional workers). The diversity umbrella also includes white men. Collins (1997) found that black personnel managers who created affirmative action programs in Chicago corporations are part of the first wave of diversity specialists when corporate priorities shifted. Work and organization scholars and researchers in the sociology of race, gender, and class examine employer motivations for adopting diversity strategies. John P. Fernandez (1991), Thomas R. Roosevelt (1990), Kelly and Dobbin (1998), Zweigenhaft and Domhoff (1998, 2006), Thomas and Ely (1996), John Skrentny (2014), Dobbin and Kelly (2013), and Kalev et al. (2006) are examples. In large part, the "diversity explosion" in human resources is driven by the diminishing proportion of white males in the US labor force, by the political agenda of minorities and women, and by the globalization of labor. Table 2.2 summarizes the differences between affirmative action and diversity initiatives.

In 1987 the Hudson Institute report *Workforce 2000* forecast white male workers would become the minority during the 21st Century. According to this report, by 1990 more than half the workforce would consist of immigrants, minorities, and women; white males, although still dominant, would be the statistical minority. Among other challenges the changing labor pool meant that employers would have to address the unique needs of women balancing work and families and the integrate black and Hispanic workers more effectively (Johnston and Packer 1987). Indeed, an increasingly urban and college educated black population, gains in the Hispanic population, and the greater labor force participation rates of women and meant that women, racial minorities and immigrant labor would compete more intensely with the traditional pool of white male workers to make claims on corporate resources in the 21st century.

In 1990 R. Roosevelt Thomas asserted that globalization, managing the new demographics of labor, and attracting more consumers demanded a new construct for diversity in US businesses. Whether or not he was the first to articulate this vision his *Harvard Business Review* article, *From Affirmative Action to Affirming Diversity* (1990), was widely acknowledged and embraced by management consultants, personnel specialists, and forward thinking CEOs. The article helped to initiate a strong pushback among change agents—particularly black management consultants and personnel specialists (e.g. Cobbs 1990, 1994; Fernandez 1991, 1995)—to challenges to affirmative action by providing a perspective on non-traditional workers that corporate culture could embrace. To be sure, the article received immediate criticism when read as dismantling affirmative action programs in favor of launching a broader diversity agenda (e.g. letters to the editor, *Harvard Business Review*, 1990, Issue 3). Somewhat provocatively Thomas concludes that "affirmative action will die a natural death" and that prejudice "has suffered some wounds that may eventually prove fatal." Here he seems to side with opponents of affirmative action who argued that

TABLE 2.2   Differences between affirmative action and managing diversity

	Affirmative action	Managing diversity
Context	Mid 1960s–early 1980s	Mid- to late 1980s–1990s
Triggering issues	Discrimination on basis of race, gender	Demographic change leading to diverse workforce, labor market, and customer/ client base
Intended to benefit	Blacks, women, Hispanics, Native Americans, Asians	Corporate bottom line, white able-bodied males; also "non-traditional" employees
Focus	Numerical representation, hiring, compliance	"To learn about others," i.e. those who are "different"
What drives implementation	Federal regulation and enforcement; legal complaints and settlements	Voluntary decisions by top management
Typical applications	Collection and monitoring of workforce data; goals and timetables; targeted recruitment and selection	Training (usually by external consultants) to provide information and promote awareness
Intended results	Representative workforce at all levels; access to employment for disadvantaged groups	Awareness of difference; improved interpersonal and intragroup communication; "human relations" skills; attitude change
Demonstrated results	Improved representation and pay for Black men and white women; some increase in representation of Blacks, women, and Hispanics	Few evaluations—but under some conditions, improved awareness and communication skills

Source: Collins, Sharon M. 2002. "Organizational Remedies to Allocation Processes." Unpublished paper. Presented at the Annual Meetings of the American Sociological Association. Chicago: August 16-19. Also see summaries of differences at:
https://saharconsulting.wordpress.com/2009/09/15/affirmative-action-eeo-diversity/
https://www.shrm.org/resourcesandtools/tools-and-samples/hr.../cms_013810.aspx
https://www.hrexchangenetwork.com/.../diversity-affirmative-action-in-the-workplace
https://communityforum.typepad.com/files/affirmative-action-vs-diversity.pdf

the expanding presence of minorities in corporate settings meant bias had been effectively censored and affirmative action programs were not needed, although he later clarifies his support for affirmative action. At the same time, however, Thomas (in particular) and the diversity rationale (in general) resituated diversity as a "business necessity" in a new global economy. Diversity positioned in this way provides employers with an intrinsically more meaningful logic for incorporating nontraditional groups than the ideal of social justice that drove affirmative action. Thus, corporate diversity programs gained momentum in the 1990s as part of a strategic response among equal opportunity experts and minority group advocates to attacks on affirmative action also see Kelly and Dobbin 1998, Edelman 1992. These constituencies viewed diversity as a way of preserving the cultural momentum and the hard won gains won by affirmative action in employment.

Past and contemporary discourse in the business world typifies the shift away from affirmative action and towards diversity as a forward-looking development (Cobbs 1990, 1994; Fernandez 1991, 1995). Under the rubric of diversity, some of the older affirmative action personnel initiatives remained intact, but other programs were rebranded, while different programs went into effect. A question presents itself: Do diversity programs work? Given the initial positive employment effects of affirmative action on government contractors, of interest is whether or not diversity builds on this trend. Does diversity have positive effects on labor market outcomes of previously excluded groups and change workforce composition?

I pose answers to this question using research on corporate diversity programs that conflate diversity with affirmative action, relying primary on Dobbin and Kalev (2013) and research of my own (Collins 2011). There is no study in my knowledge that attempts to tease out the programmatic effects of policies and procedures under diversity from those of existing under affirmative action; most likely this is due to the limitations of existing data.

Many diversity and inclusion initiatives have counterparts under affirmative action but are operating in a different regulatory environment (Bureau of National Affairs 1967, 1986a, 1986b as cited in Dobbin and Kalev 2013; Collins 1997). These include writing formal EEO declarations and advertising as an Equal Opportunity Employer, affirmative action/diversity departments and task forces and affirmative action/diversity managers, affirmative action/diversity targeted recruitment, and minority management training skill development, mentoring programs, and network building.

Research shows that advertising as an EEO employer and the presence of written EEO polices for minorities and women has no effect on increasing diversity in the managerial workforce among large and mid-sized employers (unpublished data as reported in Dobbin and Kalev 2013; also see Edelman 1990), although the vast majority of these employers had them by the year 2000 (Kalev et al. 2006).

Similarly, organizational initiatives used as educational tools to increase "cross cultural" comfort levels, and to diminish managerial bias in attitudes and behavior—such as diversity training for white managers and diversity days involving all employees—have mixed or no effect on attitudes and self-reported behavior (Roberson, Kulick and Tan 2013; also see Collins 2011). Diversity training also has little aggregate effect on workforce composition and fails to increase diversity within the ranks of management (Dobbin and Kalev 2013; Kalev et al. 2006). Dobbin, Kalev, and Kelly (2007) find that the black proportion of women in management declined 7 percent while the proportion of Hispanic women in management increased 10 percent following training.

Dobbin and Kalev (2013) assert that the role played by diversity performance evaluations in increasing workforce diversity is either negative or unclear. However, important yet unspecified variables are whether or not performance evaluations are tied to objective outcomes (i.e. numerical goals), and if such evaluations have positive, negative, or no impact hiring managers' compensation and chances for promotion.

A somewhat different picture emerges in research showing positive effects for programs targeting the recruitment of minority and women managers, for example the placement of job ads in magazines targeting women and African Americans and target recruitment at job fairs at HBCUs, and at women's colleges (Holtzer and Neumark 2000, Edelman and Peterson 1999, Konrad and Linnehan 1995). Similarly, the impact of gender and race-based management training programs to build skills among women and minorities may be positive (Bills and Hodson 2007). However, the access racial minorities and women have to such training is uneven (Hight 1998; Lynch and Black 1998.) Likewise, diversity taskforces and mentoring programs are also shown to be effective.

The effects of accountability structures–that is, having diversity departments and diversity managers, is thought to be effective in improving diversity by reducing discretionary actions and subjective bias (Bielby 2000; Reskin and McBrier 2000). However, some scholars contest this perspective (Edelman and Peterson 1999; Konrad and Linnehan 1995) and conclusions about the role formal personal systems in decreasing inequality may not be resolved. Earlier research on organizations indicates that bureaucratic structures—that is, formalizing hiring and promotion practices—protects to some degree against race and gender employment bias (Reskin and McBrier 2000; Walker 1990 as cited in Dobbin and Kalev 2013). This formalization means systematic and well defined job requirements and promotion and pay ladders, open job postings,

and centralized hiring and firing decisions. Most recently, researchers find accountability structures are instrumental in increasing the share of women and
minorities in management (Kalev et al. 2006).

Table 2.3 is based on 32 respondents to a 2001 diversity survey I conducted
with personnel managers in Chicago-based *Fortune* 500 companies. In 2009,
I conducted interviews with 40 personnel managers and management consultants. The Table shows the types of diversity programs reported and what
percent of the responding companies are involved in a program. For example, in a finding similar to the survey conducted by Dobbin and Kalev in 2002
(as cited in Dobbin and Kalev 2013), we see that diversity training is a widely
popular program. Seventy-three percent of reporting companies invested in
an awareness-training module to educate participants on cultural differences
and reduce race and gender bias. Eighty-seven percent of reporting companies
have targeted recruitment initiatives to increase workforce diversity. In the last
column I created a dichotomized variable (+/-) indicating interventions that
are more (+) and less (-) likely to change the workforce composition in companies. This variable is coded based on the research of organizational scholars
(for example, Morrison 1992, Dobbin and Kalev 2013; Leonard 1990) and interviews with knowledgeable informants.

Training has a minus (-) sign. The long term positive impact of training on
attitudes and behavior is not supported, although training seminars could be
effective as educational tools (Collins 2011). In a similar vein, diversity task
forces have a minus (-) sign. Dobbin and Kalev 2013 find that diversity task
forces add value for changing the workforce composition. On the other hand,
personnel and management consultants view as them as advisors to top management more than as change agents. Activist councils are the exceptions. Vision statements and diversity days are symbolic not efficacious, and received
a minus (-) sign.

Targeted recruitment, training internships, management skills training, and
mentorship programs are beneficial (Leonard 1990). Hiring goals are also beneficial (Freeman 1976; Leonard 1990). These programs received a plus (+) sign.
Similarly, corporate minority business procurement programs direct a percent
of corporate contracts to minority-owned businesses and have real (if highly
selective) benefits (Collins 2011). Minority supplier programs received a "+"
sign.

What is most striking in this Table is that companies engage in a wide variety of programs, but engage most in programs with the least demonstrable
benefits. The real impact of diversity programs—as opposed to affirmative
action practices—is subjective and equivocal, at best. Most companies had
no objective, quantifiable metrics to measure success. Since diversity is not

TABLE 2.3   Diversity functions in companies

Policies and programs	Percent of reporting	Effectiveness
Vision Statement	98%	–
Diversity Day	98%	–
Diversity Task Force	98%	–
Awareness Training	73%	–
Recruitment	87%	+
Mentoring/ Skill building	68%	+
MBE Procurement	70%	+
Numerical hiring goals	85%	+

Note: n=32
Source: Collins, Sharon M. 2002. "Organizational Remedies to Allocation Processes." Unpublished paper. Presented at the Annual Meetings of the American Sociological Association. Chicago: August 16–19.

a legal mandate it decouples hiring outcomes from financial consequences. Moreover, the sets of protocols and metrics to which companies conform are self-generated and self-regulated. This self-scrutiny stands in distinct contrast to federal scrutiny and tangible incentives to correct long-standing bias.

The evolution from affirmative action to diversity constitutes (at least) two shifts in human resource policy and goals that may be contradictory. One shift is the softening of goals that (ambivalently) prioritized the hiring and promotion of US ethno-racial groups and women. The contemporary focus is on widespread (including global) inclusiveness (Collins 2011; Embrick and Rice 2010; Embrick 2008, 2010, 2011). Broadening notions of corporate inclusiveness may mean that all groups are better off under diversity. Conversely, the decline in affirmative action and the rise of diversity may replace goals oriented towards some protected groups for programs and goals favoring others protected groups (Collins 2011; Embrick 2008, 2010, 2011; Smith 2002). For example, in tandem with the feminization of personnel specialties during the 1990s, human resource departments focused less an African Americans to focus more on problems facing working women, such as childcare and work-life balance (Collins 2011, unpublished interview data;[8] Kalev et al. 2006). Kalev et al. (2006) show that the effects of affirmative action plans and its organizational supports benefit white women, followed by back women. Black men benefit least. Finally, diversity may mean that protected groups—particularly

---

8   Between 2007 and 2010, I conducted 37 interviews with black senior managers working for Chicago's major employers.

black men—simply tread water or lose ground overall in favor of white men. The broader diversity rubric may downplay differences in demands for fairness and homogenize group differences (Collins 2011; Embrick and Rice 2010; Embrick 2011; Edelman, Fuller, Mara-Ditra 2001; also see Anderson 1999 as cited in Bell and Hartmann 2007).

Second and related is the shifting ideology supporting corporate inclusiveness away from protecting minorities against bias and discrimination. The idea now is that utilizing minorities increases the competitive advantage (and profitability) in emerging markets (Collins 1997; Skrentney 2014). Grounding diversity in corporate profit rather than antidiscrimination policy may protect minority group interests only if their work product contributes quantifiably to the "bottom-line" Thomas 1990). However, the simplistic business case for diversity is contested in research (cf. Kochan, et al. 2003 versus Herring 2009). Moreover, my analysis of unpublished data suggests that a globalized economy means the concept of diversity becomes internationally defined. Attention to international definitions tied to where companies do business may dampen corporations' sense of social responsibility and citizenship along with their awareness and responsiveness to US ethno-racial minorities. What constitutes diversity in the US has different meanings and different implications compared to other national contexts (Ferree 2008 as cited in Bell and Hartmann 2007). Within the global and the national contexts diversity is here to stay but the jury assessing the long-term impact on US minorities and women is still out.

References

Abram, Morris B. 1983. "Racial Quotas: 'Road to Conflict and Tragedy'." *New York Times.*

Ashenfelter, Orley and James J. Heckman. 1976. "Measuring the Effect of an Anti-discrimination Program." Pp. 46–89 in *Evaluating the Labor Market Effects of Social Programs*, edited by Orley Ashenfelter and James Blum. Princeton: Industrial Relations Section, Princeton University.

Bell, Joyce, and Douglas Hartmann. 2007. "Diversity in Everyday Discourse: The Cultural Ambiguities and Consequences of 'Happy Talk.'" *American Sociological Review*, 72: 895–914.

Belz, Herman. 1991. *Equality Transformed: A Quarter Century of Affirmative Action.* New Brunswick: Transaction Publishers.

Bielby, William. 2000. "Minimizing workplace gender and racial bias." *Contemporary Sociology*, 29 (2): 120–129.

Bills, David B. and Randy Hodson. 2007. "Worker training: a review, critique, and extension." *Research in Social Stratification and Mobility* (25): 258–272.

Blumrosen, Alfred W. 1993. *The Law Transmission System and Equal Employment Opportunity*. Madison, WI: University of Wisconsin Press.

Braddock, James H., and James M. McPartland. 1987. "How Minorities Continue to be Excluded from Equal Employment Opportunities: Research on Labor Market and Institutional Barriers." *Journal of Social Issues*, 43: 5–39.

Cobbs, Price M. 1990. "Businesses Must Learn to Motivate a Diverse Staff." in *The San Francisco Chronicle*. San Francisco.

Cobbs, Price M. 1994. *The Promise of Diversity: Over 40 Voices Discuss Strategies for Eliminating Discrimination in Organizations*, edited by Edith W. Seashore, Judith H. Katzm, Frederick A. Miller, and Elsie Y. Cross. New York, NY: McGraw-Hill.

Chicago Reporter. 1975. *In the Red on Blacks*.

Citizens' Commission on Civil Rights. 1984. "Affirmative Action: To Open the Doors of Job Opportunity: A Policy of Fairness and Compassion that has Worked." *Washington, DC: Citizens' Commission on Civil Rights*.

Civil Rights Fact Sheet. Retrieved December 2015: http://www.civilrights.org/equal-opportunity/.

Collins, Sharon M. 2011. "Diversity In The Post Affirmative Action Labor Market: A Proxy For Racial Progress?" *Critical Sociology*, 37 (5): 517–520.

Collins, Sharon M. 1997. *Black Corporate Executives*. Philadelphia, PA: Temple University Press.

Ditomaso, Nancy. 2013. *The American Non-Dilemma: Racial Inequality Without Racism*. New York, NY: Russell Sage Foundation.

Dobbin, Frank and Alexandra Kalev. 2013. "The Origins and Effects of Corporate Diversity Programs." Pp. 253–281 in *Oxford Handbook of Diversity and Work*. New York, NY: Oxford University Press.

Dobbin, Frank, John R. Sutton, and John W. Meyer. 1993. "Equal Opportunity Law and the Construction of Internal Labor Markets." *American Journal of Sociology*, 99 (2): 396–427.

Dobbin, Frank, Alexandra Kalav, and Erin Kelley. 2007. "Diversity Management in Corporate America." *Contexts*, 6 (4): 21–28.

duRivage, Virginia. 1985. "The OFCCP Under the Reagan Administration: Affirmative Action in Retreat." *Labor Law Journal*, 3 (6): 360–368.

Duster, Troy and David Wellman. 1999. "The Theory and Practice of Corporate Diversity: A comprehensive survey of available evidence." Ford Foundation Grant: 985–1604.

Edelman, Loren B. 1990. "Legal Environments and Organizational Governance: The Expansion of Due Process in the American Workplace." *American Journal of Sociology*, 95: 1401–1440.

Edelman, Lauren B. 1992. "Legal Ambiguity and Symbolic Structures: Organizational Mediation of Civil Rights Law." *The American Journal of Sociology*, 97: 1531–1576.

Edelman, Lauren B. and Stephen M. Petterson. "Symbols and Substance In Organizational Response to Civil Rights Law." Miami Beach, Florida: Paper presented at the annual meeting of the American Sociological Association. August, 1993.

Edelman, Lauren B., Sally Riggs Fuller, and Iona Mara-Drita. 2001. "Diversity Rhetoric and the Managerialization of the Law." *American Journal of Sociology*, 106 (6): 1589–1641.

Embrick, David G.. 2011. "Diversity Ideology in the Business World: A New Oppression for a New Age." *Critical Sociology* 37(5):541–556.

Embrick, David G. 2008. "The Diversity Ideology: Keeping Major Transnational Corporations White and Male in an Era of Globalization." In *Globalization and America: Race, Human Rights & Inequality*, edited by Angela Hattery, David G. Embrick, and Earl Smith. Lanham, MD: Rowman and Littlefield.

Embrick, David G., and Mitchell F. Rice. 2010. "Understanding Diversity Ideology in the United States: Historical and Contemporary Perspectives." In *Diversity and Public Administration: Theory, Issues, and Perspectives* (2nd ed.), edited by Mitchell F. Rice. Armonk, NY: M.E. Sharpe.

Federal Glass Ceiling Commission. 1995. "A Solid Investment: Making Full Use of the Nation's Human Capital." Washington D.C.

Fernandez, John P. 1995. "The Diversity Advantage: How American Business Can Outperform Japanese and European Companies

Fernandez, John P. 1991. *Managing A Diverse Work Force: Regaining the Competitive Edge*. New York, NY: Wiley.

Fernandez, John P. 1995. "The Diversity Advantage: How American Business Can Outperform Japanese and European Companies" *Administrative Science Quarterly*, 40 (3).

Ferree, Myra Marx. 2008. "Framing Equality: The Politics of Race, Class, Gender in the US, Germany, and the Expanding European Union." Pp. 237–256 in *The Gender Politics of the European Union: Mobilization, Inclusion, Exclusion*, edited by Silke Roth. New York, NY: Berghahn.

Freeman, Richard. 1976. *The Black Elite*. New York, NY: McGraw Hill.

Granovetter, Mark. 1995. *Getting A Job: A Study of Contacts and Careers*. Chicago, IL: University of Chicago.

Heckman, James J., and Kenneth I. Wolpin. 1976. "Does the Contract Compliance Program Work? An Analysis of Chicago Data."

Heckman, John J. and Brook S. Payner. 1989. "Determining the Impact of Federal Antidiscrimination Policy on the Economic Status of Blacks: A Study of South Carolina." *The American Economic Review*, 79: 138–177.

Herring, Cedric. 2009. "Does Diversity Pay?: Race, Gender, and the Business Case for Diversity." *American Sociological Review*, 74: 208–224.

Herring, Cedric and Sharon M. Collins. 1995. "Retreat From Equal Opportunity? The Case of Affirmative Action." in *The Bubbling Cauldron*, edited by Joe Feagin. New Haven, CT: Yale.

Hight, Joseph E. 1998. "Young worker participation in post-school education and train-ing." *Monthly Labor Review*, 121: 13–21.

Hill, Herbert. 1977. "The Equal Employment Opportunity Acts of 1964 and 1972: A Criti-cal Analysis of the Legislative History and Administration of the Law." *Industrial Relations Law Journal*, 2 (1): 1–98.

Hirschman, Charles, Richard Alba, and Reynolds Farley. 2002. "The Meaning and Mea-surement of Race in the U.S. Census: Glimpses in the Future." *Demography*, 37: 381–393.

Holtzer, John and David Neumark. 2000. "What does affirmative action do?" *Interna-tional Labor Relations Review*, 55: 240–271.

Holzer, Harry J. 1987. "Informal Job Search and Black Youth Unemployment" *American Economic Review*, 77 (3): 446–452.

Johnston, William B. and Arnold E. Packer. 1987. *Workforce 2000, Work and Workers for the Twenty-First Century*. Indianapolis, IN: The Hudson Institute.

Kalev, Alexandria, Frank Dobbin, and Erin Kelly. 2006. "Best Practices or Best Guess-es? Assessing the Efficacy of Corporate Affirmative Action and Diversity Policies." *American Sociological Review*, 71: 589–617.

Kelly, Erin and Frank Dobbin. 1998. "How Affirmative Action Became Diversity Man-agement: Employer Response to Antidiscrimination Law, 1961 to 1996." *American Behavioral Scientist*, 41 (7): 960–984.

King, Mary C. 1993. "Black Women's Breakthrough into Clerical Work: An Occupational Tipping Model." *Journal of Economic Issues*, 27 (4): 1097–1127.

Kirschenman, Jolene and Kathryn M. Neckerman. 1991. "'We'd love to Hire them, but…': The Meaning of Race for Employers." pp. 203–232 in *The Urban Underclass*, edited by Christopher Jencks and Paul E. Peterson. Washington, D.C.: Brookings Institution.

Kochan, Thomas, Katerina Bezrukova, Robin Ely, Susan Jackson, Aparna Joshi, Karen Jehn, Jonathan Leonard, David Levine, David Thomas. 2003. "The Effects Of Diver-sity On Business Performance: Report Of The Diversity Research Network." *Human Resource Management*, 43: 3–21.

Konrad, Alison M., and Linnehan, Frank. 1995. "Formalized HRM structures: Coordi-nating equal employment opportunity or concealing organizational practices?." *Academy of Management Journal*, 38 (3): 787–820.

Leonard, Jonathan S. 1982. *"The Impact of Affirmative Action on Minority and Female Employment."* Berkeley, CA: University of California Press.

Leonard, Jonathan S. 1984. "The impact of Affirmative Action on Employment." *Journal of Labor Economics*, 2 (4): 439–463.

Leonard, Jonathan S. 1985. "What Promises Are Worth: The Impact of Affirmative Ac-tion Goals." *Journal of Human Resources*, 20 (1): 3–20.

Leonard, Jonathan S. 1989. "Employment and Occupational Advancement Under Af-firmative Action." *The Review of Economics and Statistics*, 66 (3): 377–385.

Leonard, Jonathan S. 1990. "The Impact of Affirmative Action Regulation and Equal Employment Law on Black Employment." *The Journal of Economic Perspectives*, 4: 47–63.

Lin, Nan. 2001. "Building a Network Theory of Social Capital." Pp. 3–30 in *Social Capital: Theory and Research*, edited by Nan Lin, Karen Cook, and Ronald S. Burt. New York, NY: Academic Press.

Lynch, Frederick R. 1997. The diversity machine: The drive to change the "White male workplace." New York, NY: Free Press.

Lynch, Lisa M. and Sandra E. Black. 1998. "Beyond the Incidence of Employer-Provided Training." *Industrial & Labor Relations Review*, 52 (1): 64.

Malonis, Jane A. and Gale Cengage (Ed.). 2000. *Affirmative Action*: sNotes.com. Retrieved from: http://www.enotes.com/biz-encyclopedia/.

Mattison, E.G. 1965. "Integrating the Work Force in Southern Industry." In *The Negro and Employment Opportunity: Problems and Practices*, edited by H.R. Northrup and R.L. Rowan. Ann Arbor, MI: Bureau of Industrial Relations, Graduate School of Business Administration, University Michigan.

Morrison, Ann M. 1992. *The New Leaders: Guidelines on Leadership Diversity in America*. San Francisco, CA: Jossey-Bass.

Reskin, Barbara and Debra McBrier. 2000. "Why Not Ascription? Organizations' Employment of Male and Female Managers." *American Sociological Review*, 65: 210–233.

Roberson, Loriann, Carol T. Kulik, and Rae Yunzi Tan. 2013. "Effective Diversity Training." pp. 341–365. in *The Oxford Handbook of Diversity and Work*, edited by Quinetta M. Roberson. New York, NY: Oxford University Press.

Roberts, Paul C. and Lawrence M. Stratton. 1995. *The New Color Line: How Quotas and Privilege Destroy Democracy*. Washington, D.C.: Regnery Publishers Inc.

Roosevelt, Thomas R. 1990. "From Affirmative Action to Diversity." *Harvard Business Review*, 68 (2): 107–17.

Shrum, W., N.H. Cheek, and S.M. Hunter 1988. "Friendship in School: Gender and Racial Homophily." *Sociology of Education*, 61: 227–239.

Silberman, Lawrene H.. 1977. "The Road To Racial Quotas." In *Wall Street Journal*.

Skrentny, John D. 1996. *The Ironies of Affirmative Action: Politics Culture and Justice in America*. Chicago, IL: University of Chicago.

Skrentny, John D. 2014. *After Civil Rights: Racial Realism in the New American Workplace*. Princeton, NJ: Princeton University Press.

Smith, Ryan A. 2002. "Race, Gender, and Authority in the Workplace: Theory and Research." *Annual Review of Sociology*, 28: 509–542.

Stetson, Damon. 1963. "More Salaried Positions are Opening to Negroes." In *New York Times*.

Thomas, David A., and Robin J. Ely. 1996. "Making Differences Matter: A New Paradigm for Managing Diversity." *Harvard Business Review* (September–October): 79–90.

Thomas, Roosevelt R. 1990. "From Affirmative Action to Affirming Diversity." *Harvard Business Review* (April): 107–117.

Tomaskovic-Devey, Donald T., and Kevin Stainback. 2007. "Discrimination and Desegregation: Equal Opportunity Progress in U.S. Private Sector Workplaces since the Civil Rights Act." *The ANNALS of the American Academy of Political and Social Science*, 609: 49–84.

Topa, Giorgio. 2001. "Social Interactions, Local Spillovers And Unemployment." *Review of Economic Studies*, 68 (2): 261–295.

United States Commission of Civil Rights. 1969. Staff Memorandum. Febuary 4. Washington D.C.: U.S. Government Printing Office.

United States Glass Ceiling Commission. 1995. "Good for Business: Making Full Use of the Nation's Human Capital." Washington, DC: United States Department of Labor, Office of Federal Contract Compliance Programs.

Walker, James Titus. 1990. "Relative Black Male Employment among Business Establishments: Relation to Management Orientation toward Affirmative Action, Organizational Context, and Organizational Characteristics." University of Michigan, Ann Arbor.

Wilson, Cynthia A., James Lewis, and Cedric Herring. 1991. "The 1991 Civil Rights Act: Restoring our Basic Protections." Chicago, IL: Chicago Urban League and Chicago Lawyer's Committee for Civil Rights Under the Law.

Zweigenhaft, Richard L., and G. William Domhoff. 1998. *Diversity in the Power Elite: Have Women and Minorities Reached the Top?* New Haven, CT: Yale University Press.

Zweigenhaft, Richard L., and G. William Domhoff. 2006. *Diversity in the Power Elite: How It Happened, Why It Matters* (2 ed.): Rowman & Littlefield Publishers, Inc..

CHAPTER 3

Is Diversity Racial Justice? Affirmative Action in Admissions and the Promises and Perils of Law

Ellen Berrey

1   Introduction

On April 1, 2003, a chilly gray day with cherry blossoms in bloom, thousands of people flooded the sidewalks of Washington, DC and the steps of the U.S. Supreme Court. The Court was in the midst of hearing oral arguments in two historic cases, *Gratz v. Bollinger* and *Grutter v. Bollinger,* which challenged the University of Michigan's practice of considering race in admissions decisions. The crowd was energetic. People had come from across the country to make their positions heard, almost all of them in support of affirmative action, representing many different racial groups. A sea of marchers with a national organization called BAMN held up red and White posters, "DEFEND Affirmative Action and Integration. FIGHT for Equality." Those with Students Supporting Affirmative Action, a multi-racial collective of Michigan college students, wore blue and maize t-shirts with the slogan, "Race is a factor because racism is a factor." A Black college student had on a button, "40 acres or 20 points," referring both to a phrase that asserts the right to land for formerly enslaved Southern black farmers, as compensation for their unpaid labor, and to the number of additional points that the Michigan undergraduate admissions office gave to African American, Latino, or Native American applicants.

Others chanted about diversity. "Unity! Diversity! A better university!" repeated a group of marchers, one with a sign "Diversity is educational." Activists with the National Association for the Advancement of Colored People carried professionally made posters, "NAACP recognizes UNITY & STRENGTH in DIVERSITY."

Small groups of counter-protesters, nearly all of them White men, made their way through the crowd with handwritten signs. "Affirmative Action is Racist," read one. Another referenced a line from the famous I Have a Dream speech by Dr. Martin Luther King, Jr.: "Content of Character, Not Color of Skin."

The various slogans at the DC march reflected political activists' passionate views about the controversial practice of considering race in college admissions. These same slogans also reflect the three major legal frameworks that have, since the 1970s, guided the actions of colleges that do affirmative action:

1.   *Remedial racial justice:* An argument *for* affirmative action. According to this position, considering race in admissions is a means of rectifying past and ongoing barriers that have cut off opportunity for people of color because of their race. Example: "Fight for equality."

2.   *Diversity:* An argument *for* affirmative action. According to this position, considering race in admissions is a means of achieving diversity, which is socially beneficial because students learn best and become more capable citizens when they attend college with students of different racial backgrounds. Example: "Diversity is educational."

3.   *Colorblindness:* An argument *against* affirmative action. According to this position, any consideration of race in decision-making, even if the objective is to further opportunity for people of color, is discriminatory, denies individual liberties, and violates the U.S. Constitution. Example: "Affirmative action is racist."

To understand the pursuit of racial equality in the United States, we need to understand what, exactly, law permits us to do regarding race and what it prohibits. This includes where these legal frameworks come from and how they are applied. We also need to understand how colleges and universities actually do affirmative action. College admissions policies can determine who has access to upward mobility and who is cut off. Overall, college admissions favor affluent, predominantly White students, but when admissions officers do affirmative action—when they account for the race of minority groups as a positive factor—they can improve the life circumstances of people of color. Affirmative action evens the playing field in the competition for admissions and opens up post-college opportunities.

Since the 1970s, the U.S. Supreme Court, in response to challenges by conservative activists, has made it increasingly difficult for admissions officers to make decisions based on an applicant's race. The Court has narrowed the justification that colleges can use for voluntary race-conscious admissions, so that the goal of "diversity" is *the* acceptable rationale. How has law cut off an argument for remedial intervention and advanced arguments for diversity and colorblindness? What are the promises and perils of diversity under law? How do higher education leaders interpret the mandate for diversity? Ultimately, is diversity racial justice?

This chapter draws on legal doctrine, my ethnographic-historical study of affirmative action and the *Gratz* and *Grutter* litigation at the University of Michigan, my analysis of diversity discourse at other universities, and insights from socio-legal theories of law. It analyzes affirmative action through the lens of empirical critical race theory.[1] Critical race theory understands the U.S. legal system as a source of racial meanings and power relations (Crenshaw et al. 1996; Moore 2008). It foregrounds how law socially constructs race in ways that primarily (but not invariantly) support racial domination and perpetuate injustice. This theoretical approach casts doubts on the supposed neutrality of legal concepts such as principles, rights, and state protection. By applying critical race theory to the empirical study of affirmative action, I show the creation, implementation, legal context, and effects of the policy in relation to both institutional racism and anti-racism efforts.

This chapter presents two key insights. First, law has established the official terms of debate over race-conscious college admissions policies. Legal contests have helped to make such policies culturally significant and politically controversial. Further, they have limited—but not (yet) altogether ended—colleges' ability to give some favor to students of color in the admissions decision. Second, administrators at many selective colleges and universities have adopted diversity discourse, but not simply as a justification for affirmative action. They have made diversity an identity for their institutions. That identity symbolizes institutional values they want to project and, at least superficially, defines their actions.

As I show, diversity—as legal doctrine, organizational identity, and popular discourse more generally—provides an inadequate basis for a politics of racial justice. It affirms the cause of racial minority inclusion, but the term itself and the actions taken in its name usually fail to adequately address the structural foundations of racism. All too often, diversity placates the conversation, with the apparent intention of putting white people at ease rather than unearthing their privileges.[2]

2   Affirmative Action and Its History

Affirmative action is a form of decision making that intentionally considers an individual's race, ethnicity, or sex for the purposes of expanding opportunities for racial minorities and women (Harper and Reskin 2005). It can happen in many domains of social life, but it is most prevalent in the workplace and in

---

1   For a statement on eCRT, see Obasogie, Osagie. *Blinded by Sight: Seeing Race Through the Eyes of the Blind.* Palo Alto, CA: Stanford University Press, 2014.

2   See also Berrey, Ellen. "Diversity Is for White People: The Big Lie Behind a Well-Intended Word," *Salon.* Oct. 26, 2015.

college admissions. In contrast to colleges and universities, when companies practice affirmative action, they take additional steps to ensure that they are recruiting, hiring, and promoting racial minority and female employees to the same extent that they treat White and male employees (Skrentny 1996). Companies typically do affirmative action when they are large government contractors and thus are required by the federal government to do so.

Universities and colleges, on the other hand, typically do affirmative action in admissions voluntarily.[3] In higher education, the goal is to improve racial minorities' chances of being admitted to, attending, and graduating from universities and colleges—without requiring universities and colleges to radically change their standard admissions process (Berrey 2015a). The targets are African Americans, Latinos, and Native Americans. Admissions officers take many different kinds of actions to reach and enroll these students, from outreach and recruitment activities ("soft" affirmative action) to admissions and financial aid decisions ("hard" affirmative action), the most extreme of which reserve slots exclusively for members of a disadvantaged group (Kennedy 2013). The "harder" the form of affirmative action, the more contentious. These decisions are moments when universities distribute valuable, zero-sum resources to applicants, so, to critics, administrators appear to be picking winners (underrepresented minorities, i.e. African Americans, Latinos, and Native Americans) and losers (White students and Asian American students).

Affirmative action is a surprising departure from the legacy and ongoing dynamics of institutional discrimination, which have long kept students of color off college campuses. Through most of U.S. history, simply being a racial minority almost always barred a person from becoming a college student. There have been, since the 1830s, historically Black colleges and universities, first created to educate freed slaves and, since the late 1960s, Tribal Colleges and Universities on Indian reservations (Gasman 2015).[4] But the vast majority of the country's institutions of higher education were exclusively for White people up until the 1960s. The most elite schools were for White, affluent males from the eastern seaboard, particularly Protestants (Karabel 2005). This exclusion has had cumulative racial effects into the present. The benefits of higher education are passed down through families, generation by generation.

---

3   Or "affirmative admissions" cf Skrentny, John David. *The Minority Rights Revolution.* Cambridge, MA: Belknap Press of Harvard University Press, 2002. Some universities have faced court-ordered desegregation mandates to do affirmative action or have pursued consent decrees. The main ones are states in the deep south, such as Alabama and Mississippi.
4   Gasman, Marybeth. "Minority-Serving Institutions: A Historical Backdrop." In *Understanding Minority-Serving Institutions*, edited by Marybeth Gasman, Benjamin Baez and Caroline Sotello Viernes Turner. Albany, NY: SUNY Press, 2015.

One specific way this plays out today is through legacy preferences, which give favoritism to the children of alumni. Legacy admissions are commonplace at selective institutions. That is a huge strike against underrepresented students of color, who are more likely to be first generation college students compared to their White counterparts (Lemann 1999).[5]

In the period after World War II, in the face of changing demographics and growing social pressures, admissions procedures changed. Elite universities moved away from admissions based on family lineage. They adopted standardized testing with the pretense of making colleges more open and meritocratic, particularly for Jewish students whose enrollment was prohibited or limited by admissions quotas. Consequently, a relatively wider range of types of students were admitted.

A few elite universities and colleges first began to do affirmative admissions in the mid-1960s, University of Michigan included. Top university officials were inspired by the Southern civil rights movement, which fought against discriminatory Jim Crow laws and for full citizenship rights for Black people (Stulberg and Chen 2014). These officials believed their institutions had some responsibility to support civil rights aims. Later that decade, other elite universities adopted race-conscious admissions in response to campus-based student protest (Stulberg and Chen 2014). By the early 1970s, the practice was widespread throughout higher education (Grodsky 2007). At that point, such interventions targeted African Americans, as the Black-White divide was not only the most pronounced racial division in American life but also the focus of the 1960s civil rights reforms that banned discrimination in public education, employment, and housing (Skrentny 2002). At this time, there was relatively more social, political, and legal support for race-based interventions intended to remedy racial injustice and enable people of color to fully participate in American life.

Affirmative action is used at selective colleges and universities, which by definition are not open access and only admit a portion of applicants. The exact number of the colleges and universities that make admissions and financial aid decisions based on race is difficult to pin down. The simplest way to measure this (although not necessarily the most reliable) is based on institutions' self-reports. In the 1990s and early 2000s, a far-reaching assessment of U.S. colleges and universities estimated that 20 percent of selective colleges and universities and about half of comprehensive ones used a race-attentive policy.[6]

5   US DEPT OF ED Web Tables: Profile of Undergraduate Students: 2011–02, Table 3.11.
6   On selective institutions, see Bowen, William G., and Derrick Bok. *The Shape of the River: Long-Term Consequences of Considering Race in College and University Admissions*. Princeton,

More recently, a 2012 national survey found that approximately 45 percent of colleges and universities give some consideration to race in undergraduate admissions decisions.[7] Almost 25 percent of those institutions rated it as of considerable or moderate importance—which is more weight than they gave to personal characteristics such as applicants' ability to pay or alumni status. According to a 2015 national survey, 60 percent of the most competitive institutions (where 40 percent or less of applicants are admitted) do affirmative admissions (Espinosa et al. 2015). In that study, racial and ethnic diversity was the second highest priority for 30 percent of colleges and universities (after admissions tests scores and high school grades), and it was the highest priority for 12 percent. Racial and ethnic minority status continues to be one of the attributes valued by administrators at the country's top institutions. As political scientist Daniel Lipson found, admissions officers have some top schools have adopted affirmative action as part of their responsibilities of diversity management and view it as a professional norm (Lipson 2007).

The U.S. is not alone in its use of affirmative action. It has been adopted in countries ranging from Canada to South Africa to Brazil where, for example, approximately 70 percent of public universities had such policies in 2011 (Schwartzman and Paiva 2014).

Since its early implementation, affirmative action has been effective. It increases the odds that African American, Latino, and Native American students are admitted to and graduate from college. In a 2007 study, Eric Grodsky compared African American and Latino students to White students with similar academic records and socioeconomic status, to find out whom was admitted to college with what credentials. He found that, between the early 1970s and early 1990s, BA-granting universities and colleges across the spectrum—from the most competitive to least—gave an edge to African American applicants over White ones. In 1972, that edge was the equivalent of a 281-point boost in SAT scores. At the more competitive institutions, this advantage was upwards of 343 points or more. Between the early 1980s and early 1990s, Latino applicants received a boost of somewhere between 108 and 118 SAT points. According to another study of the top 146 institutions, the policy tripled the enrollment of African Americans and Latinos (Carnevale and Rose 2003).

N.J: Princeton University Press, 1998. On comprehensive institutions, see Grodsky, Eric, and Demetra Kalogrides. "The Declining Significance of Race in College Admissions." *American Journal of Education* 115, no. 1 (2008): 1–33.

7   National Association of College Admissions Counseling. "Diversity and College Admission in 2003: A Survey Report." 1–44. Arlington, VA, 2003.

The benefits of affirmative action extend beyond the college campus. In a major study, William Bowen and Derrick Bok demonstrate that the policy improves African Americans' career prospects and Black communities' leadership capacity (Bowen and Bok 1998). According to the authors, affirmative action beneficiaries who graduate from top universities constitute as the backbone of the Black middle class.

3   Affirmative Action in the Context of Selective College Admissions

Since the 1980s, with a ballooning number of college applicants and increasingly stricter criteria for gaining admittance, admissions to selective schools has become a high-stakes competition (or at least it feels that way to applicants).[8] The cost of college has also skyrocketed. Adjusting for inflation, the cost of attending a public four-year university in 2014 was 3.25 times more expensive than in 1984 and the cost of attending a private one was 2.46 times more expensive.[9]

There is good reason for the push to go to college. According to the Pew Research Center, young college-educated workers now earn on average $45,500 year, compared to $28,000 for high school graduates, and they are more satisfied with their careers.[10] Those who go to selective institutions are even better off when it comes to earning an advanced degree, getting a desirable job, career promotion, and future income (Espenshade and Radford 2009).

In higher education, affirmative action is an addendum to the larger system of admissions. Understanding this is crucial to understanding institutional discrimination and the counterweight that affirmative action provides. Contrary to popular myths that White students are hurt by affirmative action, bias against students of color continues to pervade that larger admissions system. Colleges and universities give unacknowledged favoritism to applicants from

---

8   Contrary to popular perception, though, 80 percent of top students are accepted to at least one elite school, according to Parchment.com, a website that college applicants can use to manage the admissions process. Carey, Kevin. "For Accomplished Students, Reaching a Good College Isn't as Hard as It Seems." *New York Times* Nov. 29 (2014). What has, in fact, changed over the past few decades is that a larger number of students with less accomplished academic records are applying to elite schools.

9   College Board. "2014 College-Bound Seniors: Total Group Profile Report." New York, NY, 2014.

10   Pew Research Center. "The Rising Cost of Not Going to College." Washington, DC, 2014. http://www.pewsocialtrends.org/2014/02/11/the-rising-cost-of-not-going-to-college/. Accessed Dec. 4, 2015.

wealthy, predominantly White families. Admissions decisions are by and large based on what administrators refer to as merit-based criteria, which include an applicant's grade point average, standardized test scores, the high school they attended, and the rigor of the classes they took. Affluent, White students are far more likely to excel on such merit-based criteria for reasons unrelated to their actual intellectual ability. Test scores are highly correlated with family income, so that the richest students do best.[11] Advantaged youth more often attend private and college-preparatory high schools, which provide test preparation, rigorous curricula, and better teachers.

In contrast, Black and Hispanic students are more likely to attended underfunded high schools that lack advanced classes. Furthermore, they consistently score lower on standardized test compared to their White and Asian American counterparts. Importantly, thought, they do *not* score lower on performance-based measures such as grades and class rank which, in fact, are better predictors of academic success down the road (Alon and Tienda 2007). Stereotype threat is a major obstacle for Black test-takers.[12] Because of widespread and inaccurate stereotypes about African Americans' inferior intellect, these students experience anxiety about being judged and treated in a stereotypical manner or about fulfilling those negative stereotypes. That anxiety, in turn, undermines their performance.

Even with affirmative action, Black, Latino, and Native American students are underrepresented in selective institutions compared to their representation in the U.S. population and to the enrollment numbers for White and Asian American students (Alon and Tienda 2007). However, the policy has been the focus of political and legal disputes for decades, with critics framing it as reverse discrimination biased against White and (more recently) Asian American students.

4   Affirmative Action Politics and the Mobilization of Law

Public opinion on affirmative action depends on the wording of the question, but a 2014 poll found that 63 percent of Americans say that affirmative action

---

11   College Board. "2014 College-Bound Seniors: Total Group Profile Report." New York, NY, 2014; Fischer, Claude S., Michael Hout, Martìn Sànchez Jankowski, Samuel R. Lucas, Ann Swidler, and Kim Voss. *Inequality by Design: Cracking the Bell Curve Myth*. Princeton: Princeton University Press, 1996.

12   Steele, Claude M., and Joshua Aronson. "Stereotype Threat and the Intellectual Test Performance of African Americans." *Journal of Personality and Social Psychology* 69 (1995): 797–811.

programs designed to increase the number of Black and Latino students on campus are a "good thing."[13] Pew found similar support in 2003.[14] Even with this support, affirmative action arguably is the most politically contentious racial policy in the United States—more so than troubled city schools, mass incarceration, immigration law, or other problems that affect far more people of color. It has become what legal scholar Christopher Edley, Jr. (Holmes 1997: (1) describes as "the highest pole in the storm." According to political scientist Jennifer Hochschild, affirmative action policy is a weapon in the culture wars, more so than a strategy to aid people of color and women or a real threat to White people. Controversies over it are a petri dish for contention over the American dream. The policy touches on deeply held, contrary sentiments about the meaning of success and the role of ability, effort, opportunity, and unfair obstacles therein. By arguing against affirmative action, she explains, White people unapologetically claim White privilege and favoritism in their pursuit of the good life.

Disputes over affirmative action have taken place from panels on college campuses to the editorial pages of major newspapers. But nowhere has these disputes been more important than in the U.S. Supreme Court. Law is central to affirmative action politics. Law defines the acceptable treatment of race in admissions decisions. Likewise, as I argue elsewhere, conflicts over affirmative action have been channeled into the courts, such that the dynamics of litigation have organized the terms of debate (Berrey 2015b). Litigation institutionalizes affirmative action politics as an oppositional contest between polarized sides, with opponents arguing for color blindness and defenders arguing for diversity, remedial justice, or some other position. Law also defines much of the popular discourse on affirmative action.

The involvement of the Supreme Court in affirmative action politics also is significant. As the highest court in the country, the Supreme Court is the foremost authority on the Constitution. Its decisions formalize what is lawful or not. The Court makes laws more precise and creates precedents that others must follow.

Since the mid-1970s, a series of important legal cases have established the acceptable use of affirmative action in admissions and the officially-sanctioned discourses on affirmative action, as outlined at the opening of this chapter. *Bakke v. Regents of the University of California* (1978) was the first of these and the most complicated one (see Table 3.1). In this case, Allan Bakke

---

13   Pew Research Center (2014a).
14   Pew Research Center (2014a).

TABLE 3.1   Major legal cases on affirmative action in college admissions, 1978–2015

Case	Legal frames	Majority opinion	Also significant
Bakke v. Regents of the University of California (1978, U.S. Supreme Court)	Colorblindness v. remedial justice/ diversity/role models	Affirmative action allowed but not racial quotas	Powell's opinion on the benefits of diversity
Hopwood v. State of Texas (1996, Fifth Circuit)	Colorblindness v. diversity	Affirmative action banned in Texas, Louisiana, and Mississippi	Overturned by *Grutter*
Gratz v. Bollinger and *Grutter v. Bollinger* (2003, U.S. Supreme Court)	Colorblindness v. diversity	Affirmative action is permissible if the goal is diversity and admissions decisions are individualized	In the lower courts, intervenors argued for remedial justice and integration
Fisher v. University of Texas (2013, U.S. Supreme Court)	Colorblindness v. diversity	*Grutter* holds, but universities have a greater burden to prove that they need to consider race	*Fisher* will be heard again by the Court in the 2015–16 term.
Coalition to Defend Affirmative Action v. Schuette (2014, U.S. Supreme Court)	Colorblindness v. political pro- cess theory	State bans on affirmative action are lawful	Not governed by the standard of strict scrutiny

SOURCE: CREATED BY AUTHOR

and his attorneys made a colorblind argument against affirmative action. They claimed that the University of California-Davis medical school used an unconstitutional racial quota (meaning, a fixed numerical admissions goal based on race). The university defended its admissions policies on many grounds. It made an argument for remedial racial justice; at this time, many college administrators across the country justified their race-conscious policies along these lines: as a means of countering Black disadvantage (Berrey 2011; Stulberg and Chen 2014). UC-Davis also argued for the benefits of diversity; this was a rationale that some of the country's most elite universities had developed in the late 1960s. And the university made an argument for the importance of racial minority role models in the medical profession (this position has never gained the prominence or legal footing that arguments for remedial justice and diversity have gained).

In a complicated, divided opinion, the Supreme Court found in *Bakke* that universities could engage in race-conscious admissions but could not use racial quotas. There was no consensus on the proper rationale.

What has received most attention out of the *Bakke* case is not the Court's final decision but, rather, a solo-authored opinion by Justice Lewis Powell. Powell's opinion offered a non-remedial defense of affirmative action. Pulling from a brief submitted by Harvard, Columbia, and a few other prestigious universities, he wrote about the value of diversity. According to Powell, students have a variety of characteristics that contribute to the mix on a college campus, and race is one of many "pertinent elements of diversity." He viewed race-conscious admissions as acceptable so long as the admissions counselors treated a student's ethno-racial identity as a "plus factor" and with the intention of achieving the social benefits of diversity. This was the first legal justification for the policy based on the instrumental pay-offs of diversity.

As legal scholar Ian Haney-López argues, Powell was influenced by policy elites who had a neoconservative assimilationist agenda (Haney-López, Ian F. 2006). These elites were responding to civil rights activists' structural analysis of racism by advancing a conception of race as ethnicity. According to that thinking, there are not dominant and subordinate racial groups but instead culturally defined groups in a pluralistic competition—giving little credence to white privilege or to institutional and interpersonal discrimination against people of color. So Powell's opinion preserved affirmative action, by taming its rationale with a logic of race as cultural difference.

Over the years, Powell's opinion became the touchstone for admissions offices that did affirmative action, as his was the safest opinion to follow. College administrators alit on the rhetoric of diversity as a description of their values and their student bodies (Berrey 2011, 2015a). That said, we do not know the extent to which schools actually eliminated any racial quotas they may have been using.

Meanwhile, those who opposed affirmative action—or, in their words, racial preferences—were becoming more politically influential. Their cause gained momentum with the growing conservative movement, which fueled White hostility against Black people.[15] This movement buoyed, and was buoyed by, the election of President Ronald Reagan in 1980, and it helped to put into place many more conservative judges. *Bakke* was the first of a number of court cases that restricted affirmative action. In the 1980s and 1990s, in the face of this movement, those who wished to argue that corporate and government policy should rectify systemic inequalities found the legal climate even more inhospitable. Significantly, the *City of Richmond v. Croson* case, which concerned affirmative action in employment, found that "remedying past societal discrimination" was not an acceptable defense for voluntary race-conscious policies. By the mid-1990s, the movement against racial preferences was winning victories in court and in state referenda. Proposition 209, passed in 1996, ended affirmative admissions in California. That same year, the Fifth Circuit Court's decision in *Hopwood v. State of Texas* halted voluntary, race-conscious admissions based in the diversity rationale in Texas, Mississippi, and Louisiana.

Through court cases and political actions such as these, and also through public opinion, the conservative movement has successfully made colorblindness a popular viewpoint and legal argument against affirmative action (Haney-López 2006). According to the colorblind position, race-conscious, equality-seeking policies are discriminatory. The reasoning is that such policies grant opportunities to people of color based solely on their racial group membership, and this violates the U.S. Constitution's protections for individuals. Political supporters of colorblindness frame their position in terms of protecting individual rights and preventing government overreach. When successful, colorblind advocates have redirected government away from progressive, collective objectives—specifically, away from earmarking resources specifically for the upward mobility of disadvantaged groups—and toward individual or private interests (Duam and Ishiwata 2010). Their actions have the effect of furthering entrenching White privilege while leaving it unacknowledged.

In contrast to the firm jurisprudential grounding for colorblindness, a diversity-based legal argument for affirmative action was not elaborated fully until the early 2000s.

4.1   The Law of Affirmative Admissions in the Early Twenty-First Century
In the late 1990s, the Center for Individual Rights, a libertarian public interest law firm, and three plaintiffs brought *Gratz* and *Grutter* against the University

---

15   Edsall, Thomas Byrne. *Chain Reaction: The Impact of Race, Rights, and Taxes on American Politics*. New York: W.W. Norton, 1992. For a review, See Gross, Neil, Thomas Medvetz, and Rupert Russell. "The Contemporary American Conservative Movement." *Annual Review of Sociology* 37 (2011): 325–354.

of Michigan. Arguing for colorblindness, *Gratz* challenged the university's main policy for undergraduate admissions, which awarded twenty additional points to African American, Latino, and Native American for their racial status out of a 150-point scale. *Grutter* challenged the law school's policy, which took race into account in a holistic review of each individual application. *Gratz* and *Grutter* turned out to be the most important affirmative action cases since 1978.

The University of Michigan administration mounted a remarkable legal and political campaign to defend its policies (Berrey 2015a; Stohr 2004). Given the legal record, diversity was the most viable argument in court. Drawing on Powell's opinion in *Bakke* and extensive social scientific research, the university administration argued what became known as the diversity rationale: that student learning improves and other benefits accrue when students interact with peers of different backgrounds, which include but are not limited to race and ethnicity.[16] The reasoning is that cross-racial interactions expose students to unfamiliar experiences and perspectives. Political support for Michigan came from all corners, including former U.S. president Gerald Ford, retired military officers, corporate executives, and the grassroots activists who organized the April 1 March on Washington.

The university had a high legal bar to pass. It needed to prove that its policies passed strict scrutiny—a difficult-to-achieve legal standard that, since *Bakke*, the conservative movement had successfully extended to race-conscious decision-making. If an institution wants to use racial classifications lawfully and still receive federal funding, it must demonstrate that its policies pass a two-prong test: that they serve a compelling governmental interest and that they are narrowly designed to achieve that interest.

Although the *Gratz* and *Grutter* litigation was framed in terms of a color-blind critique and a diversity defense, arguments for remedial justice could sometimes still be heard in popular debates and the news media, as they had been for decades (Gamson and Modigliani 1989). Notably, BAMN (or, the Coalition to Defend Affirmative Action and Fight for Equality by Any Means Necessary) intervened in *Grutter* in the lower court to argue that affirmative action was both corrective of social inequities and transformative in that it furthered integration.[17] The activists claimed that the policy offset discrimination

---

16   On the social scientific evidence, see Gurin, Patricia. "The Compelling Need for Diversity in Higher Education: Expert Report of Patricia Gurin in *Gratz, Et Al. V. Bollinger, Et Al.*, No. 97-75321(E.D. Mich.) and *Grutter, Et Al. V. Bollinger, Et Al*, No. 97-75928 (E.D. Mich.). January." (1999).

17   See also Gurin, Patricia. "The Compelling Need for Diversity in Higher Education: Expert Report of Patricia Gurin in *Gratz, Et Al. V. Bollinger, Et Al.*, No. 97-75321(E.D. Mich.) and *Grutter, Et Al. V. Bollinger, Et Al*, No. 97-75928 (E.D. Mich.). January." (1999).

in the university's admissions criteria, particularly standardized testing. However, while their claims resonated with many affirmative action supporters, the activists ultimately had little impact on decisions either at the Sixth Circuit or the Supreme Court (Berrey 2015b).[18]

In its 2003 majority decision in *Grutter,* the majority of the Supreme Court justices (5-4) rescued affirmative action from a colorblind challenge. It found that the Law School's policy of individualized, holistic review passed the test of strict scrutiny. The Court made clear that the diversity rationale was *the* legally defensible justification for voluntary affirmative action. Its majority opinion emphasized diversity's instrumental benefits for learning, the economy, and national defense. In *Gratz,* which proved to be a less important case, the Court found unconstitutional Michigan's policy of awarding additional points to the applications of students of color.

The university declared victory to much fanfare. After the Court's decisions, voices in support of diversity grew even louder. For instance, pro-affirmative action newspaper editorials overwhelmingly relied on an argument about diversity's productive benefits after the decisions were announced, in contrast to their more mixed opinions prior to the decisions.[19] Ten years later, diversity continued to hold sway as the most popular justification for affirmative action.

Michigan's impressive victory came with real compromises. The diversity rationale can be understood as a Hobson's choice: a choice between what is available and nothing at all (Berrey 2015a). This defense of affirmative action protects a modest yet effective corrective policy. It does so by leaving unacknowledged the United States' troubling problem of racial injustice. Its justification caters to White people's fears of losing privilege. The cost is that we are left without a trenchant, accurate, legally grounded diagnosis of racism.

5   The Ongoing Retreat from Affirmative Action

Although *Grutter* overturned the *Hopwood* decision, thus making affirmative action lawful in public universities in Texas, Louisiana, and Mississippi, the

---

18   The university could have made an argument about remedying discrimination, but it would have to argue that it was remedying its *own* history of discrimination—which it had no interest in doing, as it would mean admitting wrongdoing and, thus, opening the floodgates for lawsuits.

19   Richardson, John D., and Karen M. Lancendorfer. "Framing Affirmative Action: The Influence of Race on Newspaper Editorial Responses to the University of Michigan Cases." *Press/Politics* 9, no. 4 (2004): 74–94.

use of race-based affirmative action has been declining across the country. Most significantly, conservative activists succeed in created numerous state-level bans via ballot initiatives, executive action, and legislation. By 2015, the policy had been prohibited in eight states—California (1996), Washington (1998), Florida (1999), Michigan (2006), Nebraska (2008), Arizona (2010), New Hampshire (2011), and Oklahoma (2013)—and also by the University of Georgia (2000). Those eight states are home to 29 percent of U.S. high school students (Kahlenberg 2014). In Michigan, Jennifer Gratz and other activists spearheaded a misleadingly worded ballot initiative, which was fought by the university, BAMN, and other affirmative action supporters, to no avail (Lipson 2007). At the most prominent universities in those eight states, African American and Latino enrollment dropped—suggesting that affirmative action is particularly efficacious (and necessary) where admission is most competitive, perhaps because those selective institutions rely heavily on standardized test scores.[20] I return to this topic later in this chapter.

Affirmative action remains legally vulnerable. Thus far, two relatively minor Supreme Court cases have followed *Gratz* and *Grutter*. *Fisher v. University of Texas at Austin* (2013) charged that UT-Austin's admissions policy was not in line with *Grutter*. Again, a conservative/libertarian colorblind argument against affirmative action was met with a liberal/centrist diversity defense. The majority of the Court upheld *Grutter*. But it also returned the case to the lower court, stressing that UT-Austin would need to demonstrate that using race in admissions decisions was "necessary." In other words, in order to do affirmative action, universities would need to demonstrate that there was no other way to achieve a diverse student body but for considering race. Many observers read this as the Court making it all the more difficult for universities to do race-conscious admissions.

Schuette v. Coalition to Defend Affirmative Action (2014) was an altogether different sort of case. Led by BAMN and another group, it challenged the constitutionality of the state of Michigan's ban on affirmative action in public education and employment. This case was not specifically about college admissions and the legal standard was different than in *Gratz, Grutter,* and *Fisher*. It was not about strict scrutiny but, instead, political process doctrine, a thirty-year-old theory allowing people of color to advocate for public policies that support equality. According to the challengers, the ballot initiative in Michigan created a racially unfair political process: people of color, but not

---

20   For informative graphs, see *New York Times*. "How Minorities Have Fared in States With Affirmative Action Bans," June 30, 2015. http://www.nytimes.com/interactive/2013/06/24/us/affirmative-action-bans.html?_r=0.

any other group, would have to engage in an expensive, long-term campaign to amend the Michigan constitution if they wanted to contest a university's admissions policies to ensure that those policies reflect their interests. The challengers' argument was about structural inequality and civil rights. While they did not specifically argue for remedial racial justice, their claims made central problems of racial inequality. Ultimately, the majority of the Supreme Court justices decided against them. With that decision, the Court gave the green light to state-based affirmative action bans.

With each of these cases, the debate over affirmative action—and the broader question of how racial discrimination can be addressed—has continued to narrow. *Fisher* and *Schuette* are exemplary of the eagerness of the majority of the Court to undermine race-conscious, equality-seeking policies. They have been under the watch of Chief Justice John Roberts, who notoriously argued in *Parents Involved in Community Schools v. Seattle School District No. 7* (2007) that "the way to stop discrimination on the basis of race is to stop discriminating on the basis of race." At this point, the centrist, watered-down case for diversity is the only viable defense that remains, and it applies only to higher education, not even at the K-12 level.

6   The University of Michigan's New Identity of Diversity

Law has defined how colleges and universities can do race-based admissions and the justifications they must provide. However, these institutions do not simply adopt what law dictates, point blank. Neo-institutional research on law and organizations is instructive here. A rich body of research has shown that colleges—like companies, non-profit agencies, and other organizations—look to each other to figure out how to comply with laws.[21] A related insight is that, in a field such as higher education and within each individual organization, law is remade. Lauren Edelman and collaborators call this legal endogeneity.[22] Law offers fairly vague mandates, so organizations create structures like offices and policies that signal (but do not necessarily ensure) their compliance. As they do this, they mediate law's impact on society and

---

21   E.g., DiMaggio, Paul, and Walter W Powell. "The Iron Cage Revisited: Institutional Isomorphism and Collective Rationality in Organizational Fields." *American Sociological Review* 48, no. 2 (1983): 147–160.

22   E.g., Edelman, Lauren B. "Legal Ambiguity and Symbolic Structures: Organizational Mediation of Civil Rights Law." *American Journal of Sociology* 97, no. 1 (1992): 531–576.

reframe it according to their interests such as effective management or profit making.[23]

These findings prompt us to ask what universities and colleges have done with law on affirmative action, beyond retooling the technicalities and rhetorical justifications of their admissions policies. My own historical-ethnographic research on the politics and policies of affirmative action at the University of Michigan, which I conducted between 2002 and 2005, shows how law can prompt organizations to redefine what they stand for.[24] Over the past thirty-five years, Michigan has made diversity part of its distinctive public identity—one of the distilled, essential features it projects.[25] The university has done so by connecting diversity to its status as a research powerhouse and to its core objective of providing elite, public education. This is evident, for instance, on the university's Diversity, Equity, and Inclusion website portal, a letter from the university president Mark Schlissel opens, "The University of Michigan cannot be excellent without being diverse in the broadest sense of that word."[26] In addition, the university has developed an entire organizational infrastructure of diversity that includes organizational offices, positions, pedagogical programs, and funding dedicated to advancing diversity. Through initiatives such as the National Center for Institutional Diversity, it has directed some of its research resources towards studying how diversity works and can best work at colleges and universities.

The university first made a commitment to diversity central to its identity in the years following the *Bakke* decision (Berrey 2011). In fact, officials at Michigan all but copied-and-pasted their new rhetoric text from Powell's opinion. Take, for example, Michigan's 1987 undergraduate admissions brochure, which is that glossy booklet for applicants. In his opening letter, university president

---

23   Edelman, Lauren B., Sally Riggs Fuller, and Iona Mara-Drita. "Diversity Rhetoric and the Managerialization of Law." *American Journal of Sociology* 106, no. 6 (2001): 1589–1642.

24   For this study, I did field research on the political and public relations activities surrounding the *Gratz* and *Grutter* litigation prior to the Supreme Court's 2003 decisions and then, after the decisions, I did field research on changes in the undergraduate admissions office. This included participant observation on the public activities of a range of organizations, 30 formal interviews, and legal and document analysis. I also analyzed historical and archival documents to understand the development of affirmative action and the emergence of the push for diversity at Michigan since the 1960s. For details, see Berrey, 2015a.

25   Albert, Stuart, and David Whetten. "Organizational Iden Tity." In *Research in Organizational Behavior*, edited by Larry L. Cummings and Barry M. Staw, 263–295. Greenwich, CT: JAI Press, 1985.

26   http://diversity.umich.edu. Accessed December 4, 2015.

Harold Shapiro justifies the university's commitment to being "a racially, ethnically, and religiously heterogeneous community" by stating: "diversity is essential to creating an intellectual and social climate which promotes the freedom of thought, innovation, and creativity so fundamental to an academic community."

As evident in this quote, the Michigan administration did not simply make diversity their new description of affirmative action. In fact, their public rhetoric downplayed affirmative action policy altogether. Rather, university leaders—along with faculty, staff, and even students—made the diversity rationale a description of the admissions process, the student body, and the university at large. The university's promotional materials characterized students as coming from varied racial backgrounds, ethnic identities, geographic origins, religions, cultural traditions, philosophical leanings, and socio-economic circumstances. And students were repeatedly described as expressing unique cultural viewpoints, open to others' perspectives, and academically and socially enriched for being so. Photographs of students of different racial backgrounds, sitting on lush green grass, perhaps around a professor, deeply immersed in conversation became a mainstay.[27] Meanwhile, the administration kept the undergraduate affirmative admissions policy essentially the same—with different numeric thresholds for underrepresented racial minorities and majority students based on quantified factors liked standardized test scores—until it adopted the points system in 1997.[28] (The law school adopted a policy of holistic review in 1992.)

In the 1990s, the university engaged in an aggressive affirmative action policy, the Michigan Mandate, which was notably subtitled: "A Strategic Linking of Academic Excellence and Social Diversity." At the same time, the tone of the admissions and promotional materials became more focused on individual applicants and their personal experience. These materials also de-emphasized the theme of race. The 1996 undergraduate admissions brochure stressed that *everyone* contributes to diversity through their distinctive points of view: "We want your perspectives to find a place at Michigan, because we want to benefit from it, just as we believe you will benefit from the perspectives of others." During the litigation, from 1997 to 2003, the university's public discourse presented

---

27   Stevens, Mitchell. *Creating a Class: College Admissions and the Education of Elites.* Cambridge, MA: Harvard University Press, 2007.

28   Hirschman, Dan, Ellen Berrey, and Fiona Rose-Greenland. "Dequantifying Diversity: Affirmative Action and Admissions at the University of Michigan." *Theory and Society* (forthcoming).

Michigan as a place where academic excellence and diversity were deeply intertwined, where the expression of individual viewpoints generated instrumental benefits for all.

Following the 2003 *Gratz* and *Grutter* decisions, the university revamped the undergraduate admissions policy to comply with *Grutter*'s mandate for holistic, individualized review of applications. It also revised the names and criteria for scholarships and other special programming that had previously targeted students of color, relabeling them as "diversity" initiatives. Meanwhile, the administration continued its public education and public relations campaign to inform stakeholders about the legal cases. In their public discourse, administrators made Michigan's victory in *Gratz* and *Grutter* part of its identity, referencing the university's legal defense as evidence of its diversity commitment. They played up the theme of diverse perspectives and downplayed race even more. The Office of the Vice Provost produced a full-color glossy brochure about the cases, called "The Educational Value of Diversity: A Landmark Decision," which highlighted campus initiatives for gender, religious, and political diversity. No initiatives were identified as specifically about race. At the end of the brochure, the two main programs serving students of color, Multi-Ethnic Student Affairs and the Office of Academic and Multicultural Initiatives, were described as "open to all students."

By the early twentieth century, Michigan's notion of diversity was expansive enough that it need not include special attention to race at all. Even though administrators used the word to characterize university programs that worked toward racial minority representation and inclusion, the term diversity had been whitewashed, reduced to a code word for race and a palatable affirmation of cultural distinction.

7   Universities' Identities of Diversity: Beyond Michigan

Do these insights hold true at other colleges and universities? Have other institutions made diversity central to their identity? Diversity rhetoric and institutional diversity work—involving meeting, workshops, positions, programs, practitioners, and the like—have become common features throughout higher education in the U.S and beyond.[29] A national survey of 1,470 colleges and universities showed that 74 percent had mission statements that included

---

29   Ahmed, Sara. *On Being Included: Racism and Diversity in Institutional Life.* Durham, NC: Duke University Press, 2012.

a commitment to diversity.[30] The mission statements had fairly similar conceptions of diversity: 68 percent specified an ethnic and racial mix of students on campus, and 64 percent referenced other forms of diversity—most often geographic (77 percent) and socio-economic diversity (66 percent).

To understand the generalizability of what I observed at Michigan in my ethnographic-historical research, I did a separate analysis of the contemporary web sites of a random sample of 10 percent (20) of the nation's top 196 college and universities.[31] While Michigan is at the extreme in terms of its legal, political, and pedagogical campaign around diversity, and it is difficult to parse out fact from fabrication on a university web site, there nonetheless are similar patterns in how Michigan construed its diversity and how other colleges and universities do so.

Of the twenty colleges and universities analyzed, every single one had indications on its website that it supported diversity, inclusion, or racial minority access. Half (10) mentioned diversity in their mission statement, had a diversity and inclusion statement, or did both. Twelve had web pages specifically featuring diversity in campus life or human resources (beyond undergraduate admissions), and thirteen referenced diversity offices, positions, councils, and centers. All of the schools prominently posted at least one photograph or video with students of color and white students interacting in academic or social activities, although a handful of schools had very few of these images. Many described diversity as a self-evident attribute of an institution of higher education.

There was more variation in the extent to which the schools incorporated diversity into their distinctive identity, beyond these indicators. Eleven schools, to varying degrees, *strongly identified* with diversity by, for example, emphasizing their administrations' proactive institutional action around diversity. Four had explicit narratives that represented diversity as interwoven with their institutional identity, tailoring their value of diversity to the essential features of the institution. The website of Grinnell College, a small liberal arts college in Iowa with "an incredibly close-knit community," describes one

---

30   National Association of College Admissions Counseling. "Diversity and College Admission in 2003: A Survey Report." 1–44. Arlington, VA, 2003.

31   The pool of 196 colleges and universities was selected based on Barron's 2014 rankings of "highly competitive" and "most competitive" institutions. In March 2015, for each of the sampled schools, I reviewed the home page, the "about" pages, any mission/vision/inclusion statements, the admissions pages, and the main pages of any section devoted specifically to diversity or multiculturalism. Text, images, and videos were analyzed according to themes identified deductively, based on the secondary literature and my observations at Michigan, and inductively based on the materials themselves.

of the institution's three core values as "A diverse community." This includes "a wide diversity of people and perspectives" and "personal, egalitarian, and respectful interactions among all members of the college community."[32]

Three other colleges and universities *moderately identified* with diversity by, say, simply spotlighting it in the student body with generic, boilerplate language. The College of Mount Saint Vincent, for example, a Catholic liberal arts college, described its student body as diverse and open to diverse viewpoints. Its discussion of diversity was largely limited to one page of its online brochure, titled, "0 percent homogenous, 100 percent inclusive: Diversity at the Mount," with no connection to, say, the school's Catholic mission.[33] The six other colleges and universities analyzed had *no identification* with diversity, making little or no meaningful reference to it in the student body life (although one provided Spanish translation of some web pages).

On their websites, the twenty colleges and universities defined diversity broadly. Fourteen mentioned race specifically as a part of diversity, and fifteen mentioned other forms of diversity—most consistently geography, but also group-based differences such as sexual orientation and gender as well as cultural qualities such as backgrounds and perspectives. The schools noted various institutional objectives that involve diversity: fostering inclusiveness and heterogeneity (11 or 55%), teaching appreciation of difference (11 or 55%), and opening access to underrepresented groups (9 stated doing so for only racial minorities). Some rationales for diversity clearly echoed the legal conception of diversity by stressing exposure to students to different backgrounds (9 or 45%), students' self-expression and personal growth (6 or 30%), or else instrumental purposes (13 or 65%)—namely, better learning (11); preparation for a diverse world (7); excellence, innovation, and creativity (7); and career and leadership preparation (5). Only three schools cited an objective of understanding inequality and challenging discrimination. Kalamazoo College's student life page on multiculturalism stated, "Addressing issues of diversity with students and issues of institutional racism within the College is a very important part of a liberal arts education and the work of Kalamazoo College."[34]

This analysis indicates how colleges and universities have incorporated the principle of diversity into their institutional activity—into their public relations at the very least, and sometimes as something more. The push for diversity throughout higher education should be understood in social and

---

32 http://www.grinnell.edu/about/si/mission. Accessed December 4, 2015.

33 http://issuu.com/cmsvpubs/docs/final_cmsv_viewbook_high_quality/16. Accessed March 30, 2015.

34 http://www.kzoo.edu/studentlife/?p=multi. Accessed December 4, 2015.

economic context, in addition to the legal factors discussed earlier. The popularity of diversity has been connected to the growing multiculturalism on college campuses (Berrey 2011). It is a catchall word that characterizes students of many different backgrounds, including those who are gay and lesbian, low-income, of different faith traditions, or—increasingly important for financially strapped institutions—from outside the U.S. and more likely to afford full tuition. Diversity rhetoric and imagery get circulated through admissions offices' slick promotional materials, which are part of the neoliberalization of higher education as colleges and universities compete for top applicants. For many, diversity is part of the sales pitch to prospective students.[35]

As a mediator of power dynamics, diversity simultaneously reinforces and denies white privilege. It validates whiteness by marking who is "different" just as it gets used to mask the homogeneity of an all-white campus.[36] Research shows that college brochures create an image of college campuses with a far greater percentage of students of color than actually attend. The diversity photoshopping can go to extremes. The University of Wisconsin-Madison published a photograph on its admissions brochure that had been doctored so that the all-white crowd at a football game appeared to include an African American student, Diallo Shabazz.[37]

So, how does the push for diversity actually matter for the conditions of inequality and exclusion on college campuses? The experience of the University of Michigan is instructive.

8   Overcoming Inequality at the University of Michigan

That the University of Michigan saved affirmative action nationwide and identifies as a diversity champion does not necessarily mean that it has been successful at improving problems of racial inequality on campus. The results are mixed and the data limited and, again, the line between window

---

35   Urciuoli, Bonnie. "Excellence, Leadership, Skills, Diversity: Marketing Liberal Arts Education." *Language & Communication* 23, no. 3–4 (2003): 385–408. Kreiter and Scarritt 2015

36   Ahmed, 2012.

37   Pippert, Timothy D., Laura J. Essenburg, and Edward J. Matchett. "We've Got Minorities, Yes We Do: Visual Representations of Racial and Ethnic Diversity in College Recruitment Materials." *Journal of Marketing for Higher Education* 23, no. 2 (2013): 258–282. On the doctored photo and fallout, see Lisa Wade, "Doctoring Diversity: Race and Photoshop," The Society Pages, Sept. 2, 2009. http://thesocietypages.org/socimages/2009/09/02/doctoring -diversity-race-and-photoshop/ Accessed December 4, 2015.

dressing and organizational efficacy can be difficult to discern. The university's implementation of the Michigan Mandate coincided with higher enrollment and graduation rates of students of color. Between 1988 and 1998, the percentage of undergraduate and graduate students who were African American, Latino, Native American, and Asian increased from 15 percent to 25 percent.[38] The university's longitudinal Michigan Student Study examined the student experience of diversity. In 2004, the vast majority of Michigan college seniors—from 68 percent of white seniors to 79 percent of African American ones—reported that diversity had "quite a bit" or "a great deal" of an impact on their college experience. For most of those individuals, the impact was positive.[39] The 2004 seniors and alumni of the university, reflecting on their years on campus, felt their exposure to different types of people and perspectives had enhanced their intellectual development and cross-cultural awareness.

Yet problems for students of color on Michigan's campus have persisted and the promise of diversity, as formulated by the university, has not been realized. Some of this has been caused by factors outside the university's control: the state-level ban on affirmative action caused a major drop in the enrollment of students of color. In fall 2013, Black, Latino, and Native American student made up 10 percent of the first-year undergraduate class, which was the first admitted solely under the university's race-blind admissions policies.[40] This was a decrease from 15 percent in fall 2003, the last class admitted under the point system. The percentage of African American students declined even more dramatically.[41] In fall 2013, African American students made up 4.6 percent of the undergraduate student body—down from a peak of 9 percent in 1997 and below their 5 percent representation in the early 1980s.[42]

38   University of Michigan, Board of Regents. "Proceedings of the Board of Regents," 1988; University of Michigan. *Undergraduate Enrollment, Ann Arbor Campus*, 2003. http://obp .umich.edu/wp-content/uploads/pubdata/factsfigures/enrollment_umaa_fall13.pdf. Accessed Mar. 15, 2014.

39   Office of Academic and Multicultural Affairs, University of Michigan. "About the Michigan Student Study: Current Research Synopsis." No date. www.umich.edu/~oami/mss/ about/research.htm. Accessed September 18, 2006.

40   University of Michigan. *University of Michigan-Ann Arbor: Freshman Class Profile, Fall 2009-Fall 2013*, 2003. obp.umich.edu/root/facts-figures/students/. Accessed Mar. 15, 2014.

41   University of Michigan, Office of the Registrar. *Report 844: University of Michigan-Ann Arbor, New Freshmen by School or College, Citizenship and Ethnicity*, 2013. http://ro.umich .edu/report/03fa844.pdf Accessed Mar. 23, 2011 University of Michigan. *Undergraduate Enrollment, Ann Arbor Campus.* http://obp.umich.edu/wp-content/uploads/pubdata/ factsfigures/enrollment_umaa_fall13.pdf. Accessed Mar. 15, 2014.

42   University of Michigan, Office of the Registrar. *Report 872a: University of Michigan-Ann Arbor, Undergraduate Enrollment by Race, Opportunity Program, and Entry Type, 1993–1999*, 1999. http://www.umich.edu/~regoff/. Accessed Mar. 23, 2011.

Many issues of exclusion remain under the university's control, however. A study of the law school showed that opportunities for diversity discussions in the classroom were repeatedly missed.[43] Some faculty members and students lacked interest in race and other issues of identity and the topic of exclusion in the classroom, or they were uncomfortable with such conversations. More recently, as their numbers have dwindled, students of color at Michigan have found themselves isolated in what for many is a hostile campus environment. Students launched a Twitter campaign, Being Black at University of Michigan (#BBUM) in fall 2013, after a Michigan fraternity threw a "Hood Ratchet Thursday" party for "bad bitches" and "ratchet pussy," The purpose of BBUM was to voice "unique experiences of being Black at Michigan." Students tweeted comments such as "When every room you stand in on campus 9x out of 10 your [stet] the only one that is Black." The group organized protests, calling for greater representation of Black students on campus. The hashtag quickly trended on Twitter and captured the media spotlight. Similar campaigns at University of California – Los Angeles (UCLA), Harvard University, and other predominantly White campuses raised similar issues.

The movement against campus racism caught fire in fall of 2015. Activists from Yale University to University of Missouri to Claremont McKenna College mobilized to demand greater hiring of racial minority faculty members, mandatory training, and other interventions to make predominantly white colleges and universities more hospitable for students of color.[44] We have yet to see just how receptive university and college administrators will be, but the high profile resignations of a few campus leaders and the ubiquity of "town hall" campus sessions suggest that at least some schools will implement modest reforms. While many activists have couched their demands in terms of a desire for greater diversity, they rely largely on a discourse of anti-racism in their diagnosis of the problems at hand.

9   Is Diversity Racial Justice?

Diversity's advocates have institutionalized, in the name of diversity, a conception of race as a cultural identity, expressed in interaction and instrumentally

---

43   Deo, Meera E. "The Promsie of *Grutter:* Diverse Interactions at the University of Michigan Law School." *Michigan Journal of Race and Law* 17, no. 63 (2011). See also Moore, Wendy Leo, and Joyce M. Bell. "Maneuvers of Whiteness: 'Diversity' as a Mechanism of Retrenchment in the Affirmative Action Discourse." *Critical Sociology* 37, no. 5 (2011): 597–614.

44   For a compendium of campus activists' demands, see thedemands.org. For a summary analysis, see http://fivethirtyeight.com/features/here-are-the-demands-from-students-protesting-racism-at-51-colleges/. Both accessed December 4, 2015.

valuable for learning, leadership, and personal enlightenment. The Supreme Court's *Grutter* decision gave legitimacy to this formulation of race-as-diversity. Many universities portray their institutional identity and student body in similar terms. As both legal doctrine and organizational identity, diversity can provide a politically palatable cover for a progressive race-based policy. At the same time, it can facilitate a turn *away* from an analysis of group-level racial dynamics and institutional problems of racial inequality. Put to use, it affirms the cause of minority inclusion while routinely failing to recognize the structural foundations of racial inequality.

Critical race scholar Derrick Bell has made the astute point that progress toward racial equality for Black people is only politically viable when White people see it is as expedient for themselves.[45] He was writing about the historic *Brown v. Board of Education* (1954) case, but his observation holds true for the diversity rationale. Affirmative action supporters seem to perceive that White people see themselves in diversity or at least find the idea appealing and non-threatening. Likewise, according to psychologists, White people have more positive associations with an all-inclusive conceptualization of diversity than one that seems to be just for minorities (although, overall, White people associate diversity as exclusive of themselves).[46]

Today, racism in college admissions—like racism throughout American society—has become subtler in many respects than prior to the 1960s civil rights reforms. Nonetheless, it remains pernicious and consequential and tightly bundled up with class discrimination. A decline in the enrollment of students of color at top public universities and colleges due to affirmative action bans means that capable students are unfairly blocked from opportunity. The same will hold true throughout higher education if opponents succeed in banning the practice. Such declines also mean that our country is missing out on affirmative action's many positive social effects, both on campus and beyond. The prospects of these changes are deeply troubling. Even with affirmative action policies, those who attend highly selective, predominantly White campuses routinely report feeling isolated and unsupported by administrators, faculty, and other students. Without affirmative action or effective alternative policies, their enrollment numbers plummet, and their sense of isolation becomes ever more acute.

---

45   Bell, Derrick A., Jr. "Brown v. Board of Education and the Interest-Convergence Dilemma." *Harvard Law Review*, 93 (1980): 518–533.

46   Plaut, Victoria C., Flannery G. Garnett, Laura E. Buffardi, and Jeffrey Sanchez-Burks. "'What About Me?' Perceptions of Exclusion and Whites' Reactions to Multiculturalism." *Journal of Personality and Social Psychology* 101, no. 1 (2011): 337–353.

10   Affirmative Action's Future

At the time of this writing, a few important developments bear on the future of affirmative action. The first of these is the ongoing mobilization of opponents, combined with the ideological opposition of numerous Supreme Court justices toward race-conscious admissions and employment decisions. That the Court has agreed to hear the *Fisher* case again in the 2015–16 term suggests that it considers the issue unresolved. Critical observers predict that, under the guise of incremental approach to decision-making associated with Chief Justice Roberts, the Court is making the activist move of trying to overturn *Grutter*.[47]

Two new cases filed in federal court in late 2014 add a new twist to affirmative action challenges. These cases contest admissions policies at Harvard College (*Students for Fair Admissions Inc. v. President and Fellows of Harvard College*) and University of North Carolina (*Students for Fair Admissions Inc. v. University of North Carolina*). Brought by investment broker Edward Blum (who also brought *Fisher*) and groups of applicants who were rejected by both schools, the litigation is developing a case that will likely reach the Supreme Court in a few years. While the plaintiffs' charges in these cases are for colorblindness—they take issue with the universities' practice of continuing to "unconstitutionally use racial preferences in admissions decision"—the specifics of the argument are new. The claim against Harvard alleges that, just as the university discriminated against Jews in the past, it now engages in racial discrimination by setting admissions quotas on Asian American students and doing "racial balancing." The activists also have put pressure on a number of other elite colleges, including Yale Law School, regarding the transparency of their admissions processes. Given the conservative voting record of the majority of the Supreme Court justices, the legal fate of affirmative action seems quite dire.

Another development influencing the future of affirmative action is the growing popularity of alternative policies that, at face value, are racially neutral, especially those that seek to increase enrollment of low-income students. In fact, in a surprising convergence of political agendas, some conservative and progressive intellectuals and scholars have rallied behind the cause of class-based affirmative action (Kahlenberg 2014). In most of the eight states where

---

47   For a compelling prediction, see Melissa Hart's discussion on the respected SCOTUS blog. http://www.scotusblog.com/2015/09/symposium-incremental-in-name-only/. Accessed December 4, 2015.

affirmative action has been banned, the flagship universities subsequently adopted alternative admissions strategies designed to boost enrollment of students of color and low-income students without giving explicit attention to race. The best known of these strategies are the percent plans used in California, Florida, and Texas. Such admissions plans give preferential treatment to top graduates from every high school. These policies are sure to bring in students from a range of geographic locations, and because American communities and high schools are racially and economically segregated, they also can bring in students from a range of such backgrounds.

At some schools that implemented alternative strategies, the enrollment of African Americans and Latino/as recovered to pre-ban levels—although not at the most elite schools, University of California-Berkeley, UCLA, and University of Michigan (Kahlenberg 2014). Other forms of class-based affirmative action are in use, as well. A national survey by the American Council on Education found that 71 percent of universities and colleges survey do targeted recruitment and outreach to encourage low-income and/or first-generation students to apply and 73 percent see those strategies as effective for increasing racial minority enrollment.[48] There also is a much smaller chorus of people who argue that eliminating standardized tests would offset obstacles for students of color; rigorous sociological research supports this claim.[49]

The criticisms of these so-called race-blind strategies of percent plans and class-based affirmative action have been many, including that they fail to meaningfully offset White favoritism in admissions, that they rely on the problematic geographic segregation that currently exists at the secondary school level[50] and that simply keeping up with the pre-ban representation of Black and Latino students is not an adequate measure, particularly given the exploding nonwhite population in states such as Texas (Tienda 2014). According to an amicus brief signed by 823 academics in *Fisher II*:

---

48 Espinosa, Lorelle, Matthew N. Gaertner, and Gary Orfield. *Race, Class, and College Access: Acheiving Diversity in a Shifting Legal Landscape.* Washington, DC: American Council on Education, 2015.

49 Strauss, Valier. "What one college discovered when it stopped accepting SAT/ACT scores," *Washington Post,* Sept. 25, 2015. https://www.washingtonpost.com/blogs/answer-sheet/wp/2015/09/25/what-one-college-discovered-when-it-stopped-accepting-satact-scores/?postshare=981443292600992. Accessed Dec. 4, 2015.

50 Brief of 823 Social Scientists as Amici Curae in Support of Respondents. *Fisher v. The University of Texas-Austin, et al.,* 2015. http://civilrightsproject.ucla.edu/legal-developments/legal-briefs/amicus-brief-of-social-scientists-in-fisher-case/14-981-823-social-scientists-fisher.pdf Accessed Dec. 4, 2015.

Giving weight to socioeconomic status alone does not produce the diversity needed to further UT Austin's academic mission, and relying largely or solely on socioeconomic status to achieve diversity is not a feasible alternative. The extensive experience of selective colleges and universities using alternatives to race-sensitive admissions decisions in other states, including California and Michigan, underscores the need for UT Austin's holistic policy. This evidence compels the conclusion that there are no effective substitutes for race-sensitive admissions decisions in generating the diversity required to further UT Austin's educational mission.

Perhaps endorsements of class-based affirmative action are a sign that, at least in the public imagination, the meaningful cleavage in American society is not the color line but the deepening class divide between rich and poor. Such a shift is promising for addressing serious issues of class inequality, but questions remain about its efficacy at addressing vexing, unresolved problems of racial injustice.

References

Alon, Sigal, and Marta Tienda. 2007. "Diversity, Opportunity, and the Shifting Meritocracy in Higher Education." *American Sociological Review*, 72 (4): 487–511.

Berrey, Ellen. 2015b. "Making a Civil Rights Claim for Affirmative Action: Bamn's Legal Mobilization and the Legacy of Race-Conscious Policies." *Du Bois Review*.

Berrey, Ellen. 2015a. *The Enigma of Diversity: The Language of Race and the Limits of Racial Justice*. Chicago, IL: University of Chicago Press.

Berrey, Ellen. 2011. "Why Diversity Became Orthodox in Higher Education, and How It Changed the Meaning of Race on Campus." *Critical Sociology*, 37 (5): 573–596.

Bowen, William G., and Derrick Bok. 1998. *The Shape of the River: Long-Term Consequences of Considering Race in College and University Admissions*. Princeton, NJ: Princeton University Press.

Carnevale, Anthony P., and Stephen J. Rose. 2003. *Socioeconomic Status, Race/Ethnicity and Selective College Admissions*. New York, NY: The Century Foundation, March.

Crenshaw, Kimberlé, Neil Gotanda, and Gary Peller. 1996. *Critical Race Theory: The Key Writings That Formed the Movement*. New York: The New Press.

Duam, Courtenay W., and Eric Ishiwata. 2010. "From the Myth of Formal Equality to the Politics of Social Justice: Race and the Legal Attack on Native Entitlements." *Law & Society Review*, 44 (3/4): 843–875.

Espenshade, Thomas J., and Alexandria Walton Radford. 2009. *No Longer Separate, Not yet Equal: Race and Class in Elite College Admission and Campus Life*. Princeton, NJ: Princeton University Press.

Espinosa, Lorelle, Matthew N. Gaertner, and Gary Orfield. 2015. *Race, Class, and College Access: Acheiving Diversity in a Shifting Legal Landscape*. Washington, DC: American Council on Education.

Gamson, William A, and Andre Modigliani. 1989. "Media Discourse and Public Opinion on Nuclear Power: A Constructionist Approach." *American Journal of Sociology*, 95 (1): 1–37.

Gasman, Marybeth. 2015. "Minority-Serving Institutions: A Historical Backdrop." In *Understanding Minority-Serving Institutions*, edited by Marybeth Gasman, Benjamin Baez and Caroline Sotello Viernes Turner. Albany, NY: SUNY Press.

Grodsky, Eric. 2007. "Compensatory Sponsorship in Higher Education." *American Journal of Sociology*, 112 (6): 1662–1712.

Haney-López, Ian F. 2006. "A Nation of Minorities: Race, Ethnicity, and Reactionary Colorblindness." *Stanford Law Review*, 59: 985–1064.

Harper, Shannon, and Barbara Reskin. 2005. "Affirmative Action at School and on the Job." *Annual Review of Sociology* 31: 357–379.

Holmes, Steven. 1997. "Thinking About Race with a One-Track Mind." New York Times Dec. 21: p. 1, section 4. In Hochschild, Jennifer. "Affirmative Action as Culture War." In *A Companion to Racial and Ethnic Studies*, edited by David Theo Goldberg and John Solomos, 282–303. Malden, MA: Blackwell, 2002.

Kahlenberg, Richard D. 2014. *The Future of Affirmative Action: New Paths to Higher Education after Fisher V. University of Texas*. New York, NY: The Century Foundation Press.

Karabel, Jerome. 2005. *The Chosen*. New York: Houghton Mifflin, 2005.

Kennedy, Randall. 2013. *For Discrimination: Race, Affirmative Action and the Law*. New York, NY: Vintage.

Lemann, Nicholas. 1999. *The Big Test: The Secret History of the American Meritocracy*. New York: Farrar, Straus, & Giroux.

Lipson, Daniel N. 2007. "Embracing Diversity: The Institutionalization of Affirmative Action as Diversity Management at Uc-Berkeley, Ut-Austin, and Uw-Madison." *Law & Social Inquiry*, 32 (4): 985–1026.

Moore, Wendy Leo. 2008. *Reproducing Racism: White Space, Elite Law Schools and Racial Inequality*. Lanham, MD: Rowman & Littlefield.

Schwartzman, Luisa Farah, and Angela Randolpho Paiva. 2014. "Not Just Racial Quotas: Affirmative Action in Brazilian Higher Education 10 Years Later." *British Journal of Sociology of Education*. DOI: 10.1080/01425692.2014.973015.

Skrentny, John David. 2002. *The Minority Rights Revolution*. Cambridge, MA: Belknap Press of Harvard University Press.

Skrentny, John David. 1996. *The Ironies of Affirmative Action: Politics, Culture, and Justice in America*. Chicago: University of Chicago Press.

Stohr, Greg. 2004. *A Black and White Case: How Affirmative Action Survived Its Greatest Legal Challenge*. Princeton, NJ: Bloomberg Press.

Stulberg, Lisa M., and Anthony S. Chen. 2014. "The Origins of Race-Conscious Affirmative Action in Undergraduate Admissions: A Comparative Analysis of Institutional Change in Higher Education." *Sociology of Education*, 87 (1): 36–52.

Tienda, Marta. "Striving for Neutrality: Lessons from Texas in the Aftermath of Hopwood and Fisher." In Kahlenberg, 2014: pp. 91–98.

CHAPTER 4

Disfavored Subjects: How Liberalist Diversity Fails Racial Equity in Higher Education

Joyce M. Bell and Wendy Leo Moore

1   Introduction

In the spring of 2014, legal scholar Kimberlé Crenshaw visited the campus of Texas A&M University to discuss contemporary issues of racial inclusion at historically white colleges and universities. Professor Crenshaw noted that the strategic decisions of civil rights activists, particularly in the legal profession, focused on civic and political participation and lifting the barriers to access to white institutions like education and employment for people of color. The 1964 Civil Rights Act was crafted to eliminate discrimination in public spaces, employment, education, and other social arenas, to provide access for people of color, and the 1965 Voting Rights Act was crafted to protect the political participation of people of color (especially African Americans). Much less consideration was given to how the dynamics of previously exclusively white institutions—like colleges and universities—would manifest when people of color actually had access to them. As a result, people of color often entered institutional spaces that operated on a logic of exclusion that worked to reproduce marginalization within them.

Lyndon B. Johnson spoke to this issue in the commencement address he gave at Howard University in 1965. On the cusp of signing the Voting Rights Act, Johnson argued that equality of opportunity was a beginning—not the end. "But freedom is not enough..." he told the new graduates, "You do not take a person who, for years, has been hobbled by chains and liberate him, bring him up to the starting line of a race and then say, 'you are free to compete with all the others,' and still justly believe that you have been completely fair." Making the case that access wasn't enough, he argued that meaningful access was the "next and more profound stage of the battle for civil rights," and that we needed "not just equality as a right and a theory but equality as a fact and equality as a result."

Johnson was speaking at a historical moment when it looked like there would be reform: Colleges and universities started implementing affirmative action policies and attempting to heed Johnson's call to provide meaningful access. But within a short period, the Courts reacted to this reform project with a project of retrenchment, substantively dismantling affirmative action policies. As a result of the Supreme Court's treatment of affirmative action cases, affirmative action was reduced to a tool for diversity—completely stripped of potential to remedy the racial inequities that Johnson suggested would be needed in the pursuit of true equality. But more than that, the Court's decisions actually reinforced the idea that institutions of higher education were fundamentally white institutional spaces and should remain such. By favoring the rights of "innocent whites" to unfettered access to educational institutions over the rights of people of color to gain remedial access to them, the Court provided a legal frame for the reproduction of white space in higher education in the United States.

Even more troublesome, is the fact that next to the abstract individualistic and colorblind racist frames that characterize white institutional space, a sporadic, but relatively consistent, pattern of racial hostility existed—a pattern that continues to this day. Incidents of white racist speech, white symbolic violence and white physical violence are a persistent feature of US college campuses. As a result, several colleges and universities attempted to create policies to protect people of color from racist harassment. These anti-harassment policies, however, came under fire from free speech activists and with a logic that paralleled the affirmative action jurisprudence: an abstract-individualistic framing of the notion of freedom of speech that situated all speech as structurally the same and part of a diverse market-place of ideas, and therefore asserted a Constitutional right to racially hostile expression. U.S. courts responded once again with a logic that protected white space, constructing a fierce absolutist protection of free speech resulting in the functional dismantling of racial harassment policies in higher education.

This chapter examines the role that the diversity rationale, and its concomitant abstract liberalistic frame, plays in shaping race-based higher education law and policy concerning racial equity. Further, we make the case that the reliance on a diversity rationale that ignores racial relations of power normalizes and reproduces racial inequality in higher education, and thus re-instantiates these institutions as fundamentally white spaces. We use the idea of abstract liberalistic diversity to capture a set of discursive and rhetorical tools that (1) purport to value racial difference; (2) dissociate racial differentiation from racial inequality; and (3) provide the basis for race-based praxis (including everyday practices, policies, and legal structures). We examine the effect of abstract liberalistic diversity on affirmative action jurisprudence and in the legal resistance to racial harassment policy in higher education.

1.1   *Mapping the Rhetorical Maneuvers of the Abstract Liberalistic Diversity Rationale*

Contemporary race scholars note that in the post-civil rights era, racial discourse relies on an abstract liberalism that avows ideological commitment to racial equality, but simultaneously rhetorically minimizes the relevance of a racialized social structure characterized by white racial privilege, power, and wealth (Bonilla-Silva, 2010, 1997). Utilizing this discursive tactic, whites are able to normalize white domination without ever expressing racial animosity. One manifestation of this normalization occurs through the assertion of colorblindness, a principle that minimizes the relevance of race and racism, and discursively divorces structural racial inequality from historical and present day racism (Carr, 1997; Crenshaw, 1994; Eliasoph, 1999). As Ian Haney Lopez argues, "the perversity of colorblindness [is that it] redoubles the hegemony of race by targeting efforts to combat racism while leaving race and its effects unchallenged and embedded in society, seemingly natural rather than the product of social choice" (2006: 125).

As a vast body of social scientific research has documented, the United States, in all its major institutions, is characterized by racism and racial inequality. As a result of a history and legacy of legally constructed and enforced racial oppression, deep structural inequalities permeate U.S. society today (Harris 1993; Haney Lopez 2006; Moore 2008). The United States is one of the most residentially racially segregated countries in the world, and this geographical segregation (which is the result of historical and contemporary legal, political and economic racist practices) corresponds to severe structural economic inequality (Jargowsky 1997; Massey and Denton 1998; Bell 2000; Oliver and Shapiro 2006). The history of racism produced contemporary structural inequalities affects nearly every facet of American society. Education in the K-12 system is as segregated and unequal in many instances as it was pre-*Brown v. Board of Education*[1] (Kozol and Perluss 1992; Lewis 2003; Orfield and Eaton 1996). People of color are under-represented in higher education and historically white educational institutions remain demographically disparate and ideologically organized around white norms, making them fundamentally white institutional spaces in which students of color struggle to perform to their full capabilities (Feagin, Vera and Imani 1996; Moore 2008). Furthermore, African Americans are vastly over-represented in jails and prisons and under the authority of the ever-expanding criminal justice system (Davis 2011; Tonry 1995).

In spite of this structural inequality, the dominant post-civil rights ideological and discursive frame seemingly incorporates civil rights conceptions of

---

1   *Brown v. Board of Education,* 347 U.S. 483 (1954).

color-blindness, equality and democracy, yet covertly protects white privilege, power, and wealth by rhetorically divorcing these concepts from the structural realities of racial inequality (Bell 1992). Rhetorical manipulations of civil rights language makes it possible for individuals to assert, for example, an opposition to racial segregation in schools, and a simultaneous opposition to having their own children bussed in a desegregation plan (see Wellman 1993). This is accomplished through color-blind discursive tactics which deploy an abstract liberal recognition of race as a superficial set of cultural differences, which should be accepted and celebrated, but simultaneously ignores that race has any real effect on the life chances of individuals or that race shapes social life in any significant way (see Bonilla-Silva 2001, Carr 1997; Crenshaw 1997; DiTamaso et al. 2003; Doane and Bonilla-Silva 2003; Gallagher 2003). It is this framing of race as superficial, largely aesthetic, and disconnected from structure and power that has become the basis for a construction of the concept of "diversity" which U.S. courts have utilized as a tool of white retrenchment to deemphasize the relevance of the racial social structure, which merges into a minimization of racial power with regard to legal definitions of racial discrimination. This conception of "diversity" relies on a thin and tenuous foundation based in a larger color blind racist frame that works to simultaneously celebrate perceived cultural contributions of people of color and disavow the existence of historical and contemporary structures of racism (Andersen 1999, Bell and Hartmann 2007). The effect of this rhetorical maneuver is that the goal of achieving racial equity can be replaced with an amorphous goal of achieving "diversity."

2   Retrenchment, Diversity, and Affirmative Action

As reflected in the Howard University speech of President Johnson noted above, institutional policies of affirmative action were designed to give substantive meaning to the promise of access for people of color into institutions of education and employment from which they had been previously excluded. Affirmative action policies in higher education were meant to recognize the dynamics of structural white domination and create equitable avenues of access to people of color who did not have the same resources as their white peers as a result of the racist social structure. White resistance and retrenchment, beginning at nearly the same moments these policies were first enacted, influenced the legal analysis of the US Supreme Court, and the Court rejected generalized historical legal racial exclusion and oppression, as well as resulting structural racial discrimination as a basis for use of affirmative action practices.

In constructing its legal analysis of affirmative action policies, the Court asserted that Constitutional principles of equal protection are and should be color-blind. The 1978 case of *Regents of the University of California v. Bakke* was the first case to examine affirmative action in the context of higher education and the court explicitly affirms a color-blind racial legal analysis:

> The guarantee of equal protection cannot mean one thing when applied to one individual and something ... else when ... applied to a person of another color. If both are not accorded the same protection, then it is not equal. (1978: 289–290)[2]

As a result of this case, and others in the line of cases involving affirmative action (as well as other areas of law falling under the rubric of equal protection of the law) equal protection with regard to race essentially means treating all people the same, and never explicitly taking account of race or past racism. The Court does recognize, however, that there are limited circumstances in which race may be considered, yet it ultimately holds that race can only be recognized in government policies when there is a compelling state interest which requires explicit consideration of race, and even then the policy must be "narrowly tailored" to meet that compelling interest. This language has come to be known as "strict scrutiny" with equal protection jurisprudence.

The *Bakke* case involved an affirmative action policy that set aside specific seats in the medical school at the University of California at Riverside for under-represented racial minorities and was so contentious that no Court written opinion was unanimous. Instead the opinion of Justice Powell, who sat on the proverbial fence in the case, came to be regarded as the authoritative opinion. In his opinion, Justice Powell confirmed that historical discrimination was not a compelling justification to use race in higher education admissions, and he further noted that the system used by UC-Riverside was an illegal quota. However, Justice Powell suggested that institutions of higher education could "consider" race, though in a less formalistic manner; Powell suggested that the goal of "diversity" was relevant in education. Thus, the concept of "diversity" became the only compelling justification recognized by the Court as a legal basis for utilizing the policy of affirmative action in admissions into institutions of higher education.

Nearly the instant that "diversity" in education became a rationale recognized by the Court as an interest so compelling as to justify the use of race-conscious

---

2   The dots within the quotations from Court opinions indicate editing for readability.

policies like affirmative action, the concept was de-racialized; securely fitted into the color-blind sub-frame. Justice Powell thus notes in *Bakke* that, "preferring members of any one group for no reason other than race or ethnic origin is discrimination for its own sake" (307). However, he says that "race or ethnic background may be ... deemed a 'plus' in a particular applicant's file ... [such that] the file of a particular black applicant [can] be examined for his potential contribution to diversity without the factor of race being decisive when compared, for example, with that of an applicant identified as an Italian-American if the latter is thought to exhibit qualities more likely to promote beneficial educational pluralism." (1978: 317). Further, Justice Powell noted that the decision making process involved in such a use of affirmative action must be, "flexible enough to consider *all pertinent elements of diversity* (our emphasis) in light of the particular qualifications of each applicant" (1978: 317).

Justice Powell's conception of diversity is grounded in a color-blind frame, which includes, but is not limited to, an amorphous form of racial diversity (race as a "plus factor" along with other "pertinent elements of diversity") which limits the legally recognized basis for affirmative action policies in higher education admissions. The framing of the legal analysis thus reduces the power of this policy to significantly alter the racial hierarchy. By placing race alongside any number of "pertinent elements of diversity" the court buys directly into what Margaret Anderson calls "diversity without oppression" (1999: 5) This broad conception of diversity as divorced from the context of white supremacy and anti-black racism in the United States feeds into the colorblind notion that to be black or white or a top French horn player or from the Upper Peninsula of Michigan are all equally important elements of difference.

Diversity as a larger racial project has worked in US society to provide a comfortable framework for talking about real social differences without ever having to face the uncomfortable reality of social inequality. This is because, as Bell and Hartmann suggest, "the discourse of diversity rests on a white normative perspective" (2007: 907). Mobilizing the concept of a white racial frame, Bell & Hartmann argue that diversity discourse is based on an "assumption of a white center to which color is harmoniously added" (2007: 909) This assumption, they argue embeds the discourse of diversity within a frame that fundamentally excludes consideration of racial inequality, as well as white power and privilege.

Relying on a diversity justification for affirmative action creates limitations on its potential as a tool for redistributive or corrective racial justice. By arguing that the primary justification for affirmative action is the potential benefit of an individual's contribution to educational diversity, the Court (as well as anyone else who may utilize this frame) buys into the colorblind notion that the only relevant reason to talk about race is to celebrate difference. The Court also establishes the rhetorical groundwork whereby white people, white ideas, and white ways of being in the world remain central. Diversity discourse neutralizes and conceals whiteness through language and practices that treat institutions as inherently white and exoticizes, criticizes, trivializes, and compartmentalizes the cultural objects of people of color as contributions to ... a presumably neutral "us" (Bell and Hartmann, 2007). One effect of neutralizing the power and privilege of whiteness in the discourse around affirmative action in a society based on white supremacy is that it silences people of color and denies the existence of unequal power relations among the races. As Estrada and McLaren (1993) argue, through dominant discourses, those who occupy privileged positions in our society forge a universalized, sanitized and naturalized "we" that prevents the "they" from speaking for themselves. This function of relying on "diversity" as a justification for affirmative action ensures that the larger white narrative around the policy remains intact.

The discursive legal framing of race issues in the *Bakke* decision severely limited the potential force of affirmative action policies to effect racial change in higher education. In 2003 the two most recent Supreme Court decisions on affirmative action in higher education, *Gratz v. Bollinger* and *Grutter v. Bolinger* further enforced the color-blindness frame in the legal analyses of race and affirmative action. Reaffirming color-blindness, and noting its solid foundation in much affirmative action case law by citing and using the language of several relevant cases relating to affirmative action in areas other than higher education, the Court in *Gratz*, said:

> It is by now well established that 'all racial classifications reviewable under the Equal Protection Clause must be strictly scrutinized.' *Adarand Constructors, Inc. v. Pena* ... This 'standard of review ... is not dependent on the race of those burdened or benefited by a particular classification.' ...Thus, 'any person, *of whatever race* (our emphasis) has the right to demand that any governmental actor subject to the Constitution justify any racial classification subjecting that person to unequal treatment under the strictest of judicial scrutiny.' (2003:270)

The Court emphasizes here that any person has the right to challenge race conscious policies, and enforces a framing of race which views all individuals (*of any race*) as similarly and equally situated. Thus Jennifer Gratz, a white woman who was not admitted to the University of Michigan, and who alleged that she would have been if not for the university's affirmative action policy, is viewed by the Court as having the same structural position with regard to the equal protection of the law as would a person of color who was explicitly discriminated against in college admissions. The fact that US society remains fundamentally racially structured as a result of a long legacy of explicit legal and governmentally sanctioned and enforced racial oppression is ignored in the Court's analysis. The result is a discursive frame that contains a fundamental assumption about equality—one that is grounded in a falsehood. In the *Gratz* case the University of Michigan's affirmative action policy, a policy which allowed admissions points for various forms of diversity, including racial, geographical, and socio-economic diversity was held to be in violation of the law. Thus the potential reach of affirmative action policies was further limited.

The Court itself recognizes that it would be going too far to state that there actually exists a racially level playing field in the United States, which explains the contradictory decision in the *Grutter* case, the case that accompanied *Gratz*. Here the Court held that race was appropriately being used as a plus factor in the pursuit of diversity at the University of Michigan Law School. The Court affirms the "diversity rationale" originating in Bakke by citing Justice Powell's discussion concerning diversity at length concluding, "we endorse Justice Powell's view that student body diversity is a compelling state interest that can justify the use of race in university admissions" (2003: 325). The Court implicitly recognizes that race and racial inequality have some bearing upon the life experiences of United States citizens yet even here remains committed to a color-blind principle by imposing an arbitrary time limit on the use of race even for diversity purposes. The Court says:

> We are mindful, however, that '[a] core purpose of the Fourteenth Amendment was to do away with all governmentally imposed discrimination based on race.' Accordingly, race-conscious admissions policies must be limited in time. This requirement reflects that racial classifications, however compelling their goals, are potentially so dangerous that they may be employed no more broadly than the interest demands. Enshrining a permanent justification for racial preferences would offend this fundamental equal protection principle. We see no reason to exempt race-conscious admissions programs from the requirement that all governmental use of race must have a logical end point. The Law School, too, concedes that all 'race-conscious programs must have reasonable durational limits.' We take the Law School at its word that it would "like nothing better than to find a race-neutral admissions formula" and will terminate its race-conscious admissions program as soon as practicable (2003: 341–342).

In the dissenting opinions in *Grutter,* Justices of the Court also attempted to assert an absolute adherence to color-blindness as their basis for dissent. Stating, for example, "preferment by race, when resorted to by the State, can be the most divisive of all policies, containing within it the potential to destroy confidence in the Constitution and in the idea of equality" and the "Constitution proscribes government discrimination on the basis of race, and state-provided education is no exception" (2003: 388 and 2003: 349 respectively). Thus, several members of the Supreme Court would impose a complete adherence to color-blindness using a discursive framing of equality, which would preclude any policy which attempted to consciously redistribute resources along lines of race. As it stands, the legal discursive framing of affirmative action that prevailed, held tirelessly to a concept of diversity entrenched in the principle of color-blindness which made it impracticable for the vast majority of institutions of higher education to consider race in any meaningful way.

The diversity rationale that the court used to justify the most limited forms of affirmative action worked to stall the potential for racially equitable access to higher education. In other words, binding race-based admissions within the abstract liberalist diversity frame disallows the consideration of actual dynamics of structural racism and the real consequences of white domination by institutions of higher education. This failure to deal with the reality of racial inequality, racial domination, and white hostility towards people of color in institutional spaces has also meant that when people of color do gain access, they experience racial hostilities that reify their place as interlopers in white institutional space (Moore 2008). But more than that, these racial hostilities will be provided legal protection – not through an explicit discussion of diversity per se, but through a similar logic path, which disconnects the racial structure from an analysis of the law of freedom of speech and expression. This commitment to a power-blind approach to race in higher education also leads to a policy environment that privileges the right of white racist speech over the right of people of color to be free from racial harassment on college and university campuses.

3   Retrenching the Boundaries of White Institutional Space

In February 2010, at the University of California at San Diego (UCSD), a group of white students organized a party called a "Compton Cookout," which they claimed to be in "celebration" of Black History Month. The invitation was posted publicly on Facebook, asking people to dress and behave in "ghetto" fashion and indicating that chicken, watermelon and malt liquor would be served. In response to this provocation, black students organized an on-campus protest, criticizing the racist depiction of blackness and black culture. The protest sparked a burst of racist activity at UCSD, including a campus television broadcast on which white students called the black student protestors "ungrateful niggers," the hanging of a noose from a bookcase in the main library and the placement of a white pillowcase in Ku Klux Klan (KKK) style over a campus statue, all of which drew national media attention to the issue of racism on University of California campuses (Archibold 2010; Gordon 2010).

Although the incidents at UCSD received widespread national media coverage, they were not unique. For decades, there have been comparable incidents of racist expression and activity on college and university campuses, across the country, cropping up in schools from some of the largest and most prestigious to the smallest. Just a small sampling of these incidents reveals the nature of racist expression on campuses. In the fall of 1986 at the Citadel Military College, five white cadets wearing KKK-type garb stormed into the dormitory room of a black freshman, yelling racial epithets and burning a paper cross (UPI 1986). In February 1995 at UC Berkeley's renowned School of Law, 14 students of color received letters in their student mailboxes, calling them "niggers," "wetbacks" and "chinks" and suggesting that Boalt was "for whites only" (Koury and Koh 1995). In April 2000 at the University of Iowa College of Dentistry, faculty members received an e-mail message demanding that the school dismiss its minority students within three days, and after that three-day period had passed, students of color in the college received racist, threatening e-mails (Leonard 2000). In the spring of 2002, a white student at Harvard Law School used the law school website to outline the facts of a property case involving racially restrictive covenants and used the term "nigs" to refer to African Americans. After a protest in reaction to this incident, another white male student sent an anonymous e-mail (though he was later identified) to a first-year black woman law student that said, among other things, "We at the Harvard Law School, [are] a free, private community, where any member wishing to use the word 'nigger' in any form should not be prevented from doing so."[1] In 2007 at Hamline University, six white student-athletes dressed in what they called "mock African tribal outfits," donning blackface, black Lycra suits, large afro wigs and necklaces for Halloween. On the morning of November 4, 2008, the day on which Barack Obama became the first African American president of the United States, a noose was found hanging from a prominent tree on campus at Baylor University (Hoffstrom 2008).[2]

These examples are illustrative of incidents that have taken place at all types of historically white colleges and universities across the nation, beginning after the legal changes of the civil rights era when people of color gained entry to these institutions. In 1990, the National Institute Against Prejudice and Violence said that incidents of "hate speech" on college campuses and universities could be calculated at between 800,000 to 1 million per year (Matsuda and Lawrence 1993). Indeed, a 1994 report conducted by the University of Houston Institute for Higher Education Law and Governance noted that U.S. colleges and universities are characterized by a "climate of bigotry" (Agguire 1994). Yet when instances like the 2010 incidents at UCSD occur in these spaces, individuals in the media and in the academy often seem surprised, and the discourse around these incidents frames them as "recent trends" or "increasing hostilities," something new and unique (see Matsuda et al. 1993). The reality, however, is that racist expressions and activities on historically white college and university campuses have been a consistent and relatively regular occurrence throughout the post-civil rights era.

In the 1980s and early 1990s, many colleges and universities across the country, generally responding to what they asserted was an increase in racial hostilities in their institutions, attempted to create policies to sanction racist and other hate-motivated activities on campuses (Murray 1997). Most of the policies attempted to establish broad guidelines delineating which behaviors constituted discriminatory harassment, thus creating a hostile academic climate, in the campus community. These policies included targeting and sanctioning actions and expressions motivated by animus based on race, (as well as religion, sex and sometimes sexuality), in other words policies to facilitate the full and meaningful participation of people of color in previously exclusively white institutional educational spaces. Yet just as had occurred with policies of affirmative action, these policies were almost immediately challenged by whites who asserted that such policies violated their right to freedom of speech and expression as guaranteed by the First Amendment.

In 1989, the University of Michigan was the first school to experience a challenge to a harassment policy. The policy, which the university argued was a response to racist incidents and other hate-based activity on campus, penalized "stigmatizing or victimizing" individuals or groups on the basis of race, ethnicity, religion, sex, sexual orientation, creed, national origin, ancestry, age, marital status, handicap or Vietnam-era veteran status. In *Doe v. University of Michigan*, the District Court in Michigan stated, "While the Court is sympathetic to the University's obligation to ensure educational opportunities for all of its students, such efforts must not be at the expense of free speech." In a discursive maneuver that managed to convey a commitment to abstract principles of both non-discriminatory institutions and freedom of speech, the court noted that the university policy was too broad, prohibiting speech that was protected by the First Amendment. The next lawsuit came against the

University of Wisconsin System, which enacted a policy with the advice of legal scholars, including Richard Delgado, an expert in the area of racist speech
and expression (see Matsuda et al. 1993). In an effort to avoid the failure experienced by the University Michigan, the Wisconsin system drafted a policy that
applied only to hate-based expressions directed at individuals. The goal was
to restrict only that speech and expression which constituted "fighting words,"
a form of speech that the U.S. Supreme Court had previously recognized as
not protected by the first Amendment. So-called fighting words have been defined by the Court as expression that, by their very utterance inflict injury, are
targeted toward a specific individual and will naturally incite an immediate
breach of the peace. These forms of expression, the Supreme Court concluded
in 1942, were not protected by the First Amendment because they are considered to have very slight social value in a marketplace of ideas, and any benefits
arising from these expressions are outweighed by the potential social damage (see Murray 1997; Tsesis 2010). With this legal precedent in mind, the creators of the Wisconsin harassment policies attempted to create a policy that
sanctioned and penalized only those expressions that fit into the definition of
fighting words. Despite this careful crafting, however, the district court in *The
UWM Post et al. v. Board of Regents of the University of Wisconsin System* held
that the policy was too broad and, as written and enforced, did not include
restricted expressions that were legally considered "fighting words; rather, the
policy included expressions that were merely demeaning to particular individuals as opposed to expressions that would na[12]turally incite a breach of the
peace."

These challenges to harassment policies were important to colleges and
universities across the country, for they signified that U.S. courts seemed
disinclined to uphold policies that included limitations on racist speech and
expression. There remained a possibility, however, that a policy could be constructed which would only sanction racist expression that fell within the legal definition of fighting words. In 1992, that possibility was defeated by the
Supreme Court in the case of *R.A.V. v. City of St. Paul*. The *R.A.V.* case did not
involve higher education policies regarding racial/ethnic harassment but an
ordinance passed by the city of St. Paul, which prohibited the placing of a
"symbol, object, appellation, characterization or graffiti ... which one knows
or has reasonable grounds to know arouses anger, alarm, or resentment in others on the basis of race, color, creed, religious, or gender." Such an action was
considered a misdemeanor. In an opinion written by Justice Antonin Scalia,
the Court invalidated the ordinance despite the city's assurance (and the State
Supreme Court's finding) that it limited the enforcement of the ordinance to
conduct that would be legally considered fighting words, which the Supreme

Court ruled in *Chaplinsky* was not protected by the First Amendment. In a decision that was widely viewed to be a message directed toward colleges and universities attempting to create racial harassment policies (see Gould 2001), the Court stated that St. Paul's ordinance, even if limited to fighting words, was unconstitutional because it was "underinclusive" on the basis of content. In other words, the Court noted that while the city could prohibit fighting words in accordance with *Chaplinsky*, it could not prohibit *only* those fighting words that were based on race, color, religion, etc. The Court said:

> We conclude that … the ordinance is facially unconstitutional. Although the phrase in the ordinance, "arouses anger, alarm or resentment in others," has been limited by the Minnesota Supreme Court's construction to reach only those symbols or displays that amount to "fighting words," the remaining, unmodified terms make clear that the ordinance applies only to "fighting words" that insult, or provoke violence, "on the basis of race, color, creed, religion or gender." Displays containing abusive invective, no matter how vicious or severe, are permissible unless they are addressed to one of the specified disfavored topics…. The First Amendment does not permit St. Paul to impose special prohibitions on those speakers who express views on disfavored subjects.

The *R.A.V.* case, in combination with the lower court cases concerning racial and ethnic harassment policies, elucidates a commitment by U.S. courts to abstract liberalist legal framing of freedom of speech, an approach to speech that arbitrarily (without any explicit consideration) disconnects racist speech and expression from racist action and social organization. The courts employ the same kind of structurally disconnected, abstract liberalist logic characteristic of their approach to affirmative action—the discourse of color-blind racism. Framing overt, hostile and threatening racism as "speech that merely hurts the feelings of those who hear it" and framing policies or laws against such expressions as "special prohibitions on those speakers who express views on disfavored subjects," illustrate a tendency by the U.S. courts to minimize racism and divorce discussions of the mechanisms of racial oppression from liberalist discourses about individual rights and liberty. In considering policies regarding racist expressions on college campuses, the courts have consistently ignored the long history of racial violence in this country and the connection between forms of racist expression and that history.

The result is a post-civil rights Constitutional right to be racist in colleges and universities, which administrators may not restrict in any meaningful way. The legal result is that whites can invoke state-centered protection for their racist speech and expression on college and university campuses whereas students of color have no right to attain higher education free from these dehumanizing, oppressive and tacitly threatening communications. Through a structurally disconnected analysis, framed by the same type of abstract individualism utilized to create a diversity rationale to limit the reach of affirmative action policies, the courts created a powerful legal support for one of the most powerful mechanisms of white institutional space—racist mockery and threatening speech and expression.

The Supreme Court's assertion concerning the necessity of free speech absolutism in democratic society rings dishonest. The Court's previous allowance of legal restrictions on forms of speech (such as fighting words, obscenity, child pornography, certain instances of fraudulent or libelous speech) illustrate that when a social value is considered important enough, content-based speech restrictions have been and continue to be permitted. Moreover, many other democratic countries in the world that constitutionally protect and respect freedom of speech and expression do, in fact, prohibit some forms of racist and ethnocentric expression. Their restrictions have been historically based precisely on the kinds of structural connections between such expression and the histories of racial violence and oppression we discuss herein. In fact, after World War II, the United Nations General Assembly adopted the Convention on the Prevention and Punishment of the Crime of Genocide, obligating signatories to create sanctions for "direct and public incitement to commit genocide" (see Tsesis 2010: 645). With the lessons of World War II revealing startling connections between rhetorical manipulation and racial/ethnic genocide, many democratic states responded by enacting criminal and civil penalties for certain forms of expressions of racial/ethnic animus and incitement. For example, the Canadian Supreme Court has prohibited hate speech, noting that the purpose of protections of free speech include "(1) seeking the truth and the common good, (2) promoting self-fulfillment of individuals by allowing them to develop thoughts and ideas as they see fit, and (3) ensuring that the political process is open to all persons" (quoted in Tsesis 2010: 647). Noting that racial/ethnic hate speech is not compatible with these goals, the Canadian Supreme Court has permitted "reasonable" limitations on such forms of speech (Tsesis 2010). In addition, the United Kingdom, Germany, France and many other Western democracies permit criminal and civil penalties for racist and ethnocentric speech, including speech that creates hatred for an entire race/ethnicity, incites violence or argues for the mass oppression of racial and ethnic groups (Delgado and Stefancic 2004; Matsuda et al. 1993; Tsesis 2010). Moreover, in Canada, the United Kingdom and Germany, government policies have been created with special regard to such forms of hate speech on college and university campuses to prevent racist and xenophobic ideologies from "taking root" in these settings (Tsesis 2010: 646).

In the United States, however, the courts have prohibited such government interventions with regard to racist expression. The courts have utilized an abstract individualistic frame to treat all speech and expression as functionally the same, in the process disconnecting expression from racial history and social structure. This first amendment absolutism, justified through a logic of a marketplace of ideas and expression where all expression is equivalent, is yet another example of the abstract individualistic diversity frame in that ignores racial relations of power, and creates a legal fiction situating all expression as equivalent, and all individuals in the institutional community as if they have equal access to expression. As a result, whites have been granted the legal protection to patrol the boundaries of white institutional space—protection to utilize a history of white supremacist imagery and language to continually remind people of color of their outsider status and their inferiority in the space.

4   Conclusion

In *R.A.V. v. The City of Saint Paul*, the Supreme Court held that the city did not have a right to limit "speakers who express views on disfavored subjects" including race, color, creed, religion or gender. The Court uses the term "subjects" to mean topics, but the Court's usage of the word could just as easily be taken to mean disfavored *subjects of the state*—those who are subject to the rule of law in the United States, but lack its favor. The Court, in shaping race-based policy in higher education, has employed a rhetoric of equality that is detached from the reality of both historical and contemporary racial oppression. The result is an overarching adherence to the frame of abstract liberalist diversity in the realm of higher education in the United States. Behind the language of diversity in US colleges and universities sit policies that disfavor the rights of people of color to obtain higher education free from racial harassment and instead protect the right to be racist. The truth, then, is that even with all the talk of diversity in institutions of higher education, we are still miles away from the meaningful access that Johnson called for in that brief moment of high expectations when civil rights legislation was in its infancy in this country. Indeed, his call to ensure "not just equality as a right and a theory but equality as a fact and equality as a result" is as necessary today as it was when he first spoke the words in 1965.

References

Aguirre, Adalberto Jr. 1994. *Racism in Higher Education: A Perilous Climate for Minorities. Report of the Institute for Higher Education Law and Governance.* University of Houston Law Center.

Andersen, Margaret. 1999. "Diversity without oppression: race, ethnicity, identity and power." In pp. 5–20 *Critical Ethnicity: Countering the Waves of Identity Politics,* edited by M Kenyatta, and Tai R. Totowa, Boulder, CO: Rowman and Littlefield.

Archibold, Randal C. 2010 (February 26). "California Campus Sees Uneasy Race Relations." *The New York Times.* Retrieved from http://www.nytimes.com/2010/02/27/education/27sandiego.html.

Bell, Derrick A. 1992. *Race, Racism, and American Law.* Boston, MA: Little, Brown.

Bell, Joyce and Douglas Hartmann. 2007. "Diversity in Everyday Discourse: The Cultural Ambiguities and Consequences of 'Happy Talk'." *American Sociological Review,* 72 (6): 895–914.

Bonilla-Silva, Eduardo. 1997. "Rethinking Racism: Toward a Structural Interpretation." *American Sociological Review,* 62: 465–480.

Bonilla-Silva, Eduardo. 2001. *White Supremacy and Racism in the Post-Civil Rights Era.* Boulder, CO: Lynne Reinner.

Bonilla-Silva, Eduardo. 2010. *Racism Without Racists: Color-Blind Racism and the Persistence of Racial Inequality in the United States.* Boulder, CO: Rowman & Littlefield.

Carr, Leslie G. 1997. *"Color-Blind" Racism.* New York, NY: Sage.

Crenshaw, Kimberle William. 1994. "Forward: Toward a Race-Conscious Pedagogy in Legal Education."

Davis, Angela Y. 2011. *Are Prisons Obsolete?* New York, NY: Seven Stories Press.

Delgado, Richard, and Jean Stefancic. 2004. *Understanding Words That Wound.* New York, NY: Westview Press.

Di'Tomaso, Nancy, R. Parks-Yancy and C. Post 2003. "White views of civil rights: color blindness and equal opportunity." Pp. 189–198 in *White Out: The Continuing Significance of Racism,* edited by Ashley Doane, and Eduardo Bonilla-Silva. New York, NY: Routledge.

Doane, Ashley, and Eduardo Bonilla-Silva. 2003. *White Out: The Continuing Significance of Racism.* New York, NY: Routledge.

Eliasoph, Nina. 1999. "Everyday racism" in a culture of political avoidance: civil society, speech, and taboo. *Social Problems,* 46 (4): 479–502.

Estrada, K., & P. McLaren 1993. "A dialogue on multiculturalism and democratic culture." *Educational Researcher,* 22 (3): 27–33.

Feagin, Joe R., Hernan Vera, and Nikitah Imani. 1996. *The Agony of Education: Black Students at White Colleges and Universities.* New York, NY: Routledge.

Gallagher, Charles A. 2003. "Color-Blind Privilege: The Social and Political Functions of Erasing the Color Line in Post-Race America." *Race, Gender, and Class*, 10 (4): 22–37.

Gordon, Larry. 2010 (February 18). "UC San Diego Condemns Student Party Mocking Black History Month." *LA Times*. Retrieved Feb. 18, 2017: http://articles.latimes.com/2010/feb/18/local/la-me-ucsd18-2010.

Gould, Jon B. 2001. "The Precedent That Wasn't: College Hate Speech Codes and the Two Faces of Legal Compliance." *Law & Society Review*, 35 (2): 345–392.

Harris, Cheryl. 1993. "Whiteness as property." *Harvard Law Review*, 1707–1791.

Hoffstrom, Amanda. 2008 (November 17). "Campuses Combat Racism." *UWIRE: The College Network*.

Jargowsky, P.A. 1997. *Poverty and Place: Ghettos, Barrios, and the American City*. New York, NY: Russell Sage Foundation.

Koury, Renee, and Barbara Koh. 1995. (February 16). "Students at the College of San Mateo and UC-Berkeley Rally Against Racism Hate Fliers Evoke Sadness at Colleges." *San Jose Mercury News*, p. 1B.

Kozol, J., & D. Perluss 1992. "Savage Inequalities: Children in America's Schools." *Clearinghouse Review*: 26, 398.

Leonard, Jill. 2000 (April 18). "Racist E-mails Target U. Iowa Students; Unrelated to Incidents at Penn State." *Daily Collegian*.

Lewis, Amanda. 2003. *Race in the schoolyard: Negotiating the Color Line in Classrooms and Communities*. New Jersey: Rutgers University Press.

Lopez, Ian Haney. 2006. *White by Law: The Legal Construction of Race*. New York, NY: New York University Press.

Massey, D. and N. Denton 1998. *American Apartheid: Segregation and the Making of the Underclass*. Cambridge, MA: Harvard University Press.

Matsuda, Mari J., and Charles R. Lawrence III. 1993. "Epilogue: Burning Crosses and the R.A.V. Case." Pp. 133–136 in *Words That Wound: Critical Race Theory, Assaultive Speech, and the First Amendment*, edited by Mari Matsuda, Charles R. Lawrence III, Richard Delgado and Kimberle Williams Crenshaw. New York, NY: Westview Press.

Moore, Wendy Leo. 2008. *Reproducing Racism: White Space, Elite Law Schools, and Racial Inequality*. Lanham, MD: Rowman and Littlefield.

Murray, S. Douglas. 1997. "The Demise of Campus Speech Codes." *Western State University Law Review*, 24: 247–281.

Oliver, Melvin and Thomas Shapiro. 2006. *Black Wealth, White Wealth: A New Perspective on Racial Inequality*. New York, NY: Taylor & Francis.

Orfield, Gary, and Susan E. Eaton. 1996. *Dismantling Desegregation: The Quiet Reversal of Brown v. Board of Education*. New York, NY: The New Press.

Tonry, Michael. 1995. *Malign Neglect: Race, Crime, and Punishment in America*. New York, NY: Oxford University Press.

Tsesis, Alexander. 2010. "Burning Crosses on Campus: University Hate Speech Codes." *Connecticut Law Review*, 43: 617–672.

UPI. 1986 (December 2). "F.B.I. to Investigate the Citadel for Racism." *The New York Times*. Retrieved from: http://www.nytimes.com/1986/12/02/us/around-the-nation-fbi-to-investigate-the-citadel-for-racism.html.

Wellman, David T. 1993. Portraits of White Racism. Cambridge, MA: Cambridge University Press.

CHAPTER 5

"Boatloads of Money" in the Great Equalizer: How Diversity Furthers Inequality at the Neoliberal University

Michael Kreiter and Arthur Scarritt

1   Introduction

Universities have shifted their funding models towards running like a business: having their core operations directly generate income. This contrasts the traditional format in which the university provides society with a wide variety of trained people whose actions generate wealth, part of which gets invested back into the university. Rather than being invested in, students have become the principal customer and thus have borne a dramatically increased financial burden, tuition doubling every ten years. Among other questions, this brings up the issue of how universities convince students to keep attending as costs skyrocket.

This is an important question because it addresses broader shifts in society—termed neoliberal reforms—wherein the profit motive drives the outcomes of social institutions. Instead of adhering to politically determined redistributive priorities, such as providing food security or other rights, market competition governs resource allocation. Advocates argue that providing more resources to the wealthy enables them to be job creators and the engines of the economy so that wealth trickles-down to the general populace. The actual outcomes of neoliberal reforms, however, have been highly regressive, concentrating wealth at the top while dramatically undercutting the middle class and poor (Hacker and Pierson 2010). Looking at these results leads David Harvey to conclude that neoliberalism amounts to "draconian policies designed to restore and consolidate capitalist class power" (Harvey 2011:10).

The widespread application and regressive outcomes of these shifts give rise to an important question: how do neoliberals construct consent amongst a sufficient population to get their reforms implemented? That is, these massive changes could not simply be imposed, but under democratic principles had to gain widespread popular support. As the work of Antonio Gramsci points out, a critical engagement with such issues will reveal their elitist nature. But reformers can draw from a full host of cultural values, traditions, fears, and political sloganeering to help generate a common sense consensus about the correctness of such policies. For instance, many works stress the harnessing of the culturally conservative Christian movements to help the economically conservative neoliberal agenda (Frank 2004; Hacker and Pierson 2010). Indeed, the issue of constructing consent to neoliberalism has received considerable attention (*inter alia* Harvey 2005; Klein 2007; Peck 2010; Zizek 2009).

In this context, we investigate how campus diversity engages with the neo-liberalization of the university. Concurrent to higher education seeking more funding from students, universities proclaim commitments to increasing multiculturalism on campus. This stands in contrast to the business model because increasing diversity means investing resources to provide improved college opportunities to historically marginalized groups. And race-based affirmative action programs provide one of the primary methods. Thus, universities face the paradoxical position of cutting resources to students while investing in multiculturalism. This leads us to ask: how does the way that universities reconcile this contradiction affect the spread of the business model?

To address these issues, we interviewed white students at Boise State University about their perspectives on increased tuition, multiculturalism, and affirmative action. How do these students variously contend with rising tuition? And how do they regard diversity and affirmative action in conditions of increased austerity? We found that students understood increased tuition as an unproblematic necessity, even as they struggled to meet their financial obligations. It was their own individual problem, not a problem with the way the university was run. But we also found a stark contradiction between white students adamantly embracing diversity while simultaneously deriding affirmative action, the very policies geared to enhance multiculturalism and diversity. That is, white students were not politicized about increased tuition, but were politicized against affirmative action. And they saw no connection between affirmative action and diversity.

These findings lead us to argue that the particular ways that students reconciled their contradiction between affirmative action and diversity helps explain why they understand increased tuition as unproblematic. Or to put it another way, universities constructed student consent to neoliberalism through promoting a diversity devoid of redistributive content. Pushing this kind of diversity relied on white students' own colorblind racism. In colorblind racism, white people eschew racial bigotry, instead asserting a well-meaning belief that race is only skin deep. But such downplaying of difference blinds white people to the systems that confer privileges and disadvantages according to skin color, and therein significantly determine people's life chances according to their race (Bonilla-Silva 2010; Gallagher 2009). This leads white people to believe that equality of opportunity pervades society. They therefore conclude that racial inequalities reflect the poor choices made by individual people of color.

We found students employing their colorblind logic to internalize multiple depoliticized diversity ideologies (Embrick 2008, 2011) that obscure the contradiction between their pro-diversity and anti-affirmative action stances: (1) snowflake diversity seeing everyone as meaningfully different, (2) constructing wealthy international students as the new model minority, and (3) instrumental diversity that views diversity as providing tradable skills. In thus championing a depoliticized diversity, these students came to advocate for reshaping the university to serve elite interests. The depoliticized diversities brought them to support a neoliberalized university. In essence, the positive elements inherent in these different forms of diversity argued against the public model of higher education serving the needs of the general populace. Instead, celebrating depoliticized diversities promoted the neoliberal trickle-down model of catering to the privileged. In other words, students' colorblind racism also blinded them to their class interests.

Thus, our full argument: the university promotes depoliticized diversity ideologies that harness white students' colorblind racism to the task of neoliberalizing higher education. In the following sections we flesh out the concepts of colorblind racism and neoliberal higher education, and explain how the diversity ideologies we identified lead from one to the other. Please note that we are by no means saying that this is the only means through which universities construct consent. We are not even saying these are the only diversity ideologies. Further, we are not saying that the university is the only organization promoting such ideologies, just as much as we are not saying this is anything close to the university's core activities. Rather, we focus on the university and its unique function of training citizens, identifying a robust process here that is one piece of a much larger puzzle.

2 Colorblind Racism

Colorblind racism is highly potent precisely because it argues against overt racisms that view whites as inherently superior. Instead, colorblindness hides under a well-meaning acceptance of racial diversity. Colorblindness mistakenly takes Martin Luther King's dream that "people will not be judged by the color of their skin" as suggesting people ignore race rather than understand it.

Colorblindness dictates that people disregard both phenotype and judgment, excising King's emphasis on empathizing with the situation of other people, on the need to judge from an informed position.

Accordingly, whites see other races as merely different in skin color. And this trivializing of difference blinds whites to the meaningful differences, the structural sources of racial inequality, such as those generated through residential segregation, employment discrimination, and a biased criminal justice system to name but three (Alexander 2010; Massey and Denton 1993; Neckerman and Kirschenman 1991; Pager 2003; Rugh and Massey 2010; Sites and Parks 2011; Wacquant 2009). Indeed, colorblind ideology constructs speaking about meaningful racial difference as racist, as judging people solely on their skin color (Guinier and Torres 2009).

More than simply ignoring the plight of minorities, colorblind racism enables whites to participate in the structures that perpetuate racial hierarchy without believing they are doing so. Colorblind racism emphasizes individual effort in a supposed environment of equality of opportunity. Whites thus perceive observable racial disparities as the result of "lethargic, incorrigible, and often pathological behavior of people who fail to take responsibility for their own lives" (Brown et al. 2003:6). Conversely, colorblind racism enables whites to believe that their own accomplishments come exclusively from their individual efforts rather than any systemic conferring of privilege (Gallagher 2009). Attempts to redress systemic inequalities, such as affirmative action, whites therefore view as personal attacks punishing them for past events of which they are wholly innocent. Whites therein come to endorse the system that provides privileges to whites and disadvantages to people of color.

Importantly, colorblind ideology does not fully ignore race, but recognizes it in a very circumscribed way: as choice and cultural inclination. Colorblindness therein embraces a shallow version of multiculturalism that helps perpetuate racial hierarchy. Businesses, for example, superficially embrace multiculturalism as an ideal expression of international capitalism, and an ideology that bridges gaps between the supply and the demand sides of a growing economy (Zizek 1997). Nearly every major business has a diversity program as a way of marking its inclusion in the modern spirit of capitalism. David G. Embrick (2011) argues that diversity is an ideology that obscures the gender and racial inequalities that continue to persist. Businesses market themselves as "equal opportunity employers" that "care about diversity" (Embrick 2011: 3), yet they have no observable dedication to equality. Rather than constructing diversity as something critical of the status quo, diversity ideology revitalizes colorblind racism. Our work investigates how such diversity ideologies play out in the arena of higher education.

3   Neoliberalism and Higher Education

Neoliberal reforms initially adopted a laissez-faire stance, weakening government regulations over existing markets (Harvey 2005). Over time, though, reformers became more ambitious, creating market-like mechanisms in institutions where they did not exist before (Brown 2006; Peck and Tickell 2002). This brought non-market organized fields such as health care and education into the neoliberal fold.

For higher education, the core idea involves turning the university into a self-sustaining business. The university generates revenue out of its main functions, with upper administrators becoming CEOs, professors turning into entrepreneurs, and students converting into discriminating consumers buying the educational commodity they desire the most. These conditions generated what Jeff Selingo (2012) terms the "lost decade" of the aught years in which colleges "advertised heavily and created enticing new academic programs, services and fancy facilities" in an attempt to attract ever more income from corporations and tuition. Universities advertised their fun qualities to students over their educational possibilities. Boise State's own "A+ for Adventure" sells skiing rather than the thrill of new knowledge. This, coupled with the exponential rise in tuition costs, has created a massive student debt bubble doubling in a few short years to over a trillion dollars (Selingo 2013).

Like businesses, the ranks and salaries of upper management swelled. As Johns Hopkins professor Benjamin Ginsberg (2011) tells it, neoliberal universities proliferate new administrative positions with such vague job descriptions that these "deanlets" would not be missed if abducted by aliens. In fact, their absence would make universities better off as such positions largely function to enable the increased power and salaries of upper administration. While administrative costs skyrocket, professors' salaries stagnate or decline (Clawson and Page 2011). Further, the professoriate splinters, the few rock star researchers constantly seeking external research money, separated from the increasingly contingent and low paid teaching labor force. Faculty power declines precipitously through such strokes as eviscerating the cogovernance of the faculty senate, and increasingly open attacks on tenure. As a result, faculty and their programs face increased scrutiny through deeply flawed quasi-market analytics and benchmarks. In practice, these mainly serve to provide the administration with greater, more business-like power.

Schools began to focus on competition, selectivity, and rankings rather than serving the diverse population. State universities in particular have shifted from providing for state needs to catering to higher tuition-paying out-of-state students. Administrators invested in raising median SAT scores while lowering entering students' median age so as to attract what they un-apologetically term the right student customers: a homogenous group of the best prepared (Harrison-Walker 2010). Attrition rates increased dramatically, especially among minorities. Given US wealth inequalities and the tight correlation of wealth and educational success, these right students are white and upper middle class (Guinier and Torres 2009). The skyrocketing attrition rates, for example, hit minorities the hardest. In sum, the business model involves concentrated executive power focused on advancing the most lucrative fields while prioritizing spending on incentives to attract the wealthiest students. We address the question of how white students consent to this regressive remaking of higher education.

4   Methods

Higher education offers a telling example of how neoliberalism is remaking a public institution into a business as well as an institution that reproduces business logic. Foremost, education is one of the worst fits with the market model, relying instead on a host of odd and contradictory proxies. Tuition, for instance, is a poor approximation of business profit, as it is not generated directly out of the core productive activities, and does not discipline upper management. Instead, tuition amounts to collecting arbitrary rents from people to access a now privatized public service. Higher education therein represents one of the greatest neoliberal victories. What happens in higher education can speak to most other institutions. At the same time, this poor fit potentially highlights key means to creatively resist and roll back neoliberalization. As a unique training ground, the university can robustly inculcate neoliberal ideologies. But this same function can generate some of the greatest challenges to neoliberalism.

To explore this issue, we conducted qualitative interviews (Weiss 1995) with 31 students at Boise State University (BSU). Students were recruited from required upper-division classes in different disciplines. Recruits provided contact information for other potential participants in a snowball sampling method (Rubin and Babbie 1993). All the participants were white with a median age of 22. Participation was limited to upper-division students to ensure an adequate number and salience of experiences within the university. Interviews lasted between 30 and 90 minutes and took place in private offices on campus between November 2012 and February 2013. Each was recorded and transcribed. We replaced their names with pseudonyms. We promised participants confidentiality and compensated them $20 for their time. The BSU Sociology department provided funding for this research.

We selected BSU based on access to participants and as a case study of a traditionally working-class, mostly white, commuter university with a politically disengaged and fragmented student body. As reported by Boise State (Belcheir 2002), most students are first-generation college students and nearly 80 percent work in order to afford their education. Because of lower incomes, students contribute "more to the cost of their education than students elsewhere" (Belcheir 2002:5). Unlike major flagship universities where issues of affirmative action receive national attention (Berrey 2011; Katznelson 2005), BSU has little history of political confrontation. The limited political engagement from the student body enables uncontested neoliberal changes instituted from the top down.

One drastic change has been the tuition increase. Like many other neoliberalizing universities, BSU has more than doubled tuition since 2003, from $2,984 to $6,292 in 2013 (National Center for Education Statistics 2015). The increased costs place additional strain on local students, most of whom are working to support themselves and their education. All but five of the respondents reported earning an annual income of less than $20,000.

During the interviews, we asked questions like "What does the term 'diversity' mean to you?" "How do you feel about affirmative action?" and "In what ways does the university operate as a business?" in order to explore issues of diversity and neoliberalism in their college experiences. The vagueness of the "diversity" question gave the participants the freedom to construct their own meanings of diversity, which we compare to their thoughts about affirmative action specifically. We analyzed the transcripts using a qualitative approach where our analysis was based on our intimacy with the data and the university itself. Next, we examine the processes students use to depoliticize diversity and how these processes deepen colorblind racism and further propel neoliberalization.

5   Getting Neoliberalism through Race

When talking to white students about their educations, we were intrigued by how they adamantly embraced diversity while at the same time condemned affirmative action. Students demonstrated little ability to speak substantively about either term. We found, in other words, two contradictory hegemonic ideologies. And the reconciliation of these demanded explanation.

Students in our study used various processes that we argue compose a set of beliefs about the fundamental equality between people (Embrick 2008, 2011), which depoliticize diversity by removing confrontational elements in lieu of palatable misconceptions about existing inequality. Depoliticization refers to a process that "limits or circumscribes the political choices offered to the citizen" (Swyngedouw 2011: 372).

Each of these processes deepens colorblind racism and animosity toward affirmative action. For example, Kara, a 23 year old white female, articulates this sentiment:

> *Interviewer:* So how do you feel about affirmative action?
> *Kara:* Well I guess you kinda have to do it. I don't know, like, I didn't get a scholarship because I'm not Native American or whatever, but I don't know. I guess you kinda need to do it. Because, I guess cultures that we've done bad to–certain individuals or groups of individuals–I guess we have to make up for it, I guess. It's unfortunate that we're paying for it now when it happened so long ago.
> *Interviewer:* Do you think you should be paying for it now?
> *Kara:* I mean, I don't want to be totally against it because it has a good idea, but at the same time, it is frustrating for me to not get special attention when I didn't do anything wrong. You know, like, in a sense, I'm being punished when I did not scold Native Americans back in the day, but that's life. We have to pay for our predecessors mistakes, I guess.
> *Interviewer:* OK, do you think that's something that should continue or should it end at some point?
> *Kara:* Eventually, I mean it's natural for humans to take advantage, and when we give something, we can't give it forever because they'll just keep taking advantage. And at some point, when can they forgive us?

Kara uses a colorblind logic that denies any responsibility for past wrongs. Its inherent argument is that racism would end if people would quit playing the race card, despite the fact that many social structures continue to stratify people by race (Bonilla-Silva 2010; Bonilla-Silva, Lewis and Embrick 2004, 2008; Guinier and Torres 2009). She holds to a sincere fiction (Feagin, Vera and Batur 2001; Vera, Feagin and Gordon 1995) that "scolding" was the worst atrocity inflicted upon Native Americans.

Similarly, George, a 22 year-old white male, laments his loss of heritage in response to a question about how the university could be more inclusive:

> I don't know how you would. The only thing I can think is just not being discriminatory to people who are applying. Just have them based on their

test scores and not on their race. Which is why on that little thing [the demographic questionnaire for this study] I always put English-American instead of Caucasian, because I feel like my heritage is lost because of my skin color. So I feel, like, to not have Caucasian would be great.

George argues that the university should not consider race (read affirmative action) in admissions because that would be "discriminatory to people who are applying." He bases his argument on the colorblind belief that such a policy would come at the "expense of more qualified white victims of 'reverse discrimination'" (Jones and Mukherjee 2010: 403). He goes on to construct a white ethnic identity that highlights his continued victimization. He implicitly argues for the return of an idyllic world that existed before nefarious affirmative action policies disappeared his identity (Maly, Dalmage, and Michaels 2012). Students like Kara and George call upon ideological processes to depoliticize diversity in order to celebrate it while simultaneously deriding affirmative action.

We argue that the way in which students draw upon diversity ideologies is shaped by the practices of the university and the discourses of the administration. Diversity is already a depoliticized concept as a result of colorblind racism; however, how it is depoliticized is particularly telling. We found three recurring ideological themes among students we interviewed (see Table 5.1) that show the unique ways that they incorporated university approaches to diversity in their own depoliticizing logic.

These ideologies of white students show that the university has little interest in addressing substantive racial inequality in higher education. It does, however, have an interest in maintaining an apolitical student body, with little to no fluency in the language of inequality, in order to enact further regressive

TABLE 5.1   Processes of depoliticizing diversity ideologies

Ideology	Racist process:	Depoliticizes diversity as:	Neoliberalizes by:
Snowflake Diversity	Dismisses group inequality	Individuals	Liberal individualism
New Model Minority	Marginalizes domestic minorities	International Students	Commodification
Instrumental Diversity	Constructs inequality as product differentiation	Providing tradable skills	Marketization

SOURCE: CREATED BY AUTHORS

neoliberal policies without pushback from students. For instance, one of the most articulate interviewees, Drake, said he thought the university is "very much a business and I don't know how it wouldn't be one." Explaining the commoditized nature of education, he continued: "I'm consuming education in college and I'm consuming food at the grocery store. In that sense I think we're the consumer." When asked for the downside he emphasized that: "education is really expensive, so that's a disadvantage. You have to sacrifice a lot to go to college because you have to pay for it and your family sacrifices." And when asked what else to do about rising tuition he said "to me it's just like, 'oh, tuition is rising' or, 'gas is rising.' It's just one of those things you have to take." Drake therein embraces the business model as inevitable. And while he finds rising tuition problematic, he regards it as a necessity that can only be addressed through individual sacrifice. That is, he lacks the understanding to socially challenge skyrocketing tuition, even though he regards society as the ultimate beneficiary of education.

Putting these together, we argue that the depoliticized diversity that white students internalize helps eliminate the conceptual tools that address their deteriorating situation as students; a lack of racial consciousness brings a lack of class-consciousness. Table 5.1 outlines the process through which students move from their different diversity ideologies to ultimately endorse neoliberal higher education. The following sections explain each one in turn.

6   Snowflake Diversity

Through the process of what we term "snowflake diversity," students expand their constructions of diversity to the point that everyone and everything is diverse. When asked to define diversity, Byron, a 23 year-old white male responded:

> Yeah, I think of phrases like "Diversity Today" and things like that, where they are sort of moments that are dedicated to recognizing diversity. Which is really weird to me, because I understand that it's not a cultural diversity that exists, but there is also a human individual element of diversity. So you can have a whole culture of, say, punk rock kids, that you know, we can all say that they are diverse, different from a religious group, or something like that. But, within those two groups you are going to find that every individual is slightly different.

Byron takes the approach of trivializing diversity as simply any and all kinds of difference. For example, punk rock kids—who are typically white youth (Moore and Roberts 2009)—are distinct from an abstract religious group. While issues of inequality may exist between punk rock kids and religious groups, Byron uses this example to downplay the significance of cultural diversity. He uses the process of snowflake diversity to move conceptions of diversity from the "weird" recognition of group/cultural differences to the recognition of individuality. Byron's statement that "every individual is slightly different" exposes the source for our term "snowflake diversity," which is based on the idiom that we are all unique and special little snowflakes.

All individuals are perceived as just humans, thus nothing in particular. The problem is that without conceptual categories for people, diversity ideology has no language for inequality. Instead, it promotes diversity that is devoid of any substantive group meaning, obscuring historical and present-day inequalities, and sanitizing diversity to become a non-threatening, apolitical, and hollow concept.

This policy of diversity is embraced by the university, communicated to students, and visible in some students' ideological constructions. As BSU has restructured itself to become a "Metropolitan Research University of Distinction," it has established the new Institute for STEM and Diversity Initiatives. This combines diversity with its market-oriented approach of emphasizing STEM (science, technology, engineering, and mathematics), which should be recognized as a strategy to attract corporate and government research funding (Giroux 2002). BSU promotes the Inclusive Excellence statement, set forth by the Association of American Colleges and Universities (2015), which defines diversity as "Individual differences (e.g., personality, learning styles, and life experiences) and group/social differences (e.g., race/ethnicity, class, gender, sexual orientation, country of origin, and ability as well as cultural, political, religious, or other affiliations)." This statement does recognize group categories, but it first emphasizes individual differences, a problematic addition to the definition of diversity.

White students embrace university efforts to increase diversity based on celebrating (white) snowflakes. The students demonstrate their inclusive morality by stating and reveling in the obvious fact that every individual is different. At the same time, in celebrating each individual as an equal incarnation of diversity, the snowflake version denies key aspects more traditionally associated with the concept of diversity. It leaves no place for meaningful group experiences, especially those of shared oppression. And it categorically dismisses inequality between groups. Claims based on membership in a group, let alone

one with a long history of discrimination, become meaningless as everyone has the same rights.

The following exchange with Max, a 32 year old white male, demonstrates this sentiment:

> *Interviewer*: Have you ever experienced any of these things [campus resources for diversity]? Like have you been to the multi-cultural center?
> *Max*: I've been in the multi-cultural center, I've been part of the tunnel of oppression [an on-campus event about oppression], [and] things of that sort of nature.
> *Interviewer*: What were your experiences there? What sticks out to you?
> *Max*: We're all people, we're all human beings, and we all need to be treated equal. It doesn't matter who you are or where you come from, your background. That's what diversity is about.

Out of an experience designed explicitly to grant empathy for people oppressed due to their group membership, Max emerged from the tunnel reinforced in his individualistic beliefs. Max moves the discussion from the multi-cultural center, as a campus resource aimed at reducing inequality between groups, to the idea that "we're all human beings," an expression of meaningful individuality. The problem for Max was not of oppression but group membership. If people do not want to be oppressed because of their group membership, all they have to do is quit their group. This is a classic colorblind trope based on misunderstanding Martin Luther King's dream of people not being judged by the color of their skin (Brown et al. 2003). The idea holds that fighting racism involves seeing everyone as equal. And in so doing, this enables white students to believe they are not racist by overlooking the very things that cause racial inequality, the structures that confer privilege and disadvantage according to skin color.

Snowflake diversity builds upon the findings of previous research on culturalist racism (Dalton 2008; Dyer 1988; Frankenberg 1993). These seminal works showed that white people do not recognize their own race or culture, but instead recognize themselves as just normal, while people of color are marked by the category of race and culture. This is a colonial dialogue that frees whiteness and its attendant privileges from interrogation because it is simply normal. Well-meaning white folk can therein lament their lack of culture and consequently spread their culture of domination.

Snowflake diversity extends beyond culturalist racism in that it continues the phenomenon of whites failing to recognize their own whiteness while adding the phenomena of failing to recognize any categorization and the self-congratulating embrace of a rich multiculturalism. Because diversity is a moral framework, students demonstrate their morality by participating in diversity. Under snowflake diversity, whites achieve the moral imperative to celebrate diversity through focusing on one's own unique individuality. In other words, snowflake diversity is a hegemonic appropriation of difference, granting white students equality in their diversity claims. It not only undermines minority claims to redress from historic and systematic oppressions. It now wields diversity as a means to further white domination.

Through this racist process, snowflake diversity helps the neoliberal transformation of the university. Overall, it enhances the American culture of liberal individualism through harnessing the moral strength of diversity. As George Lipsitz (1995) pointed out, liberal individualism is the core idea that blinds whites to the concept of group experiences, and therein safeguards their group privileges. The appropriation of diversity increases the potency of individualism, enhancing white people's blindness. Now in addition to not seeing their own privileges, white students lack the conceptual language to grasp their most immediate group membership: students. Instead, they see themselves as individuals with similar chances of educational success based on effort. This only makes it more difficult for them to identify with their class interests in the regressive restructuring of the university and society in general.

With the opening up of college to a wider population, activism by different groups in the 1960s and 1970s began challenging higher education's traditional elitism. Specifically, through employing the group experience of being students in higher education, in combination with diverse membership in oppressed groups, these movements aimed to reconstruct college as a foundation of egalitarian democracy. Students had the time and inclination to challenge the system explicitly because they were students.

Forty years later, neoliberal higher education and its snowflake diversity show instead the harnessing of working class austerity to preserve university exclusion. Elite schools avoided austerity through intensive privatization processes such as creating massive endowments and partnerships with corporations. State schools, meanwhile, have become more like professional vocational colleges, turning from the rich liberal arts tradition to champion applied fields. Juggling work, family, and school, these students find the college experience highly individualized and anomic. With commuting to school between other responsibilities, heavy cost burdens prevent them from identifying as students and mounting the challenges of the previous generation.

Working students therefore push for the most direct way to acquire the degrees that promise to increase their lifetime earnings. Ideas such as peer to peer learning make little sense as everyone is there only for themselves. Instead, peers only represent competition. These students have therein internalized the business model of individuals competing against each other, with the most deserving supposedly coming out on top. Time and money constraints combine with this ideology to push students to advocate for highly individualized styles of learning, such as online classes. This gives them the flexibility they need. But it undermines their ability to identify as beset students. And, it cuts them off from the group university experiences so jealously safeguarded by elite institutions that most effectively translate into enhanced incomes: the skills to create new knowledge and social connections, including group identities.

7   International Students as the New Model Minority

In the next construction of diversity that we identified, white students idealized wealthy international students as the paragon of multiculturalism. For example, when asked what promotes diversity in the university, George, the English-American from earlier, responded:

> Well obviously our acceptance of international students at the university. Not everyone does that. Even though they're paying us boatloads of money, which is mostly the reason that we're doing it. But I think it's good anyways. And I do have a couple Mexican professors, which I think is great... Mostly, the diversity that I've seen has mostly gone unnoticed. Nobody is like, "oh, our teacher is Mexican."

George constructs his diversity ideology entirely through international frames. Even diverse faculty are referenced by foreign nationality. His elucidation is illustrative of why many students construct international diversity as ideal. These particular minorities are desired because they bring culture and diversity that are unthreatening, while economically they bring wealth—a diametric opposite from minority students and their so called special needs.

Students like George celebrate how international students help create novel income streams for the university. They also recognize the opportunity to demonstrate their moral inclusivity by accepting them because "not everyone does that." Students thus embrace international students because they bring no challenge to the inequitable structures already in existence. This model of diversity is not only sanitized of acrimony around inequality, it becomes a new way to generate revenue. Students eagerly endorse this diversity because it promises to increase everyone's wellbeing in the most immediate economic terms, to say nothing of cultural richness.

Importantly, the university itself stresses this understanding. For instance, the provost's flagship reworking of the core student requirements generated new mandatory University Foundations (UF) courses outside the purview of traditional disciplines. And this is part of a larger project facilitating the "internationalization of curriculum" (Boise State University Task Force on Internationalization 2006). The only UF course treating diversity, UF 200, lumps together "written communication," "ethics," and "diversity and internationalization" as its three learning outcomes, diversity is not even worthy of its own category let alone its own course.[1] Further, though, the course description stresses an ethical need to learn about diversity, while framing that diversity solely through a global or international perspective (Boise State University 2013). The university thus explicitly trains students to think of internationalization and not racial hierarchy when addressing diversity.

As an unthreatening, depoliticized diversity, internationalization retrenches racism. White students perceive international students as the deserving students. They are the new "model minority" stereotype for others to emulate, a moniker previously applied to Asian Americans (Lee 1994; Ng, Lee and Pak 2007; Suzuki 1977, 2002). With the Asian-American case, there is some recognition (however incorrect) that they have overcome inequality, but yet, also represent a threat due to their perceived above-normal success, which causes places like schools to be too competitive for supposedly normal whites (Lee 1994, 1996; Ng et al. 2007). At the same time, this stereotype frees whites from responsibility for inequality and reinforces their anti-affirmative action stances as Asian Americans provide a route for upward mobility for other minorities to follow.

While similarly giving whites both an excuse and an out, the international model minority represents a more extreme case. First, while the Asian American stereotype emerged from some plausibility, the new standards for success for minorities have become simply impossible. In effect, white students are saying: "if you want to succeed, be a member of the global elite." The point, though, is that students are not stating or even implying this because they no longer feel they have to account for inequality. Rather, they completely reverse the original meaning of diversity: an acrimonious process of confronting differences emerging from a society steeped in inequalities. Instead, students work backwards, embracing diversity as inherently valuable and believing that importing a trouble free variety is the best way to achieve their desires. The

---

1   In contrast, many other universities have made classes in race and ethnicity mandatory, some of which successfully present these relations as contestatory. Boise State had its own initiative for a diversity requirement of which UF 200 is one depoliticized offspring.

international model minority then becomes a colorblind ideological tool of expulsion, providing no place for minority students in higher education.

In another major difference from the Asian American model, white students we interviewed did not perceive the high status of the international model minority as a threat. Perceived academic success made Asian Americans both ideal and threatening, helping to keep them and other minorities in their places in the racial hierarchy. However, in the international model, the new standard is simply that "they're paying us boatloads of money," educational achievement be damned. Participants felt that international students benefited from these arrangements because they would return to their home countries with high value US credentials. Thus, white students saw international students as unthreatening partially because they were not going to compete on the same job markets. Students also saw them as unthreatening because there was no institutionalized way of regularly interacting—except during such events as international student day when domestic students could consume unthreatening products of physical culture like food.

More than providing the model for racial minorities, though, international students represent an ideal for all students. The business model holds that students as customers (and alumni eventually) bring money to the university to purchase their degrees.[2] International students become particularly praiseworthy in this logic because they import "boatloads of money," the vital trait of a student once the university becomes a business.

This ideology, which is bolstered by colorblind racism, calls for a regressive remaking of the university. For example, Kara, who earlier stated that she opposed affirmative action in part because she did not "scold Native Americans," argues for increasing diversity through recruitment, based on her own study abroad experiences:

> *Interviewer*: Do you think there's other ways for them to get more diversity in the school?
> *Kara*: Besides study abroad? Well, definitely advertising and recruiting, I guess. I think–I don't know really know how much football helps outside of the U.S. I'm thinking that only brings people from other states. That's a good question because I know it's very important because education at BSU is a good international export for Idaho.
> *Interviewer*: Do you think the university should put some time and effort into promoting that kind of diversity?
> *Kara*: Absolutely!

---

2   Or they are purchasing the services that will eventually provide them with their degrees.

We already saw that Kara disliked the idea of affirmative action as a way to promote inclusivity of historically marginalized groups. But here, Kara "absolutely" supports dedicating limited resources to promote diversity. Her unapologetic use of business terms, such as "advertising" and "international export," links diversity and education to market practices. This engenders the notion that the university is a business, which expands its market and exports internationally via advertising (Clawson and Page 2011; Harvey 2005).

Her logic holds that, especially in times of budget constraints, investing money to attract wealthy students generates better outcomes for all, especially as this also enhances the diversity she values. Indeed, BSU, along with most other universities, explicitly highlights recruiting out-of-state and international students as a solution to budget shortfalls.[3]

This ideology extends even more, holding that diverse students receive marketing and pay more to attend the university, but students should not expect anything resembling a welfare state/university with policies like affirmative action. Indeed, many students condemned financial aid as a stigmatized government handout. Ironically, while these students have no problems with foreign governments paying tuition for international students, they do not want the same for themselves.

Five students specifically noted Saudi Arabia in their responses. Zane, a 23 year old white male, says:

> I know that the Saudi Arabian government has this program where they pay tuition for everything for people. They will just pay everything. So if you take a foreign student versus, like, an in-state student, a foreign student is worth four times as much because they have to pay out of state tuition, everything is paid for, they don't have any loans, so I feel like that is the easiest way to make money.

Zane recognizes how diversity is used to increase revenue rather than address systemic inequities. He goes even further, illuminating the logic behind this system that values a foreign student at four times that of an in-state student— at a state university. Mason, a 21 year old white male, is optimistic about the influx of Saudi students. He says:

---

3 BSU's President Kustra places the blame for budget problems on flat enrollment, ignoring the fact that demand for degrees remains high but skyrocketing tuition rates, caused by the imposition of the business model, provide the largest barriers to people acquiring their bachelor's (see Goldrick-Rab et al. 2013).

I know that [university president] Bob Kustra is working on increasing the percentage of Saudi students, and this year there was a big improvement, and he has got a certain percentage of the whole student population he is trying to get.

Mason recognizes the university's focus on marketing to international students, and celebrates their improved attendance.

Herein we see how deepening colorblind racism works to acquire the consent necessary for neoliberalizing higher education. In embracing international multiculturalism, what these students do not recognize is how the university is using its resources to recruit international students as a way of demonstrating campus diversity in order to increase university prestige, and thus its exclusivity (Berrey 2011). A higher profile from the international student presence helps the university compete for the best prepared and wealthiest students with the highest test scores (wealth being the greatest predictor of the other two), therein shifting the university mission from serving the state to serving the elite. The business model parlance proudly calls selectivity and highlights it as a key way to increase overall revenue (Clawson and Page 2011). Further, seeking new income streams is only half of the equation. Without concurrent cost containment measures, new income translates to higher tuition (Goldrick-Rab et al. 2013). White students' endorsement of international diversity therein saddles them with higher tuition costs.

Beyond simply advocating for budget choices to recruit international students over some other expense, these students actually endorse reshaping the university to serve the wealthy at the expense of the traditional working class. Once here, elite students must be served in the way that fits them best. They are much more likely than other students to transfer to institutions they like better. Retention also translates more readily into alumni dollars, of which wealthy students are more likely to give.

Importantly, their demands differ markedly from the majority of students. The business model envisions the traditional college student as: living in dorms, attending classes during the day, partying with peers, and never juggling responsibilities of work and children. All of these factors clash with the majority of BSU students, 80 percent of whom work at least part time, with many providing the bulk income for families. Indeed, the Boise State administration regularly celebrates a demographic shift as indicative of a higher quality education (because of increased competitiveness and selectivity), providing frequently disingenuous statistics to prove that incoming students are getting much younger while their test scores are vaulting upwards. Thus, in advocating the importation of a wealthy and conflict-free diversity to supplant the acrimonious local variety, white students endorse an elite university not designed to serve their needs.

In this way, the students in this study internalize one of the most regressive ideas behind neoliberalism, the notion that making the wealthy better off will improve everyone's wellbeing. They are envisioning a university customized to ability to pay: rich students get what they need from the university while others have to make do. Or to put it another way, wealthy students should get the best service while everyone else has to struggle through their castoffs, because the elite disproportionately enable the university to function.

8   Instrumental Diversity

The third process of depoliticization we identified relies on an instrumental diversity that views multiculturalism as providing tradable skills for the marketplace. For example, when asked how she needed diversity for the future, Laura, a 22 year old white female, responded:

> Specifically, with marketing because I need to be able to see the way that people think or the way that they make their decisions and why they buy products—absolutely influences the way I see people because I'm very aware of other people, or I try to be very aware of that so I can learn from that.

This is a market multiculturalism that differs from other forms. In her embrace of diversity training for the job market, Laura reconstructs society as the marketplace. The way people think is reduced to why they buy products. Her heightened awareness of other people is just about what they buy.

This ideology depoliticizes diversity by viewing everyone as an equal participant in market transactions. Differences are important, but only as a form of product differentiation, and the opportunity to make more money on the market. As with the above ideologies, this builds on the classic colorblind trope constructing people as not unequal but simply different (Gallagher 2009). Now, however, students want difference. Indeed, this is an aspect of what Luc Boltanski and Eve Chiapello (2005) call the New Spirit of Capitalism, in which people are not buying products so much as meaningful experiences, in this case in the form of cultural exchange. And, in not seeing this difference as inequality, students are also endorsing the neoliberal processes of economic polarization: inequality masked as diversity is good because it creates more opportunities for profit.

This kind of diversity training goes further, however. Mark, a 22 year old white male, gave us his take:

> I think being able to work with different people and get along with different people. When I get out in the world, there's going to be all kinds of different problems that I'll need to be able to communicate and get along with other people and work through problems. So, I think that's just exposure to being flexible.

For Mark, this skill set will enable him to create peace at work and help everybody just get along. This idea hinges on the trope of tolerance, that if we all just understand each others' different practices we will rid the world of its problems. Again, we are not unequal, just different and misunderstood. As a traditionally white paternalistic concept, tolerance ideology places the blame on people who actually do see inequality and act on it. Such people are perceived as hostile because they do not "tolerate" injustice, but rather act to end it, and thus represent the wrong kind of diversity. This is a kind of training, then, in how to not see inequality. Moreover, it trains students to become proselytizers of depoliticized diversities and the myth of the end of racism.

Instrumental diversity, however, retrenches racism even more. In reconstructing society as the equally accessible marketplace, it constructs human value strictly in terms of market success. This is a change from the paternalistic welfare understanding of helping minorities to survive where markets fail. It instead treats minorities as entrepreneurs of the self whose own failure in the market will result in bare life conditions. Failing in the market is failing in society, eliminating any conceptual place for such individuals.

This ideology ignores the legacy of inequality and assumes that everyone has the same chance to succeed in the market—minorities perhaps with better chances since they have culture and whites supposedly do not—relegating minority groups to enhanced marginality. There is no place for them because of their own individual failing in the market. This is a logic of expulsion. But it is also a new and more extreme version of blaming the victim in that it does not even provide for the charity aspects of Keynesian capitalism. It rather builds disadvantage on top of disadvantage.

This racist process in turn helps bolster the overall neoliberal project and the university business model more specifically. Neoliberal ideology provides the notion of equating society with the market. But this brand of diversity provides hegemonic content, a part of the substance that makes the reshaping of higher education appear worthwhile. By creating new and innovative ways for ever more diverse people to interact through the market—Harvey's

(2005) accumulation by dispossession—everyone seems better off, even as they are being marginalized. Students therein not only deepen their color-blind racism, in doing so, they demand an acceleration of the regressive processes of appropriating non-market relations for the sake of private profit. In other words, this kind of diversity training requires ever more market relations to succeed, with any and all marketization of social relations, including of the university itself, appearing as opportunities for meaningful multicultural profit.

9   Reversing the Depolitcization of Diversity

While most students in our study bought into the depoliticized discourses about diversity, some actively opposed the depoliticized and sanitized ways that the university uses diversity. These students argue that affirmative action policies are necessary to achieve equity in education. Jack, a 22-year-old white male, expresses his desire to politicize diversity:

> *Jack*: I think more opportunities should be given to students with those marginalized identities. More effort should be given to finding out how those marginalized identities are, in many ways, disallowed from attending university, and efforts should be made to compensate for that—in whatever way is possible.
> *Interviewer*: So how do you feel about affirmative action?
> *Jack*: I feel that it is good for what it is. But, there should be some sort of a shift. There should be a slight shift in the way that it is run, and a slight shift in the way that the discourse around it is being run. It should be communicated from the university, and from people within the university, not as, like, a welfare program—that it is often talked about as—it should start off as "here are the reasons that this exists," which could feed into a lot of diversity education that should be happening, a lot of the diversity research that should be happening, and overall I think that would make for a stronger university as well.

Jack's biggest concern is that affirmative action is too often misrepresented as a "welfare program." Instead, he argues that a shift in its operation should be made to actively engage the ways that people with "marginalized identities" have been excluded from the university. Students like Jack argue that a program engaged in this type of critical "diversity education," would "make for a stronger university."

To achieve real equality requires a model of diversity that "includes celebrating cultural differences, but also it requires an analysis of exclusion and discrimination, and it challenges hegemonic notions of colorblindness and meritocracy" (Herring and Henderson 2012:630). Jack demonstrates this ability in his desire to transform the discourse about affirmative action from one that constructs it as superfluous charity to one that integrates it as an engaging program positively affecting all students. The ideologies that depoliticize diversity are flexible in order to retain their hegemony (Jackman 1994), thus they create opportunities for dialectical processes to emerge that do give attention to parity and equity.

The politicized discourses of students like Jack indicate that white students' critical consciousness about race creates a class consciousness about their marginalized positions as students. By embracing inequality discourses, these students have the ideological resources necessary to recognize multiple inequitable structures. For example, in discussing how the university operates as a business, Jack stated, "I have experienced being a customer in some classes that are way too overfilled, where the professors are just not interested." The business model of the university hinders educational experiences.

Depoliticizing diversity eliminates discourses of inequality. Thus, politicizing diversity has the potential of challenging and reversing this relationship. Recognizing real structures of inequality creates discourses that give attention to inequality and challenge the neoliberal remaking of the university. Administrators exploit vapid, meaningless constructions of diversity to train students to embrace neoliberal reforms. Yet, remaking the university increasingly undermines the education of students. A leveling out of admissions shows that the outcomes of the business model are becoming less tenable, illustrated by skyrocketing tuition and outstanding student loans. Administrators use this to impose austerity and retrench neoliberalism. But the ideological clothing also becomes more transparent. Thus, since issues of race, class, and neoliberalism are inherently intertwined, all of these issues can become simultaneous fronts for undoing the business model and asserting a more human-centered education system. A challenge on the front of racial inequality inherently informs the challenge on the class front, for instance, and challenges to neoliberalism work to undo racism.

10   Conclusion

In this chapter we revealed an intimate relationship between the deepening of racism and the regressive neoliberal remaking of society. Racially privileged white students came to advocate for the university business model through vitalizing their colorblind racist beliefs. We argued that there are at least three particular processes used to depoliticize diversity that resolve the contradiction between opposing affirmative action and supporting diversity. Students draw upon multiple diversity ideologies shaped by the university, including (1) "snowflake diversity" that sees everyone as meaningfully different, (2) constructing wealthy international students as the "new model minority," and (3) an "instrumental diversity" that views diversity as providing tradable skills.

Each process reinforces the neoliberalization of higher education. The depoliticization of diversity removes language for inequality, ultimately undermining the interests of the local, white, working-class students that make up the majority at Boise State University and across the United States. This leaves working-class, white students with no outlets to express the loss of access to higher education caused by ever-increasing tuition rates and lower returns on degrees. Each process variously employs depoliticizing colorblind logics. In so doing, each affirms the neoliberal remaking of the university by removing the language of inequality. White students end up advocating against their own class interests while they use colorblind discourses to privilege themselves racially.

The ideological work of white students who occupy the contradictory nexus of supporting diversity while opposing affirmative action reveals the multifaceted ways that neoliberalism strengthens its grasp over public institutions like higher education. Rather than instituting market reforms through force, institutional leaders entice people to embrace policies with an ethic of multiculturalism and inclusivity. However, that ethic depoliticizes, and thus disregards, inequality and instead employs logics that affirm neoliberalism, such as liberal individualism, meritocracy, and entrepreneurship (Harvey 2005, 2011). Students are able to support diversity measures while opposing affirmative action because they utilize constructions of diversity that differ depending on context. By embracing depoliticizing processes, students vitalize color-blind racism through disentangling issues of inequality from their constructions of diversity. Thus, celebrating diversity becomes an expression of white privilege. But that privilege is tempered by exploitative neoliberal reforms that, above all, dispossess a growing numbers of students of access to higher education. Racial minorities continue to be underrepresented (Giroux and Giroux 2004), and those admitted are forced to pay exorbitantly high tuition costs (Clawson and Leiblum 2008; Clawson and Page 2011).

Considering the three diversity ideologies together, our work also indicates a self-reinforcing cycle typical of the spurious logic linking race and neoliberalism: relative successes by minorities occur just as the university becomes less accessible along class lines. Instead of blaming the business model policies reshaping higher education, students blame the more proximate minorities, even though minorities are more vulnerable to these changes. Much the same occurred in the labor market: the affirmative action inroads to good manufacturing jobs occurred just as corporations offshored these jobs (Lipsitz 1995). Working class white males therein became enlisted into the neoliberal cause because they believed it confronted the problem of minorities and women taking "their" jobs, when in actuality neoliberalism brought about the decline of the middle classes (Harvey 2005).

Herein, our analysis provides a vista for better understanding the complexities of an increasingly unequal society. While we focus on students, the institutional level emerges as paramount. The university and higher education in general has enacted massive changes, aiming ultimately to be free of the state—and its unique capacity to provide an egalitarian education. Yet the tuition-inflating actions of visionary administrators do not come under scrutiny. Instead, through simultaneously championing the twin hegemonic ideologies of diversity and anti-affirmative action, that is, through shaping depoliticized diversities, the university successfully trains students to advocate for the very changes that undermine their educational outcomes.

This brings up a major point that has been underemphasized in critical race theory: our study clearly shows the relativity of white racial privilege. White students get significant head starts. But in jealously hewing to these, they make themselves worse off. We give a clear demonstration that white students undermine their most narrowly conceived educational wellbeing by holding on to racist ideologies. In clinging to their colorblind racist beliefs, students advocated against their own class interests. While this point was made strongly about the birth of whiteness (Zinn 1980), its emphasis has been lost in other topics, a point that needs rectification.

While the poor fit of education to market relations shows a great triumph for the neoliberal project, it also allows for greater potential resistance. Higher education cannot abandon its training function, and indeed has employed this well to inculcate neoliberal ideologies. At the same time, however, an educated populace finds more and creative ways to crack open the contradictions. The university still remains an important site for acquiring critical consciousness. And with the dynamic relationship between race and class, working class white students can and do become empowered through understanding racial oppression. While pressed for time like no other generation, these students can still employ these critical understandings to challenge the overall business model. They therein set about reversing the cycle such that racial consciousness undermines neoliberalism and brings about greater racial and class equality. The bigger lesson for resistance then, centers on exploiting the contradictions of neoliberalism and colorblind racism, and employing non-market or poorly marketized resources to undermine the outlined framework upon which neoliberalism depends.

References

Alexander, Michelle. 2010. *The New Jim Crow: Mass Incarceration in the Age of Color-blindness*. New York, NY: New Press.

Association of American Colleges and Universities. 2015. "Making Excellence Inclusive."

Belcheir, Marcia J. 2002. "A Profile of Boise State First Year and Senior Students with Comparisons to Other Urban Universities." *Boise State Office of Institution Research*.

Berrey, Ellen. 2011. "Why Diversity Became Orthodox in Higher Education, and How It Changed the Meaning of Race on Campus." *Critical Sociology* 37 (5): 573–596.

Boise State University. 2013, "Uf 200: Foundational Studies Program." Retrieved May 12, 2013 (http://academics.boisestate.edu/fsp/students/uf-200/).

Boise State University Task Force on Internationalization. 2006. "Making the Global Connection: Recommended Pathways to Internationalizing the Campus." Retrieved September 18, 2013 (http://academics.boisestate.edu/provost/files/2009/01/itffinal report.pdf).

Boltanski, Luc and Eve Chiapello. 2005. "The New Spirit of Capitalism." *International Journal of Politics, Culture, and Society* 18 (3–4): 161–188.

Bonilla-Silva, Eduardo. 2010. *Racism without Racists: Color-Blind Racism and the Persistence of Racial Inequality in the United States*. Lanham, CO: Rowman & Littlefield Publishers.

Bonilla-Silva, Eduardo, Amanda Lewis and David G. Embrick. 2004. "'I Did Not Get That Job Because of a Black Man...': The Story Lines and Testimonies of Color-Blind Racism." *Sociological Forum* 19 (4): 555–581. doi: 10.1007/s11206-004-0696-3.

Brown, Michael K., Martin Carnoy, Elliott Currie, Troy Duster and B. David Oppenheimer 2003. *Whitewashing Race: The Myth of a Color-Blind Society*. Berkeley, CA: University of California Press.

Brown, Wendy. 2006. "American Nightmare Neoliberalism, Neoconservatism, and De-Democratization." *Political theory* 34 (6): 690–714.

Clawson, Dan and Mishy Leiblum. 2008. "Class Struggle in Higher Education." *Equity & Excellence in Education* 41 (1): 12–30.

Clawson, Dan and Max Page. 2011. *The Future of Higher Education*. New York, NY: Routledge.

Dalton, Harlon. 2008. "Failing to See." pp. 15–18 in *White Privilege : Essential Readings on the Other Side of Racism*. New York, NY: Worth Publishers.

Dyer, Richard. 1988. "White." *Screen* 29 (4): 44–64.

Embrick, David G. 2008. "The Diversity Ideology: Keeping Major Transnational Corporations White and Male in an Era of Globalization." In *Globalization and America: Race, Human Rights & Inequality*, edited by Angela Hattery, David G. Embrick, and Earl Smith. Lanham, MD: Rowman and Littlefield.

Embrick, David G. 2011. "The Diversity Ideology in the Business World: A New Oppression for a New Age." *Critical Sociology* 37 (5): 1–16.

Feagin, Joe R., Hernan Vera and Pinar Batur. 2001. *White Racism: The Basics*. New York, NY: Routledge.

Frank, Thomas. 2004. *What's the Matter with Kansas?: how conservatives won the heart of America*. New York, NY: Metropolitan Books.

Frankenberg, Ruth. 1993. *White Women, Race Matters: The Social Construction of Whiteness*. Minneapolis, MN: University of Minnesota Press.

Gallagher, Charles A. 2009. "Color-Blind Privilege: The Social and Political Functions of Erasing the Color Line in Post-Race America." pp. 100–108 in *Rethinking the Color Line*, edited by C.A. Gallagher. New York, NY: McGraw-Hill.

Ginsberg, Benjamin. 2011. *The Fall of the Faculty*. London, England: Oxford University Press.

Giroux, Henry A. 2002. "Neoliberalism, Corporate Culture, and the Promise of Higher Education: The University as a Democratic Public Sphere." *Harvard Educational Review* 72 (4): 425–464.

Giroux, Henry A. and Susan Searls Giroux. 2004. *Take Back Higher Education: Race, Youth, and the Crisis of Democracy in the Post-Civil Rights Era*. New York, NY: Palgrave Macmillan.

Goldrick-Rab, Sara, Lauren Schudde and Jacob Stampen. 2013. "Making College Affordable: Rethinking Voucher-Driven Approaches to Federal Student Aid." Paper presented at the The trillion-dollar question: Reinventing student financial aid for the 21st century.

Gratz V. Bollinger, 539 U.S. 244 (2003).

Guinier, Lani and Gerald Torres. 2009. "The Ideology of Colorblindness." pp. 109–113 in *Rethinking the Color Line*, edited by C.A. Gallagher. New York, NY: McGraw-Hill.

Hacker, Jacob S and Paul Pierson. 2010. "Winner-Take-All Politics: Public Policy, Political Organization, and the Precipitous Rise of Top Incomes in the United States." *Politics & Society* 38 (2): 152–204.

Harrison-Walker, L Jean. 2010. "Customer Prioritization in Higher Education: Targeting 'Right' Students for Long-Term Profitability." *Journal of Marketing for Higher Education* 20 (2): 191–208.

Harvey, David. 2005. *A Brief History of Neoliberalsim*. New York, NY: Oxford University Press.

Harvey, David. 2011. *The Enigma of Capital: And the Crises of Capitalism*. London, England: Oxford University Press.

Herring, Cedric and Loren Henderson. 2012. "From Affirmative Action to Diversity: Toward a Critical Diversity Perspective." *Critical Sociology* 38 (5): 629–643.

Jackman, Mary R. 1994. *The Velvet Glove: Paternalism and Conflict in Gender, Class, and Race Relations*. Berkeley, CA: University of California Press.

Jones, Bradley and Roopali Mukherjee. 2010. "From California to Michigan: Race, Rationality, and Neoliberal Governmentality." *Communication and Critical/Cultural Studies* 7 (4): 401–422.

Katznelson, Ira. 2005. *When Affirmative Action Was White: An Untold History of Racial Inequality in Twentieth-Century America*. New York, NY: W.W. Norton & Company, Inc.

Klein, Naomi. 2007. *The shock doctrine: the rise of disaster capitalism*. New York, NY: Metropolitan Books/Henry Holt.

Lee, Stacey J. 1994. "Behind the Model-Minority Stereotype: Voices of High-and Low-Achieving Asian American Students." *Anthropology & Education Quarterly* 25 (4): 413–429.

Lee, Stacy J. 1996. *Unraveling the "Model Minority" Stereotype: Listening to Asian American Youth*: Teachers College Press.

Lipsitz, George. 1995. "The Possessive Investment in Whiteness: Racialized Social Democracy and the" White "Problem in American Studies." *American Quarterly*: 369–387.

Maly, Michael T., Heather M. Dalmage and Nancy Michaels. 2012. "The End of an Idyllic Wold: Nostalgia Narratives, Race, and the Construction of White Powerlessness." *Critical Sociology*: 1–23.

Massey, Douglas S. and Nancy A. Denton. 1993. *American Apartheid : Segregation and the Making of the Underclass*. Cambridge, MA: Harvard University Press.

Moore, Ryan and Michael Roberts. 2009. "Do-It-Yourself Mobilizations: Punk and Social Movements." *Mobilization: An International Journal* 14 (3): 273–291.

National Center for Education Statistics. 2015. "Ipeds Data Center." 2015.

Neckerman, Kathryn M. and Joleen Kirschenman. 1991. "Hiring Strategies, Racial Bias, and Inner-City Workers." *Social Problems* 38 (4): 433–447.

Ng, Jennifer C., Sharon S. Lee and Yoon K. Pak. 2007. "Contesting the Model Minority and Perpetual Foreigner Stereotypes: A Critical Review of Literature on Asian Americans in Education." *Review of Research in Education* 31 (1): 95–130.

Pager, Devah. 2003. "The Mark of a Criminal Record." *American Journal of Sociology* 108 (5): 937–975.

Peck, Jamie. 2010. *Constructions of Neoliberal Reason*. London, England: Oxford University Press.

Peck, Jamie and Adam Tickell. 2002. "Neoliberalizing Space." *Antipode* 34 (3): 380–404.

Rubin, Allen and Earl Babbie. 1993. "The Logic of Sampling." *Research Methods for Social Work*: 367–371.

Rugh, Jacob S and Douglas S Massey. 2010. "Racial Segregation and the American Foreclosure Crisis." *American Sociological Review* 75 (5): 629–651.

Selingo, Jeff. 2012. "Fixing College." *New York Times* 26: A23.

Selingo, Jeffrey J. 2013. *College (Un)Bound: The Future of Higher Education and What It Means for Students*. New York, NY: Houghton Mifflin Harcourt.

Sites, William and Virginia Parks. 2011. "What Do We Really Know About Racial Inequality? Labor Markets, Politics, and the Historical Basis of Black Economic Fortunes." *Politics & Society* 39 (1): 40–73.

Suzuki, Bob H. 1977. "Education and the Socialization of Asian Americans: A Revisionist Analysis of the 'Model Minority' Thesis." *Amerasia Journal* 4 (2): 23–51.

Suzuki, Bob H. 2002. "Revisiting the Model Minority Stereotype: Implications for Student Affairs Practice and Higher Education." *New Directions for Student Services* (97): 21–32.

Swyngedouw, Erik. 2011. "Interrogating Post-Democratization: Reclaiming Egalitarian Political Spaces." *Political Geography*: 370–380.

University of California Regents V. Bakke, 438 U.S. 265 (1978).

Vera, Hernan, Joe R. Feagin and Andrew Gordon. 1995. "Superior Intellect?: Sincere Fictions of the White Self." *Journal of Negro Education*: 295–306.

Wacquant, Loïc J.D. 2009. *Punishing the Poo : The Neoliberal Government of Social Insecurity*. Durham, NC: Duke University Press.

Weiss, Robert S. 1995. *Learning from Strangers: The Art and Method of Qualitative Interview Studies*. New York, NY: Simon and Schuster.

Zinn, Howard. 1980. *A People's History of the United States*. New York, NY: New Press.

Zizek, Slavoj. 1997. "Multiculturalism, or, the Cultural Logic of Multinational Capitalism." *New Left Review*: 28–51.

Zizek, Slavoj. 2009. *First as Tragedy, Then as Farce*. London, England: Verso, New Left Books.

PART 3

Pedagogy and Transformation in Higher Education

.:

Teaching in Black and White: Reflections of Teaching the Social Construction of Race

Tiffany Davis, Wendy Leo Moore and Joyce M. Bell

1 Introduction

One of the most enjoyable aspects of teaching sociology is to get students to understand the value and utility of understanding society from a sociological perspective. As C. Wright Mills (1959) reminded us, our task as sociologists is to unite history and biography in such an intricate way that it is virtually impossible to attempt to understand an individual or event separate from the historical, political and social contexts in which it is embedded. This is one of the reasons that teaching about race and racial inequality is such an exciting, yet challenging, endeavor. As Omi and Winant (1996) highlighted in their work, race is an ongoing project and how it is understood, experienced and contested is a consequence of larger social processes that are occurring at the time. Given the often fast pace with which social change occurs today, pinpointing best practices of teaching about racial inequality can almost feel like trying to nail down a moving target.

There is one aspect of race not subject to this type of continual change that sociologists must confront when teaching race; that race is a social construct. All students come to the classroom with some understanding of inequality along the lines of race, class, gender and possibly other identities. However, few have the sociological or historical knowledge needed to understand the root of these inequalities and even more importantly, to understand that they are based on social categories that are socially constructed, which in theory means they could be deconstructed. Teaching students that race is socially constructed and not a biological phenomenon is one of the most important elements of a sociological pedagogy of race. Of equal importance, however, is balancing the teaching of this new perspective of race with an acknowledgment that the consequences of race are very real, despite the fact that "race" is not. Correspondingly, the focus of this chapter is how each author has used this lecture as a conceptual tool to push students beyond essentialist notions of race. It is our hope that practitioners can glean from our experiences equally effective and creative ways to teach the social construction of race and challenge students long held assumptions.

Introducing race as a social construct is particularly important today because in this post-civil rights era and with the nation currently being led by its first Black president, young people are increasingly buying into a colorblind framework. At an individual level, students often assert the idea that "not seeing" race will end racial inequality, yet as Bonilla-Silva (2001, 2010) warns, the color blindness being infused into our nation's political and economic policies ultimately reproduces the structural racism that currently plagues our nation. This contradiction makes teaching race as a social meaning not a biological fact both more important and more challenging. Letting go of the belief that race is biological or "real" can be a natural segue to adopting a color blind notion of race; if race is "merely" a social construction and essentially not real, then colorblindness appears to be a suitable approach to viewing race and thus, racial inequality. As critical race scholar Patricia Williams (1997) has noted, this tendency facilitates an abstract individualistic and color blind ideological frame, which ignores the reality that in order to confront and deconstruct racial inequality and structural racism, we must first take explicit account of race and the long history of white supremacy, which has led to this racial inequality.

When the three of us (co-authors Davis, Bell, and Moore) began teaching about race and racism as young sociologists we frequently discussed the challenges of teaching about the socially constructed nature of race in a meaningful way, while simultaneously balancing the reality of the consequences and lived experiences of race and racism. Working together to construct effective teaching approaches to this process, we were informed by the pedagogical scholarship of bell hooks (1994) and Paulo Freire (1996) in that we viewed the teaching process as a potentially transgressive act embedded with the power to identify the dynamics of racial power and challenge the boundaries of the white normativity. As a result, we strived to engage in a pedagogy that re-centered the experiences of people of color as normative and deployed a critical dialogical approach to actually *doing* race in the classroom. This led us to create a class lecture and inter-active discussion by using our own bodies and racial identities as the questioned racial subject in the classroom. Having introduced our undergraduate students to the idea that race is socially and historically constructed (which is sometimes captured quite quickly by students, and other times takes much more time), we ask students simply to identify our race. Our goal is to get students to engage in the process of racing people in the same way that we all do in our everyday lives—but subsequently to explicitly challenge their process of racing other individuals by asking them to critically consider *why* they perceive us racially in particular ways.

Alicea and Kressel (1997) have experimented with a similar approach in their intermediate sociology/history course that covered issues of immigration and ethnicity. In their activity, on the first day of class, they had the students go around and guess one another's race and ethnicity and write it down. From there, students were assigned as homework to journal about the activity as a way of reflecting on the choices they make in regard to their own racial identity along with the criteria they use in racially classifying others. One of their biggest takeaways from the assignment was that it "makes very clear the fallacy that one can determine (biological) ancestry from physically visible characteristics" (Alicea and Kressel 1997: 68).

Although using Alicea and Kressel's (1997) approach in having students guess one another's racial background has its benefits, we argue that formulating this activity into a dialogical exercise where we highlight the racialization process using ourselves, the teachers, as the target of the racialization exercise, has benefits over the student based approach. First, we recognize that by putting ourselves in the subject position, we are inviting students to discuss our race and thereby not putting students in the position of racializing another person who might be uncomfortable with their racial judgment. Moreover, in this context, students are able to work as a collective in guessing the race of their teacher, and as a result their individual racial judgments are less highlighted—in this group context we are also able to highlight the ways in which social constructions take place through social negotiations.

In spite of this range of responses and interactions we have received from students, we have found that this exercise is often successful in getting students to begin to move away from biological and essentialist notions of race and racial categories to get them to engage the sociological imagination. In addition to this, through the process of this exercise students come to understand their deep reliance on biological assumptions and as a result our discussion of the real relevance of race, despite its socially constructed nature, becomes salient for students. We believe that laying the foundation of the socially constructed nature of race is critical before delving into more substantive issues, as it is key to helping students develop more sociological grounded interpretations of racial inequality. Below we lay our stories side-by-side to illuminate the patterns we have found, and the ways we have utilized these patterns to push students to think critically about race, racialization, and white domination.

2   Davis' Experience

As an African American female professor of sociology at a Minority Serving Institution (MSI), my teaching strategies continue to evolve to meet the needs of young people of color, who in my opinion need to have a deft ability to recognize and confront racism and racist structures in this current era of neo-liberalism. In light of this, teaching about the social constructedness of race provides an alternative and critical foundation from which my students can examine and question some of the ways race impacts their day lives and interactions with the social world. Having been trained at a mainstream university and my previous teaching experience being with predominantly white students, when I initially began teaching at my current university, I naively assumed that it would be "easier" to teach students of color about the socially constructed nature of race and issues of racial inequality. I thought the personal experiences they may have had with discrimination and inequality would have easily and inevitably translated into a conceptualization of race as a social construct. It is true that my students do have a complex and very personal understanding of race and its political, economic and social consequences for their lives, but sometimes they need some assistance with fully grasping the idea that race itself is a social construct.

I typically use this lecture in my introduction to sociology or diversity courses that I regularly teach. I open the section on race and ethnicity with the "What is my Race" discussion and ask students to guess my racial background. More often than not, in response to this question the whole class will immediately blurt out "BLACK" or "African American" usually with a collective tone of indignation as if I have insulted their intelligence by asking such an obvious question. I then asked whether they would be surprised to learn that I was not Black in spite of having a dark complexion and wearing my hair in locks. The responses range from that being impossible to perhaps it is possible that I had some other race in my bloodline countless generations ago. Typically, they begin to make guesses about ethnic ties that I may have and assume that I am of Jamaican descent (presumably because of my hairstyle) or that I descend from some other ethnic group in the Caribbean or Africa. I usually have to take a step back to explain the sociological difference between race and ethnicity and try to get them to contemplate about my racial identity again. From here, they usually return to their original response that I am Black and there really are not any other alternatives to how I can identify.

From here, I try to complicate the issue by asking whether how I racially identify could change if they knew that I have non-black relatives on both sides of my family. I do have non-black relatives on both sides of my family as my maternal great-grandmother was white and my paternal great-grandmother was Native American and was very close to her Cherokee roots. To this, students tend to respond that my great-grandparents whom I knew quite well as a child, didn't matter and in their eyes I was still Black. I follow this response by asking how many know or have a relationship with any of their great-grandparents.

Usually, an overwhelming majority of the class responds in the affirmative. I challenge them and ask why then is it expected that I deny my family members even though they are allowed to claim theirs. Again, they deny my potential biological roots and say that it is not the case that I cannot claim my family, but having non-black family members does not make me any less black in terms of how others will view and treat me. This shows that in many ways, students are very clear on the fact that the social determinants of race are often more important than biological claims.

I can distinctly recall one response that I got from a student early on in the exercise. While students were going back and forth, tossing out responses, one young man smugly replied, "maybe you think you are white since you talk white." At this point, the class erupted in laughter, including myself. His response stands out in my mind, not because I was offended, but rather because it was an early experience with being called out by my students as an African American woman for using mainstream English while amongst my racial peers. This was perceived as a cultural offense and in some regards, rightfully so. In her research on young African American students, Carter (2003) defines "non-dominant" cultural capital as "a set of tastes, appreciations, and understanding, such as preferences for particular linguistic, musical, and dress styles, and physical gestures used by lower status group members to gain 'authentic' cultural status position in their respective communities" (138). Hence, "non-dominant" cultural capital can serve as an invaluable tool for African American students in settings that are also predominantly African American. However, in mainstream spaces that are structured along racial lines, what was once a valuable resource transforms into a potential liability. As such, my students are protective of their claims to and participation in non-dominant cultural capital and value the opportunities when they can engage in it freely and Minority Serving Institutions often do the work of creating these safe spaces for students to do so. Therefore, as a Black woman, my use of mainstream English at that time, along with the very idea of me problematizing my race in the classroom led my students to believe that I was openly rejecting my Blackness—something that is connected to white domination and the oppression of people of color (Steinburg 2007).

By the end of the exercise, rarely have I been able to convince students that I am anything other than Black. At the most, they may come up with hypothetical situations where I could potentially identify as something else, but these responses are usually ethnic identities as mentioned above. Unlike my co-authors, as a result of my phenotype, students immediately categorize me as Black or African American. Instead spending a lot of time considering the different ways I can identify, we tend to spend more time on why it is that I can only identify as black. This then creates a segue into a reflective discussion of how the "one-drop rule" is still very much alive and used by both Blacks and non-Blacks to situate individuals on the racial hierarchy. We discuss the ways our continued reliance on the one-drop rule undermines individuals' ability to truly identify as bi- or multiracial. Subsequently, many of them have adopted a white/non-white view of race relations in the U.S. in terms of who has access to privilege and resources. In all, I have found the exercise to be successful in getting students to understand, through the use of their own responses, that previous and current biological claims about racial attributes are scientifically impossible to prove and have and continue to be embedded in larger social and cultural constructions of race.

3   Bell's Experience

When I teach about racial identity in my typically predominantly white class-rooms, I begin by talking about how Tiger Woods crafted his own racial label—Caublanasian. I ask them to think about the relative importance of his own identity and the way that other people perceive him racially; and I ask them to reflect upon the relevance (both personally, to Woods, and socially, to how others perceive Woods) of Woods' attempt to construct a new individualized racial label. After this discussion I begin the "What is my race" lecture by asking the classroom "So what is my race?" They always start with blank stares, and there is awkward silence—I assure them that I want them to guess and that I won't be offended. Over the years of doing this exercise I've gotten all sorts of answers attempting to make sense out of my racially ambiguous body. "Latina?" "Puerto Rican?" "Mixed with black and something." "Somoan." "Native American." "Vietnamese." "Something Middle Eastern." The range of answers I've gotten over the years is astounding.

After they populate a list of guesses I start with a series of hints. "What if I told you that I have at least one white great-grandparent?" The students always say it doesn't matter—it doesn't help them understand my race. "Ok, what if I told you I speak fluent Spanish." Here someone always chimes in to say, "you could have learned Spanish." Then I say, "ok, the truth is I identify as white. What do you think about that?" The responses here are particularly interesting and offer students an important illustration of the power of whiteness as a category of exclusivity. The core of the discussion that follows every semester is "I don't know what you are, but you're not white." Some students do this by questioning my definition of "white." By the time we do this exercise we've talked about how race operates differently in different societies and how some people who are considered black in the United States couldn't pass for black in Brazil for example. They think it's a trick question and I'm saying that I'm white in Brazil. So I clarify that I mean I'm both American and white. Their faces generally belie their disbelief. Alternately, they'll say something like, "I guess if you identify as white, that's your business." With the implication that it's fine for me to think whatever I want, but that other people won't see me that way. This response leads directly into my lecture on labeling theory and racial identity where I explain that our racial identities are not simply of our own making. Rather, they are formed out of a complex interaction between how we view ourselves and how others see us.

The responses I've gotten from Black students over the years are particularly interesting. They generally outright reject my claim to whiteness. When I ask what they would say if I told them I was white, many black students will say, "I would want to know what happened that made you feel that way." Or just, "yeah, right." I had a young black woman in my class who said, "I would feel really bad about that because we don't have very many black professors and I would feel like you abandoned me." So beyond the clear rejection of the idea that I could actually *be* white, she is also making the claim that in the event I had mixed racial heritage, choosing whiteness was not only a rejection of my own blackness but a rejection of her as a black student. In this instance this exercise exposes two powerful elements of race and racialization. First, it illustrates the power of the notion of whiteness as purity—and Blackness as a form of taint on that purity—the ideology underlying the "one drop rule" which characterizes US racial categories and holds that one-drop of "Black blood" makes one Black (Gross 2010). Secondly, it reveals the political nature of race and racialization resulting from a racist social structure that devalues and marginalizes Blackness so that a rejection of Blackness is viewed as an embracing of that devaluation and participation in the ideology of white domination (Johnson 1998, Steinberg 2007).

The truth is that I'm a biracial woman with a black father and white mother. I'm light skinned and I identify as black. So eventually after the discussion, I tell them this and help them to think about how they denied my access to whiteness even though I have a white parent. I help them to think about why this is. It opens up a discussion about the one-drop rule, the exclusivity of whiteness and how our internal racial identities are only a part of our racialized experience. In this way we are able to discuss the power of social structure in a meaningful way as we take note of the fact that the external definition of my racial identity (a definition resulting from a contemporary system and historical legacy of white supremacy) is more pragmatically relevant than any identity I may wish to choose for myself. Moreover, we discuss how the racial

category "white" has been closely guarded and protected as an exclusive category garnering social, economic, and political privilege since its invention
(Harris 1993, Gross 2010).

Having this discussion with students, as a person who could make a 50%
biological claim to whiteness, helps the students to see the absurdity of understanding race as a biological truth. In our discussions that follow and in their
writings, many students comment on how they did not even know they thought
about race biologically—it was simply taken for granted. But more than that,
it helps them to see how whiteness in particular is constructed as a category of
exclusivity. In many ways, my students would be willing to hear that my brown
skin reflects any other racial category besides white—they themselves point
me to other "racial" identities like Latina, Native American, Middle Eastern or
Vietnamese. The fact that they give such a wide range of answers points to the
complex analysis that my students go through when asked explicitly about my
racial identity. Often when we debrief, students will tell me that they assumed
I was black, but since I was asking, maybe they were wrong. It also speaks to
the students' deep-seated need to assign me to any racialized category other
than white. I could stand in front of them and make the case that my racial
identity was anything they guessed, or something they had never heard of and
my guess is that they would believe me and try to interact with me as such; this
is a phenomenon related to my phenotypical racial ambiguity which leads the
students to look for more information about my race in order to understand
their interactions with me (Omi and Winant 1994, Lopez 1994). However, even
a trace or hint of something in one's physical characteristics that mark one
as non-white means that you are outside the boundaries of whiteness, and as
such any personal claims to whiteness you may attempt to make will be viewed
as problematic.

4   Moore's Experience

When I teach race and ethnicity, I begin the first several weeks of my class
with materials developed to facilitate students' understanding of the social
constructedness of race, and the connection between processes of racialization and white supremacy. I generally use the "what is my race?" lecture in the
second or third week, after I have already problematized the racist roots of biological determinism and racial formations (Gould 1996). Like my co-authors,
I set up this discussion by asking my class "what is my race?" but unlike my
co-authors, the responses I have gotten over the years have been more varied,
and my claims to alternate racial identities have been accepted or challenged

in different ways. Although Davis and Bell both attempt to push their students by asking them how they would respond if they claimed their racial identify as white, in my classes I ask students how they would respond if I told them I self-identify as Black in light of the fact that I actually identify as a white woman. In the process of the discussion, I note that I have an African American brother, that much of my family is Black, and that I have a great-grandmother who was Black. All of these are true, yet none of my African American family is biologically related to me; they are all adopted or adoptive kin. This allows me to push the students to think about my race in a way that calls into question the relevance of self-identification, culture, and biology. Here I share a few of the responses I have encountered in this process to illustrate.

When I ask students the question, "what is my race?" they respond with the same silence and apprehension noted by my co-authors. I always have to push them, and I explain to them that this is a space in which we can actively engage in and discuss the process of racialization that takes place implicitly in their everyday lives. Generally speaking, two things happen when I ask the question; first, the majority of the students say that I'm white, but second, they feel that I must not be just white because I am asking the question—and they generally attempt to extend their guess by pointing to ethnic identities. The most frequent ethnicities I have been assigned are Italian, Greek, or Spanish—none of which represent my ethnic ancestry, but all of which appear to be a negotiation of them viewing me as white, but perhaps not quite white (Jacobson 1999). I push students to move back to race, away from the ethnic identifications, and then I ask them, "would it change your mind if I told you I have an African American great-grandmother." Generally, most students, particularly white students, respond to this by saying it would, but only if I was culturally connected to the African American community and/or if I self-identified as African American. There is generally a feeling that if I want to be Black, they are willing to see me as Black—and on occasion (although this has only happened a few times), I have had students respond by telling me that once I informed them of my Black heritage, they could see it in my phenotypical features. Once student said she could see it because of my olive toned skin and my curly hair, and one student told me he could see it in the shape of my eyes and my nose.

The next thing I do is explain to my students that I am not biologically related to my African American great-grandmother, or other African American family I have mentioned. This is generally embarrassing to the students who said they believed I was Black as a result of my Black family (particularly those who explained they could see the physical markers of Blackness in my phenotype), however it raises a perfect opportunity to discuss the depth of assumptions about biology and genetics as a so-called basis for race. As well, it enables me to discuss the notion of the exclusivity of whiteness, and the way that one African American relative can change perceptions about my race, whereas one white relative would not, generally, change peoples' assumptions about a person's race from African American to white. In quite a few instances, I still have students (mostly white students) who say that I am free to identify as Black if that is my self-identification, despite the fact that I am not biologically related to the African American people who I consider my family. They rely both on a notion of culture, as well as a desire to affirm my ability to self-identify in any way I wish to identify. At this point I generally say to the class, "ok, so if I had walked into class on the first day of class and said: As an African American woman, I plan to teach this class...." I never need to go further, because generally everyone laughs at the idea of me asserting that I am African American. This allows me to really problematize the notion that self-identification or cultural connections can overcome the dominance of phenotype in the U.S. racialization process, particularly when individuals have phenotypical characteristics that fit neatly into dominant racial classifications—in other words are not racially ambiguous.

I generally push students in this way to get them to think clearly about the continued significance of phenotype and biology in racialization processes, despite our understanding that race is socially and historically constructed. There is one other reaction that I often receive during my process of questioning the class about whether I can self-identify as Black, which comes from Black students and other students of color. That response is one of hostility—a reaction against someone with my white phenotype claiming access to a Black identity (despite any claim I make to African American heritage and/or cultural connection). Viewed together, the responses of students of color that express anger come from a very clear understanding of the connection between race and racism—the structural and political consequences of our racialization process in the U.S. and its connection to white domination. In what I view as the inverse of the responses that Davis and Bell received, a disappointment in their attempt to identify themselves as something other than Black, my attempt to claim Blackness angers these students because I have not had to experience the everyday heavy burden of racism in a society structured by white domination. My claim to a social identification with Blackness resembles the affectation that occurs when whites misappropriate Black culture and Black experience. This response provides me with an excellent opportunity to talk about both white domination, and the political nature of racial identification. It also allows me to discuss contemporary white misappropriation of Black culture and how we must problematize our notions of culture, particularly when culture is racialized, and make connections between power, white domination, and the social production of culture. All of these responses also provide me with an opportunity to note that my white phenotype conveys particular privileges, for example not being racially profiled, which contribute to my everyday life in such a way that I believe I must self-identify as white because that is the life experience I receive as a result of the racial social structure, without regard to who my family is, or what kinds of cultural forms I find appealing.

Except. Most of my classes contain variations of the examples I discuss above. But there was one class that was different. One semester I had an evening class, and I decided to take my son (who was in the 6th grade at that time). My son is Black (although he is often racially identified as Latino or Mexican-American, likely because we live in Texas in a community with a high percentage of Latinos). I never identified him to the class, although it is likely they heard me call him son; I would bring him in early find him a seat near the back in case he needed to leave for anything, and then proceed to the front to prepare for class. In that class, in approximately the third week, I conducted the "what is my race?" exercise, and nearly two-thirds of the class said I was Black. There were still those who said I was white, but there were far fewer comments about my ethnicity, and before I identified any of my background a majority of the class racially identified me as Black. When it happened, I realized that it was because I had brought my son to class—and I raised the issue to the class, telling them it was unusual, and asking them to reflect. They noted two key elements that led them to the conclusion I was Black, or at least not white. The first was that my son was clearly Black or bi-racial, and so they thought that I was likely Black or bi-racial. The second, very much related to the first, was that I was asking them to identify my race, and they did not believe I would ask them to do that if I was "just white." In this instance, once again we were able to problematize the exclusivity of whiteness, and the manner in which whiteness gets tacitly viewed as something racially "pure," such that if you display any possible racial otherness your whiteness is in question. But, as well, we were able to discuss and problematize the assumption that race, and processes of racialization, are not something white people participate in—that white people are not compelled to think about race (largely because of the white normalization that occurs as a component of white domination) and thus, I would not be asking about race if I were white.

I have used all of these instances and examples to illuminate the social structural dynamics of race and racism. We discuss the fact that we, as individuals, are born into an already racially organized society, and thus we are assigned our race largely through the racial gaze of others. As well, we talk about the fact that our racially organized society is organized based upon assumptions and ideologies of white supremacy, which means that processes of racialization can evoke powerful and potentially painful reactions. This indicates the necessity for exercises like this one, which push students to understand that race is socially constructed, that this means that an important element of our identity is largely externally defined, and that the social constructions of race connect to racial oppression and white domination. It also indicates that we must be sensitive to the historical and contemporary violence of the racist social structure and white domination.

5   Conclusion

The varied responses that each of us have received over the years in the process of teaching that race is a social construct has taught us several things. First, introducing students to the idea of race as a social construct can often be a process that requires dialogical teaching, attention to the structural dynamics of racism and white domination, and sensitivity to the pain that is frequently a component of negotiating the violence of a racist social structure. Even after spending considerable time on this topic, invariably at some point later in the semester students make comments about race that were embedded in belief that race and the characteristics that we attribute to it are biological, comments that reify white racist notions of race. In subsequent sections in the course when topics like race and education or income inequality are being discussed, some students' comments revealed that they still believed in and relied upon inaccurate stereotypes attached to different racial groups to explain their placement on the racial hierarchy. We take this to be indicative of the fact that a long history of biologically deterministic "science" of race, and contemporary popular notions of race as biological and genetic, are challenging to disrupt, and students do not easily give up their long held implicit understandings of race. We use these moments for reflection, asking students to think back to the "what is my race?" exercise and reminding them that as we learn about and engage in discussions of the politics of race, we are, indeed, making race—reproducing or disrupting racial meanings. This challenges students to think critically about their own views, and the language they use to discuss race, and how it contributed to either racial reproduction or the disruption of normative racial meanings.

The second powerful lesson we have learned about race from teaching this exercise is how the depth of the ideology of white purity informs the racialization process. As discussed, Moore was given far greater latitude in challenging students' assumptions about her race then either Davis or Bell, who were presumed to be black regardless of any assertion of other racial heritages. This was true despite the fact that Davis and Bell can point to a great deal of variation in their phenotypical characteristics, suggesting that *any* phenotypical indication of black heritage results in an assumption of blackness— or at least non-whiteness. Negotiating these assumptions through the "what is my race?" exercise provides us with an dialogical and reflective process by which to illustrate to students the white supremacist assumptions in notions of white purity, legal constructs like the one-drop rule, and the tacit ways in which white power and privilege are evoked in the process of racialization. The exercise provides us with an illustration of white domination in a way that both exposes how students' assumptions about race are framed by the legacy of white domination, and that illuminates the "real" consequences of social constructs like racial categories.

Lastly, we noted that our white students were much more willing to deny the phenotypical relevance of race and assert that culture or self-identification were most relevant racially, whereas students of color recognized the relevance of phenotype and connected it explicitly to racial hierarchy. We suggest that this reveals the way in which white students and students of color are differently situated in the racial hierarchy; students of color have a more tacit understanding of the implications of race, racism, and white domination, because they experience the consequences of the racist social structure. White students, on the other hand, are able to ignore and minimize the relevance of racism, because they are not experiencing this racism as a part of their daily lives. The "what is your race?" exercise gives us an opportunity to discuss this in two important ways. First as we engage in the discussion about race, we are able to uncover the tacit white framings of race and the structural implications of racism as part of the process of racialization. This enables us to use the class discussion as a springboard to discuss the racist social structure, as well as the political implications of race and the way that we racialize one another in society. Second, because the three of us have been doing the same lecture for so long, we are able to draw upon our own and each other's experiences in teaching this exercise and discuss these in class to draw students into an even more self-reflective discussion about race and racism. As we discuss the implications of one-another's experiences, students are able to look at their own assumptions, compare them to the assumptions of students in other classes, and give thought to the racial meanings that inform our processes of racialization and how those racial meanings are connected to the white racist social structure.

References

Alicea, Marisa and Barbara Kessel. 1997. "A Socially Awkward Question: A Stimulation Exercise for Exploring Ethnic and Racial Labels." *Teaching Sociology*, 25 (1): 65–71.

Bonilla-Silva, Eduardo. 2001. White Supremacy and Racism in the Post-Civil Rights Era. Boulder, CO: Lynne Reinner.

Bonilla-Silva, Eduardo. 2010. Racism Without Racists: Color-Blind Racism and the Persistence of Racial Inequality in the United States. Boulder, CO: Rowman & Littlefield.

Carter, Prudence. 2003. "Black Cultural Capital, Status Positions, and School Conflicts for Low-Income African American Youth." *Social Problems*, 50 (1): 136–155.

Freire, Paulo. 1996. *Pedagogy of the Oppressed*. New York: Penguin Education.

Gould, Stephen J. 1996. The Mismeasure of Man: Revised edition. New York: W. W. Norton & Co. Gross, Ariela J. 2010. *What Blood Won't Tell Us: A History of Race on Trial in America*. Cambridge, MA: Harvard University Press.

Harris, Cheryl. 1993. "Whiteness as Property." *Harvard Law Review*, 106: 1707–1798.

Hooks, bell. 1994. *Teaching to Transgress*. New York, NY: Basic Books.

Jacobson, Matthew Frye. 1999. *Whiteness of a Different Color: European Immigrants of Race and the Alchemy of Race*. Cambridge, MA: Harvard University Press.

Johnson, Kevin. 1998. "Race, the Immigration Laws, and Domestic Race Relations: A Magic Mirror into the Heart of Darkness" *Indiana Law Journal*, 73: 1111.

Lopez, Ian Haney. 1994. "The Social Construction of Race: Some Observations on Illusion, Fabrication, and Choice." *Harvard Civil Rights—Civil Liberties Law Review*, 29 (1).

Mills, C. Wright. 1959. *The Sociological Imagination*. Oxford, London: Oxford University Press.

Omi, Michael and Howard Winant. 1994. *Racial formation in the United States*. New York, NY: Routledge.

Steinberg, Stephen. 2007. *Race Relations: A Critique*. Stanford, CA: Stanford University Press.

Williams, Patricia. 1997. *Seeing a Colorblind Future: The Paradox of Race*. New York, NY: Farrar, Starus, Giroux.

CHAPTER 7

"Formed, Transformed, Destroyed, and Re-formed": Diversity Formation at a Majority-Minority University

Shan Mukhtar

1   Introduction

In the four decades since *Regents of the University of California at Davis v. Bakke*, diversity "seems to have become one of the most commonly used words in the U.S.," and has "become the postmodern, post-Obama mantra of equality (Embrick 2006: 541–542, 2011)." In higher education, colleges and universities create federally compliant diversity, affirmative action, and anti-discrimination policies; they also hire diversity-focused administrators to promote and implement "campus diversity." And for their efforts they are presented with diversity awards, such as the *Diversity Insight* magazine's Higher Education Excellence in Diversity (HEED) award,[1] and are included in diversity rankings, such as the *U.S. News and World Report* "Campus Ethnic Diversity" index.[2] In this way institutions engaging in diversity work acquire a certain amount of social capital; though, it does not protect them from legal and public scrutiny. There have been four landmark cases at the district and Supreme Court levels since *Bakke* that have considered the "merit" of diversity in higher education. All of them have focused on racial and ethnic identity as a factor in college and university admissions. The most recent of these have had increasingly *diverse* plaintiffs: *Fisher v. University of Texas* argued twice in the Supreme Court between 2012 and 2015 filed by white female college applicant Abigail Fisher; lawsuits against race consciousness in college admissions at Harvard University and University of North Carolina Chapel Hill by Asian American applicants.

Thus even though diversity *seems to be the most commonly used word in the U.S.*, its place in higher education has been redefined almost to the point of

---

1   "About the HEED Award," Insight into Diversity, accessed December 21, 2015, http://www.insightintodiversity.com/about-the-heed-award/.

2   "Campus Ethnic Diversity Methodology," US News and World Report, accessed December 21, 2015, http://www.usnews.com/education/best-colleges/articles/campus-ethnic-diversity-methodology.

abnegation; so much so that Justice Antonin Scalia declared in the first *Fisher v. Texas* decision in 2013 that diversity's "bell may soon toll."[3] Because of this, the higher education structures created through diversity are made up of multiple "racial meanings" (Omi and Winant 1994). They are an extension of colorblind ideology, reproducing rote narratives of racial progress and positive cross-cultural interaction. But, they are also under attack by proponents of colorblind ideology on the basis of "equal treatment" under the law for whites and Asians, and therefore they develop alongside fear of litigation. Omi and Winant wrote that "most theories" in the post-civil rights era sought to bind racial identity to "other supposedly more fundamental social and political relationships," "reduc[ing] race to a mere manifestation of ... ethnicity and class" (Omi and Winant 1994: 2). They offered *racial formation* as a revitalized, critical framework for exploring the social construction of racial categories and the enforcement of racial order. I suggest that what Omi and Winant described as the racial "ambivalence" of the post-civil rights period can most readily be observed in the social construction of diversity in higher education. I refer to it as *diversity formation*, or the dual process by which "social, economic and political forces" determine how diversity is institutionalized in higher education settings, and in turn how the structures and narratives created through diversity work and by diversity workers "create, inhabit, transform, and destroy" racial discourse and race consciousness (Omi and Winant 1994: 55).

Sociologists and higher education researchers have already written on diversity in higher education extensively as both critics and advocates. However, research on diversity has primarily focused on either the results of racially diverse and racially homogenous educational environments,[4] or on the top-down institutional structures that have suppressed "efforts to take seriously race as a factor in admissions, hiring, and promotion."[5] But, the "everyday lifeworld" (Feagin et al. 1991: 7) of diversity and the language of identity, demography, and merit produced through it has only recently emerged as subjects of analysis (Berrey 2014). The narratives of diversity workers at a large, public university and the structural parameters within which they work are the primary focus of this study. Diversity worker interviews showed the ambivalence and contradictions inherent within diversity discourse. They further demonstrated

---

3 *Fisher v. University of Texas at Austin, et al.,* (631 U.S. 213 2013).

4 See Gurin et al., 2002; Gurin et al., 2004; Jayakumar, 2008.

5 Mark Chesler, Amanda E. Lewis, and James Crowfoot, *Challenging Racism in Higher Education,* (Lanham, MD: Rowman and Littlefield Publishers, 2005), 3. See also Giroux, 1988; Takagi, 1993; Goldberg, 1995; Essed, 1996; Massey, et al., 2006; Sharma, 2004; Searls Giroux, 2010.

that diversity formation takes place both in a top-down fashion as part of an established ideology of colorblindness and class-blindness *and* through a discomfited social process that includes moments of successful counter-narration and micro-level change. The study that informed this chapter sought to contribute an approach that focused on the relationship between the structural and social, and how that relationship was expressed through the performance of diversity work, the construction of the campus as a place, and the development of a diversity-focused institutional master narrative at a university I referred to by the pseudonym, *Public U.*[6] This chapter focuses on a segment of those findings: the racialized narratives of diversity workers and the majority-minority institutional context in which they were doing diversity work.

The participants were university staff, faculty, and students working in one or more of the university wide diversity-focused initiatives or within localized efforts in academic departments and in a variety of student life units. They were either paid administrative staff, or in service positions. Between August 2011 and July 2013, I conducted 40 individual interviews and 9 group observations of diversity workers at Public U. I documented the social and structural processes through which diversity workers at the university negotiated their individual definitions of what diversity means and their perceptions of how it could be practiced at Public U. I also studied what I called "top-down" institutional narratives on diversity at Public U. These included: admissions brochures, posters, fliers, PowerPoint presentations, and issues of the student newspaper and university magazine that were current during the study; the university blog, current and past institutional research documents, student newspaper, university magazine, strategic plans and campus expansion plans, meeting minutes, university office and committee website pages (both for current and inactive offices and committees), and one non-university weekly magazine local to the city that has published significant coverage of the university.

For reasons related to worker anonymity, in this chapter I identify diversity workers in one of four ways: staff, faculty, graduate student, undergraduate student; and when necessary for context I provide information about the specific work they did. Because diversity workers were a racially and ethnically visible population at the university, they were vulnerable to identification. Aside from certain identity characteristics (race, ethnicity, or gender) are relevant

---

6 All documents and other media specific to Public U in this chapter were researched by the author. The references and quotes come from hard copies of current sources, active university websites, web-based archives of university and external news media, and archived inactive sites.

to the context of the worker's narrative, I do not describe the participants or allude consistently to their identities. Diversity workers at Public U were part of two main diversity work spaces (staffed offices; faculty- and student-led service committees). Therefore, the way I identify them here signals particular ways of working on diversity. For example, the small number of undergraduate students I interviewed were leaders within student organizations focused on diversity or assistants in university offices participating in the recruitment or mentorship of students of color. Their work most often emphasized diversity as social, interpersonal exchanges. Faculty and graduate student workers focused most heavily on structural diversity. The committees on which they served worked largely on making recommendations for the hiring and tenure, advocating for the recognition of diversity- and community- focused research, and addressing local diversity issues within academic departments. Staff diversity workers were greatest in number in the study and at the university. They also had the broadest range of responsibilities. They worked on policy, such as writing the diversity strategic plan for the university. They also coordinated a variety of diversity-focused events. For instance, one office planned the annual MLK Day activities for the campus; another organized a monthly cross-cultural learning event for residents in one of the dorms. Further, some staff diversity workers did not work in a "diversity" office, but they were part of diversity-focused programs or initiatives that their office coordinated in addition to its primary mission.

2   The 'DNA' of Diversity at Public U

Public U is a large public university of over 30,000 students. It is located in a city center and describes itself on its website as a "true urban university" with "diversity in [its] DNA." Public U is also a majority-minority, majority women university that has received national recognition for awarding high numbers of bachelor's degrees to African-American students. It advertises itself as "a place where all students succeed," and its demographic make-up, graduation statistics, and the descriptions of Public U by diversity workers at the university all seem to support this assertion. As the university blog stated in 2013:

> There are no disparities in graduation rates here. Graduation rates for African-American students have climbed 30 points in the last 10 years— one of the largest increases at any college or university in our nation.

An African-American freshman enrolling at [Public U] is just as likely to graduate as a white freshman.

In 2012 Public U won national accolades for its "inclusion initiatives related to gender, race, ethnicity, veterans, people with disabilities and members of the LGBT community." The award committee stated that Public U's "programs for minority students ... exemplify the outstanding efforts that make [Public U] a leader in opportunity to students who otherwise would not be able to receive a quality education or be able to study in another country." However, the university did not focus the salience of race, ethnicity, and gender as political and social identities on its campus other than in the diversity strategic plan. For example, "enterprising," "urban lab," and "global" appeared in university materials much more than "diversity," "race," or "ethnicity," accompanied by images of women and men of color and white women in laboratories and classrooms, and the city skyline. The result was a constructed image of Public U that depended on the visibility of racial and ethnic difference to make good on its promise of a diverse student body, but also mediated this difference through a language of business and research. Descriptions that reimagined Public U as a "greener, cleaner" place also reframed the university's story from a lower income, majority-minority space to a social laboratory with a global student body and a rapidly expanding campus footprint.

Further, the university's recruitment, retention, and promotion of faculty and management-level administrators of color—particularly black and Latino/a faculty and administrators—does not show the same successes. For instance, Public U appointed a "taskforce" for minority faculty recruitment and retention twice in the last twenty years, and later created a faculty-led "office" for this purpose. But in 2014–2015 according to the institutional research office, the university had just 26% non-white and 9% black "full-time instructional faculty." That same academic year the Public U's total student population of "approximately 32,500" was 70% non-white and almost 36% black. Putting these statistics into the context of diversity formation, I found that despite the inclusion of multiple identity categories under the umbrella of "diversity" at Public U, diversity work at the university was *race work*; that is, it was labor that helped produce the racial and ethnic make-up and culture of the institution.

Studying diversity formation at Public U was further complicated by the fact that most of the diversity workers were people of color and women. For example, only four of the respondents identified as white men, and two of the four were in a tenured faculty or managerial administrative position. This was important because it illustrated the distribution of resources for diversity work, and the ways in which diversity labor became marked by the participation of people of color and women in it. For instance, professional staff comprised the largest group doing diversity work at Public U and thus represented almost half of the participants in the study. During that time, about 50% of all staff at Public U identified as African American, 38% as White, 5% as Asian, 2.4% as Hispanic, and all other ethnicities and those who chose not to identify comprised 4.6% of the total.[7] In the "Office Admin & Support" category under which most diversity staff positions fell, black women made up over 58% of the total number of individuals working in that area. Participants in the study identified racially and ethnically in the following ways: 13 African American or black; 5 multi-racial black; 6 Asian, out of which 4 identified with a specific Asian nationality while 2 identified as Asian American; and 16 white or Caucasian, out of which none identified with any nationality or ethnicity outside of their racial identity. Thus the disproportionate representation of black diversity workers in the study was both expected and an indicator of how diversity labor was racialized at Public U.

Also, 24 of the participants identified as women and 16 as men. This again had to do with the number of women across all racial and ethnic identities who worked in non-managerial administrative staff positions at Public U, and the number of women faculty and graduate students who became involved in service work related to diversity. For example, one faculty diversity committee discussed at length the dilemma of women faculty in their field, particularly women of color, showing greater interest in doing diversity-focused work but also getting the least rewarded for their participation. Similarly, an assistant professor who identified as an Asian American woman, stated that her department chair had discouraged her from becoming involved with campus issues until she secured tenure. "When you're an assistant professor," she said, "it's head down and publish, publish, publish. They really don't like us ... bothering with anything else." All four women faculty of color in the study indicated that the pressure to be published and promoted was at odds with the pressure to "be there for" and "advise" graduate students of color who sought them out professionally due to shared research areas or personally because of shared racial, ethnic, and gender identities. To the graduate diversity committee members that I interviewed, the devaluation of labor performed by women faculty of color at Public U became apparent when in the previous

---

7   These were the specific racial and ethnic categories used by the university within its demographic reports.

year, "A very important faculty member [who is Latina] didn't get tenure." Graduate students in the department "rallied around" the issue and "the university found a way to keep her." However, the students felt that the incident was "telling" of the "culture" at Public U.

But, while diversity labor itself is marginalized in higher education settings, the presence of diversity workers on university and college campuses—particularly highly visible diversity workers of color such as deans, provosts, and vice presidents of diversity, equal opportunity, or multicultural affairs—is often constituted into the institution's broader narrative of racial progress. Like students of color, diversity workers' bodies and the identities they express become representations of diversity itself. In one meeting that included both staff and faculty diversity workers, the group was acutely aware of how their racial and ethnic identities would "play out" at a diversity-focused event they were planning for the next semester. They wished to attract "all students ... not just the usual groups." A black staff member in the meeting worried that white students would be in low attendance and stated that the office needed to find someone other than "people who look like this" (pointing to his own face) as the emcee and speakers.

During an interview, the graduate diversity committee chair who identified as a white woman, expressed frustration that her participation in diversity work was marginalized by her white faculty advisor:

> Just the fact that there is such a thing as a 'diversity person.' That's the problem in the first place, right? I can literally lead the [graduate diversity committee] for a whole year and my advisor is like, 'Oh you're on that committee? Why did you get a diversity award?' Because I'm part of the majority, the faculty don't see me as a diversity person. There are those people who are considered diversity people. And that kind of thinking is usually very black and white, very concrete.

Thus diversity, a concept often critiqued for being too racially abstract and ideological in its colorblindness was experienced as "very concrete" by those doing diversity work at Public U because of the stereotypes embedded within diversity work spaces and the professional realities of performing diversity labor. On one hand, how diversity is framed in the current era promotes an abnegation of race consciousness. On the other hand the racialization of diversity workers creates a sense of determinism which links racial identity to diversity labor in a way that must be addressed as workers negotiate their roles and try to produce diversity-focused outcomes for their offices or committees.

3   The Language of Staff Diversity Work

Diversity offices and committees at Public U were charged with the bulk of ground-level work on racial and ethnic difference and ethno-racism on campus. In that capacity they created a variety of diversity-focused products that ranged from the structural (interpreting and enforcing federal anti-discrimination law; coordinating, writing, and implementing diversity strategic plans; overseeing diversity-focused institutional research), to the material (producing brochures, posters, websites, press releases, and public reports and statistics), to the social (sponsoring identity-focused public events and student organizations). In examining the discourse created through these diversity products, it became apparent that diversity has given rise to a particular institutional language of difference at Public U.

It was not surprising when a staff member who worked in student recruitment referenced one of the most promoted demographic statements in Public U's official literature. When asked if he felt Public U was a diverse place, he replied, "We have people from over 150 countries here and then we have a lot of other identity groups too." The term "more than 150 countries," or a variation of it, was in the university's one-page admissions flier, on multiple pages of the admissions website, and was quoted on academic department websites and external websites that referenced Public U. Another common statement from multiple participants focused on diversity in the U.S. context rather than a global one: "We have students that come from every county, and every state." The power of short descriptive narratives like these was in the consistency with which they were used across different people and mediums. The workers I interviewed discussed Public U's demography as a permanent, defining aspect of the university's landscape. One graduate student who had recently joined the graduate diversity committee, stated, "I heard [before I came here] ... that it is like one the most diverse universities ... in the US." The combination of hearing about the diversity at Public U and later "see[ing]" it further established racial and ethnic diversity as an empirical fact of life at Public U. The presence of large numbers of non-whites, whether "colorful," "different shades," from different "ethnic groups," or representing "more than 150 countries," was the first way that all forty participants defined Public U's diversity. But as each of the interviews progressed, most diversity workers recognized that demographic facts were "things" that people generally knew about Public U, but the social and political context of this demographically diverse place was not as easy for diversity workers to articulate or navigate.

The terminology used in diversity work at Public U included a variety of common offshoots of the word diversity, such as "inclusion," "engagement," "multicultural," "intercultural," "community" and "opportunity." But these were, in practice, synonyms that referred to the same basic approach. First, when diversity workers talked about advocacy for specific underrepresented groups such as black or Latina/o faculty, the need to address micro-aggressions in the workplace, or the recruitment and promotion of administrators of color into management positions, they consistently referred to things "the university" or "they" could do about these issues. Workers generally did not connect words like "equity" to the diversity work that was already going on at the university or to work they could see themselves doing at Public U either presently or in the future. They felt that structural change required top-down intervention. Faculty and student workers especially saw themselves as removed from administrative decision-making processes. The level of disempowerment was exacerbated by their sense that the work being done at the executive leadership level, such as the development of a diversity strategic plan, was not something they could "trust." They instead saw it as a gesture that existed to impart symbolic rather than social or economic value. One faculty participant responded, "To the best of my knowledge the diversity strategic plan is a bunch of flags that we can salute." Similarly, another stated that the language within the plan was too abstract to be effective, "They say diversity is important and then they talk as vaguely as it could be, as supportive as they want to look to be." During one faculty committee meeting and in the university senate meeting minutes, workers spent considerable time discussing the presence of diversity work "silos" at the university and saw administrative diversity offices as both "fragmented" and existing mainly to address "student body" issues.

Staff members did not express an overall distrust of administrative processes but they also variously named the "the president" and "the regents" as the primary agents of change at the university. This perception was further supported by the limited structural scope of their office missions and by their own narratives about how they envisioned diversity at Public U. For instance, the primary mission of the equal opportunity office was to "foster interaction amongst diverse people around compelling ideas and questions" and "assist the university in becoming a center for learning about [a] vast array of issues." The multicultural center was charged with "educating students to participate in a global economy with individuals different from themselves" and "provid[ing] opportunities for intentional, meaningful programming and dialogue to assist students to learn more about themselves and others." And, the intercultural relations program was "committed to providing opportunities for students to engage in meaningful dialogues around cultural and diversity issues." In addition to these missions overlapping in their goals for teaching about "issues" with an emphasis on "global" and "cultural" learning, the method by which they sought to do this work was almost exclusively *cross-cultural interaction*. Here I use a variation on Chang, Denson, Saenz and Misa's *cross-racial interaction*, which they defined as, "the understanding of and willingness to interact and exchange ideas with others who are racially different."[8] Chang, Denson, Saenz and Misa pointed out an absence of "consensus regarding what exactly institutions must do to achieve [a 'nonracist' cultural climate]."[9] They found that "each college or university faces a set of unique circumstances that cannot be easily addressed by ready-made ... strategies."[10] But within diversity work spaces at Public U, staff members focused heavily on "getting [people] together." They seemed to perceive a strong operational relationship between demography, social interaction, and the implementation of diversity at the university. One staff member who saw cross-cultural interaction as the primary "work to be done" at Public U stated, "We have so many different nationalities and other groups here but you wouldn't know it because everyone is still, pretty much set up a little, whatever the name of the country is, here, and another one there. [There's] no cross dialogue."

Another staff member, when asked how she thought cross-cultural interaction could be done on a practicable level, constructed an ideal, imaginary social space that was organized and supported by the upper-level leadership of Public U, but also embodied egalitarianism and a freedom from institutional hierarchy:

> I would have some kind of event for staff that would have some draw. So we wouldn't be in silos all the time. You need something where people want to go. And it doesn't matter who you are... Things to get people outside of their comfort zone but not culture specific. I don't really like forums and things like that. But it would be, I don't know, something like a party. But you have everyone there. The president [of the university] is there and other upper level administration. We do that kind of thing for students but not for faculty and staff.

Through the characterization of an ideal diverse space, the participant indirectly elaborated on what she saw as barriers to meaningful interaction among staff and faculty: the exclusion of staff and faculty from most existing

---

8   Mitchell J. Chang, Nida Denson, Victor Sáenz, and Kimberly Misa, "The Educational Benefits of Sustaining Cross-Racial Interaction Among Undergraduates," *The Journal of Higher Education* 77 (2006): 433.

9   Chang, Denson, Sáenz, and Misa, 434.

10   Ibid.

cross-cultural programming, and the absence of the upper-level administration of from staff- and faculty-focused diversity events. These were concrete issues that signaled specific structural problems such as the isolation of university leadership from the public life of the university, and a lack of attention to the workplace environment experienced by university employees. But the narrative itself reproduced abstract terminology and vague goals similar to those in Public U's various diversity mission statements. At various times, workers called it "cross dialogue," "interaction," "mix[ing]," or "a party," which articulated an emphasis on cross-cultural interaction over structural change. But when asked, they were not able to provide concrete ideas for meaningful interaction; not in general or as work that their positions or offices could support.

Staff members and undergraduate students also generally emphasized the need to construct overtly casual spaces of interaction on campus. The staff member above had attended and presented at multiple off-campus diversity conferences and seminars over the year I observed her office. She had participated in planning two student events—one for MLK Day and the other a health and wellness fair for men. Both events involved speakers, facilitated discussions or panels, and the distribution of promotional materials. But the idealized diversity event she described was more free form. Its appeal was that it had no expectations or agenda. Based on observations, this was significantly different from how all the diversity-focused events and spaces at Public U actually functioned. Staff did a lot of work to create diversity social events, trainings, conferences, and community dialogues. They were expressive about their belief that diversity would not just happen through "osmosis." But they also seemed to experience burn-out from developing and planning these spaces of interaction. They worried that attendance would be low. And, they often discussed about how to frame diversity-focused conversations when, as one black staff member asked during an off-campus professional development conference for diversity professionals, "Affirmative action is already a dirty word."

Narratives regarding the relationship between the campus and the city also brought out tensions between ideal diversity and the racialized and classed settings which diversity workers experienced. One undergraduate student mentor who identified as multi-racial, stated that when he first arrived at Public U he quickly learned that he did not like to be "hit over the head" with diversity. This was because he felt at Public U racial and ethnic diversity was something students "can't avoid"; they would only learn about it by "living with it." For him, living in the city center in university dorms during his freshman and sophomore years was how he got "used to" the demographic diversity on campus and in the city. Consistent with this perspective, a significant part of the diversity programming led by staff members in the housing office focused on living in the city. One staff member stated that students needed to understand that they were "not the only people living downtown." Dorm events included faculty-led walking tours of historically black neighborhoods close to campus, and an outdoor "sit-in" event during which students spent 36 hours "living" in the parking lot of one of the dorm facilities in order to raise money for a homelessness services organization. However during campus tours I attended in the same time period, tour guides consistently introduced the residential halls by noting that parents often "worried about" students "living on campus" in an "urban" "downtown" location. Guides first emphasized that the campus is policed "24-7" because the "main priority" was the "safety" of students. They then reiterated that the downtown area was a home to several "major corporations" as well as a number of "restaurants" and "museums."

These conflicted perspectives on the city as a diverse place were apparent across multiple observations and interviews. The university did not have on-campus housing until the early 2000s. Institutionally the fact that approximately 4000 students were living in dorms on Public U's campus during the course of this study was related to two important changes. During the previous decade, the university had begun to transition from a commuter institution with a lower income, older, and working student body to a more spatially and academically "traditional campus" matriculating younger, more middle income, and increasingly residential college students. Additionally, the razing of public housing throughout the city resulted in extensive redevelopment of the streets and neighborhoods surrounding the campus (in large part, by the university itself). The same processes that contributed to a diminishment of age and socioeconomic diversity on campus and a near erasure of both historically black neighborhoods and affordable housing throughout the city, produced what were now the primary places for student life at Public U. Students were being encouraged to "experience" "the diversity of cultures and lifestyles" in downtown at time when these spaces were becoming increasingly controlled and branded by the university.

Despite this, the majority of staff diversity workers emphasized the inescapability of diversity at Public U. They used terms such as, "It's everywhere," "It's obvious," and, "You don't come [here] if you don't want to be around different people." There was also a sense that the borders between the university and the city were still very porous. Multiple diversity workers discussed the prevalence of individuals "asking [them] for change" as they walked on or near campus. One staff member who identified as white commented that the city was the most "intermixed" place she had lived, and that at Public U, you sometimes couldn't tell, "Who's a student, who's homeless, who's just someone walking through." She stated that she had now become accustomed to seeing difference on and around campus, and she wanted the student organizations she worked with to do the same. When asked if she lived in the city, she replied that she chose to live in an area just outside of the city center where she "could meet more people" who did not fit the "traditional ... diversity" present in the downtown area. Another staff member who identified as black, talked extensively about the "need" for young black students to "understand the privileges" they had as a result of the "activism" and "sacrifices" of previous generations. Her efforts to organize alternative spring breaks and form partnerships with community organizations off-campus were directly related to her sense of civic responsibility toward black communities. About the racial and ethnic diversity on campus and in the city, she said, "I think no matter where you go, you cannot escape the cultural diversity... It is here. It is a beautiful thing." But she added that while she "[did not] want to displace [herself] from certain racial groups ... or socioeconomic groups..." she had moved to a suburban area that was largely white, East Asian, and Persian, in order to "get into a certain mentality" of "advancing past" the "lower rung." Neither of the above staff members stated explicitly that the presence of lower income and poor black residents in the city affected their decision not to live near campus; but it was clear that this was the reason. In this way the difference between seeing the diversity at Public U and "living with it" everyday created tension for some diversity workers. It also showed that while class diversity is generally not met with the same intense resistance as racial and ethnic diversity, when the bodies of people with different socioeconomic backgrounds were black and brown, the appeal of their diverseness diminished.

3.1   *Faculty Diversity Workers and the Construction of Merit*

Torres' approach to agency focused on "the culturally constructed variations of human agency and the concrete forms of discursive and non-discursive means expressed through different actor strategies and conceptions of power."[11] I similarly argue here that a focus on "rationales" faculty diversity workers at Public U used to form their approaches to addressing the lack of racial and ethnic diversity among faculty is critical to understanding how diversity works, and the ways in which it simply does not. For example, among faculty workers on the departmental diversity committee I observed, there was a clear conflict when it came to recommendations for hiring new faculty. Members of the

---

11   Gabriel Torres, "Plunging into the Garlic: Methodological Issues and Challenges," in *Battlefields of knowledge: The interlocking of theory and practice in social research and development*, eds. Norman Long and Ann Long, (London, UK: Routledge, 1992), 86.

committee often debated the value of increased racial and ethnic diversity versus the value of hiring on the basis of "merit," which they constructed as race neutral. One faculty member on the committee explained the tension related to hiring decisions:

> Diversity within the faculty is a very touchy subject to tell you the truth. So even if we have goals for [diversity] we can, cannot just simply say we should get more people of color, or those who have particular [research] subjects. I think that doesn't fly well with people. So we, you know we have to have some kind of angle... We cannot [assign] an ethnicity or particular cultural background as a way of defining the future.

Because racial and ethnic diversity was a "touchy subject," one "angle" that the diversity committee came up with was a faculty diversity award for existing faculty in the department. The award included a small grant and a smaller teaching load to encourage faculty of color and faculty conducting community- or social identity-focused research to publish their work and write more grants in order to make themselves more competitive for tenure.

Faculty also pointed to the intensity of hiring processes, during which an increasing divide between faculty who supported addressing racial and ethnic underrepresentation and those who supported hiring junior faculty who would be more easily tenured made for heavy contestation. Diversity committee members also expressed during one meeting that their department was under increasing "pressure" from "the university" to maximize publications and grants. In his interview, one committee member talked about a hiring committee in which he had participated as a representative from the diversity committee:

> We ... were really fortunate for a rare occasion to have a couple of candidates we interviewed that were from underrepresented groups.... There were reasons why we did not feel they weren't going to come in and be able to be tenured you know, a few years later. So we had that value [of tenure] and then we have diversity as a value, and we spent three hours arguing in a faculty meeting... Ultimately the decision was made not to make offers to those candidates and it was the right decision but a lot of people were really upset about it because we say that we value diversity but when we had the chance to build on it we didn't.

Officially the diversity committee's goals included support[ing] affirmative action policies and other recruitment and retention initiatives that promote a demographically diverse faculty, staff, and student body. But structurally, the hiring of "demographically diverse faculty" was sporadic, and was marked by turmoil in the department. A faculty member from another department described her experience on a hiring committee that successfully hired the department's only Latina/o faculty member:

> This last hire we actually got a queer Latina, but it was an interesting fight and we won by one vote. And it was like, rallying people around to get that... Instead of having departments like ours having to fight for that internally, I want institutionally that to be a goal, something that was, highly encouraged. I know there's the threat of uh, affirmative action being struck down most likely that some universities don't want the hassle of having written something written in the books. But it's extremely important for a place like this.

Much like the staff member who asked how diversity offices could discuss recruitment and retention when "affirmative action was already a dirty word," this faculty member linked the "fight" for one candidate to both to the inaction of university leadership and the broader "threat" of "affirmative action being struck down." But, none of the faculty interviewed indicated that the conflict between diversity and merit was itself problematic. They saw it as a central struggle between opposing values: diversity was as a social or political value; merit was an economic or academic value. Also on a more practical level, they saw it as the difference between a junior faculty member for whom the department would have to fight again during the tenure process, and one who would be retained more easily. Wherever they stood on the issue, all but one of the faculty workers accepted the distinction between the two. Also, the "diversity" moniker placed on faculty of color by the very institutional mechanisms that undervalued racial and ethnic representation further intensified the experience of representing departmental diversity. A faculty member who identified as Asian expressed this view when discussing the experience of being hired as an assistant professor:

> I'm grateful for affirmative action but it is a kind of subtle racism, isn't it? A subtle way of undermining [people] in it I think. So it would be nice. Not that we ignore it but that it's not such a factor that contributes to things like academic performance at [Public U].

This statement illustrated the broader issue of racial and ethnic identity becoming a barrier to acceptance and recognition in academic settings.

Because the fight over diversity did not just cause conflict among faculty already in the department, but it also affected the professional climate within which faculty of color had to work.

3.2   *Graduate Students Enacting Micro-level Change*

All the members of the graduate diversity committee I interviewed stated as matter of fact that diversity work was going to diminish their marketability for academic jobs in their field. Committee members discussed what it meant that "there is such a thing as a 'diversity' person" and weighed the effects of being perceived as "pushy" or "demanding" in their pursuit of diversity training in their program. They felt that they had become known for "criticizing" their supervisors and professors and understood that "people don't like it." Also, the fact that they were all women, all but one of them were women of color, and they were all conducting research on social identity created more motivation for their work, but also an increased sense of isolation from the department. Committee members were also highly conscious of having very little power in department level decision-making, and none at all on the institutional level. As such the graduate diversity committee was housed within a smaller program in the department and restricted its activities to that program only. Committee members viewed the group as improving "[their] own graduate training" and cross-cultural interactions that took place in the specific spaces where they worked. While they petitioned for and got student representation on the faculty diversity committee, they did not feel that committee "could do much" to address current issues in the department. This was in part because the visibility of white men within the department's leadership and also because almost all faculty and students of color were in the community-focused programs in the department. One graduate committee member described a moment when the demographics of the department became clearer to her:

> The other day the fire alarm in this building went off and all the students had to come out while the fire department investigated. I was in the front of the building... I looked around. It was all white men. Maybe a white woman here, a black man there, one black woman, but most of the people were white men.

The student's observation about the representation of white men in the department was particularly important because throughout the study, the dominant narrative about Public U was that diversity is "part of [its] DNA." But this counter-narrative provided an alternate view of Public U's campus by focusing on the distribution of power. In response, the graduate diversity committee formed an approach that members characterized as both very direct, and at other times "covert" and "behind-the-scenes." Students described how they worked to "address gaps in [their] education" and to challenge the program when they felt their supervisors were only "trying to maintain" a diversity status quo. When advocating for cultural competency in the program's workplace and training for teaching faculty, the students approached the issues directly with department leadership. They conducted a cultural competency evaluation of their learning space, surveyed other graduate students in the program regarding training experiences, and took their recommendations to the Chair. These included a request for formal diversity training for program supervisors and faculty charged with teaching and evaluating students in the field. The goal was "to address diversity issues" that had emerged from faculty "not talking about diversity when [they] really should be" "as if our identities weren't a part of what was happening." It also involved seeking out "more diverse experiences." For instance, students experienced overt racial matching between themselves and community members with whom they were assigned to work. Because a majority of students in the program were black women, their training became linked to the knowledge they had based on their own identities, rather than the program providing them with skills to work effectively in a variety of settings. One student explained:

> I know for at least a couple of us, sexual minority and other minority colleagues ... it's kind of like we feel people of certain race ethnicities and or minority statuses get those [community members] to [interview] more so than other people do. It's like, you can't tell me that the only people who are [coming here] are black women. You can't tell me that. So can I get a non-black woman? I mean not to say I don't enjoy it but I'd like to round out the [training] experience.

However, when it came to recruitment of graduate students of color into the department, the committee worked covertly. Current graduate students spoke about how the students that recruited them into the program had come together "unofficially" or in "sporadic" ways to help advocate for students of color entering the program. In turn, they did the same thing for future applicants:

> We'll ... secretly get together and say okay, who is coming in [during recruitment], make sure you talk to them. The same thing happened when I applied here. And you know, it's part of what made me want to come here. I found out the students who interviewed me on interview day had

a clandestine plan to interview me and other applicants of color ... it [was] all on their own. It's nothing that's official.

The range of organized and "clandestine" actions that graduate committee members took simultaneously counteracted the larger mechanisms of diversity at Public U and reflected the instability of diversity measures at the university. When juxtaposed with the faculty diversity committees, the graduate students were able to create very specific definitions regarding the racial, ethnic, gendered, and classed meanings of diversity and equity in their program. And, their work resulted in substantive changes to their educational and work experiences. But while the graduate committee's work on training and professional development could serve as a model for micro-level progress, their "unofficial" actions were more complex in their contribution to the department and the university. The passing on of this mode of organizing from graduate cohort to graduate cohort lent it some consistency. But the ephemeral aspects of the graduate committee's involvement in recruitment were similar to faculty descriptions of "arguing [for three days]" about whether to make an offer to a "diverse" candidate, or staging a "fight" for a minority candidate that was "won by one vote." These actions took place in ad hoc spaces in which diversity was not a priority for the whole group. The processes that diversity workers followed did not work in cohort with any official institutional mechanisms for increasing diversity at Public U. Their work highlighted the inefficacy of existing diversity structures at the university rather than complementing similar efforts in other departments or within the university senate. For instance, when students from the graduate diversity committee "rallied" to retain a professor of color who had been denied tenure, "the university found a way to keep" her. But while the professor was able to remain in the department, neither her position as an untenured faculty member who now had diminished job security nor the department or university's tenure policies changed.

4   Conclusion

As researchers have already shown, the dominant ways of articulating what racial and ethnic diversity means in higher education, what value it has for U.S. society as a whole, and how it can be operationalized in institutional settings, most often prioritize race neutrality and an equal rather than equitable distribution of resources. At Public U, the language of diversity included words such as, "opportunity," "success," "achievement," and "enterprising," alongside blanket terms for racial and ethnic difference (multicultural, cross-cultural, intercultural, diverse community, urban, and global) in ways that allowed room for race awareness while minimizing race consciousness. The number of non-white people at Public U was the first thing that diversity workers in the study talked about. A university with a majority-minority population could not engage in the kind of overt race neutrality that a predominantly white campus might, for example as we saw in in Mitchell Steven's study of "The College."[12] However, what happened at Public U was an overemphasis on the ability of the university to mediate racial and ethnic difference so that, "an African-American freshman ... is just as likely to graduate as a white freshman." Black student graduation rates became the fight song of this "place where all students succeed." Much less visible were narratives about black students' experiences of Public U as people of color in a traditionally white university that had only recently become majority-minority. Or, the leadership roles students of color had taken in order to form spaces that were culturally relevant for them. The university's identity was increasingly "global," which was not white, but for U.S. institutions was also not fraught with the histories and pervasiveness of American ethno-racism as an "urban" university.

In addition to Public U's top-down public narratives that intertwined racial and ethnic difference with race neutrality, diversity formation at the university also occurred in place-based contexts. It generated its own set of categories and values specific to diversity workers at Public U and the spaces where diversity work was being done. For instance, white race consciousness at Public U had become very visible during the years that I conducted the study. Diversity workers indicated that white students had begun to distance themselves from campus life. Especially during the diversity event-planning process, staff workers frequently discussed the issue of white student attendance. In 2013, a student at Public U student attempted to follow the Towson University example and start a White Student Union.[13] The proposed organization's flier found on posting boards on campus, described it as, "a place [for white students] to unite and celebrate their own unique heritage." This garnered both protests by students across racial and ethnic lines and local media attention. While the student affairs division maintained that the White Student Union never submitted an official application to become a student organization at Public U, neither the dean of students at the time nor the president of the university

---

12   Mitchell L. Stevens. *Creating a Class: College Admissions and the Education of Elites.* (Cambridge, MA: Harvard University Press, 2007).

13   Charles M. Blow, "The meaning of minority," *New York Times*, December 12, 2012, http://www.nytimes.com/2012/12/13/opinion/blow-the-meaning-of-minority.html?_r=0.

made statements to address the underlying issue of ethno-racism on Public U's campus.

Through a study of diversity workers at Public U, I sought to demonstrate the micro-level struggles that took place in diversity work spaces. Workers reproduced dominant definitions of diversity and ways of doing diversity work. But they also expressed a need for alternatives, such as a comprehensive stance by university leadership on the hiring of more faculty of color. But because diversity had already become Public U's primary social capital, diversity discourse and the professional and service-based work that accompanied it had to continue moving forward, despite structural barriers and lack of communication across different diversity work spaces.

Staff members, who performed most of the diversity work at Public U, were largely fragmented into specialized offices and initiatives. However the study showed that most of these had overlapping missions and goals that reflected the institution's diversity terminology more than the practice of diversity work. Staff members worked in varied ways across a large number of units at the university. But how staff viewed the potential outcomes of diversity work was largely through a lens of social interaction and cultural learning opportunities. Meanwhile faculty focused on hiring and promotion. But conflicts within departments regarding "diversity hires" and looming tenure processes created an environment where the goals of diversity work were continually at odds with the academic discipline. And though the faculty diversity committee I observed officially sought to "support [the university's] affirmative action" goals of the university, they also expressed a distrust of Public U's institutional mechanisms for promoting diversity. Faculty and graduate diversity workers shared many of the same concerns related to diversity work and academic marketability. But the graduate diversity committee was the only working diversity group in the study that was able to bring about concrete changes to their program. But the "clandestine" nature of the work they did to recruit graduate students of color into the department was similar to the fights faculty waged in order to hire faculty of color—while at times effective, they relied heavily on the motivation of the individuals in the group and power relations in the department favoring one side over the other.

Those who want to bring about the formation of more critical diversities and counteract the systematic marginalization of non-white race consciousness in U.S. colleges and universities must be willing to contend with diversity workers and the labor they perform. As the study showed, diversity workers at Public U were mostly people who identified as women of color, men of color, and white women (in that order of prevalence). As professional staff and volunteer committee members, they did work which was highly racialized, but opposed to race consciousness; and that was based on the promotion of cross-cultural interaction, but could not support racial and ethnic difference or oppose ethnoracism in a critical or transparent manner. And if they worked in an academic environment, becoming a diversity leader or being someone who was seen as benefitting from diversity policies and programs made them more rather than less vulnerable in their educational and work spaces. In addition, as agents of the institution who were trained and professionalized in the university, diversity workers also espoused many of the same tropes of positive race relations employed by Public U's institutional narratives. This was true even when diversity workers saw their work as isolated from "the university" power structure. These findings signal a need for more research on diversity formation across different types of higher education institutions, different cadres of diversity workers, and diversity work spaces. An attention to local processes of diversity formation alongside the robust discussion on colorblind racism in higher education that is already in progress would allow for a deeper critical discourse on race in higher education.

References

Berrey, Ellen. 2014. *The Enigma of Diversity: The Language of Race and the Limits of Racial Justice.* Chicago, IL: University of Chicago Press.

Blow, Charles M. "The Meaning of Minority." *New York Times*, December 12, 2012. Retrieved 2014 from: http://www.nytimes.com/2012/12/13/opinion/blow-the-meaning-of-minority.html?_r=0.

Chang, Mitchell J., Nida Denson, Victor Sáenz, and Kimberly Misa. 2006. "The Educational Benefits of Sustaining Cross-Racial Interaction Among Undergraduates." *The Journal of Higher Education, 77*: 430–455.

Chesler, Mark, Amanda E. Lewis, and James Crowfoot. 2005. *Challenging Racism in Higher Education.* Lanham, MD: Rowman and Littlefield Publishers.

Embrick, David G. 2011. "The Diversity Ideology in the Business World: A New Oppression for a New Age." *Critical Sociology, 37* (5): 1–16.

Embrick, David G. 2006. *The Making and Selling of an Illusion: An Examination of Racial and Gender Diversity in Post-Civil Rights U.S. Corporations.* Ph.D. diss. College Station, TX: Texas A&M University. Retrieved 2011 from: http://oaktrust.library.tamu.edu/handle/1969.1/ETD-TAMU-1201.

Essed, Philomena. 1996. *Diversity: Gender, Color and Culture.* Amherst, MA: University of Massachusetts Press.

Feagin, Joe R., Anthony M. Orum, and Gideon Sjoberg. *A Case for a Case Study.* 1991. Chapel Hill, NC: University of North Carolina Press.

Fisher v. University of Texas at Austin, et al. 2013. 631 U.S. 213.

Giroux, Henry A. 1988. *Teachers as Intellectuals: Toward a Critical Pedagogy of Learning.* Westport, CT: Bergin & Garvey.

Gurin, Patricia, Eric L. Dey, Sylvia Hurtado, and Gerald Gurin. 2002. "Diversity and Higher Education: Theory and Impact on Educational Outcomes." *Harvard Educational Review*, 72: 330–366.

Gurin, Patricia, Jeffrey S. Lehman, Earl Lewis, Eric L. Dey, Gerald Gurin, and Sylvia Hurtado. 2004. *Defending Diversity: Affirmative Action at the University of Michigan.* Ann Arbor, MI: University of Michigan Press.

Insight into Diversity. "About the HEED Award." Retrieved December 21, 2015 from: http://www.insightintodiversity.com/about-the-heed-award/.

Jayakumar, Uma M. 2008. "Can Higher Education Meet the Needs of an Increasingly Diverse and Global Society? Campus Diversity and Cross-cultural Workforce Competencies." *Harvard Educational Review*, 78: 615–651.

Massey, Douglas S., Camille Z. Charles, Garvey Lundy, and Mary J. Fischer. 2006. *The Source of the River: The Social Origins of Freshmen at America's Selective Colleges and Universities.* Princeton, NJ: Princeton University Press.

Omi, Michael and Howard Winant. 1994. *Racial Formation in the United States: From the 1960s to the 1980s.* New York, NY: Routledge.

Searls Giroux, Susan. 2010. *Between Race and Reason: Violence, Intellectual Responsibility, and the University to Come.* Palo Alto, CA: Stanford University Press.

Stevens, Mitchell L. 2007. *Creating a Class: College Admissions and the Education of Elites.* Cambridge, MA: Harvard University Press.

Takagi, Dana Y. 1993. *The Retreat from Race: Asian-American Admissions and Racial Politics.* Rutgers, NJ: Rutgers University Press.

Torres, Gabriel. 1992. "Plunging into the Garlic: Methodological Issues and Challenges." In *Battlefields of Knowledge: The Interlocking of Theory and Practice in Social Research and Development.* Edited by Norman Long and Ann Long, London, UK: Routledge.

US News and World Report. "Campus Ethnic Diversity Methodology." Retrieved December 21, 2015 from: http://www.usnews.com/education/best-colleges/articles/campus-ethnic-diversity-methodology.

PART 4

Diversity and STEM

∴

Diversity in STEM: How Gendered Structures Affect Women's Participation in Science

Marie des Neiges Léonard

1   Introduction

Women are underrepresented, outnumbered, out networked, outranked and out salaried in the scientific work force (NCWGE 2012; Catalyst 2013; NSF 2013, 2015). The metaphor of the leaky pipeline for women in science refers to the idea of a persisting loss of women in Science Technology Engineering and Mathematics (STEM) fields, particularly geoscience, engineering, economics, mathematics/computer science, and the physical sciences, as they climb the career ladder. This phenomenon has prompted multiple studies from different disciplines (psychology, sociology, history, education) attempting to provide sometimes contradicting explanations for a pattern that has universities worried.

This chapter provides a critical overview of the different perspectives explaining gender disparities in STEM disciplines, from individual-level explanations (biology, human capital, socialization) to structural-level explanations. Furthermore, based on the works of feminist theorists (Acker 1990, 1992; Longino 1990, 2001; Haraway 1991, 2001; Harding 1991, 2001; Keller 2001), this essay argues that women working in science have to contend with gendered institutional structures, cultures, practices that pose barriers to their advancement and acceptance. We have to acknowledge that those layers of gendered barriers exist, and we have to understand them within the context of a gendered culture and workplace if we are to improve women's participation and experience in STEM fields. The following chapter contributes to shedding a light on existing and persisting gender inequities in STEM.

I begin with a review of the key findings, trends and data regarding the presence and participation of women in science fields. I then critically assess the current literature that explains the causes for gender inequities in science. Finally, using feminist frameworks, I examine alternative additional explanations that focus on the gendered cultures and structures in STEM fields.

2   Reality Check: Gender Disparities in STEM

There has been some progress for women in science since Title IX passed in 1972. Under Title IX, educational programs that receive federal funding are prohibited from discriminating on the basis of sex. Particularly, Title IX covers all educational activities and ensures that women are not discriminated against in fields like science or math education.

However, despite some progress due to efforts and remedies to promote women's participation in STEM disciplines (NCWGE 2012), and even though women outnumber men in undergraduate enrollments, they are still underrepresented in most science fields. According to the National Science Foundation statistics (NSF 2013), women comprise 47% of the total U.S. workforce, including more than half of all professional and related occupations, but only 24% of workers in STEM fields. Similarly, data from the Bureau of Labor Statistics (2013) show that women in the U.S. are still underrepresented in most of the STEM occupations (see Table 8.1).

Additionally, according to the National Science Foundation (NSF 2012), women's presence in STEM fields tends to decline over the years, sometimes dramatically as in the fields of mathematics, physical science and engineering (see Table 8.2).

Furthermore, according to National Science Foundation (NSF 2013), women are also underrepresented in academia in faculty positions in STEM disciplines and it decreases even further with rank (see Table 8.3).

TABLE 8.1   Employed Persons by Detailed Occupation, Sex, Race, and Hispanic
             or Latino Ethnicity 2012

Occupation	Percent women
Biological Scientists	50.1%
Medical Scientists	52.8%
Chemists and Materials Scientists	44.2%
Computer and Mathematical Occupations	25.6%
Environmental Scientists and Geoscientists	25.7%

SOURCE: BUREAU OF LABOR STATISTICS, CURRENT POPULATION SURVEY, "TABLE
11: EMPLOYED PERSONS BY DETAILED OCCUPATION, SEX, RACE, AND HISPANIC OR
LATINO ETHNICITY 2012," *ANNUAL AVERAGES 2012* (2013)

TABLE 8.2   Employed Doctoral Scientists and Engineers in 4-Year Educational Institutions, by
Broad Field of Doctorate, Sex, Faculty Rank, and Years since Doctorate: 2008

Field of doctorate	Percent of women in positions (working less than 10 years)	Percent of women in positions (working 10 or more years)
Mathematics/Statistics	33.3%	16.9%
Biological/Agricultural/ Environmental Life Sciences	45.0%	30.2%
Health Sciences	70.1%	62.5%
Physical Sciences	28.9%	15.0%
Social Sciences	47.0%	31.5%
Psychology	66.4%	47.1%
Engineering	22.9%	7.2%

SOURCE: "TABLE 3. EMPLOYED DOCTORAL SCIENTISTS AND ENGINEERS IN 4-YEAR EDUCATIONAL
INSTITUTIONS, BY BROAD FIELD OF DOCTORATE, SEX, FACULTY RANK, AND YEARS SINCE DOCTOR-
ATE: 2008" (NSF 2012)

TABLE 8.3   Science, Engineering, and Health
Doctorate Holders Employed in
Universities and 4-Year Colleges, by
Broad Occupation, Sex, Years since
Doctorate, and Faculty Rank: 2010.

Faculty title	Percent
Professor	21.9%
Associate Professor	38.0%
Assistant Professor	44.4%

SOURCE: "TABLE 9-23: SCIENCE, ENGINEERING,
AND HEALTH DOCTORATE HOLDERS EMPLOYED IN
UNIVERSITIES AND 4-YEAR COLLEGES, BY BROAD
OCCUPATION, SEX, YEARS SINCE DOCTORATE, AND
FACULTY RANK: 2010," *WOMEN, MINORITIES, AND
PERSONS WITH DISABILITIES IN SCIENCE AND ENGI-
NEERING* (2013)

In the same fashion, data from the NSF shows that women make up about half of the doctorates in science and engineering in the US, but only 21% of full professors in science disciplines and 5% of professors in engineering. Of all physics professors in the US only 14% are women. The pattern of underrepresentation of women in STEM fields is consistent across race and ethnicity. The numbers of black and Hispanic scientists are even lower; in a typical year, 13 African-Americans and 20 Latinos of either sex receive PhDs in Physics. A 2006 NSF survey of doctorate recipients shows that only 3% of Asian American women (out of 12% Asian Americans doctorate students), only 1% of Black women (out of 3% of Black doctorate students), and only 1% of Hispanic women (out of 3% Hispanic doctorate students) obtain a doctoral degree in science and engineering (Burrelli 2009). Additionally, a 2013 NSF survey of science and engineering occupation distribution (see Table 8.4) shows that only 5% Asian American women (out of 12% Asian Americans in science and engineering), only 2% Black women (out of 5% Blacks in science and engineering), and only 2% Hispanic women (out of 6% Hispanics in science and engineering) are represented in STEM occupations (NSF 2015). Therefore, across all racial and ethnic groups, more men than women work in science and engineering occupations and white men constitute about one-half of the science and engineering workforce (NSF 2015).

Moss-Racusin et al. (2012) document gender disparities in the science field with regards to salaries. Particularly, their study involved sending out identical resumes of potential candidates seeking a position as a lab manager to science professors of both sexes. The results of the study show that no matter what the respondent's age, sex, area of specialization or level of seniority, the hypothetical male candidate named "John" was rated an average of a half a point higher than the hypothetical candidate named "Jennifer" in all areas except likability. Hypothetical candidate John was offered an average starting salary of $30,238 versus $26,508 for hypothetical candidate Jennifer.

This discrepancy in salary expectations is reflected in real-life data as seen below, showing the differences in salaries for men and women scientists.

The absence of women is progressive (gets worse as we move up the ranks) and persistent (problem remains despite periodic treatments). The problem is not new. Educators have been working for over 20 years to encourage more girls and women to participate in school science through programs like Global Innovation through Science and Technology (GIST) or Women in Science and Engineering (WISE). However, existing efforts to attract women to science have not worked.

The section below intends to examine the array of explanations for this continued pattern of gender disparities in science fields.

TABLE 8.4 Median Annual Salary of Scientists and Engineers Employed Full Time, by
Highest Degree, Broad Occupation, Age, and Sex: 2006

Occupation	Women's salary as a percent of men's salary	Women's median salary	Men's median salary
Mathematical Scientist	87.5%	$70,000	$80,000
Biological/Life Scientist	83.1%	$54,000	$65,000
Computer and Information Scientist	91.9%	$79,000	$86,000
Physical Scientist	78.9%	$60,000	$76,000
Social Scientist	81.9%	$68,000	$83,000
Psychology	87.0%	$60,000	$69,000

SOURCE: NATIONAL SCIENCE FOUNDATION, "TABLE 9-16: MEDIAN ANNUAL SALARY OF SCIENTISTS
AND ENGINEERS EMPLOYED FULL TIME, BY HIGHEST DEGREE, BROAD OCCUPATION, AGE, AND SEX:
2006" (2013)

3   Explaining the Gap and the Leak

Whether in terms of the participation, presence or retention of women in
STEM disciplines and occupations, progress has been slow, has stagnated or
in some cases even declined (as seen in the percentage of women in computer
science which has decreased since 1991). Why has progress been so slow? Why
has women's participation in the STEM disciplines stalled? Is it a leaky pipeline, a gender filter or both?

Explaining these patterns has brought disputes and disagreements amongst
scholars. In this section we explore the different perspectives and frameworks
that have sought to explain the gender gap in STEM fields. Current approaches
can be divided into two categories, a set of individual-level approaches and
structural frameworks.

3.1   *Individual Level Explanations: Genetics and Human Capital*
Biology—Biological/genetic and psychological approaches explain women's
low achievement and participation rate in the STEM fields in terms of individual innate or biological characteristics (Hyde 1996; Sadker and Sadker 1994;

Browne 2002; Sax 2006). However, according to the STEM report regarding equality issues with the achievement gap in STEM fields (NCWGE 2012), scientific studies show no innate differences between boys and girls in their scientific abilities. Other abilities (math performance, spatial reasoning) are not "biologically programmed by gender" (NCWGE 2012). Thus we have overwhelming scientific data showing no correlation between genetic make-up and achievement/outcome for women in science fields (Guiso et al. 2008; Hyde et al. 2008; Hyde and Mertz 2009). Despite the fact that such scientific research has debunked the stereotype about male and female abilities in math and science, such stereotype is still pervasive in the U.S. and is largely perpetuated by society, including academia. As Reuben, Sapienza and Zingales (2014) remind us, then President of Harvard University Larry Summers advanced in a 2005 speech that one of the hypotheses for the underrepresentation of women in science was different innate aptitudes among men and women at the high end of science-based fields. Despite recent trends in achievement and despite years of scientific research demonstrating that the aptitude-based hypothesis for a gender gap in STEM is simply incorrect, the stereotype continues and as Reuben, Sapienza and Zingales (2014) argue, it impairs women's careers in science.

Human Capital and Gender Socialization—The human capital/gender socialization approaches explain inequalities in terms of individual achieved abilities. Human capital theory comes from economists and makes the claim that differences between men and women on the job market can be explained by the relative differences between men and women in skills, experiences, and commitment to their jobs. From the human capital standpoint, if women invested in the same human capital as men do, sex inequality would not exist (Polacheck 1981; Blau, Ferber, and Winker 1998; Bojars 2005).

On the one hand, the human capital perspective assumes that gaps persist because of the different investments men and women make. These investments include education, training, experience and different career-related preferences among men and women. For example, Ceci et al. (2014) argue that the major barriers to women's presence and participation in STEM disciplines are women themselves in the form of their early educational choices and in their occupational and lifestyle preferences. However we know that women want to be in STEM fields. In fact, girls are encouraged to study in traditionally male-dominated disciplines at school, but often they later abandon those subjects. In a report for the UK Resource Centre for Women in SET and the Royal Society of Chemistry, Newsome (2008) shows that at the beginning of their studies, 72% of women express an intention to pursue a scientific career in academia or industry (when only 61% of men express the same intention).

However, Newsome's report (2008) also shows that by their third year, only 37% of women and 59% of men have the same intentions. Numbers are even lower for academia, where only 12% of women and 21% of men see academia as their preferred choice for a career in STEM. We see here that the so-called career choices that women are supposedly making isn't in fact proper to just women, since both men and women's attitudes and beliefs about scientific careers in academia are somewhat similarly negative.

On the other hand, the human capital approach focuses on individual deficiencies that women learn through socialization. For example, a 2012 survey by the American Institute of Physics shows that female scientists received less financing, lab space, office support and grants for equipment and travel (even after controlling for differences other than sex). A human capital approach would look at the gap in wages or funding in terms of how women lack the ability to interact and negotiate in professional situations. Therefore, such an approach leads to the concluding advice that women should "lean in," a term popularized by Facebook COO Sheryl Sandberg in a book where she advises women to "take a seat at the table" and speak up, negotiate their salaries and choose a mate carefully. The problem with such an approach is that it blames women for their drawbacks and their "faulty" behavior. It reflects an essentialist framing of gender which implies, as Rhoton (2011) explains, that certain practices stereotypically perceived as feminine are construed as tendencies inherent to women and are therefore somehow in their essence or nature. It also implies that women themselves are hurting their career path (in science for example) and their success and advancement.

Additionally, a focus on women's human capital and socialization assumes that if women would only be socialized differently they would acquire the "normal" necessary attitudes and behaviors to be successful in STEM. This argument presents the attitudes and behaviors necessary to be successful in a work environment (such as science) as a gender-less or gender-neutral norm which becomes "normal." But in fact, as we will examine further in this chapter, these norms (be assertive, aggressive, etc...) are socially based on normative masculine behaviors and accepted as if they were gender-less. So instead of challenging the quality of such behaviors, we are asking women to "elevate" themselves to behave and perform normative masculine behaviors, without declaring them gendered or masculine.

Both the biology/genetics and the human capital approaches are complementary in that they emphasize women's individual presumed innate abilities or personally chosen preferences, which such approaches claim have shaped women's outcomes on the scientific job market. What is problematic and dangerous with both the biology and human capital frameworks is that they tend to either essentialize individual characteristics (where biology becomes destiny) or frame the outcome as an individual preference or choice without taking account for social, cultural and structural barriers. Indeed, by focusing on individual abilities only, without taking into account structural and systemic patterns and contexts, such approaches support the view that academic science "reflects gender fairness, rather than gender bias" (Williams and Ceci 2014). This approach assumes that the market is essentially gender-blind. However, despite its popularity, the human capital approach in particular fails to explain persisting gender inequalities and disparities in STEM.

4   Structural Level Explanations and Feminist Frameworks: Gendered Structures

The structural approach argues that women face significant structural, cultural and social barriers that undermine their ability to achieve the same outcomes as men. Such approach takes into account institutional barriers as well as the role of the social and cultural environment (role models, mentors, values, expectations, attitudes and experiences) showing that these barriers affect women's experiences in preparation for and throughout their careers.

Women working in science have to contend with gendered institutional structures, cultures, practices that pose barriers to their advancement and acceptance. What follows is an examination of the literature, using feminist frameworks, explaining the barriers women face in STEM in terms of the gendered construction of scientific knowledge and of the internalization of the gendered structures of STEM fields amongst women scientists.

4.1   Science as Gendered Knowledge

Although science is still a male dominated field, science as an institution is largely perceived as a gender-neutral meritocracy, because as a discipline it is largely based on positivist principles of objectivity and rationality coming from the Enlightenment, which have passed as gender-neutral or gender-less principles over the years. However, as noted by Blickenstaff (2005), feminist theorists (Acker 1990, 1992; Longino 1990, 2001; Haraway 1991, 2001; Harding 1991, 2001; Keller 2001) have argued that, "science is inherently masculine in its structure, epistemology, and methodology." In other words, science is a gendered institution. As Acker (1992, 567) explains, "the term 'gendered institutions' means that gender is present in the processes, practices, images and ideologies, and distributions of power in the various sectors of social life." Science (academia in general) is an institution that has historically been developed by men, is still dominated by men, and has been "symbolically interpreted from the stand-point of men in leading positions" (Acker 1992, 567). Therefore, in order to explain the persisting gender filter and leaky pipeline in STEM for women, we must examine the institutional structures in science fields as gendered as they simultaneously maintain the appearance or illusion of gender neutrality.

In fact, using Acker's (1990) argument, we can say that disparities between genders persist in STEM because they are built into the structure of science as an institution and as a workplace. In that regard, Harding's standpoint episte-mology (1991, 2001) has helped us uncover the relationship between knowledge and politics. Harding (2001) points to the masculine production of science where the dominant group (men scientists) has organized knowledge in its image and has set limits for others. For example, Smith (1996) explains how the ideal of objectivity in science is a masculine construction that corresponds to androcentric practices and carries androcentric values. For Harding (2001), the implication and problem with objectivity as the conventional approach to scientific research is that it can only be acquired by breaking ties from local or historical values and life as if to "purify" science to make it value-free. Production of scientific knowledge through objectivity then supposes suspending our gender, our knowledge of who is speaking, so the body of knowledge produced in the name of objectivity is separated from the practitioners (the knowers) who are expected to practice science outside and independent of the situation. One of the consequences is that knowledge is constructed in binary opposites like rational/emotional, objective/subjective, science/nature, masculine/feminine where one side is associated with men and the other side with women, and we are socialized to value the masculine qualities (Gilbert 2001).

Feminist scholars like Harding, Haraway (1991, 2001) and Longino (1990, 2001) argue that instead of blinding themselves with the illusion of neutrality, scientists should recognize and acknowledge the political nature of scientific knowledge. Furthermore they claim that scientists should acknowledge that all knowledge is "situated" and plural and that it can take many different standpoints. As Blickenstaff (2005, 383) explains, one of the significant contributions of such feminist scholars is to have unveiled the gendered nature of scientific research, particularly showing that "political and social power affects the kind of questions that scientists ask and how scientists interpret the answers they obtain." Scientists must therefore seek to detect and confront the limiting aspect of the current scientific epistemology due to masculine bias and recognize science and the work of scientists as gendered work in order to alleviate if not eliminate the inherent masculine bias. One of the outcomes for scientific research will be the improvement of "the diversity of its practitioners across gender, ethnic and racial lines" (Blickenstaff 2005, 383). Of course, one of the challenges is precisely for the scientific community to start with the recognition that a gender bias exists at all in science disciplines. Indeed, a study by Moss-Racusin, Molenda and Cramer (2015) shows that men scientists are more likely to react negatively to and doubt evidence of gender bias in STEM fields. Particularly, the study shows that respondents either trivialized evidence of gender bias or avoided altogether acknowledging the actual existence of gender bias in science despite the evidence, for it would be a threat to the perceived fairness of the gender-neutral meritocratic institution that is science. One concerning finding for Moss-Racusin, Molenda and Cramer (2015) is the fact that when acknowledging the evidence of gender bias in STEM, respondents justified it with biological arguments. For example, respondents focused on perceived innate gender differences, say Moss-Racusin, Molenda and Cramer (2015). The use of essentialist arguments by men scientists to justify gender disparities in STEM is problematic because it has been linked to heightened endorsement of gender stereotypes (Moss-Racusin, Molenda and Cramer 2015). And we know from Reuben, Sapienza and Zingales (2014) that the stereotype of women's perceived inferior performance in science related field (such as mathematics) hurts them in their career prospects in STEM.

4.2   *Internalizing Gendered Structures*

Padavic and Reskin (2002, 11) explain that the social construction of gender in the work place is a "by-product of the ways that employers organize work." Additionally, both Padavic and Reskin (2002) and Acker (1999) acknowledge that gender is constructed and performed at work through organizational practices and interactions. Acker (1990) even argues that jobs are defined with a reference and therefore preference for male workers. Amongst the processes at the heart of organizations reproducing the gendered structures in the work place, Acker (1990, 147) identifies "organizational logic" which refers to "underlying assumptions and practices" at the core of work organizations. Elements of organizational logic include work rules, contracts, directives, evaluation systems and other documents which all contain "symbolic indicators" (Acker 1990, 147) of the gendered structure of organizations. All of these elements constitute taken-for-granted policies and principles that rationalize and legitimize gender hierarchies in organizations. Acker (1990) argues that these processes are the key to the reproduction of gender inequality, even more so because they are performed and acted every day in practical work activities. The way that organizational logic enables the reproduction and persistence of gender hierarchies in organizations is by appearing gender neutral so that these practices and assumptions seem natural and normal. This process takes place through the disembodiment of the worker where the job, not the individual, becomes the basic abstract unit in the organization. Therefore Acker (1990, 149) claims, in organizational logic, the job prevails as an abstract concept, category and norm without "occupants," "human bodies" or gender.

> Rational-technical, ostensibly gender-neutral, control systems are built upon and conceal a gendered substructure in which men's bodies fill the abstract jobs. Use of such abstract systems continually reproduces the underlying gender assumptions and the subordinated or excluded place of women.
>
> ACKER 154

Therefore, Acker (1990, 1999) and other feminist scholars (Scott 1999; Padavic and Reskin 2002) have well demonstrated that organizations are not gender neutral, and that gendered practices and discourses are embedded in organizations and continue to perpetuate gender hierarchies and inequality.

In STEM fields, the gendered cultures and structures impose a set of masculinized expectations on scientists that limit the range of acceptable behaviors and professional demeanors. Many of the harmful practices in which men scientists engage are not intentional but we have to acknowledge they exist and we have to understand them within the context of a gendered culture and workplace because scientists may inadvertently reproduce gendered barriers for women in STEM disciplines.

Building on the works of Acker (1990, 1999), Longino (1990, 2001), Haraway (1991, 2001), Harding (1991, 2001) and Keller (2001), we can examine STEM fields as gendered disciplines and spaces that create and construct gendered norms and practices defining the role of scientist and the reality of "doing of science" (Keller 2001). Rhoton (2011) defines gendered practices as a set of activities available to be performed in accordance with cultural gender expectations and may be manifested in discourse, or the ways in which people talk about concepts or verbally position themselves relative to others (Rhoton 697). For example, disciplinary norms dictate that scientists be decisive, methodical, objective, unemotional, competitive and assertive, characteristics often associated with men and masculinity. Disciplinary norms also dictate that scientists adopt a work style that demonstrates complete dedication to their work at the expense of any other obligations (a pattern most often possible for men as childbearing activities mostly likely fall on women). As Acker (1990:149) explains, the disembodied "hypothetical worker cannot have other imperatives of existence that impinge upon the job." Outside imperatives (such as family life) are therefore not acknowledged in the worker's life and the concept of the scientist's job assumes a particular organization of domestic life and social production that corresponds to the image of the male worker. However, once again, the paradox, underlined by Acker (1990) and Keller (2001) is the fact that the language and the practice of "doing science" is simultaneously constructed on masculine principles or qualities, while being presented as gender neutral, similar to the idea of "laws of nature."

The same socialization processes that impress the gender neutrality ideal on all scientists also influence the way women scientists may interpret gender bias or gender discrimination. Women have internalized oppression and discrimination and women scientists often come to expect and even accept gender discrimination and bias as normal. Women may even support hegemonic masculinity and the gender order as a whole by engaging in gender practices that devalue some women or certain types of femininity. Indeed, through the internalization of the gender bias, women scientists engage in gender practices that reproduce the gender order of society, the status quo and the gendered relations within it, particularly the gendered barriers in STEM fields. Rhoton (2011) argues that one way women scientists internalize norms takes place when women scientists participate in the practice of distancing, a "discursive separation or dissociation" from behaviors women scientists see as too feminine. They do so either by distancing themselves from other women scientists who are perceived as displaying typically feminine behaviors, or by avoiding engaging in practices they consider typically feminine. For example, women scientists equate giggling with femininity and lack of professionalism and will distance themselves from other women doing it, or they may suppress any emotions because of a connection between emotions and femininity they perceive as negative. Distancing can also be observed in the types of choices women scientists make about their careers or in the denying of gender inequality (Rhoton 2011). For example, women scientists distance themselves from women who make claims about gender barriers to success or who engage in efforts to address gender discrimination. Similarly, women scientists distance themselves from women who are viewed as overreacting or otherwise viewed as responding inappropriately to instances of gender bias. Instead, through the internalization of a masculine worldview of science, women scientists tend to accept the dominant ideology that presents STEM disciplines as gender-neutral meritocracies.

The purpose of this work of distancing is about not displaying femininity which women scientists perceive as a threat to their legitimacy as scientists. For Rhoton (2011) indeed, adopting such distancing practices allows women scientists to situate themselves as professionals in ways that are consistent with the imposed cultural norms and expectations of their occupation coming from hegemonic masculinity. Therefore, women in STEM try to become "one of the boys" and one of the ways they do it is by avoiding engaging in what might be perceived as overtly feminine practices or feminine gender display.

Consequently, women scientists indicate that to avoid complications or barriers women must either postpone childbearing until after tenure or ensure that support structures are in place for child care before deciding to have children, which means making sure that family obligations do not interfere with their career. Women scientists then conform to the "ideal worker" norm that is part of the gendered culture and structure, or organizational logic, of academic STEM disciplines. In that regard, the ability to privilege career over family is most often associated with men whereas privileging family over career is most often associated with women. However, family formation seems to damage the academic careers of women but not of men: indeed, having children is a career advantage for men, but for women it is a career killer. Men experience "fatherhood bonus" or "fatherhood premiums," which means that men get pay increases when they have children (Kelly and Grant 2012). Goulden and Wolfinger (2013) also show that family formation is a career advantage for men in academia. In the STEM fields, among those working in academia, men who have early babies are more successful in earning tenure than women who have early babies. Generally, having babies seems to help men: they achieve tenure at slightly higher rates than people who do not have early babies, and they are more likely to be promoted than men without children (Mason and Goulden 2002). Benard and Correll (2010) argue that fatherhood enhances the perception of highly valued social skills. It seems to signal positive interpersonal qualities in male workers (for example that they are more stable and more committed to work), but not for female applicants. Women who do advance through the faculty ranks do so at a high personal price. A big proportion of women scientists and engineers are unmarried, and generally women scientists are far less likely to be married with children. On the other hand, we see many more women than men who are married with children working in the adjunct-faculty ranks (one of the fastest growing sectors in academe).

And so, Rhoton (2011) concludes, women who engage in feminine practices within an environment that values masculine practices may undermine their own legitimacy since femininity is constructed as subordinate to masculinity.

5   Conclusion

Whether we call it gender filter or leaky pipeline, the phenomenon of persisting gender disparities in STEM disciplines can be explained in terms of gendered institutional structures, cultures, practices that pose barriers to the advancement and acceptance of women in science. Women's presence, participation and career advancement in STEM fields has not improved over the years because science (and scientists) is male.

Based on the works of feminist theorists (Acker 1990, 1992; Longino 1990, 2001; Haraway 1991, 2001; Harding 1991, 2001; Keller 2001), this essay argues that women working in science have to contend with an organizational logic that is gendered in favor of a hegemonic masculinity while portraying science as a gender-neutral meritocracy. The organizational logic in STEM means that gender inequality is institutionalized through every day values, discourses and practices justifying the gendered order as normal and neutral. Therefore, because of the association of science with masculinity, women scientists will likely come to view masculine practices as more professional than feminine practices and adopt/promote the view that STEM disciplines are gender-neutral meritocracies. So they tend to see failures or problems as personal or individual rather than structural and systemic. They also tend to essentialize gender differences and abilities or handicaps. These tendencies are precisely at the heart of their denial of structural barriers facing women in STEM disciplines. Scientists in general, men or women, do not view the practice-based expectations as gendered. The image of science as a gender-neutral vocation (skill and merit determining success) is learned by both men and women through socialization and maintained through professional discourse. We know that gender bias and stereotypes affect women scientists' careers and women scientists are expected to adhere to cultural ideals demonstrating solidarity with the culture. For example, successful female professors are perceived as displaying masculine characteristics such as aggression, competitiveness and they are often childless. Furthermore, as demonstrated by Rhoton (2011), because of internalized oppression, women scientists perform a distancing from women colleagues perceived as displaying feminine values and behaviors. Through the process of distancing, women thus participate in the reproduction of the gendered occupational culture and organization logic in STEM fields.

One of the consequences of the gendered organizational logic in STEM fields is the marginalization often experienced by women scientists. For example, as Pollack (2013) explains, a committee of six senior women and three senior men at MIT investigated the experience of women scientists at M.I.T. Their findings are that women in science are marginalized through differences in salary, space, awards, resources and responses to outside offers between men and women faculty, with women receiving less despite professional accomplishments equal to those of their colleagues.

In order to address gender disparities and hierarchies in STEM, we first have to acknowledge that those layers of gendered barriers exist, and we have to understand them within the context of science as a gendered organization and workplace if we are to improve women's participation and experience in STEM fields. We have to create a space for women in STEM for equal retribution, remuneration and recognition. So, first and foremost, more research is needed to identify and examine the gendered organizational logic at work in science as a discipline and work place.

Additionally, below are some institutional-level policy recommendations (Mason 2014; NCWGE, 2012):

· Enforcement of existing antidiscrimination laws (gender equity in pay).
· Assignment of women to science advisory boards, editorial boards of science journals, science policy positions.
· Better family-friendly policies:

Better/more child-care options: better day-care facilities (even including private fund raising); emergency backup childcare for all faculty.

The NSF has announced (Oct. 2014) that NSF awards may be used to pay the salaries of temporary employees hired to replace people who take a leave of absence to meet dependent-care responsibilities.

Effective dual-career policies: female scientists are likely to be married to male scientists, while male scientists (many more of them) are likelier to have a spouse who works only part time. One of the two bodies must defer, and that body is likely to be hers.

According to a NSF (Survey of Earned Doctorates), 65% of married female Ph.Ds. acknowledged that spousal-career concerns affected their search for a permanent job (compared with 38% of married male Ph.Ds.). The two-body problem is often the one problem cited by women scientists to explain why they dropped out of the science pipeline.

Childbirth accommodations: colleges and universities should establish standardized guidelines for tenure-track eligibility and offer a stop-the-clock option for women and men with small children. Also, colleges and universities should offer paid parental leave for both mothers and fathers. They could also offer relief from teaching (a semester); offer a part-time pre-tenure track for working parents; workplace flexibility for both new mothers and fathers.

· Compliance with Title IX: Title IX of the Higher Education Amendments of 1972 specifically prohibits sex discrimination in any education program receiving federal financial assistance. The most vulnerable years for a female scientist's career are the earliest. According to a NSF survey, married mothers are 35% less likely than married fathers to obtain a tenure-track job. Single women without children are almost as likely as men to get that job. College and universities are in violation of Title IX if they fail to allow pregnant mothers a reasonable period of leave for childbirth or fail to guarantee that they can return to their former positions (this includes graduate students and post-docs). These guidelines should be broadly disseminated and publicized.

· College and universities should offer mandatory leadership training on gender bias and discrimination for chairs, professors, deans, and administrators at all levels.

· All agencies or institutions receiving federal financial assistance should conduct Title IX and STEM reviews to ensure the grantee institutions are providing equal opportunities and treatment for women in STEM.

References

Acker, Joan. 1990. "Hierarchies, Jobs, Bodies: A Theory of Gendered Organizations." *Gender and Society*, 4 (2): 139–158.

Acker, Joan. 1992. "From Sex Roles to Gendered Institutions." *Contemporary Sociology*, 21 (5): 565–569.

Acker, Joan. 1999. "Gender and Organizations." In *Handbook of the Sociology of Gender*, edited by Janet S. Chafetz, 177–194. New York, NY: Kluwer Academic/Plenum.

Benard, Stephen and Shelley Correll. 2010. "Normative Discrimination and the Motherhood Penalty." *Gender and Society*, 24 (5): 616–646.

Blau, Francine D., Marianne A. Ferber, and Anne E. Winker. 1998. *The Economics of Women, Men, and Work*. Upper Saddle River, NJ: Prentice Hall.

Blickenstaff, Jacob Clark. 2005. "Women and Science Careers: Leaky Pipeline or Gender Filter?" *Gender and Education*, 17 (4): 369–386.

Bojars, George. 2005. *Labor Economics*. Boston, MA: McGraw-Hill.

Browne, Ken R. 2002. *Biology at Work: Rethinking Sexual Equality*. New Brunswick, NJ: Rutgers University Press.

Burrelli, Joan. 2009. *Women of Color in STEM Education and Employment*. CEOSE Mini-Symposium on Women of Color in STEM. NSF, Division of Science Resources Statistics.

Catalyst. 2013. *Catalyst Quick Take: Women in the Sciences*. New York: Catalyst. Accessed December 8 http://www.catalyst.org/knowledge/women-sciences.

Ceci, Stephen J., Donna K. Ginther, Shulamit Kahn, and Wendy M. Williams. 2014. "Women in Academic Science: A Changing Landscape." *Psychological Science in the Public Interest*, 15 (3): 75–141.

Gilbert, Jane. 2001. "Science and Its 'Other': Looking Underneath 'Woman' and Science for New Directions in Research on Gender and Science Education." *Gender and Education*, 13 (3): 291–305.

Goulden, Marc and Nicholas Wolfinger. 2013. *Do Babies Matter? Gender and Family in the Ivory Tower*. Rutgers University Press.

Guiso, Luigi, Ferdinando Monte, Paola Sapienza, and Luigi Zingales. 2008. "Culture, Math, and Gender." *Science*, 320 (5880): 1164–1165.

Haraway, Donna. 1991. *Simians, Cyborgs, and Women: The Reinvention of Nature*. New York, NY: Routledge.

Haraway, Donna. 2001. "Situated Knowledges. The Science Question in Feminism and the Privilege of Partial Perspective." In *The Gender and Science Reader*, edited by Muriel Lederman and Ingrid Bartsch, 169–188. New York, NY: Routledge.

Harding, Sandra. 1991. *Whose Science? Whose Knowledge? Thinking from Women's Lives*. Open University Press: Milton Keynes.

Harding, Sandra. 2001. "Feminist Standpoint Epistemology." In *The Gender and Science Reader*, edited by Muriel Lederman and Ingrid Bartsch, 145–168. New York, NY: Routledge.

Hyde, Janet S. 1996. "Meta-analysis and the Psychology of Gender Differences." In *Gender and Scientific Authority*, edited by Barbara Laslett, Sally Gregory Kohlstedt, Helen Longino and Evelynn Hammonds, 302–322. Chicago: University of Chicago Press.

Hyde, Janet S. and Janet E. Mertz. 2009. "Gender, Culture, and Mathematics Performance." *Proceedings of the National Academy of Sciences*, 106 (22): 8801–8807.

Hyde, Janet S., Sarah M. Lindberg, Marcia C. Linn, Amy B. Ellis, and Caroline C. Williams. 2008. "Diversity. Gender Similarities Characterize Math Performance." *Science*, 321 (5888): 494–495.

Keller, Evelyn F. 2001. "Gender and Science. An Update." In *Women, Science and Technology. A Reader in Feminist Science Studies*, edited by Mary Wyer, Mary Barbercheck, Donna Giesman, Hatice Ozturk, and Marta Wayne, 132–142. New York, NY: Routledge.

Kelly, Kimberly and Linda Grant. 2012. "Penalties and Premiums: The Impact of Gender, Marriage, and Parenthood on Faculty Salaries in Science, Engineering and Mathematics (SEM) and Non-SEM Fields." *Social Studies of Science*, 42 (6): 869–896.

Longino, Helen E. 1990. *Science as Social Knowledge: Values and Objectivity in Science Inquiry*. Princeton, NJ: Princeton University Press.

Longino, Helen E. 2001. "Subjects, Power, and Knowledge. Description and Prescription in Feminist Philosophies of Science." In *The Gender and Science Reader*, edited by Muriel Lederman and Ingrid Bartsch, 213–224. New York, NY: Routledge.

Mason, Mary Ann. 2014. "How to Level the Playing Field for Women in Science. The Baby Penalty in Academe Could Be Eased with Four Key Reforms." *The Chronicle of*

Higher Education, March 3. Accessed December 8 http://chronicle.com/article/How-to-Level-the-Playing-Field/145037/.

Mason, Mary Ann and Marc Goulden. 2002. "Do Babies Matter?" *Academe*, 88: 21–28.

Moss-Racusin, Corinne A., Aneta K. Molenda, and Charlottee R. Cramer. 2015. "Can Evidence Impact Attitudes? Public Reactions to Evidence of Gender Bias in STEM Fields." *Psychology of Women Quarterly*, 39 (2): 194–209.

Moss-Racusin, Corinne A., John F. Dovidio, Victoria L. Brescoll, Mark J. Graham, and Handelsman Jo. 2012. "Science Faculty's Subtle Gender Biases Favor Male Students." *Proceedings of the National Academy of Sciences*, 109 (41): 16474–16479.

National Coalition for Women and Girls in Education (NCWGE). 2012. "Science, Technology, Engineering and Mathematics. Equality Narrows the Achievement Gap." In *Title IX at 40: Working to Ensure Gender Equity in Education*. 17–27. Washington, DC: NCWGE.

National Science Foundation, National Center for Science and Engineering Statistics. 2015. *Women, Minorities, and Persons with Disabilities in Science and Engineering: 2015*. Special Report NSF 15-311. Arlington, VA. Accessed December 8, 2015. http://www.nsf.gov/statistics/wmpd/.

National Science Foundation, National Center for Science and Engineering Statistics. 2013. *Women, Minorities, and Persons with Disabilities in Science and Engineering: 2013*. Special Report NSF 13-304. Arlington, VA. Available at http://www.nsf.gov/statistics/wmpd/.

National Science Foundation, National Center for Science and Engineering Statistics. 2012. *Characteristics of Doctoral Scientists and Engineers in the United States: 2008*. Detailed Statistical Tables NSF 13-302. Arlington, VA. Available at http://www.nsf.gov/statistics/nsf13302/.

Newsome, Jessica L. 2008. *The Chemistry PhD: The Impact on Women's Retention*. UK Resource Center for Women in SET, The Royal Society of Chemistry.

Padavic, Irene and Barbara Reskin. 2002. *Women and Men at Work*. Thousand Oaks, CA: Pine Forge Press.

Polacheck, Solomon W. 1981. "Occupational Self-Selection: A Human Capital Approach to Sex Difference in Occupational Structure." *Review of Economics and Statistics*, 63: 60–69.

Pollack, Eileen. 2013. "Why Are There Still So Few Women in Science?" *The New York Times*, October 3.

Reuben, Ernesto, Paola Sapienza, and Luigi Zingales. 2014. "How Stereotypes Impair Women's Careers in Science." *Proceedings of the National Academy of Sciences*, 111 (12): 4403–4408.

Rhoton, Laura A. 2011. "Distancing as a Gendered Barrier: Understanding Women Scientists' Gender Practices." *Gender and Society*, 25 (6): 696–716.

Sadker, M and D Sadker. 1994. *Failing at Fairness: How Our Schools Cheat Girls*. New York, NY: Simon & Schuster.

Sax, Leonard 2006. *Why Gender Matters: What Parents Need to Know about the Emerging Science of Sex Differences.* New York, NY: Random House.

Scott, Joan W. 1999. *Gender and the Politics of History.* New York, NY: Columbia University Press.

Smith, Dorothy E. 1996. "Women's Perspective as a Radical Critique of Sociology." In *Feminism and Science*, edited by Evelyn Fox Keller and Helen E. Longino, 17–27. Oxford, New York: Oxford University Press.

Williams, Wendy M. and Stephen J. Ceci. 2014. "Academic Science Isn't Sexist." *The New York Times*, 31 October.

CHAPTER 9

Equal Opportunity in Science: Diversity as an Economic and Social Justice Imperative

Enobong Hannah Branch and Sharla Alegria

1   Introduction

Prior to 2001, a seemingly inexhaustible pool of international students and professionals met the ever-increasing need for a technical workforce. Post 9/11,[1] many Science, Technology, Engineering, and Math (STEM) educators predicted a crisis as international student enrollment plummeted. The heightened cries for a diverse workforce in STEM-related fields paralleled this shrinking international labor pool, as incorporating "all" of America's talents became the primary means to maintain our intellectual edge amid increasing global competition. These fears drove an urgent call to action by economic, industry, and policy leaders to incorporate the largely untapped U.S. born population of racial/ethnic minorities and white women.

While fears about immigration may wax and wane, policy advisers and Presidents alike have long recognized that the full participation of historically underrepresented minorities in the areas of science, technology, engineering, and math could fill the supply shortfall and is therefore in the national interest. President Carter signed the *Science and Engineering Equal Opportunity Act of 1980,* which codified this belief into law. However, U.S. efforts to increase diversity in STEM fields have been episodic—becoming a national priority as external political and economic pressures mounted but waning as pressures and priorities shifted.

The urgent call for a diverse STEM workforce is not an altruistic goal aimed at improving access for all. Rather, the momentum around gender and ethnic/racial diversity in STEM fields today is fueled by the desire to assure U.S. future competitiveness in the global arena as fears rise that the relatively low participation of U.S. workers will no longer be offset by qualified technical workers from outside of the U.S. We argue that this is a unique moment for the U.S. in

---

1 The terrorist attacks in the US on the World Trade Center and the Pentagon created an environment of fear in the US. In response to the attacks, the government tightened security by limited and restricting movement across and within US borders.

which increasing diversity and inclusion by drawing members of historically underrepresented groups into STEM fields meets both social justice goals and economic priorities. Hence, how we proceed from here matters. If we continue the episodic focus of the past, we are unlikely to realize long-lasting meaningful change that provides enhanced educational and occupational opportunities to historically underrepresented groups. If we embrace the push for diversity, however, not just as an economic goal but also as an important social justice project, lasting change is possible.

This chapter begins by outlining the extent to which U.S. innovation has been driven by immigration. Next we consider three historical moments that illustrate America's episodic focus on, rather than long-term commitment to, diversity. First, we discuss the beginning of the knowledge economy in Kennedy's race for space and the focus on inclusion in the Science and Engineering Equal Opportunity Act of 1980. Second, we consider the transition from manufacturing to innovation as the engine of the economy under Reagan and the unintended racial consequences. Third, we illustrate the extent to which today's concerns are motivated by global economic competition and critique the lack of sustained focus on full participation. We demonstrate that, absent external pressure, full participation of all U.S. workers in STEM work fades as a national priority. We end by making the case for full participation of historically underrepresented groups in STEM fields as both an economic and social justice aim.

2   Immigration Driven Innovation

In her acclaimed 2002 speech, *"The Quiet Crisis: Falling Short in Producing American Scientific and Technological Talent,"* Rensselaer Polytechnic Institute President Shirley Ann Jackson Ph.D. proclaimed that the declining number of U.S. students seeking careers in the sciences is indeed a national crisis and called for an immediate and comprehensive initiative to prepare underrepresented minorities to navigate the arduous STEM education pipeline. She was not alone. Business leaders, especially in information technology, warned of a "critical shortage in skilled American workers that is threatening their ability to compete in the global marketplace" (Land of Plenty 2000). The President's Council of Advisors on Science and Technology predicted a shortfall of roughly one million educated STEM workers over the next decade (Holdren and Lander 2012).

Why the clarion call? The STEM workforce in the United States is heavily dependent on highly skilled migrant workers. In the 1990s, scientific fields experienced an immigration boom, particularly among the highest educated workers, thanks, in large part, to the H-1B Visa program passed by Congress. H-1B visas provided additional paths to migration for highly skilled immigrants and Congress has consistently increased the number of visas available each year. Fully 40 percent of H-1B visas granted between 2000 and 2009 were for tech industry workers, illustrating the centrality of international talent to America's technological innovation (Government Accountability Office 2011). Further, over 57 percent of Computer Science and Electrical Engineering doctorate holders in 2003 were foreign-born (Regets 2007). According to the Council on Competetitiveness (2005), a third of scientists and engineers working in the U.S. were born in other countries (Council on Competitiveness, pp. 44–45).

As competition between governments for corporate capital has increased and corporations have become more accustomed to finding skilled workers outside of countries with the biggest Western economies, anxieties have risen that the best foreign-born scientists would stop immigrating to the U.S. In their report, *Innovate America*, the Council on Competitiveness, an organization of corporate CEOs, university presidents, and labor leaders, summarized the fragility of future US innovation saying, "For the first time in our history, the United States is confronting the possibility of a reverse brain drain—with innovators, scientists and engineers taking advantage of the growing opportunities for world-class education and research outside our borders" (2005: 45).

U.S. economic planners' fears that highly skilled foreign-born workers would stop migrating to the US were realized post 9/11 when the number of foreign students applying to take the GRE test (a pre-requisite for admission to a US graduate program) fell by a third (Council on Competitiveness, 2005: 45; National Research Council 2010). While the number of highly skilled foreign-born workers and students coming to the U.S. has recovered, the long-term sustainability of America's dependence on international talent is in question. Post 9/11 immigration controls resulted in a 35 percent increase in rejections of foreign-born students' visas in 2004 and a 32 percent decline in international student applications in the same year (Council on Competitiveness, 2005: 45). The National Academy of Sciences (National Research Council 2010) and Senators Charles Schumer and Lindsey Graham (2010), ideological opposites on many issues, describe attracting foreign-born scientists as a matter of national economic security that requires new, more flexible immigration measures.

Sending countries, such as China and India, are making strong investments in education and expanding opportunities in science and technology careers to further their own innovation driven economic ambitions, fueling fears that larger proportions of highly skilled migrant workers may return home

(National Research Council 2010; Regets 2007; Favell, Feldblum and Smith 2007). The idea that highly educated foreign-born workers may stop coming to the U.S. was among the concerns that led the National Research Council to author two foreboding reports in quick succession. *Rising Above the Gathering Storm: Energizing and Employing America for a Brighter Economic Future* (2007), and *Rising Above the Gathering Storm, Revisited: Rapidly Approaching Category 5* (2010), warn of national economic disaster if the U.S. fails to take two key steps: (1) provide easier access and more incentives for highly skilled foreign-born workers to come to the U.S. to solve the short-term problem and (2) invest in the math and science education of the broad population to solve the long-term problem.

Moving from inclusion as an aspirational goal to a large-scale actionable goal seemed unlikely until now. By and large, America lacked the collective will to tackle the problem of the severe underrepresentation of racial/ethnic minorities and white women in STEM careers until post 9/11 amid global economic threat. The once inexhaustible pool of international talent that drove American innovation is in jeopardy as we face "fierce competition from countries that seek an innovation-driven future for themselves" (Council on Competitiveness, 2005). We are in a historical moment wherein increasing diversity, defined as American born white women and ethno-racial minorities, appears to be in the national economic interest. Thus there is a call to action at all levels of government and in the private sector to recruit historically underrepresented groups into STEM jobs.

3   A Focus on Inclusion: An Opportunity Lost in Science

On May 25th, 1961, President Kennedy went before a special joint session of Congress and jumpstarted the race for space saying, "...I believe that this nation should commit itself to achieving this goal, before this decade is out, of landing a man on the moon and returning him safely to earth" (JFK, 1961). The Union of Soviet Socialist Republics (USSR) had already launched a manned spacecraft, Sputnik, into orbit around the earth and the Kennedy administration was certain that the key to winning the "minds of men" in the ideological battle against communism was through grandiose displays of scientific advancement in the form of space exploration (Kennedy 1961).

More than ideological advantage, President Kennedy made the case for space in terms of global leadership. In a speech given at Rice University on September 12, 1962 titled "We Choose to Go to the Moon," President Kennedy said "no nation which expects to be the leader of other nations can expect to stay behind in this race for space." He continued, "...our leadership in science and industry, our hopes for peace and security ... require us to make this effort." In his speeches, particularly his 1963 speech to Congress proposing major education legislation, President Kennedy emphasized math and science education as key to national security and economic prosperity. In his words, education would give the U.S. the "skilled manpower and brain power to match the power of totalitarian discipline" (Kennedy 1963).

Kennedy began and Johnson finished a race to the moon that inspired Americans to pursue math and science. They also completely overhauled education policy, providing expanded educational opportunities for all Americans, and implemented civil rights legislation that ensured race would be less of a barrier to education than ever before. Finally, the passage of Hart Cellar Immigration and Naturalization Act of 1965 reduced restrictions on immigration for highly skilled workers, particularly those from developing countries in Asia, enabling easier entry into the U.S. (Kilty 2002). These legislative and political events of the 1960s were crucial for expanding the size and diversity of the STEM workforce in the U.S.

The gears set in motion in the 1960s were sustained into the 1970s as the Cold War continued and the Equal Employment Opportunity Act of 1972 strengthened Title VII of the Civil Rights Act. In 1980, President Carter signed the *National Science Foundation Authorization and Science and Technology Equal Opportunities Act*. This legislation was significant because it codified federal recognition of the need for diversity in the STEM workforce and set in motion long-term term federal investment in equal opportunity in science (Malcolm, Chubin, & Jesse 2004). The legislation has two parts, Part A, The National Science Foundation Authorization required the President "to give due regard to equitable representation of scientists who are women and who represent minority groups in making nominations for the National Science Board." Part B, the Women, Minorities, Science and Technology Equal Opportunities Act, declared it the policy of the United States that "men and women have equal opportunity in education, training, and employment in scientific and technical fields." It continues:

> It is in the national interest to promote the *full* use of human resources in science and engineering and to insure the *full* development and use of the scientific and engineering talents and skills of men and women, equally, of all ethnic, racial, and economic backgrounds.
>
> MALCOLM et al. 2004:10, emphasis added.

The Science and Technology Equal Opportunity Act authorized the National Science Foundation to engage in wide ranging activities to increase the participation of women and minorities in scientific and technical fields. The challenges facing women were seen as one of limited access to be addressed by (1) career encouragement, traineeship and fellowship opportunities for women; (2) elementary and secondary school outreach; (3) continuing education for women in the workforce; (4) research on women in science to facilitate participation and career advancement; (5) dissemination and public outreach about women in science; (6) and grants to women scientists and supporting institutions.

The challenges facing racial and ethnic minorities, however, were less clearly understood in comparison to the specificity of the directives aimed at women. One specific recommendation to address minority underrepresentation was to address their lack of preparation by supporting comprehensive science education programs. Another program sought to initiate research at minority serving institutions. Neither set of initiatives is specific to the experiences of women who are also racial/ethnic minorities. As the book *All of the Women Are White, All Blacks Are Men, But Some of Us Are Brave* illustrates, the tendency is often to pay scant attention to the specific concerns of minority women (Hull, Scott, Smith 1982). Their challenges are assumed to fall under the umbrella of women or racial/ethnic minorities but many federal directives miss the challenges driven by the intersection of race and gender (Branch 2011).

The Science and Technology Equal Opportunity (STEO) Act established within the National Science Foundation a Committee on Equal Opportunities in Science and Technology (CEOST), with two sub-committees; one to focus on women, the other to focus on minorities, again the issue of women of color was not specifically addressed. The STEO Act required the NSF director, with the assistance of CEOST, to prepare and submit to specified congressional committees a report proposing a comprehensive program to promote minority participation. In addition, it required the submission of annual reports to Congress concerning the participation and status of women in science and technology, including an accounting and comparison by sex, race, and ethnic group, and by discipline, of the participation of women and men in scientific and technical positions.

The emphasis on inclusion in STEM in the 1960s and 1970s followed a larger ideological and social shift toward social justice and decreasing inequality that defined the Civil Rights Era. When President Reagan was elected in 1980 his administration virtually stopped enforcing affirmative action legislation and, absent the federal imperative, desegregation in the labor market stalled and in some segments segregation began to increase (Branch 2011). More broadly, the 1980s marked a definite shift in the national climate regarding the importance of creating equal opportunity and affirmatively tackling the barriers to minority participation in science, although the focus on women remained, along with its inattention to racial/ethnic differences (Bruer 1984).

4   From Manufacturing to an Innovation Economy

When President Reagan took office in 1981 a series of reforms paved the way for the U.S. economy to shift from a focus on manufacturing to a focus on innovation. Increased federal funding for research and development (R&D) took some of the financial burden associated with innovation away from corporations and made public-private partnerships more attractive[2] (Cooper 2008, Keyworth 1984). Broader sweeping changes to patent law gave increased protection against copyright infringement, giving the United States considerable advantage in attracting corporations to locate high value intangible components of production[3] within their borders (Evans 2008; Cooper 2008).

These policy directions were a direct response to the economic shifts of the 1970s, when economic growth was stagnant, gas was scarce and expensive (as a result of the oil embargo) and manufacturing was in decline as global competition, particularly from Japan, increased (Cooper 2008). Japanese firms had the advantage of a much more flexible manufacturing model that proved more efficient than the American "Fordist" production model that dominated prior to the 1980s. In that model, factories would produce goods from start to finish on an assembly line, in the case of Ford it was a car. Workers at different positions on the line would assemble their part of the car until the whole car had been assembled.

The Japanese "post-Fordist" manufacturing model sub-divided production to maximize efficiency. Its success sparked a new normal where manufacturing became increasingly geographically based depending on the availability of low-wages and necessary skills as well as technology. Thus, one plant might build the engine, another the seat, while the design team and engineering was entirely decoupled. This new "post-Fordist" model allowed companies to locate components of production wherever they could employ workers with the necessary skills at the lowest cost (Gereffi 2005). It was under these conditions that Reagan pursued policies that would locate the high value added, intangible aspects of production in the U.S. and quietly permit the movement of low-skilled line manufacturing overseas (Cooper 2008). The decision to pursue

---

2   Particularly once the Bayh-Dole of 1980 act required universities to patent and commercialize federally funded inventions.
3   Particularly R&D and branding.

knowledge-based jobs and let the market take care of manufacturing effectively pushed the U.S. economy away from producing goods; scientific innovation was to replace manufacturing as the engine of the U.S. economy.

The 1960s and 1970s were decades of relative security for working class Americans who were able to enjoy stable employment in the booming manufacturing industry. Unionized manufacturing jobs were a means for low-skilled whites to attain middle-class stability and build wealth (Honey 2002; Oliver and Shapiro 2006). American Blacks were just gaining access to manufacturing jobs, but at the moment when it might have been possible for a larger proportion of Blacks to get ahead, the economy shifted. The move towards an innovation (knowledge-based) economy reflected the national level goals for the American workforce of the future. Indeed, since the early 1980s the U.S. has moved steadily towards knowledge-based jobs and away from production-based jobs (Branch 2011). In 1965, 27 percent of non-farm workers in the US were employed in manufacturing; by 2011 only 8.9 percent were employed in manufacturing (Bureau of Labor Statistics 2012).

Every American President since Reagan has placed their hopes for future economic prosperity squarely in knowledge-based work producing scientific and technical innovation, rather than in the efficient manufacture of goods the world wants to buy (Cooper 2008). While the relationship between science and the economy is not new it has a different quality now than it did in the past. From President Kennedy to President Carter there were multiple streams for economic growth. Producing scientific and technical innovation was important, especially when it enhanced manufacturing or allowed American factories to produce new goods and export them around the world, but it was not the primary means to a vibrant U.S. economy. Under Reagan, the connection between innovation and manufacturing weakened—American workers were now meant to produce ideas not products, and innovation itself became the primary path for economic growth and global leadership (Keyworth 1984; Cooper 2008).

5   Global Competition and America's Diversity Problem

Against the backdrop of the 2008 global financial crisis caused by the collapse of the mortgage backed securities market, President Obama argued that innovation and technological advancement would not only turn the US economy around, but also reassert the global leadership of the United States. One of the key features of contemporary federal initiatives targeted at increasing innovation is a focus on broadening the pool of scientists in the United States. The

National Science Foundation, a critical funding source for a wide variety of scientific research, currently operates 19 different programs specifically focused on broadening participation in science, and an additional 19 programs that emphasize broadening participation among several goals. Expanding the pool of science workers includes efforts such as ADVANCE, which targets women, the Louis Stokes Alliance for Minority Participation, which provides support for students from underrepresented racial and ethnic groups, and changes to immigration policy that allow for more H-1B visas and longer stays for foreign born scientists and engineers. Millions of dollars in federal funding are being spent to increase the numbers of scientists from historically disadvantaged groups, not to mention substantial private investment. Increasing the size and diversity of the US science workforce is a national economic goal.

Despite these substantial investments, diverse constituencies are sounding the alarm of a quiet crisis. Norman Augustine, Retired Chairman and Chief Executive Officer of Lockheed Martin Corporation, wrote in a *Washington Post* op-ed titled "Learning to Lose? Our Education System Isn't Ready for a World of Competition":

> In the five decades since I began working in the aerospace industry, I have never seen American business and academic leaders as concerned about this nation's future prosperity as they are today... The scientific and technological foundations of our economic leadership are eroding at a time when other nations are building their innovative capacity. (December 6, 2005)

In a 2006 speech to the U.S. Securities and Exchange Commission (SEC) titled, "The Converging Forces of the Quiet Crisis," Shirley Ann Jackson, President of Rensselaer Polytechnic Institute, warned of a critical labor shortage in U.S. STEM fields driven by three factors: (1) global competition and tighter restrictions that have reduced the in-flow of scientists and engineers from around the world; (2) an insufficient scientific pipeline in the U.S. that is not producing enough new talent to replace the retiring generation; (3) a shift in U.S. demographics to include larger numbers of women and minorities whose participation in science and engineering has historically been quite low (Jackson 2006).

This reality coupled with growing concern over the "giants" of the world—China and India (which compose 40 percent of the world's population)—is driving fears about America's economic and political standing (Council on Competitiveness, 2005; National Research Council 2007, 2010). For decades, the answer to maintaining American international dominance through rapidly changing times was to be at the forefront in the areas of science and technology—to continue to be the world innovation leader. In making the case for substantial national investment in the race for space President Kennedy used exactly these terms:

> Those who came before us made certain that this country rode the first waves of the industrial revolutions, the first waves of modern invention, and the first wave of nuclear power, and this generation does not intend to founder in the backwash of the coming age of space. We mean to be a part of it–we mean to lead it.
>
> KENNEDY, 1962

Yet, threats to American leadership in innovation abound. The *Rising Above the Gathering Storm* (2007 and 2010) reports raise several concerns: (1) the increasing investment in science education by the developing world, particularly China, India and the Middle East, (2) lack of investment in science education and research by the U.S. government, and (3) increasing desirability of the developing world for top science talent. Solutions to solve these problems include proposals to better fund research and development, more incentives for business, changes to immigration laws to make it easier and more desirable for science/technology professionals and students from abroad to come to the U.S. and stay here, and finally expanding the pool of domestic science/technology workers to include more women and minorities by increasing the quality of K-12 science and math education. The fear of being outpaced in science education by countries that were not considered a real threat is now pushing U.S. education, science research, and immigration policies at the highest level. In the past, the U.S. was able to rely on the relative strength of its economy to attract talent from around the globe. The new threats to U.S. economic dominance require a renewed focus on training U.S. born racial and ethnic minorities in STEM fields in order to avert the looming crisis.

6   Episodic Focus versus Long-term Commitment

In 2016, why has the inclusion of historically underrepresented groups been so incremental? Despite the near feverish pitch of calls for inclusion to pursue innovation, American investment in equal opportunity has been episodic and driven by economic threat and international competition. Not all Americans are poised to succeed in, or contribute to, the innovation economy and they never have been. The push for math and science education in the 1960s was for every citizen to reach his or her full potential so the nation could literally shoot for the moon. We reached the moon but did not ensure that all citizens could reach their potential. The "end of the decade" deadline Kennedy set meant that its achievement could not rely on developing a pipeline of national talent to fuel the STEM workforce. Instead, the policy solution included short-term and long-term fixes. In the short term, increase the flow of highly skilled immigrants and long-term, educate a broader swath of Americans for STEM jobs. We as a society have not yet succeeded in our long-term mission.

Once we completed our goal (successfully launching a man into space and sending him to the moon) and reestablished our position as a world leader, our motivation to continue on a path of national educational uplift diminished. We were lulled again into a place of complacency regarding the need for continued progress and the incorporation of *all* U.S. talent. We maintained a verbal commitment to access and actively pursued an innovation economy but we did not address systemic inequities in the educational preparation of minorities for careers in science.

Every President since Kennedy has argued for an investment in our nation's economic future through the pursuit of innovation and education of our youth. In his 1983 State of the Union Address, President Reagan said, "We Americans are still the technological leaders in most fields. We must keep that edge, and to do so we need to begin renewing the basics—starting with our educational system." Similarly, President Bush in his 2006 State of the Union Address said:

> We must continue to lead the world in human talent and creativity. Our greatest advantage in the world has always been our educated, hardworking, ambitious people. And we're going to keep that edge. Tonight I announce an American Competitiveness Initiative, to encourage innovation throughout our economy and to give our nation's children a firm grounding in math and science.

Even President Obama who is politically far apart from Bush and Reagan sounds strikingly similar in his call for the U.S. to lead the global economy through innovation fueled by education. President Obama's proposed 2012 budget was described as targeting federal funds "to areas critical to winning the future: education, innovation, clean energy, and infrastructure" (White House, 2011).

There is a clear precedent for responding to national challenges through education. On September 2, 1958, President Eisenhower signed the National Defense Education Act (NDEA), a piece of legislation that directly responded to the fear that the Soviet Union was ahead in the race for space. The impact of NDEA was transformational:

> ...Federal expenditures for education more than doubled. In higher education, this included funding for federal student loan programs, graduate fellowships in the sciences and engineering, institutional aid for teacher education, funding for capital construction and a surge of funds for curriculum development in the sciences, math and foreign languages.
>
> Council on Competitiveness 2005: 50

However, it also cemented the idea of who was fit to do this work. This critical period of investment and definition took place at a time when minorities and white women where informally and at times legally excluded from many jobs and research universities that were the gatekeepers for entry into science and technology careers.

Currently, amid urgent calls for investment in education and innovation to build our national talent pool, we are arguably recovering, albeit slowly, from the worst educational crisis of our time. School funding from elementary to post-secondary schools has not recovered from the all-time lows that resulted from massive budget cuts instituted as states and municipalities reeled from the Great Recession. Charles Blow of the *New York Times* referred to the sheer scope of the current crisis in education as creating a generation of "lost children," i.e. those for whom the recession and subsequent cuts in education will cost their future careers (Blow 2011). How can we as a nation aspire to include and inspire the "new majority" while simultaneously abdicating our responsibility to provide them with a basic education? Teacher layoffs, class overcrowding, school closure, and building decay are happening alongside the 4.35 billion dollar federal investment in the Race to the Top, a United States Department of Education competitive grant created to spur and reward innovation and reforms in state and local K-12 education. While these funds are targeted in part to turn around low-achieving schools, they address only a fraction of school-side factors, such as teachers and test scores, and ignore the structural inequalities, such as infrastructure, inadequate facilities, and entrenched poverty, that are drivers of underperformance (Kozol 2012). We are ensuring that only those that have the private capacity to educate or an extraordinary will to persist against the odds are present at the table to pursue innovation.

Twenty-seven years ago the American Council on Education released the acclaimed report, *One Third of a Nation: Minorities in the United States.* Foremost among its findings were extensive details depicting the glaring inequities in the level of educational attainment for minority groups in the U.S. (1988). It was clear then, as it is now, that one of the chief obstacles to achieving greater numbers of minorities in STEM disciplines was inadequate preparation at the K-12 level. The American Council of Education recommended the nation adopt a comprehensive plan designed to enhance diversity in the pipeline. The key element of their plan was based on raising the educational attainment levels for members of underrepresented groups by engaging and supporting them in earlier stages of their academic development. Ironically, now, many years later, these same points are being vehemently articulated in the current discussions and debates aimed at improving the STEM discipline pipelines. Pnina G. Abir-Am (1990) noted in the late 1980s that "the economic and political costs of women's exclusion from science are rapidly becoming higher than the social cost of supporting their full participation." Her comments are equally applicable to women and students of color now.

The September 2000 report, *Land of Plenty: Diversity as America's Competitive Edge in Science, Engineering and Technology*, by the Congressional Commission on the Advancement of Women and Minorities in Science, Engineering, and Technology Development reported that "if women, underrepresented minorities, and persons with disabilities were represented in the U.S. science, engineering, and technology workforce population, this shortage [of skilled American workers] could largely be ameliorated" (2000:1).

The Commission examined the barriers that exist for women, underrepresented minorities, and persons with disabilities at different points of the science, engineering, and technology (SET) pipeline, and identified 5 problems: Precollege Education, Access to Higher Education, Professional Life, Public Image, and Nationwide Accountability. The problem of nationwide accountability, they argue, is one of episodic focus rather than long-term commitment:

> The lack of diversity in SET education and careers is an old dilemma, but economic necessity and workforce deficiencies bring a new urgency to the nation's strategic need to achieve parity in its SET workforce. Real progress demands a system of accountability so that the Commission's objectives can be met in a timely, effective manner.
>
> Land of Plenty, 2000

These persistent problems point to the importance of diversity beyond the maintenance of America's intellectual edge, and as a fundamental social justice aim. Shirley Ann Jackson, President of Rensselaer Polytechnic Institute, concluded in her speech to the SEC that, "Innovation, and the development and exploitation of new technologies require people—bright, talented, inspired, engaged, highly educated people—who, of necessity, must be drawn from the complete talent pool—including from our 'new majority.'" She continued, "This means that we MUST ... [make] sure that the entire new majority is educated, prepared for advanced scholarship, encouraged, and mentored." President Bush summarized it best saying, "If we ensure that America's children succeed in life, they will ensure that America succeeds in the world" (State of the Union Address 2006).

The post-9/11 immigration restriction and subsequent drop in international student enrollment created a peculiar moment wherein the societal imperative of equal opportunity for all, dovetailed with the economic imperative of maintaining America's global competitiveness via leading innovation. The heightened cries for a diverse technical workforce paralleled these international developments as the awareness of the need for incorporating *all* of America's talents became increasingly urgent for the maintenance of our global position. This rare moment of cross-institutional prerogatives and cooperation has focused national attention on expanding opportunities for, and removing barriers to the incorporation of historically underrepresented groups in STEM fields.

7   The Need for Diversity

Diversifying science has proven to be an ephemeral ambition. Some have argued that the need for special programs no longer exists due to the increasing numbers of members of historically disadvantaged groups in STEM fields. However, recent reports on the current state of diversity within the academy contradict this belief and show that "educational preparation and opportunity are not yet evenly distributed by race, ethnicity, gender, and geography" (Malcolm et al. 2004: 2; Herzig 2004; Jackson 2004; Woodrow Wilson National Fellowship Foundation 2005).

Underlying these differing perceptions of the state of diversity in the academy are differing notions of the aims of diversity. Some argue that the goal of fostering diversity has been reached when the numbers of women and students of color steadily increase over time. This can be inferred to be the position of those who argue against continuing outreach to women and underrepresented minority men and women. However, others argue that diversity goals will not be reached until the numbers of white women and students of color steadily increase to reach their proportions in the population at large, *full participation*. In this view, a 263 percent and 400 percent increase in the number of engineering Ph.D.s granted to African-Americans and Hispanics, respectively, from 1983 to 2003, is impressive and furthers the goal of fostering diversity (Woodrow Wilson National Fellowship Foundation 2005:15). Yet, their proportional representation in all Ph.D.s awarded, 3.7 percent and 4.9 percent, respectively, falls far short of their representation in the population and undergirds the argument that they have yet to reach *full* participation in the field of engineering.

Despite attacks on this broader view of diversity, evident in lawsuits against race targeted programs, the United States Supreme Court ruling on June 23, 2003, in *Grutter v. Bollinger* and *Gratz v. Bollinger,* "sanctioned what has been known for decades in higher education ... diversity can be an essential component of excellence in education" (Malcolm et al. 2004:9). Their decision granted constitutional legitimacy to institutions that want to continue to diversify their faculty and student body. Although the numbers of white women and underrepresented minorities have increased dramatically in recent years, "changing demographic patterns and national priorities demand that America *fully* utilize its greatest resource—its citizenry" (Malcolm et al. 2004:9, emphasis added).

White students were three times more likely than a student of color to earn a doctorate in 2003, thus "while the next generation of college students will include dramatically more students of color, their teachers will remain overwhelming white" (Woodrow Wilson National Fellowship Foundation 2005: 7). While higher education has made substantial efforts to diversify the doctorate, "the fact remains that doctoral programs have made significantly less progress in diversifying than have business and government, or for that matter other levels of the educational system" (Woodrow Wilson National Fellowship Foundation 2005:7).

In 2003, 14,300 international students earned U.S. doctorates whereas U.S. citizens who are African American and Hispanic earned approximately 3,000, merely one-fifth of the degrees awarded to citizens of other nations. Robert Weisbuch, President of the Woodrow Wilson National Fellowship Foundation, notes that "educating the world's students while neglecting significant groups of the national population is a vast inequality at the highest academic level" (Woodrow Wilson National Fellowship Foundation 2005: 8).

8   Conclusion

America is at an important crossroad for deciding if its commitment to diversity is an episodic economic imperative or a societal aim of full participation. The road we choose will have important implications for the opportunities that are ahead for the next generation of workers. International trade agreements and state level labor laws make it unlikely that the kind of manufacturing that fueled the U.S. economy in the early and mid-20th century will return. Manufacturing increasingly seeks cheap labor and has moved to places where labor costs are lower to maximize profit. The manufacturing jobs that remain require workers to have specialized technical skills. This reality is restructuring what it means to live and work in the U.S.

Despite the numerous pleas of politicians, pundits and workers to bring manufacturing jobs back to the U.S., this is not the direction that today's highly mobile corporations are likely to take or the path our economic policy encourages. Even if manufacturing jobs did return to the U.S., they are likely to require more highly specialized skills than the manufacturing jobs of the past. The new ideal U.S. worker is one with at least a college education who produces knowledge or innovation rather than tangible goods. Unfortunately, the path into knowledge production jobs is not available to all. Diversifying science matters because it is the economic engine of the future. Unless we are deliberate in ensuring sustained access there will be an escalator for some and a concrete roadblock for others.

Americans of color remain starkly underrepresented, and white women are underrepresented, in many fields. The influx of immigrant labor to fill these jobs shines a light on our continued failure to educate *all* Americans. While Title VII of the Civil Rights Act of 1964 may have formally opened the door to the innovation economy, these jobs still required access to higher education that many men and women of color had been denied through legal segregation for those of working age in the 1960s and through subtler means thereafter. Hence, the promise of equal opportunity, particularly for education and employment, was not fully realized as the science and technology workforce grew. As Tomaskovic-Devey and Stainback (2007) argue, white women were the biggest winners of the civil rights movement. Professional careers in science and technology remain out of reach for many men and women of color, particularly for those educated in America's most underserved schools where students are more likely to go to prison than college. Policy at the national level looks to a larger and more diverse pool of scientists to renew the economy through innovation, without addressing the complex and intersecting factors that shape the demographics of the scientific workforce, such as the quality of K-12 education and the cultural orientations of fields (Branch and Alegria, forthcoming).

Ethno-racial and gender equity is critical at the moment, not just because it addresses a societal imperative for social justice, but also because it helps solve an impending economic problem. Policy makers, educators, and corporate leaders are calling for broader participation in science and technology by evoking fears of future economic decline. Ensuring the economic dominance of the U.S. economy requires increasing innovation, by incubating talent at universities that will fuel the profit-making capacity of companies who drive the economic growth of the nation. The social justice slant to these programs is fueled by market logic, yet discrimination and unequal preparation keep talented people from pursuing the most profitable careers.

Investments in STEM education for historically underrepresented groups have been episodic and have not produced the long-term, sustained focus that real change will require. While lasting change has thus far been illusory, we are optimistic that the economic imperative underlying the current calls for broadening participation may have the side effect of furthering the social justice goals of decreasing racial/ethnic inequality in STEM fields. Although the calls for diversity are not actually about social justice, maybe global competition and fears of future economic decline are what it will take for the focus on diversity to be sustained. America's national economic ambition may finally facilitate the transformational social justice goal of removing barriers to access and entry in scientific careers. How we as a nation proceed from this point will be a testament to our commitment to the inclusion of historically underrepresented groups or our continued episodic focus on diversity as means to maintain world position.

References

Abir-Am, Pnina G. 1990. "Science policy or social policy for women in science?: Lessons from historical case studies." *AWIS Newsletter* 19: 12.

Alegria, Sharla and Enobong Hannah Branch. Forthcoming. "Causes and Consequences of Inequality in the STEM: Diversity and its Discontents." *International Journal of Gender, Science, and Technology.*

Augustine, Norman. 2005. "Learning to Lose? Our Education System Isn't Ready for a World of Competition," *Washington Post,* December 6. Accessed February 17, 2012: http://www.washingtonpost.com/wp-dyn/content/article/2005/12/05/AR2005 120501548.html.

Blow, Charles. 2011. "The Decade of Lost Children." *New York Times*, August 5. Accessed on February 22, 2012: http://www.nytimes.com/2011/08/06/opinion/the-decade-of-lost-children.html?_r=0.

Branch, Enobong Hannah. 2011. *Opportunity Denied: Limiting Black Women to Devalued Work.* New Brunswick, N.J.: Rutgers University Press.

Bruer, John T. 1984. "Women in science: Toward equitable participation." *Science*, 9: 3–7.

Bureau of Labor Statistics. 2012. "Industries at a Glance: Manufacturing." Accessed February 22, 2012: http://www.bls.gov/iag/tgs/iag31-33.htm.

Bush, George W. 2006. "President Bush's State of the Union Address." *Washington Post,* January 31. Accessed February 9, 2012: http://www.washingtonpost.com/wp-dyn/content/article/2006/01/31/AR2006013101468.html.

Commission on Minority Participation in Education in American Life. 1988. *One Third of a Nation.* American Council on Education. Accessed on February 19, 2012: http://files.eric.ed.gov/fulltext/ED297057.pdf.

Congressional Commission on the Advancement of Women and Minorities in Science, Engineering, and Technology Development. 2000. *Land of Plenty: Diversity as America's Competitive Edge in Science, Engineering and Technology.* Accessed on February 19, 2012: http://www.nsf.gov/pubs/2000/cawmset0409/cawmset_0409.pdf.

Cooper, Melinda. 2008. *Life as Surplus: Biotechnology and Capitalism in the Neoliberal Era.* Seattle, WA: University of Washington Press.

Council on Competitiveness. 2005. *Innovate America.* Washington, D.C. Accessed on February 22, 2012: http://www.compete.org/storage/images/uploads/File/PDF%20Files/NII_Innovate_America.pdf.

Evans, Peter. 2008. "Is an Alternative Globalization Possible?" *Politics and Society* 32: 271–305.

Favell, Adrian, Mirian Feldblum, and Michael Peter Smith. 2007. "The Human Face of Global Mobility: A Research Agenda." *Society,* 44: 15–25.

Gereffi, Gary. 2005. "The Global Economy: Organization, Governance, and Development." In *Handbook of Economic Sociology,* by Neil J. Smelser and Richard Swedberg. Princeton, NJ: Princeton University Press.

Government Accountability Office (GAO). 2011. "H-1B VISA PROGRAM: Reforms Are Needed to Minimize the Risks and Costs of Current Program." Accessed February 19, 2012: http://www.gao.gov/assets/320/314501.pdf.

Herzig, Abbe H. 2004. "Becoming Mathematicians: Women and Students of Color Choosing and Leaving Doctoral Mathematics." *Review of Educational Research.* 74: 171–214.

Holdren, John P. and Eric Lander. 2012. "Report to the President—Engage to excel: Producing one million additional college graduates with degrees in science, technology, engineering, and mathematics." *President's Council of Advisors on Science and Technology.* Accessed February 22, 2012: https://www.whitehouse.gov/sites/default/files/microsites/ostp/pcast-engage-to-excel-final_feb.pdf.

Honey, Michael Keith. 2002. *Black Workers Remember: An Oral History of Segregation, Unionism, and the Freedom Struggle.* Berkeley, CA: University of California Press.

Hull, Gloria T., Patricia Bell Scott, and Barbara Smith (eds.). 1982. *All of the Women Are White, All Blacks Are Men, But Some of Us Are Brave.* Old Westbury, NY: The Feminist Press.

Jackson, Judy. 2004. "The Story Is Not in the Numbers: Academic Socialization and Diversifying the Faculty." *NWSA Journal 16*: 172–186.

Jackson, Shirley A. 2002. *"The Quiet Crisis: Falling Short in Producing American Scientific and Technological Talent,"* Building Engineering & Science (BEST) Conference. Accessed on February 9, 2012: http://www.bestworkforce.org/PDFdocs/Quiet_Crisis .pdf.

Jackson, Shirley A. 2006. "The Converging Forces of the Quiet Crisis." U.S. Securities and Exchange Commission (SEC) African American Council, February 7. Accessed on February 9, 2012. https://www.rpi.edu/president/speeches/ps020706-sec .html.

Kennedy, John F. 1961. "The Goal of Sending a Man to the Moon." Joint Session of Congress, May 25. Accessed on February 17, 2012: http://millercenter.org/president/ speeches/speech-3368.

Kennedy, John F. 1962. "We Choose to Go to the Moon," Rice University, September 12. Accessed on February 17, 2012: http://er.jsc.nasa.gov/seh/ricetalk.htm.

Kennedy, John F. 1963. "Special Message to the Congress on Education." Joint Session of Congress, January 29. Accessed on February 17, 2012: http://www.presidency.ucsb .edu/ws/?pid=9487.

Keyworth, George A. 1984. "Four Years of Reagan Science Policy: Notable Shifts in Priority." *Science*, 224: 9–13.

Kilty, Keith M. 2002. "Race, Immigration, and Public Policy: The Case of Asian Americans." *Journal of Poverty*, 6: 23–41.

Kozol, Jonathan. 2012. *Savage Inequalities: Children in American Schools.* New York, NY: Broadway Books.

Malcom, Shirley M., Daryl E. Chubin, and Jolene K. Jesse. 2004. *Standing Our Ground: A Guidebook for STEM Educators in the Post-Michigan era.* Washington, DC: American Association for the Advancement of Science, 2004. Accessed on February 2, 2012: http://www.aaas.org/report/standing-our-ground.

National Research Council. 2007. *Rising Above the Gathering Storm: Energizing and Employing America for a Brighter Economic Future.* Washington, DC: The National Academies Press. Accessed on February 19, 2012: http://www.nap.edu/openbook .php?record_id=11463.

National Research Council. 2010. *Rising Above the Gathering Storm, Revisited: Rapidly Approaching Category 5.* Washington, DC: The National Academies Press. Accessed on February 19, 2012: http://www.nap.edu/openbook.php?record_id=12999.

Obama, Barack. 2011. "The 2012 Budget." White House, February 14. Accessed on February 19, 2012: https://www.whitehouse.gov/blog/2011/02/14/2012-budget.

Oliver, Melvin L., and Thomas M. Shapiro. 2006. *Black Wealth, White Wealth: A New Perspective on Racial Inequality.* London: Routledge.

Regets, Mark C. 2007. "Research Issues in the International Migration of Highly Skilled Workers: A Perspective with Data from the United States." Working Paper, Science Resource Statistics, National Science Foundation. Accessed on February 22, 2012: http://www.nsf.gov/statistics/srs07203/pdf/srs07203.pdf.

Schumer, Charles E. and Lindsey O. Graham. 2010. "The Right Way to Mend Immigration." *The Washington Post,* March 19. Accessed on February 22, 2012: http://www.washingtonpost.com/wp-dyn/content/article/2010/03/17/AR2010031703115.html.

Tomaskovic-Devey, Donald and Kevin Stainback. 2007. "Descrimination and Desegregation: Equal Opportunity Progress in US Private Sector Workplaces Since the Civil Rights Act." *Annals of American Academy of Political and Social Science* 699: 49–84.

The Woodrow Wilson National Fellowship Foundation. 2005. *Diversity & the Ph.D.: A Review of Efforts to Broaden Race & Ethnicity in US Doctoral Education.* Accessed on November 16, 2007: http://www.woodrow.org/wp/wp-content/uploads/2013/06/WW_Diversity_PhD_web.pdf.

PART 5

Diversity and Communities

∵

Diversity in the Church: A Comparative Analysis of Multiracial, White, and Black Congregations

Michelle S. Dodson

1 Introduction[1]

In the introduction to what he calls a "spiritual" biography of W.E.B. Du Bois, Edward Blum asserts that segregation in religious organization was particularly abhorrent to Du Bois because "it legitimated racial division by strengthening the conflation of whiteness with godliness" (Blum, 2007). In light of this Du Bois would likely have found great encouragement in the burgeoning movement toward racially diverse congregations in this country over the last few decades. While the percentage of multiracial congregations in the United States is relatively small there is evidence to suggest that they are growing.

In 1998 the percentage of multiracial congregations in the Unites States was 7.4 (based on data from the 1998 National Congregations Survey). The most recent data from the 2010 Faith Communities Survey indicates that that percentage has almost doubled to 13.7. Out of context this percentage sounds small. However, the number of congregations in this country is greater than the total number of "Subways, McDonalds, Burger Kings, Wendy's, Starbucks, Pizza Huts, KFCs, Taco Bells, Domino's Pizzas, Dunkin Donuts, Quiznos and Dairy Queens combined *and multiplied by three*" (Edwards et al., 2013: 212 emphasis added). Thus, numerically multiracial congregations represent a significant portion of American voluntry organizations on the whole. This fact alone makes them worthy of study. However, and more importantly, beyond the sheer number of them, multiracial congregations represent the intersection of two pillars of American society: religion and race.

---

1 A Note on grammar: I capitalize the term Black when referring to a racial group. Unlike most white Americans, most African-Americans who are descended from slaves do not have the option of drawing on a more specific ethnic identifier—symbolic or otherwise (see Waters 1990 for a discussion of symbolic ethnicity)—because most of us have no way of retracing our ethnic heritages apart from a general understanding that we originated from the continent of Africa. In light of this the term Black is deeply tied to the identity of a people in ways that the term white is not. My choice not to capitalize white is simply in keeping with the rules of grammar.

American life is highly segregated. Where one lives, works and attends school is often greatly constrained by both race and class. However, while those factors may constrain where one is able to worship it is to a much lesser degree; congregations are open to people regardless of race or class. Despite this, religious organizations continue to be highly segragated, which speaks to the power of race (and class) as an organizing principle in American life and makes the 13.7 percent of congregations that have "bucked this trend" particularly interesting sites of study.

Critically, even racially and ethnically integrated congregations cannot be declared a victory for racial justice. Du Bois was one of the first to argue that segregation in religious organizations serves to further conflate whitness with godliness. I argue that an integrated collection of multi-colored bodies does little to rectify this. While the growth of multiracial congregations may be a cause for celebration it is still not clear whether or not these organizations challenge or maintain the racial hierarchy. Understanding to what extent they do or do not truly buck the trend of white supremacy (and how) may yield invaluable information about the mechanisms and processes invloved in dismanteling racism (See Hughey et al. 2015). Such an understanding may further shed light on the incideousness of institutional racism and the ways that it is supported at the macro, mezo and micro levels.

One enduring affect of white supremacy is the division between Blacks and whites in this country. While the racial landscape has dramatically changed, the Black/white paradigm continues to be a powerful and enduring framework (Wu 2002). Blacks have historically been (and remain) the most highly racially segregated group in this country (Massey and Denton 1993), and this division is prevalent in our congregations. In general, African-Americans and whites are less willing than other racial/ethnic groups to let go of certain aspect of their cultural expressions of Christianity and embrace other expressions (Emerson 2000). Emerson (2000) argues that America has two indigenous cultures, white and Black; he states:

> ...white U.S. culture is no more American than black U.S. culture. Both have been present since the nation's founding. Both have contributed immeasurably to the nation's development. Both have developed unique religious cultures. And both share and contribute to the American political, educational, economic and entrainment systems. To whatever extent there is a single overarching American culture, it is as scholar Cornel West and others have said, the blending of Black and white cultural aspects (137).

These two indigenous cultures were born at the same time and were formed in opposition to each other (Emerson, 2006; Warren and Twine, 1997).

While persons immigrating to the U.S. expect to lose some of their cultural expressions and to embrace some form of Americanism, for African-Americans and whites embracing one is seen as a renouncement of the other (Emerson 2006). Thus, Emerson (2006) argues that multiracial churches typically have a dominant worship expression that is rooted in one of the indigenous cultures, and are typically comprised of either African-Americans and one or more other racial/ethnic group(s) or whites and one or more other racial/ethnic group(s).

In light of this, one sign that a multiracial church may be resisting the status quo is the degree to which they are able to attract African-American congregants. The aim of this project is to gain a better understanding of Black participation in racially diverse churches. Specifically, this paper examins what factors predict whether a multiracial church will have high percentages of Black congregants.

Much of the current research on racially diverse churches has found that it is difficult to attract and retain African-American congregants when the congregation is predominantly non-Black. Sociologists have speculated that this may be due in part to worship style preferences (Martin 2005) or larger cultural preferences (Emerson 2006 Edwards 2008). However, some scholars acknowledge that there is a need for more research in this area.

I began this research with the assumption that racially diverse churches that directly addressed race would have higher percentages of African-American congregants than those that did not. Based on this assumption I have identified three key factors that I hypothesize will positively predict Black participation in such churches: the race of the clergy, whether or not the church is politically engaged and whether or not the church sponsors race conscious programming.

2   Historical Context

Churches have historically been one of the most segregated voluntary associations in the United States (Kathleen Garces-Foley forthcoming; Emerson 2006; Christerson et al. 2005; Emerson and Smith 2000). However, throughout the history of the church there have been small movements to integrate. The most notable example is the birth of the Pentecostal movement in the United States. Led by William Seymour, an African- American man, the Azusa Street revival that began in Los Angeles, CA in April 1906 was one of the first and certainly the largest integrated religious movements in this country at that time (Creech 1996). However, such movements were typically short lived. In the case of the Azusa Street revival, the movement eventually split into a number of racially segregated denominations (e.g. The Church of God (white) and the Church of God in Christ (Black)).

After the Civil Rights movement there was a resurgence of this push toward integration within Evangelical churches (Garces-Foley 2007; Emerson and Smith 2000, DeYong, et al. 2004, Edwards et al. 2013). Racial reconciliation became the new trend. A number of conferences, books, bible studies and study guides surfaced all aimed at promoting racial reconciliation (see Emerson and Smith 2000, Edwards et al. 2013). During this time the Southern Baptist denomination issued a formal apology for not condemning slavery and for its inaction during the Civil Rights movement (Emerson and Smith 2000).

This move toward racial reconciliation reflected what was happening in the larger society. By the late 1980's the immigration boom that resulted from the Immigration Act of 1965 had significantly changed the face of America (Garces-Foley, 2007). Whites were becoming increasingly more accepting of integration and all of this was reflected in the racial reconciliation movement within the evangelical church, which continues to the present. Whereas much of the literature on American churches in the past focused on ethnic churches (e.g. the Black Church, and immigrant churches), over the last decade social scientists have begun to examine this relatively new trend toward integrated churches.

3   Framing the Discussion

In my analysis, I place multiracial churches in two categories, those in which racial/ethnic diversity is explicitly addressed in the life of the church, often being built into the very mission of the church (Emerson and Kim, 2003), and those in which racial and ethnic diversity is celebrated but where issues of race are not explicitly addressed (Garces-Foley 2007; Marti 2008, 2009, 2010). The first type I refer to as race-conscious multiracial churches; the second type I label race-blind multiracial churches.

The literature on multiracial congregations can be organized under two dominant perspectives: that of racial transcendence and race consciousness (Edwards et al. 2013). The most dominant perspective is that of racial transcendence. Most scholars on multiracial congregations have argued that one way these congregations sustain racial diversity is by utilizing a color-blind, or racial transcendent, approach (Edwards et al. 2013).

What has been observed in the studies that fall under this perspective is that congregations that utilize this strategy (race-blind congregations) tend to deemphasize race, focusing instead on uniting people around other areas of interest such as art and music (Becker 1998; Jenkins 2003; Marti 2008, 2010). Marti (2005) refers to these congregations as "havens of inclusion." While these congregations often celebrate being racially diverse, they tend to shy away from direct conversations about race (Marti 2005, 2008, 2009, 2010; Garces-Foley 2007). Directly engaging in discussions about race is seen as divisive (Marti 2005) and therefore unchristian (Christerson et al, 2005; Emerson and Smith, 2000; Edwards 2008).

Another characteristic of these congregations is that, while racially diverse, they tend to be monocultural, most often organized around white evangelical cultural norms (Garces-Foley 2007; Christerson and Emerson, 2003; Edwards 2008a, 2008b) even when whites are not the dominant race (Edwards 2008a). However, it should be noted that most of the research on multiracial congregations has been based on studies of predominantly white protestant churches, which may partially help explain this finding. There are several notable exceptions. For example, Garces-Foley (2007) and Christerson and Emerson (2003), studied predominantly Asian congregations and Edwards' (2008a) work included a case study on a predominantly Black multiracial congregation.

The second organizing perspective is that of race-consciousness. Rather than looking for the ways that race is transcended this perspective emphasizes the ways people make sense of their (and others) racial and ethnic identities (Garces- Foley 2007, Christerson et al. 2005; Emerson 2006). Notable studies that fall under this perspective have measured the racial attitudes of people who attend multiracial congregations (Yancey 1999, 2001, Emerson 2006; Daugherty and Huyser 2008) or have directly challenged the notions of colorblindness present in much of the literature (Edwards 2008a, 2008b; Pitt 2010).

As for the congregations themselves, based on the literature, those that directly engage race are less common. However, findings suggest that in such congregations, directly addressing racial inequality and/or racial reconciliation is seen as being an essential component in living out the mission of the church (Emerson and Kim 2003; DeYoung et al. 2004; Christerson et al. 2005; Daugherty and Huyser 2008).

In general, multiracial congregations tend to be younger both in terms of the average age of congregants and the average age of the organizations (Dougherty and Huyser 2008, Emerson and Kim 2003, Emerson 2006, Edwards et al. 2013).

They also tend to be comprised of highly educated members (Edwards et al. 2013) as compared to their monoracial counterparts.

Most of the studies thus far in this field have been primarily qualitative and geared towards describing multiracial congregations (and their congregants) rather than theorizing broadly about the implications of such organizations for the larger racial structure (Edwards et al. 2013). Such studies have been tremendously useful in laying the groundwork for further study, but as Edwards et al. (2013) argues what is lacking is connecting this budding field to the larger body of sociological inquiry.

4   Methods

Given the scarcity of Black people in predominantly white multiracial congregations the guiding question of this work is: what contributing factors lead to a predominantly white church having higher numbers of African-American congregants? I have four hypotheses. First, I hypothesize that multiracial churches are more like white churches than they are like Black churches. My second hypothesis is that Blacks are more likely to attend race-conscious multiracial churches than race-blind. In this study race-consciousness is operationalized as a church having race-conscious programming. Thus, my hypothesis is that among multiracial churches, having race-conscious programming is the most important variable for attracting and retaining Black congregants. My third and fourth hypotheses are that having a Black pastor and expressive worship will both be significant factors in predicting Black participation in multiracial churches respectively.

To answer my research question I used data from Wave I of the National Congregation Survey. There are three waves of this survey. The first conducted in 1998, the second 06–07 and the most recent in '12 (the first articles about this study appears in the December 2014 edition of the Journal for the Scientific Study of Religion (JSRR)). The first wave of the study is the only wave in which a specific question about race relevant programming was asked which is why I have chosen to use this data set.

Data for Wave I were collected from a nationally representative sample of 1236 congregations from all over the United States. The primary method of data collection was interviews conducted with key informants (often the clergy) from the 1236 congregations in the sample. Of these interviews 92% were conducted over the phone with the remaining 8% conducted face-to-face.

I use a subsample of 489 churches to address my hypothesis in this paper. To derive my sub-sample I excluded churches whose majority racial group constituted between ninety-nine and eighty-one percent. I end up with a sample of churches that fit one of three categories: (1) those that are one hundred percent Black (n = 64); (2) churches that are one hundred percent White (n = 234); and (3) churches that are multiracial (n = 191). I define multicultural churches similar to Michael Emersons 80:20 ratio. Emerson asserts that congregations can be classified as multiracial when no more than 80 percent of its congregants are of the same race. In other words a church can be classified as multiracial if no less than twenty percent of the congregation is racially different than the majority group. This ratio is not random; it is grounded in research that shows that twenty percent "constitutes the point of critical mass. At this percentage, the proportion is high enough to have its presence felt and filtered throughout the system" (Emerson 2006 p. 35).

I begin my analysis with a description of how multiracial churches differ from Black and White churches in a number of substantive ways. To test my hypothesis that multiracial churches are more like White churches than they are Black churches I perform both Chi Square and ANOVA tests. In this section what is evident is that in most ways multiracial churches tend to look more like White churches in terms of the structure of Sunday worship services, the types of programming/ministries that are implemented, political involvement and other characteristics.

I then present a regression model that includes a series of variables to assess the degree to which variation in Black participation in multiracial churches can be predicted by (1) the race of the clergy, (2) style of worship and finally, (3) whether race-conscious programming is offered.

4.1   Measurement of the Dependent Variable

Percentage of African-Americans in the Congregation—The percentage of African-Americans in the congregation was determined by asking the informant "What percent of the regular adult participants in your congregation are Black or African-American?" (A variation of this question was asked to determine the percentage of Latinos, Asians, and Whites as well).

4.2   Measurement of the Independent Variables

Race of Clergy—Respondents were asked to identify the race of the primary spiritual leader of the church. In this paper I was specifically interested in the effect that having a Black clergy person would have on the percentage of African-Americans in the congregation. A dummy variable was created to measure this.

Expressive Style—Here I identified several variables that capture various ways of being expressive during a worship service. I was specifically interested in a type of expressiveness that is associated with the Black church experience (Lincoln and Mamiya 1990). Those variables are: shouting amen (respondents were asked whether or not people shouted amen during the last service they attended), jumping (respondents were asked whether or not anyone jumped up and down, "shouted" or danced during the last service they attended), raised hands (respondents were asked whether or not people raised their hands during worship at the last service they attended), applause (respondents were asked whether or not there was applause from the congregation during the last service they attended) and finally testify (respondents were asked whether or not there was time allotted for people to share testimonies at any time during the worship service at the last service they attended). I created dummy variables for each of these to measure them in my regression.

My interest in these variables comes directly from the literature. Displeasure with the worship is often mentioned in the literature as a possible reason for Blacks not being comfortable in multiracial churches.

Race-conscious Programming—The survey specifically asks respondents whether the church sponsored programs in the past year to discuss race. My hypothesis is that Blacks are more likely to attend race-conscious multiracial churches, that is churches in which race is explicitly dealt with. In my regression equation I use race-conscious programming as a gauge of race-consciousness. I did this primarily because such programming is a clear indication that a church directly and intentionally engages in discussions about race. A dummy variable was created to measure this.

Findings

Table 10.1 presents the descriptive statistics for all of the variables in my analysis.

In Table 10.2 you see that multiracial churches tend to look more like White churches. When it comes to the length of the sermon multiracial churches (23.24 minutes) are almost identical to White churches (23.98 minutes). We also see that multiracial churches tend to have more members with at least a four-year degree than do Black churches (17.9%) or White churches (28.4%).

Table 10.3 shows us the statistical significance of the difference between Black churches, multiracial churches and white churches. Across all three of the variables we see that the differences between Black churches and multiracial churches are statistically significant while the differences between White churches and multiracial churches are not.

Table 10.4 is an analysis of how multiracial churches differ in terms of the style of the worship service. Participants were asked whether or not the activities listed in the table occurred in their churches during the last service.

TABLE 10.1   Descriptive statistics

	Minimum	Maximum	Mean	Std. Dev.	Variance
Service Length in minutes	0	300	82.96	37.63	1415.73
Sermon Time in minutes	0	120	24.3	16.32	266.46
Percent w/ BA	0	100	26.06	24.16	583.65
Percent Black	0	100	18.2	34.07	1160.82
Black Clergy	0	2	.28	.69	.49
Race Relevant Programming	0	1	.17	.38	.14
Shouted Amen	0	1	.56	.50	.25
Applause	0	1	.60	.49	.24
Jumped	0	1	.15	.36	.13
Raised Hands	0	1	.49	.50	.25
Testified	0	1	.73	.44	.20
Participated in Social Services	0	1	.69	.46	.22
Government Official Spoke	0	1	.09	.29	.08
Candidate Spoke	0	1	.06	.24	.06

SOURCE: NATIONAL CONGREGATIONS STUDY SUBSET OF THE GSS, 2006

TABLE 10.2   Service Time, Sermon Time, and Percent Bachelor's Degree

	Black churches	Multiracial churches	White churches
Mean length of service (in minutes)	128.8	79.05	76.06
Mean length of sermon (in minutes)	37.16	23.24	23.98
Mean % with four year degree	17.9	34.1	28.4

SOURCE: NATIONAL CONGREGATIONS STUDY SUBSET OF THE GSS, 2006

Here again we see that overall multiracial churches tend to look more like White churches.

Multiracial churches are almost identical to White churches when it comes to shouting amen and allotting time for sharing testimonies during the service. When asked whether or not congregants had shouted "amen" during the last

TABLE 10.3   Results from ANOVA

Dependent variable	Church type	Church type	Mean difference
Service time	White churches	Multiracial churches	−3.32
		Black churches	−52.47[b]
	Multiracial churches	White churches	3.32
		Black churches	−49.15[b]
	Black churches	White churches	52.47[b]
		Multiracial churches	49.15[b]
Sermon time	White churches	Multiracial churches	1.87
		Black churches	−12.23[b]
	Multiracial churches	White churches	−1.87
		Black churches	−14.09[b]
	Black churches	White churches	12.23[b]
		Multiracial churches	14.09[b]
% with a four-year degree	White churches	Multiracial churches	−2.77
		Black churches	10.22[a]
	Multiracial churches	White churches	2.77
		Black churches	12.98[b]
	Black churches	White churches	−10.22[a]
		Multiracial churches	−12.98[b]

a   The mean difference is significant at the 0.05 level.
b   The mean difference is significant at the .001 level.
SOURCE: NATIONAL CONGREGATIONS STUDY SUBSET OF THE GSS, 2006

worship service 93.8 percent of respondents from Black churches answered yes compared to 51.8 percent of respondents from multiracial churches and 51.3 percent of respondents from White churches. Similarly, when asked about testimonies being shared during the service 81.3 percent of respondents from Black churches answered affirmatively compared to 74.9 percent of multiracial churches and 71.4 percent of White churches.

When it comes to clapping during the service multiracial churches seem to be slightly more expressive than their White counter parts but still much less expressive than their Black counterparts. When asked, 65.5 percent of respondents of multiracial churches said that there had been applause during their

TABLE 10.4 Expressiveness of Worship Style

		Black churches	Multiracial churches	White churches
Shouted Amen[b]	% Yes	93.8	51.8	51.3
	% No	6.2	48.2	48.7
Applause[b]	% Yes	89.1	65.5	50.0
	% No	10.9	34.5	50.0
Jumping[b]	% Yes	51.6	13.1	7.3
	% No	48.4	86.9	92.7
Raised Hands[b]	% Yes	88.1	61.7	29.3
	% No	11.9	38.3	70.7
Testified[a]	% Yes	81.3	74.9	71.4
	% No	17.2	25.1	28.6

a   Pearson Chi Square test reveals significance at the .05 level.
b   Pearson Chi Square test reveals significance at the .001 level.
SOURCE: NATIONAL CONGREGATIONS STUDY SUBSET OF THE GSS, 2006

last service while only 50 percent of respondents from White churches answered yes to that question. However, 89.1 percent of respondents from Black churches said that there had been clapping during the service.

The most notable divergence in the table is the response to the question of whether or not members of the congregation raised their hands during the last worship service. Unlike the other ways of being expressive where multiracial churches are, for the most part, very much like White churches here we see them somewhere in the middle of Black churches and White churches. 60.7 percent of respondents from multiracial churches said that there had been raised hands during the last service. This is compared to 87.7 percent of respondents from Black churches and 29.1 percent from White churches.

Table 10.5 presents the response to two questions posed to respondents about their level of involvement with politics. Respondents were asked whether or not a government official had spoken at their church in the past 12 months. Here you see that 19.8 percent of respondents from Black churches answered yes compared to 9.5 percent of respondents from multiracial churches and 7.1 percent of respondents from White churches (differences are not statistically significant).

TABLE 10.5 Political involvement

		Black churches	Multiracial churches	White churches
Gov. Speakers[a]	% Yes	19.8	9.5	7.1
	% No	80.2	90.5	92.9
Political Candidates[a,b]	% Yes	26.2	6.5	4.3
	% No	73.8	94.5	95.7

a   Pearson Chi Square test reveals significance at the .05 level.
b   Pearson Chi Square test reveals significance at the .001 level.
SOURCE: NATIONAL CONGREGATIONS STUDY SUBSET OF THE GSS, 2006

TABLE 10.6 Participating in social services

		Black churches	Multiracial churches	White churches
Participation in Social Service[a,b]	% Yes	64.5	78	64.1
	% No	35.9	22	35.5

a   Pearson Chi Square test reveals significance at the .05 level.
b   Pearson Chi Square test reveals significance at the .001 level.
SOURCE: NATIONAL CONGREGATIONS STUDY SUBSET OF THE GSS, 2006

Respondents were next asked whether or not a person running for political office had spoken at their church in the past 12 months. 26.6 percent of respondents from Black churches answered yes compared to 6.5 percent of respondents from multiracial churches and 4.2 percent of respondents from White churches.

Table 10.6 presents the responses to the question of whether or not the church had within the past 12 months participated in or supported social service, community development or neighborhood organizing. Here we see an interesting break from the trend. Black churches and White churches are almost identical with 64.5 percent and 64.1 percent, respectively, of respondents answering yes to that question. However, 78 percent of respondents from multiracial churches answered yes.

Table 10.7 presents the results of the linear regression. I ran this regression on the 191 multiracial churches in the sample. The model that predicts the highest amount of variation is model 10. This is largely due to including the variable "Black clergy" in the model. Adding the race of the clergy (specifically Black clergy) to the model dramatically increases the variability predicted from fourteen percent to forty-two percent. Holding all other independent variables constant, having a Black clergy person increases the percentages of Blacks in a multiracial church by 19 percent.

Overall expressive worship styles (except jumping/dancing) were not strong predictors of the percentage of Blacks in a multiracial church with one notable exception. In every model, jumping, dancing and shouting is significant at or stronger than? the .01 level. In Model 3, holding all other independent variables constant, jumping, dancing or shouting at the last worship service increases the percentages of Blacks in a multiracial church by 14.5 percent.

5   Discussion

Overall my hypothesis that multiracial churches are more like White churches than they are Black churches is supported by the data. Multiracial churches are almost identical to white churches from the length of their services and sermons ways that they engage politics. This may be due in part to the fact that most of the multiracial churches in this sample are predominantly White and led by White clergy. However Edwards' (2008) argument that many of these churches adapt to accommodate White members is one that is supported by the analysis.

My second hypothesis that race-conscious multiracial churches would be more attractive than race-blind multiracial churches is not supported by the data. While the effect of a culturally sensitive liturgy is not statistically significant in any of the models in my regression, I find that it is in a negative rather than positive direction.

My hypothesis that having a Black pastor would be a significant factor in predicting Black presence in multiracial congregations is supported by the analysis, in fact it is the strongest predictor in the model. Finally, my hypothesis that having an expressive style of worship would be a significant predictor of Black participation in multiracial churches is partially supported by the analysis. Most forms of expression are not significant. However, in every model, jumping/dancing is significant at the .05 level at least.

TABLE 10.7   OLS Coefficients predicting the percentages of African-Americans in a
            Congregation

N = 191	Model 1 $R^2 = .007$	Model 2 $R^2 = .010$	Model 3 $R^2 = .077$	Model 4 $R^2 = .079$
Intercept	13.78	12.78	12.297	13.40
Race-conscious Programming	−3.21	−3.04	−1.497	−1.51
Amen	----	1.84	−1.69	−1.56
Jumped	----	----	14.45[c]	14.85[c]
Testify	----	----	----	−1.64
Applause	----	----	----	----
Raised Hands	----	----	----	----
Social Services	----	----	----	----
Gov. Officials	----	----	----	----
Candidate	----	----	----	----
Black Clergy	----	----	----	----

a $p < .05.$
b $p < .01.$
c $p < .001.$
Note: I am not using standardized and unstandardized because there is only one variable that
can be standardized.
SOURCE: NATIONAL CONGREGATIONS STUDY SUBSET OF THE GSS, 2006

While jumping, shouting and dancing during the service all have a significant positive effect on Black percentages in Multiracial churches, this would likely be a difficult thing to introduce to congregations that are not already charismatic in those ways.

Based on my findings, the best way for multiracial churches to increase the percentages of Blacks that attend is to hire Black clergy. Given that white clergy head most of the churches in the sample, this has major implications for how multiracial churches think about leadership. It may be beneficial for churches that are interested in increasing the percentage of Blacks to experiment with leadership models that will allow them to increase the presence of Black leadership. This could possibly take the form of shared leadership between white and Black pastors.

Model 5 $R^2 = .1$	Model 6 $R^2 = .13$	Model 7 $R^2 = .135$	Model 8 $R^2 = .139$	Model 9 $R^2 = .144$	Model 10 $R^2 = .419$
10.71	16.61	18.12	18.06	17.85	16.38
−1.38	−1.00	−.74	−.98	−.83	−3.19
−2.31	−.799	−.67	−.53	−.65	−.44
13.51[b]	14.52[c]	14.33[b]	14.51[c]	14.295[b]	12.19[c]
−2.07	−1.93	−1.61	−1.58	−1.53	−2.02
5.43[a]	5.06	4.77	4.84	5.08	2.53
----	−3.27	−3.08	−3.31	−3.33	−3.12
----	----	−3.11	−3.39	−3.45	−3.87
----	----	----	3.91	5.59	7.69[a]
----	----	----	----	−6.60	−5.13
----	----	----	----	----	19.07[c]

6   Conclusion

Black participation in predominantly white multiracial congregations is limited and difficult to sustain. While the data do not support my hypothesis that race consciousness is a significant predictor, my analysis suggests that the race of the clergy is an important factor. But this finding reveals an interesting conundrum. On the one hand race-consciousness (at least as it has been operationalized here) is not a significant predictor of Black participation in predominantly white multiracial congregations. On the other hand, the findings suggest that explicitly considering race in the hiring process (for example intentionally hiring a Black pastor) could go a long way in increasing the number of Black congregants.

Beyond this, the findings point to a more important problem related to the critical study of these congregations. In my regression equation I used race relevant programming as a gauge of race-consciousness. I did this for two reasons. First, such programming is a clear indication that a church directly and intentionally engages in discussions about race. Second, and more to the point, this was the only variable in the data set that came close to capturing race-consciousness. The National Congregations Study (NCS) provides a wealth of insight into congregational life in the United States. It is one of the largest and most comprehensive surveys of its kind and has been used in a number of studies of multiracial congregations. Yet questions related to race (beyond demographical data) are very limited. As the number of multiracial congregations continues to increase how will we study them? Will questions about how such congregations address (or fail to address) structural racial inequality should be at the forefront of research agendas.

References

Becker, P.E. 1998. "Making Inclusive Communities: Congregations and the 'Problem' of Race." *Social Problems, 45*: 451–472.

Blum, E. 2007. *W.E.B. DuBois An American Prophet.* Philedelphia, PA: University of Pensilvania Press.

Brad Christerson, K.E. 2005. *Against All Odds: The Struggle for Racial Intergration in Religious Organizations.* New York and London: NYU Press.

Christerson, M.O. 2003. "The Cost of Diversity in Religious Organizations." *Sociology of Religion, 64*: 163–181.

Creech, Joe. 1996 "Visions of Glory: The Place of the Azusa Street Revival in Pentecostal History." *Church History*, 65(3): 405–24.

DeYoung, Curtiss Paul. 2004. *United By Faith: Multiracial Congregations as an Answer to the Problem of Race.* New York, NY: Oxford University Press.

Dougherty, Kevin. 2008. "Racially Diverse Congragations: Organizational Identity and the Accomodation of Difference." *Journal for the Scientific Study of Religion, 47*: 23–43.

Edwards, Korie. 2008a. "Bring Race to the Center: The Importance of Race in Racially Diverse Religious Organizations." *Journal for the Scientific Study of Religion, 47*: 5–9.

Edwards, Korie. 2008b. *The Elusive Dream: The Power of Race in Interracial Churches.* New York, NY: Oxford University Press.

Edwards, Korie. 2013. "Race, Religious Organizations, and Inegration." *The Anual Review of Sociology, 39*: 211–228.

Emerson, Michael O. 2003. *People of the Dream: Multiracial Congregations in the United States.* Princeton and Oxford: Princeton Univerity Press.

Emerson, Michael O. 2000. *Divided by Faith: Evangelical Religion and the Problem of Race in America.* New York, NY: Oxford University Press.

Emerson, Micheal O., and Karen C. Kim. 2003. "Multiracial Congregations: An Analysis of Their Develpoment and a Typology." *Journal for the Scientific Study of Religion,* 42: 217–227.

Garces-Foley, K. 2007. *Crossing the Ethnic Divide.* Oxford, London: Oxford University Press.

Hughey, Matthew W., David G. Embrick, and Ashley "Woody" Doane. 2015. "Paving the Way for Future Race Research: Exploring the Racial Mechanisms within a Color-Blind, Racism and the Racialized Social System." *American Behavioral Scientist,* Vol. 59(11), 1347–1357.

Jenkins, K.E. 2003. "Intimate Diversity: The Presentation of Multiculturalism and Multiracialism in a High-Boundary Religious Movement." *Journal for the Scientific Study of Religion, 42*: 393–409.

Lincoln, C. Eric, and Lawrence H. Mamiya. 1990. *The Black Church in the African American Experience.* Durham, NC: Duke University Press.

Marti, G. 2005. *A Mosaic of Believers: Diversity and Inovation in a Multiethnic Church.* Bloomington and Indianapolis: Indiana University Press.

Marti, G. 2009. "Affinity, Identity and Transcendence: The Experience of Religious Racial Integration in Diverse Congregations." *Journal for the Scientific Study of Relition, 48*: 53–68.

Marti, G. 2008. "Fluid Ethnicity and Ethnic Trancendence in Multiracial Churches." *Journal for the Scientific Study of Religion, 47*: 11–16.

Marti, G. 2010. "The Religious Racial Integration of African-Americans into Diverse Churches." *Journal for the Scientific Study of Religion, 49*: 201–217.

Massey, Douglas, and Nancy Denton. 1993. *American Apartheid: Segregation and the Making of the Underclass.* Cambridge, MA: Harvard University Press.

Myers, Kristen. 2005. *Race Talk: Racism Hiding in Plain Sight.* Lanham, Maryland: Rowman & Littlefield Publishers, Inc.

Pitt, Richard. 2010. "Fear of a Black Pulpit? Real Racial Trancendence Versus Cultural Assimilation in Multiracial Churches." *Journal for the Scientific Study of Religion, 49*: 218: 223.

Smith, Michael O. 2000. *Divided by Faith.* Oxford, London: Oxford University Press.

Stanczak, G.C. 2006. "Strategic Ethnicity: The Construction of Multi-racial/Multi-ethnic Religious Community." *Ethnic Racial Study, 29*: 856–881.

Warren, Jonathan W. 1997. "White Americans, the New Minority? Non-Blacks and the Ever-Expanding Boundaries of Whiteness." *Journal of Black Studies, 28*: 200–218.

Waters, Mary. 1990. *Ethnic Options: Choosing Identities in America.* Berkley, CA: University of California Press.

Wu, Frank. 2002. *Yellow: Race in America Beyond Black and White.* New York, NY: Basic Books.

Yancey, George. 1999. An Examination of the Effects of Residential and Church Integration on Racial Attitudes of Whites. *Sociological Perspectives, 42*: 279–304.

Yancey, George. 2001. Racial Attitudes: A Comparision of People Attending Multiracial and Uniracial Congregations. *Journal for the Scientific Study of Religion, 12*: 185–206.

CHAPTER 11

"Not in My Backyard": How Abstract Liberalism and Colorblind Diversity Undermines Racial Justice

Laurie Cooper Stoll and Megan Klein

1   Introduction

As the population in the United States becomes more racially diverse, will we see an increase in integrated communities? If so, will these communities embrace their newfound diversity or will they seek to protect white normativity as previous research suggests (e.g., Ellen 2001; Johnson and Shapiro 2003; Maly 2005; Charles 2006)? Studies of stable, racially diverse, socially progressive communities (e.g., Goodwin 1979; Ellen 1998; Nyden et al. 1998) may provide some insights into these questions. After all, these communities have been living for decades with the kinds of racial diversity the rest of the United States will experience in the coming years.

Consistent with previous research (Burke 2012), we find that whites living in these communities often use the frames of colorblind racism (Bonilla-Silva 2006) in ways similar to whites who reside in all or almost-all white enclaves (see also Bobo 1999; Rich 2011). Moreover, whites in racially diverse, socially progressive communities may reap more rewards from the politics of colorblind racism. After all, living in these communities allows one to claim an identity marked by racial progressiveness without necessarily having to confront and address racial inequalities (Stoll 2013), particularly when other institutions in the community provide dominant group members access to racial diversity without having to live in diverse neighborhoods themselves. When this happens dominant group members are able to concentrate capital in their neighborhoods in a way that protects and reproduces white habitus while also defining themselves as racial progressives. *White habitus*, according to Bonilla-Silva (2006) refers to a "racialized, uninterrupted socialization process that conditions and creates whites' racial tastes, perceptions, feelings, and emotions and their views on racial matters" (104).

In this chapter, we add to the body of literature that illustrates how abstract liberalism and colorblind diversity discourse can undermine racial equity and maintain the status quo (Bonilla-Silva 2006; Burke 2012; Doane 2012; Stoll 2013). We use the case of racially diverse, socially progressive communities to elucidate this relationship. Specifically, we explore what happened when a new school referendum went up for a public vote in a suburban community of Chicago we call Lakeview.

2   Colorblind Racism and Colorblind Diversity

In *Racism without Racists,* Eduardo Bonilla-Silva (2006), refers to the "new form" of racism that exists in the U.S. in the post-Civil Rights era as *color-blind racism* (see also Bonilla-Silva 2001). Colorblind racism manifests in four frames used predominantly by whites to interpret information about race: abstract liberalism, naturalization, cultural racism, and minimization of racism. Of all the frames, Bonilla-Silva (2006) argues that abstract liberalism is the most important because it constitutes the foundation of the new racial ideology (26). According to Bonilla-Silva:

> The frame of *abstract liberalism* involves using ideas associated with po-
> litical liberalism (e.g., "equal opportunity," the idea that force should not
> be used to achieve social policy) and economic liberalism (e.g., choice,
> individualism) in an *abstract* manner to explain racial matters. By fram-
> ing race-related issues in the language of liberalism, whites can appear
> "reasonable" and even "moral," while opposing almost all practical ap-
> proaches to deal with de facto racial inequality. (28; emphasis in original)

In other words, abstract liberalism allows whites to express a concern for racial inequality (and to express pro-diversity attitudes) while simultaneously
opposing race-specific policies that would directly address racial inequality.
Abstract liberalism is based on the belief in individualism and meritocracy
with the conviction that no group should be singled out for "special treatment"
and that "individual freedoms" must be protected above all. Ironically, this
allows whites to protect the status quo and their own group interests by problematizing the *special* group interests of racial minorities.

For example, the logic of abstract liberalism was apparent when Lakeview
High School (which operates as a separate school district from Lakeview elementary and middle schools) wanted to eliminate freshman honors courses
in humanities in 2010 and biology in 2012. While the intent was to address the
pervasive racialized outcomes of tracking at Lakeview High School, both proposals were met with opposition from white parents in the community who
had or would eventually have children in these programs and wanted them
to have access to these classes. The white superintendent of the high school

was very public about his concern that despite having one of the most racially diverse high schools in the state, there were very few racial and ethnic minority students in honors and Advanced Placement classes. Both proposals passed, therefore eliminating honors humanities and later honors biology classes for incoming freshmen, but not without much debate and contention.

When it was proposed that the honors biology class for freshmen be eliminated, a petition was circulated to delay this initiative, spearheaded by a white woman in the community who was heavily involved in the Parent Teacher Association. Another white Lakeview resident, Ms. Turner, summed up what a number of folks who opposed the proposal argued at school board meetings when she was quoted in the local paper as saying, "[De-tracking focuses] on bringing the *bottom* up-and there's an assumption that our *bright children* will take care of themselves." Ms. Turner's comments not only reflect the notion that de-tracking represents a type of "special treatment" or "special attention" given to the "bottom" at the expense of the "bright children" but also what Bonilla-Silva (2006) refers to as a meritocratic way of defending white privilege:

> Another tenet of liberalism whites use to explain racial matters is the Jeffersonian idea of "the cream rises to the top," or meritocracy (reward by merit). And whites seem unconcerned that the color of the "cream" that usually "rises" is white. (32)

In other words, while Ms. Turner's comments may read as race-neutral because she frames the issue as a matter of difference between academically successful students who have *achieved* their rightful spots in the honors and Advanced Placement classes and students who struggle academically, what she fails to acknowledge is the "bright children" in the honors and Advanced Placement classes at Lakeview High School are overwhelmingly white and the "bottom" is overwhelmingly comprised of racial and ethnic minority students.

We provide this example of the debate regarding freshmen honors classes not to insinuate that all whites in Lakeview were opposed to eliminating these classes. After all, it was whites in the community including white educators at the high school who were able to convince a majority of school board members to vote for the proposals. We offer it as an illustration of how abstract liberalism often undergirds racial tensions that surround issues like these even in racially diverse, socially progressive communities.

Further, our analysis shows that in Lakeview the logic of abstract liberalism couples neatly with the use of diversity discourse. An example of this is found in the interview with Ms. Parker, a white second grade teacher who lives in Lakeview with her African American spouse and teaches at a mostly-white school in north Lakeview. When Stoll (2013) asked whether Ms. Parker had noticed the contradictions between the social justice ethos of Lakeview and the examples of colorblind racism Stoll documented in her research, Ms. Parker responded:

> [Mimicking white parents in Lakeview] "We moved to Lakeview for the diversity! We love the brown children in my child's class!" But those are also the parents at this grade level that don't have those kids over for the play dates, don't invite those kids to the birthday parties because, "Well, they probably wouldn't be able to get there." First, how do you know that? And so you just don't invite them? I find that to be so offensive. And, I have a very hard time holding myself to parents sometimes, but I've had parents say to me, "Well, I see on your birthday chart that it's so-and-so's birthday [a student of color] and so I thought I would bring in a treat." Why? You're assuming that that parent isn't going to? I feel like there's a judgment put on that parent.

In sum, diversity discourse, or "happy talk" as Bell and Hartmann (2007) refer to it, allows for the recognition of difference without acknowledging systematic inequalities or white normativity. In essence, diversity discourse in an era of post-racial politics allows dominant group members to engage in discussions about race while dismissing the material consequences attached to it, what Andersen (1999) refers to as "diversity without oppression." Woody Doane (2012) calls this type of diversity *color-blind diversity*. According to Doane:

> In the decades since the Civil Rights Movement, it is increasingly socially desirable for individuals to embrace diversity in order to substantiate their non-racist or post-racial standpoint. Beyond the psychological benefits of feeling virtuous (most of us want to live in a society where race does not matter) "doing" diversity also provides individuals with a credential to use in racially challenging situations. (5)

As we show in this chapter, the abstract liberalism and colorblind diversity that many white residents in Lakeview embrace generally operates to reproduce white habitus and maintain the status quo as opposed to alleviate racial inequality. We believe a quintessential example of this is the heated debate that surrounded the possibility of building a new school in a majority-minority neighborhood in Lakeview we call the Central Corridor. The public vote that followed along with subsequent actions taken by the school board served to further illuminate the racial tensions exacerbated by Lakeview's history of segregated neighborhoods and integrated schools.

3   Methods

Data for this chapter come from two separate research projects carried out independently by both authors in the Lakeview community. One source of data is an ongoing research project by Klein beginning in October 2012. In this project, she gathered archival data at the Lakeview Historical Society on Lakeview's 1967 integration of the public elementary schools. The content analysis included extensive minutes both from official school board meetings from 1964–1967 and from the meetings of the Commission on Integration, which was established by the school board to develop an adequate plan for integrating Lakeview's public elementary schools. In addition to meeting minutes, the archives include published and unpublished district reports on integration, plans for preparing teachers to navigate the process of integration, formal and informal communication with local residents and businesses, school area attendance maps with demographic information, and surveys sent to families with elementary school-aged children and other relevant documents.

In this chapter we also include interview data from two sources to supplement the archival research we discuss. Our objective for including these data is not to generalize from these experiential accounts to the entire Lakeview population, but to offer some qualitative insights on the patterns of segregation and integration we outline. The first set of qualitative data comes from a study conducted by Stoll that explored Lakeview teachers' perspectives on race and gender in schooling. During the 2010–2011 school year, Stoll interviewed, observed, and then re-interviewed eighteen teachers who work at three different elementary schools (kindergarten through fifth grade) in Lakeview. Semistructured initial interviews allowed Stoll to gather background information on each teacher before observation. In these interviews, teachers were asked about their unique educational and career trajectory, teaching philosophy and pedagogy, as well as their subjective understanding of their social location. Several questions from the initial interview schedule were adapted from Lortie's (1975) classic study of teachers and the teaching profession. After the formal period of observation was concluded, Stoll conducted a second semistructured interview that asked about teacher's attitudes toward educational policy in general and race- and gender-based policies specifically. Teachers were compensated fifty dollars at the conclusion of the final interview to purchase classroom supplies.

In addition to this data, Klein (2012–2014) conducted eighteen in-depth, semi-structured interviews with long-time residents of Lakeview's historically Black community, the Central Corridor. These residents live in the part of the community where the proposed new elementary school would be located. Interviews ranged from one to three hours with most lasting around seventy-five minutes. The interviews centered on themes of community history, culture and education. Thirteen of the residents lived in the Central Corridor for the majority of their lives (ranging from forty to seventy years) and many of them attended the all-Black elementary school in Lakeview Warren Elementary School before the district integrated in 1967. Two of Klein's respondents were born in Lakeview and attended the newly integrated elementary schools beginning in the fall of 1967. The remaining interviewees moved to the Central Corridor later in life and have children who attended the Lakeview public school system. Interviewees were compensated with a twenty-five dollar gift card at the conclusion of their interview. Finally, the names of all interview respondents as well as the names of schools, neighborhoods, and the community have been changed.

4 Lakeview: A History of Segregated Neighborhoods and Integrated Schools

We consider Lakeview a racially diverse, socially progressive community for several reasons (see also Ellen 1998). First, Lakeview's population of approximately seventy-five thousand residents is comprised of persons who identify as white (62%), Black or African American (18%), Hispanic or Latino (9%), and Asian (9%). Second, as compared with national averages, residents have a much higher level of formal education (68% of residents over the age of twenty-five have a bachelor's degree; almost 40% have a graduate or professional degree). Third, residents are politically liberal; President Barack Obama and Democratic presidential candidate, John Kerry, for example, carried the community by an overwhelming majority in previous election cycles. Finally, Lakeview is a community that prides itself on an ethos of social justice and tolerance. For example, Lakeview's diversity is mentioned in the first sentence of the *Visit Lakeview* web page on the official community web site as something that "delights" both Lakeview residents and Lakeview visitors.

These criteria make Lakeview a racially diverse, socially progressive community (see Ellen 1998), but they do not necessarily make Lakeview an *integrated* community (e.g., Charles 2006). Despite its pro-diversity reputation, Lakeview

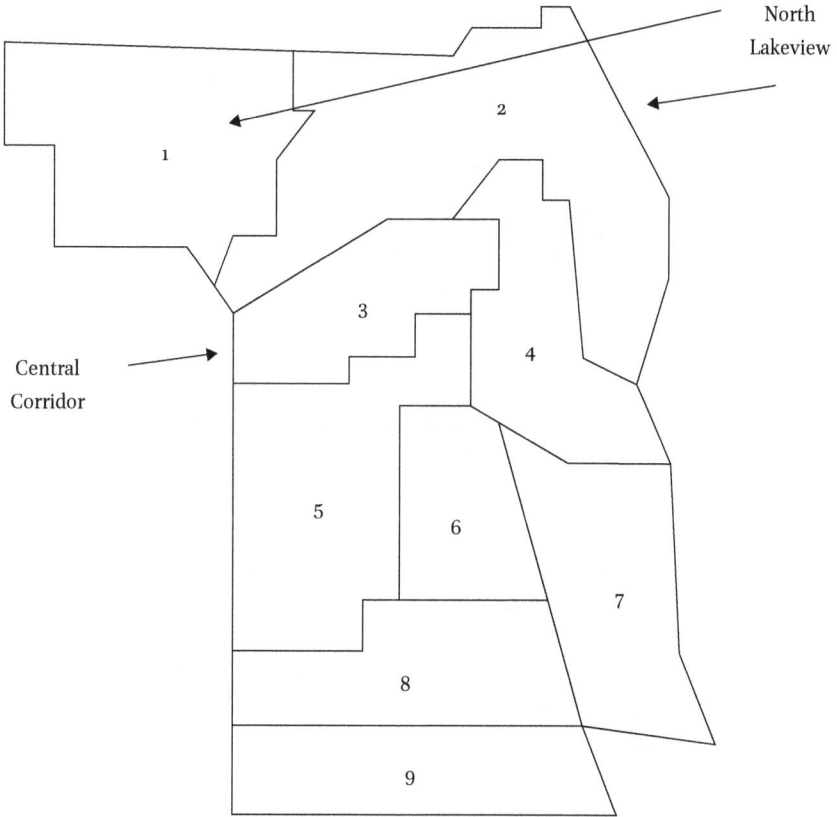

MAP 11.1   Map of Lakeview by ward
SOURCE: CREATED BY THE AUTHORS.

remains a community where many neighborhoods are racially segregated.[1] For example, three of the four northern Census tracts located in Wards 1 and 2 (see Map 11.1) range from 92% to 94% white. Further illustrating this fact, in a community where 18% of the population identifies as African American or Black, a mere 0% to 4.5% of the residents in these three northern Census tracts are

---

1   For the purposes of this paper, we define neighborhoods in Lakeview as distinguished by wards. While this is not an uncommon measure used to capture neighborhoods, it is an imperfect one. However, we believe ward designations in Lakeview do closely reflect a distinctive history, culture, and brand of politics typically used to define neighborhoods. This is especially true for the neighborhoods we focus on in this paper: those located in north Lakeview and the Central Corridor.

Black. Property tax data reveal at least one significant consequence of Lakeview's residential segregation: the four northern Census tracks have average property values ranging from $390,000 to $579,000 while the Central Corridor, which is a majority-minority neighborhood, has an average property value of $213,000.[2]

Regardless, white residents in these northern Census tracts, like Lakeview residents in general, often cite diversity as its number one selling point, especially compared to towns further north where many Lakeview residents say they would "never live" because these communities are "too white." As Mr. Gold, a white teacher who works in north Lakeview and is a Lakeview resident himself, described to Stoll:

> You don't live in Lakeview if you are a different type of person generally. Now, all the teachers generally live in Lakeview, or they are people who have been associated with Lakeview a long time. And the ones who come from outside soon learn the type of personality and the type of community we live in. And you'd be very out of place if your attitudes were racist, and you know, homophobic, or you had gender preferences.

According to Mr. Gold, racists would be "out of place" in Lakeview, yet it is a community where pervasive racial segregation continues to exist in a number of neighborhoods. Contradictions like this can often go unacknowledged in both public and private discourse in an era of post-racial politics until an issue-such as the new school referendum-emerges that forces them into the light. To fully understand the racial tensions that underlie these contradictions requires historical context. In particular, it requires an understanding of how Lakeview's history of racially segregated neighborhoods and its long history of integration policies in the local public school system continue to perpetuate an environment in which affluent whites in the community can choose to live in mostly white enclaves, but still regularly have access to racially diverse institutions.

According to Nyden et al. (1998), there are two distinct trajectories that can result in the formation of diverse communities: (1) a community can be *diverse by direction* whereby the community makes intentional efforts to create and sustain its diversity; or (2) a community can be *diverse by circumstance* in which case its diversity is mostly the result of "unintentional"

---

2   While property values vary throughout the community, per pupil expenditure is the same for all K-8 public school students.

processes. Lakeview has straddled this divide throughout its one hundred and fifty year existence. Historically, racial diversity in Lakeview has resulted from unintentional processes (e.g. proximity to employment). Affluent white landowners and working-class Black employees initially settled the community.

In the first fifty years of its existence, Black families lived in neighborhoods throughout Lakeview, including the north side. This historical fact is contrary to what many current residents believe. In fact, Ms. Hatfield, a Black, eighty-three-year-old resident who lived in Lakeview all her life, recounted an experience to Klein in which she had to correct a white Lakeview official for his lack of knowledge about the history of Blacks in the community:

> And I told him "Blacks used to live all *over* Lakeview." And he looked at me, I said, "And they had their own houses." "Oh no," he said. "They lost their houses." I said "In no way did they lose their houses when they put 'em up on wheels and *moved* them along with the people!" I said, "That's *not* lost."

Mr. Montgomery, a Black eighty-five-year-old lifelong Lakeview resident, also argued rather pointedly that Blacks were "all over the place" when Lakeview was founded in the mid-nineteenth century: Blacks lived in the northern and southern parts of the community and in neighborhoods in between. Further, while racially homogenous enclaves did exist, they were dispersed (as opposed to highly concentrated) throughout the larger community. Yet, despite some spatial integration in parts of Lakeview, there existed pervasive social segregation between racial groups.

During the first half of the twentieth century, Lakeview's Black population was congregated and segregated in the Central Corridor (see Map 11.1). Mr. Smith, a Black resident in his late sixties who lived in Lakeview all his life, recalled for Klein the story of his father's forced move:

> Yeah, so we've been in Lakeview, my dad was born in 1917 and he attended Morgan School 'til third grade and then they put the Black people out of North Lakeview. And they took his house and moved it so that he wouldn't be north. So he was eight-years-old then so that must have been 1925. But then he transferred to Warren School from that point.

While the formation of diversity in Lakeview initially reflected *diversity by circumstance* (Nyden et al. 1998), it could be argued that this period of segregation in Lakeview's history reflects *diversity by direction*, yet the end result was segregation. Blacks were discriminated against when attempting to use white institutions; consequently, the Central Corridor had its own institutions including an almost all-Black elementary school (Warren Elementary), a Black recreation center and a Black hospital.

At the time of the 1960 Census, Lakeview's population was comprised of 88.5% white residents and 11% Black residents. By this point in Lakeview's history, the overwhelming majority of Black residents lived in the segregated Central Corridor. Therefore, well into the 1960s racial diversity in Lakeview more closely resembled two spatially and socially separated communities.

In the late 1960s, Lakeview began to compensate for its pervasive residential segregation through measures Nyden et al. (1998) might also refer to as *diverse by direction*. For example, in the mid-1960s, in the wake of the landmark 1954 Supreme Court decision in *Brown vs. the Board of Education*, Lakeview became the first northern school district to "voluntarily" integrate its public school system. Lakeview had already started busing Black children out of the Central Corridor to neighboring all white elementary schools, years earlier to alleviate crowding at the all-Black Warren Elementary School in the Central Corridor. According to Mr. Smith, however, it was this experience that strengthened the community's desire to have an integrated school in the Central Corridor. When asked about the busing of children from the Central Corridor to neighboring all white elementary schools, he said:

> Yes, they could go to Morgan but they had to stay in their *own* room all day long, their lunches brought to them in their rooms and they could only get off that bus, go to class and get back on that bus and come home. And that's why the Black people wanted Warren Laboratory School. If you're gonna rebuild the school, you have to be integrated. 'Cause we wanted an integrated school in the Central Corridor.

Mr. Montgomery recounted how the Lakeview Board of Education had plans to build another school near the Central Corridor to alleviate overcrowding but residents organized and fought against it, arguing they did not want another segregated school. The new school was not built. Instead, in 1964, Lakeview's Board of Education (under a pro-integration superintendent) formed a commission to attack the problem of segregation in Lakeview's elementary schools. The commission, a seventeen member group of local residents (twelve men and five women) was challenged with the daunting task of devising a workable way to integrate Lakeview's elementary schools. Minutes from their regular meetings occurring between December of 1964 and October of 1966 (housed in the archives at the Lakeview Historical Society) reveal the challenges faced by this commission.

For example, because the Lakeview school system has historically been based on the neighborhood school concept with children attending the school closest to their home, integrating the school district required a lot of creativity as the Commission attempted to reconcile a number of contradictory aims. This included maintaining the neighborhood school concept, evenly integrating all elementary schools, and overcoming highly segregated neighborhoods. The end result of months of data collection and analysis by the Commission was: (1) to make Warren Elementary a laboratory school (Warren Laboratory School) beginning the first year with kindergarten students only; (2) accept roughly 25% of neighborhood (i.e. Black) students at Warren Laboratory School; and (3) bus in a majority of white students whose participation was incentivized by enrichment programs, free transportation and other "carrots," while sending the remaining Black children to neighboring all white schools (e.g., Rossell 1990).

The longtime residents of the Central Corridor Klein interviewed talked favorably about their own experiences during early phases of Lakeview's integration, arguing that it was "working" because it was "evenly distributed" between Black and white children. Mr. Thomas, a fifty-nine-year-old Black Lakeview resident who began his education as a student at Warren and who switched schools as a sixth grader in 1967 because of integration, articulates his understanding of the initial phase of Lakeview's integration:

> Integration seemed to work very well. For the first time in my life, white people put their five- and six-year-olds on a bus into the heart of a Black community. I know kids who are now fifty, white kids who are now fifty, who, they were one of those kids. And they love Warren School just like I do.

Ms. Houston, a lifelong Black resident of the Central Corridor in her seventies, described her children's experiences at an integrated Warren Laboratory School this way: "And so by the time my kids got there, it was very, you know, integrated. And it was, you know, it was fine. But by then, I think we'd all become accustomed to integration." Both Mr. Thomas and Ms. Houston indicated that integration, at least initially, seemed to be working well. For many longtime Central Corridor residents, the initial phase of institutional integration was one in which the work of *diversity by direction* was more evenly distributed by race.

In the 1970s, the Board of Education faced the challenge of closing a number of Lakeview's public elementary schools because of steep population declines. The ousting of the pro-integration superintendent and subsequent replacement with a conservative superintendent combined with declining enrollment led the Board to close schools, most of which were located in the central part of the community. These schools, including Warren, were more "naturally" diverse because they reflected the increasing neighborhood diversity in this part of the community as compared with other parts of Lakeview.

Regardless, Warren Elementary and a number of other schools in the central part of the community were closed while the schools in the north part of Lakeview (nestled in almost exclusively white enclaves) remained open. The laboratory school that had been in the Warren building was moved out of the neighborhood into a different building in Lakeview, leaving a large and recently renovated building shuddered and empty in the Central Corridor. Around the same time, the community's plans for institutional integration included the closing of the Black recreation center (1969) and the segregated community hospital in the Central Corridor (1980). School attendance boundaries divided up the Central Corridor and forced families to send their children to one of eight different assigned schools for the neighborhood. As residents recounted, some intersections had children going to four or five different elementary schools.

At this point, for those living in the northern half of Lakeview, the daily work of integration fell squarely on the shoulders of the children living in the Central Corridor. In the following quote, Mr. Thomas describes the conditions under which Black residents of the Central Corridor supported the Board of Education's plan for integration in 1967:

> Because, understand, a promise was made. That one, your kids would be able to go to school there [at Warren Laboratory School], yeah, you'd bus some out but after a while it was like 75% of the kids [attending Warren Laboratory School] were white. Also, that education would always remain in the Central Corridor. In 1979 [with the closing of the Warren Lab building and relocation of the school], they broke that promise. It was bait and switch.

For Mr. Thomas and other residents, the closure of Warren was seen as part of a wave of disinvestment in the Central Corridor for the purpose of investing in other Lakeview communities.

Commenting on the effects that the closure of Warren had on the community, Mr. Smith explained:

> Every community needs a basis for religion, for education and for economics. When one of those three legs on the stool collapses, the whole stool falls. You took out the social factor of the community that was

our basis, that was our organization, and remove that? Whatever it was replaced by was never supplanted what we had at Warren School. It was just like a chain reaction.

Ms. Houston similarly recounted the important role that Warren played in the community:

Warren School...it was the hub. The church and the school that was in the African American community, you know, that was it, basically what you had. I mean, there were a few institutions, we had the Black Recreation Center, you know, things like that, but the school and the church was where you spent the majority of your life.

Finally, Mr. Montgomery believed that an important consequence of the closure of Warren for the neighborhood was the lack of a space for political organization:

The political control of the system that doesn't have the influence of the Black parents is what we have now. The School Board right now is all white. That's because there's no political loci, there's no locus for power and development, political development in the Black community. That's all the more reason you need a neighborhood school.

Reflecting back on the closures of three anchor institutions, many residents viewed the process of institutional integration as one that undermined the social, political and economic basis of their formerly segregated community. At the same time, neighborhoods in the north whose schools were not closed had social and political capital concentrated in their communities.

Finally, in the mid-1980s, the school district adopted a policy that no defined racial group should comprise more than sixty percent of any one school's population. In order to remain in compliance with this policy, the district has occasionally redrawn school attendance boundaries, located magnet programs in certain schools to attract specific racial groups, as well as continue to bus students, primarily students of color, to schools outside their neighborhoods. Despite these efforts, there is currently one school located in the northern part of the community that exceeds the 60% threshold with 70% of its students identifying as white. Another school located in north Lakeview has exceeded the threshold in the past, and is not far from exceeding it again with a white population of 57%.

By comparison, two schools in the southern part of the community and one in the western part are over 70% minority. Interestingly, while two of these schools are not considered to be in violation of the attendance policy, one that is well within the sixty/forty guidelines is cited as being in violation. This is because throughout Lakeview's history of integration, racially diverse schools have explicitly been premised on a dichotomous model that is majority white with roughly 17–21% students of color. This model has assumed that to achieve "diversity" students of color must be integrated into predominantly white schools. Schools that are predominantly Black and Hispanic do not qualify as diverse schools in this equation. Instead, they are more likely to be considered what Randolph (2013) calls the "wrong kind of different" or reflect what Lentin and Titley (2011) call "bad diversity."

In sum, integration policies in Lakeview have historically been implemented in ways that reproduce white habitus and maintain the status quo. According to Burke (2011), "White habitus itself is the engine of colorblind ideologies, as the ideology of colorblindness explicitly legitimates and leaves intact the racial order that it purports to explain" (661). Integration policies in Lakeview have maintained schools in affluent white neighborhoods while closing schools in majority-minority and integrated neighborhoods. This has allowed whites within mostly white neighborhoods to regularly access racial diversity vis-à-vis the busing in of students of color while concentrating capital in their neighborhoods in the form of thriving, high-achieving neighborhood schools. As Mr. Thomas put it, "What happens is, especially on the north side, they love their diversity as long as it gets delivered to them [on a bus] and it's gone by three-thirty."

Further, by not affirmatively accounting for the historical treatment of Black Lakeview residents, the plans for integrating the public elementary schools appeared to assume that rigid neighborhood segregation was natural and thus it was left unproblematized. As a result, institutions were integrated in a way that avoided the core problem: segregated neighborhoods. Further, the fact that institutions in Lakeview are integrated is something that most dominant group residents laud and support; this allows them to claim a racially progressive identity living in a diverse community but does not require many white residents in north Lakeview to be subjected to the "consequences" of this diversity such as the closures of white institutions or the disproportionate busing of schoolchildren out of white communities. In the end, despite their good intentions, integration policies in Lakeview have resulted in highly racialized outcomes where whites have benefitted and racial minorities have been disadvantaged (e.g., Saito 2009).[3]

---

3   Other racialized outcomes that occurred as part of the institutional integration of Lakeview include the closure of both the historically Black YMCA and the segregated Black hospital.

In the next section, we discuss what happened during the 2011–2012 school year when residents in Lakeview were asked to consider a referendum to build a new school in the Central Corridor. The new school would have encompassed the Black and Hispanic neighborhood from which most of the minority students at four predominantly white schools in the northern part of the community are bused. Whites in these neighborhoods turned out in large numbers to overwhelmingly reject the new school referendum in order to "preserve the work of integration begun in the 1960s," elucidating what we believe is the fundamental contradiction of colorblind diversity: it allows whites to leverage racial "diversity" in order to protect their own group interests, including keeping their property values high, ensuring elementary schools remain within walking distance of their homes, and maintaining access to institutional diversity. Further, the new school referendum offers an excellent example of how whites can use abstract liberalism and colorblind diversity in order to reproduce white habitus and maintain the status quo.

5 Reproducing White Habitus and Maintaining the Status Quo: Findings from the New School Referendum

During the 2011–2012 school year the Lakeview school board put the building of a new school in the Central Corridor up for public referendum. The new school was expected to be racially diverse (the best estimates of racial composition were 59% Black, 28% Hispanic and 13% combined white, Asian, Native American, mixed racial, and Other). However, this model of diversity diverged significantly from the one white residents in the northern parts of the community have grown accustomed to over the past fifty years, a model that has allowed them access to diversity (vis-à-vis the busing in of black and brown students from outside their neighborhoods) without having to live in diverse neighborhoods themselves.

Along with Warren Elementary, these were the anchor institutions of a thriving segregated Black neighborhood. Ironically integration policies, while explicitly dealing with race, largely attempted to be "race neutral," thinking about Lakeview's children in colorblind terms. By not accounting for the history of race-based inequality, such policies assumed a level playing field and this assumption has worked to the detriment of the Central Corridor neighborhood. For the purpose of institutional integration, Black institutions were closed and Blacks were expected to use the white YMCA and the white Lakeview hospital, both of which had actively discriminated against them historically. These closures, like the closure of Warren, left the Central Corridor struggling to maintain its once thriving business environment.

With a neighborhood school in the Central Corridor, the Black and Hispanic students who live there would no longer be bused to schools in these predominantly white neighborhoods, severing residents' regular access to institutional racial diversity. Interestingly, there was a lot of conversation, particularly in the Central Corridor, about whether or not the Lakeview school board even needed a public referendum to build the new school. After all, they have the authority to close a school without a referendum and can build additions (even large, multi-million dollar additions) to existing schools without a referendum. Many residents in the Central Corridor perceived the referendum as a means for the school board to shift the responsibility of making a decision on building the new school to the public in an effort to avoid blame. When asked by members of the school board to help campaign for the proposed new school, Ms. Houston responded:

> I said to them, "You didn't need a referendum to close Warren School, it didn't take that. So why would you need a referendum? Why do you need a referendum to open a new school?" And of course the answer is no, they didn't. But they wanted the community to decide. So why would the overall community decide, the overall community didn't decide to close the [Warren] school.

Nevertheless, Lakeview's school board decided in October 2011 to put the issue to a vote the following March, allowing the community approximately five months to debate the issue. The referendum asked residents for more than forty-seven million dollars, less than half of which would have gone towards the construction of a new school. Very few community meetings entertained a discussion of where the additional money would be spent, which included additions at two Lakeview middle schools and locker rooms at one of the magnet schools. For the majority of residents, the "real issue" was whether or not to build the new school in the Central Corridor.

Even though there were major concerns about the proposed location of the new school, residents of the Central Corridor overwhelmingly supported building a new school in their neighborhood, pointing out that students who lived there were the only ones in Lakeview that did not have access to their own neighborhood school. Further, supporters argued that a neighborhood school would encourage greater home-school connections as parents and family members, particularly those without transportation, would be able to more easily access the school because of its physical location in the neighborhood. On the other hand, the most common reason given by whites that opposed building a new school in the Central Corridor was that the new school would re-segregate schools in a community that had a long history of integration. This may at first seem counterintuitive; after all, it suggests that many white residents in Lakeview were more concerned about segregation than residents of color. However, we believe this makes sense given the logic of abstract liberalism and colorblind diversity.

While diversity discourse is pervasive in an era of post-racial politics, "diversity" can mean very different things to different people based on their life experiences. Because diversity as a concept is not "tied down," it can be employed to achieve opposite ends (Ahmed 2007). Indeed, valuing or embracing "diversity" can pull people in opposite political directions (Berrey 2005). As Berrey writes, "the powerful, shared idea of diversity can communicate contradictory understandings of social differences that challenge, reinforce, or sidestep existing inequalities" (144).

For example, some whites in Lakeview take a paternalistic view when it comes to busing students of color in the Central Corridor to the mostly white neighborhood schools in the northern part of the community. In the following, Mr. Hamilton, a white male teacher in north Lakeview, expresses his concern about racial inequality (therefore, situating himself as "moral" and "reasonable") while simultaneously failing to acknowledge institutional discrimination in schooling and housing (e.g., Bonilla-Silva 2006: 26):

> I would say that here at Morgan [Elementary], and one of the unique, the weird thing is we have a district where our Morgan boundaries are not contiguous. We have this little square of land in a poorer area of Lakeview that kids are bused from every single day. And I do not have an answer to this question, but sometimes I think the best thing that could have happened for some of our students is that they happened to live in that little postage stamp of land that gets to come over here to one of the best schools in the state as measured by data. We know that. And, and so I think Anton [African American student in Mr. Hamilton's class] sure did get lucky that, that he has the right address to get here at Morgan. Um, and...so do I think there's racial inequalities, and do they remain? Absolutely! And it still is affecting what we do in schools! I think we've taken a lot of efforts here in Lakeview to address that very honestly, um, but it's still nagging and it's still...not solved by any means.

While Mr. Hamilton speaks passionately about enduring racial inequality in schooling, he fails to connect his concerns to the broader context of institutional discrimination. For example, his gratitude that most of his students of color are bused to Morgan even though they live in the Central Corridor does not question the patterns of residential segregation that explain why these students of color have to be bused to an almost all-white neighborhood school in order to obtain a modicum of racial parity at Morgan. Indeed, Mr. Hamilton situates the poor families who live in the Central Corridor as the "lucky ones" who have the "right address."

Abstract liberalism was also apparent in comments surrounding the new school referendum. In the months leading up to the vote, residents in favor and those opposed to the new school set up websites to stake out their positions, gave presentations at public meetings, and commented on various online forums. One local blog, *Lakeview123*, polled users regularly about their opinions regarding the referendum. The majority of public posts on this blog and on other online comment boards were opposed to building a new school because of its lack of "diversity" and the belief that the concentration of students of color from lower socioeconomic backgrounds was antithetical to Lakeview's historic commitment to diversity and integration. Illustrating a lack of understanding about how the history of racial oppression and segregation informed and shaped the standpoint of minority residents in Lakeview (e.g., Cooper 2004), these public and online conversations often reflected a colorblind understanding of diversity that positioned diversity for whites in the northern part of Lakeview as more important than the desires of Black and Hispanic residents in the Central Corridor.

In fact, when residents did make public statements or comments in favor of the proposed new school, they were often met with criticism. Some follow-up comments to blogs about the referendum accused those in favor of the new school of being "out of touch" with what "most" (white) Lakeview residents wanted out of their public school system. Some were even accused of "playing the race card." However, Central Corridor residents like Mr. Thomas told Klein not only would the new school be diverse, but if built had the potential to integrate the most segregated neighborhoods in Lakeview, something the current approach to integration does not attempt to do. According to Mr. Thomas, "Our job is to look twenty, thirty, forty years into the future and create a world-class school system. That did not take away diversity, it added to the pot. What progressive white family wouldn't want to send their kids to a state of the art, brand new school?" In this example, Mr. Thomas hypothesizes that a new, state-of-the-art neighborhood school in the Central Corridor might be enough to stimulate neighborhood integration in northern Lakeview.

Mr. Thomas' hypothesis would not be tested, however; in March 2012, the new school referendum was defeated. Ms. Landers, a white school board member, expressed her pleasure that the referendum was defeated in a story that ran in the local paper following the vote:

> I am gratified that a majority of voters in Lakeview shared my point of view that the referendum was not the best way to spend taxpayer funds. I believe the majority of voters agree that *social justice* means providing a high quality education for *all* children, no matter their race, income, or neighborhood... A new building would have pulled resources from all other schools.

While Ms. Landers attempts to justify her opposition to the referendum based on taxes and resources, she uses the logic of abstract liberalism (e.g., rejection of group-based treatment; support for "equal opportunity") to buttress her argument that social justice means providing a high quality education for "all" students regardless of their race, income, or neighborhood. Ms. Landers' statement implies that building a new school in the mostly Black and Hispanic Central Corridor would be singling out certain Lakeview residents (low-income persons of color in that neighborhood) for special treatment at the expense of other schools in the community.

On the other hand, the African American superintendent of elementary and middle schools in Lakeview, Dr. Andrews, who was very vocal in his support for the new school referendum, stated in the same newspaper story that he was encouraged by those residents who turned out to vote in favor of the referendum:

> I am encouraged by the number of voters who feel that the parents and community of the Central Corridor *deserve* the opportunity for supporting and participating in the education of their children that a neighborhood school offers. A successful referendum would have...fulfilled the dream of a neighborhood school for this *deserving community*. However, even without these resources, we will continue providing the supports and services necessary to effectively educate our students in the current array of buildings and classroom space available.

Unlike Ms. Landers who did not see the residents of the Central Corridor deserving of a new school because it would "cost too much money," "pull resources from other schools," and "undermine social justice," Dr. Andrews directly refers to residents in the Central Corridor as *deserving* of their own neighborhood school.

When votes were calculated by neighborhood the findings told a story of racial divide (see Map 11.1). The only three wards in Lakeview that had more persons vote for the referendum than against it were predominantly Black and Hispanic; the ward with the most votes in favor of the referendum

TABLE 11.1   New school referendum vote by neighborhood/ward

	No	Yes
Ward 1 (North Lakeview)	65.6%	34.4%
Ward 2 (North Lakeview)	64.8%	36.2%
Ward 3 (Central Corridor)	32.6%	67.3%
Ward 4	50.1%	49.8%
Ward 5	48.8%	52.2%
Ward 6	56.4%	44.6%
Ward 7	52.9%	47.1%
Ward 8	51.0%	49.0%
Ward 9	52.0%	48.0%

SOURCE: COOK COUNTY CLERK'S OFFICE, https://www.cookcountyclerk.com

contained the Central Corridor where the new school would have been built (see Table 11.1).[4] The vote tallies in several other wards were close, although more residents opposed the referendum than approved. In contrast, in the two mostly white wards in the northern part of the community whose access to diversity comes primarily from their interactions with the public school system, residents overwhelmingly rejected the referendum by a margin of two to one. The end result for residents in these white neighborhoods is they were able to maintain their access to institutional diversity without having to move to more racially diverse neighborhoods. The end result for the mostly Black

---

4   The overwhelming number of votes in the Central Corridor in favor of the referendum also happened despite lower than expected voter turnout. While some white residents claimed the turnout was a sign that most residents in the Central Corridor did not want the new school built, the majority of Klein's interviews negated this impression in their interviews, instead expressing logistical concerns. The location in which the district was planning to build the school, Warren Field, has major historical and cultural value. It is one of the only green spaces in the Central Corridor and it is where segregated Black residents held all their community events. In the Central Corridor, the majority of Klein's respondents were ideologically in favor of a new school but expressed frustration at both the fact that the proposal to build the school went to a public referendum and the fact that the Board of Education would build the new school on Warren Field. Mr. Wilson, a 64-year-old lifelong Lakeview resident, expressed the following when asked to elaborate on his vote against the referendum: From my viewpoint, the city, we don't have that much land in the beginning and they wanted to take our land, the little land that we have at Warren Center and put a school there. I wasn't opposed to them havin' a school in the Central Corridor, I was opposed of havin' the school in *that* spot.

and Hispanic residents of the Central Corridor is that they lost the opportunity to once again have a neighborhood school for their children to attend instead of having them bused to mostly white schools so those schools can achieve a modicum of racial diversity. Before concluding, it is important to note that although the new school referendum was defeated, Lakeview's school board went ahead and carried out many of the projects for existing schools that were part of the referendum. For many Central Corridor residents, this was seen as "throwing salt in the wound."

6   Conclusion

In this chapter, we argue that the commitment to integration in the Lakeview K-8 public school system, while in a number of ways admirable, has allowed residents in mostly white enclaves regular access to institutional diversity without having to live in diverse neighborhoods. This in turn has allowed these residents to concentrate capital in their neighborhoods, which reproduces white habitus and maintains the status quo. We also provide several examples of the ways abstract liberalism and colorblind diversity can be used to express concern about racial inequality and express support for diversity while also allowing white residents to oppose race-specific policies they believe benefit or disadvantage one group over another (see also Stoll 2013). Indeed, according to Bonilla-Silva (2006), "Abstract liberalism is the explanatory well from which whites gather ideas to account for residential and school segregation, limited levels of interracial marriage, and a host of other racial issues" (153). By combining historical analysis with interview data from both educators and community members in Lakeview we provide a case study demonstrating how colorblind racism and diversity discourse can work to undermine racial equity even within racially diverse, socially progressive communities.

In fact, while paradoxical, it is Lakeview's reputation for racial diversity and social progressiveness that in many ways shields dominant group members from being forced to acknowledge the pervasiveness of racial inequality in the community. For example, when Stoll asked Mr. Swain, a Black teacher who is a native Southerner, whether he thought there was less racism in Lakeview (something a number of people Stoll talked to in Lakeview assumed), he responded:

> No, it's, it's the same. And I think that's the thing you'll find. Or that I've found in Lakeview, too, or many places, I mean. I felt the same way about Texas. I think there you sort of know where people stand, but I think

here it's a lot more subtle. And so you may not, um, people don't say how they feel and I prefer to know. I like that about people in Texas because I knew where they stood. And I prefer people to be honest about what they think. I think here you do find that hypocrisy or just, just not being out front makes it harder to communicate those things, you know...you're not really sure what their motives, or what they're trying to get from it [initiatives to address institutional inequalities].

To be clear, we are not suggesting that whites that live in north Lakeview are explicitly motivated to do so because there are so few people of color who live there (although research on racial residential segregation would support this contention). The reality is that most persons of color in Lakeview are priced out of the affluent neighborhoods in the northern part of the community, so in general it is whites that live in these upscale neighborhoods that have greater *opportunity* to live in more racially diverse neighborhoods than vice versa. As Bonilla-Silva (2006) points out: "Because whites have more power, their unfettered, so-called individual choices help reproduce a form of white supremacy in neighborhoods, schools, and society in general" (36). In the end, it seems that "diversity" does not trump other considerations for many whites in these neighborhoods when it comes to choosing where to live in Lakeview, but it does when it comes to local school politics.

Even though most whites that live in north Lakeview are not putting their houses up for sale to move to the Central Corridor in the name of "diversity," based on the referendum vote, they do want to hold onto their access to it when it comes to the public school system. This, of course, makes sense given the ways that "diversity" has been commodified in an era of post-racial politics. A lack of commitment to or appreciation of diversity in many respects can be seen as almost anti-American in the Age of Obama, when rejecting or critiquing "diversity" can open one up to charges of bigotry and racism. Today, "diversity" is used to promote and sell all types of goods and services (Berrey 2011; Embrick 2011).

Yet, as Lakeview's history of integrated schools and segregated neighborhoods illustrates, it is a commodity that must be kept in check. According to Doane (2012: 6), "Diversity is fine in a colorblind world, as long as things do not become too diverse." While white residents in the mostly white neighborhoods of north Lakeview are willing to exert the political will to keep their schools racially diverse, they have not as of yet mustered the political will to generate systematic efforts to desegregate their neighborhoods. As Ms. López, a dual language teacher at Morgan told Stoll, "People say they want diversity, but not in *my* backyard."

In conclusion, a major historical challenge to addressing school segregation has been attempting to disentangle public and private efforts to maintain segregated neighborhoods. As Orfield and Eaton (1996) write, "The problem that confronts any effort to demonstrate the precise nature of the school-housing relationship is that public and private discrimination, past and present, are woven inextricably together" (302). While racial demographics in the United States continue to change, a decrease in the white population coupled with an increase in the population of people of color, however, does not necessarily signal greater racial unity or integration, especially given the pervasiveness of color-bind racial logic (Bonilla-Silva 2006; Doane 2012). Indeed, as long as abstract liberalism and colorblind diversity go unchallenged, even racially diverse, socially progressive communities will struggle to address the systemic inequality and privilege pervasive in an increasingly diverse United States.

References

Ahmed, Sara. 2007. "The Language of Diversity." *Ethnic and Racial Studies*, 30 (2): 235–256.

Andersen, Margaret L. 1999. "Diversity Without Oppression: Race, Ethnicity, Identity and Power." In *Critical Ethnicity: Countering the Waves of Identity Politics* edited by M. Kenyatta and R. Tai, Totowa, NJ: Rowan and Littlefield.

Bell, Joyce M. and Douglas Hartmann. 2007. "Diversity in Everyday Discourse: The Cultural Ambiguities and Consequences of 'Happy Talk'." *American Sociological Review*, 72 (6): 895–914.

Berrey, Ellen. 2011. "Why Diversity Became Orthodox in Higher Education, and How it Changed the Meaning of Race on Campus." *Critical Sociology*, 37 (5): 573–596.

Berrey, Ellen. 2005. "Divided over Diversity: Political Discourse in a Chicago Neighborhood." *City & Community*, 4 (2): 143–170.

Bobo, Lawrence D. 1999. "Prejudice as Group Position: Microfoundations of Sociological Approach to Racism and Race Relations." *Journal of Social Issues*, 55 (3): 445–472.

Bonilla-Silva, Eduardo. 2006. *Racism Without Racists: Colorblind Racism and the Persistence of Racial Inequality in the United States* (2nd ed). Lanham, MD: Rowan and Littlefield.

Bonilla-Silva, Eduardo. 2001. *White Supremacy and Racism in the Post-Civil Rights Era*. Boulder, CO: Lynne Rienner Publishers.

Bonilla-Silva, Eduardo and Ashley W. Doane. 2003. Whiteout: *The Continuing Significance of Racism*. New York: Routledge.

Burke, Meghan A. 2011. "Discursive Fault Lines: Reproducing White Habitus in a Racially Diverse Community." *Critical Sociology*, 38 (5): 645–668.

Burke, Meghan. 2012. *Racial Ambivalence in Diverse Communities: Whiteness and the Power of Colorblind Ideologies*. Lanham, MD: Lexington Books.

Charles, Camille Z. 2006. *Won't You Be My Neighbor? Race, Class, and Residence in Los Angeles.* New York: Russell Sage Foundation.

Cooper, Davina. 2004. *Challenging Diversity: Rethinking Equality and the Value of Difference.* Cambridge: Cambridge University Press.

Doane, Ashley W. 2012. "Shades of Color Blindness: Rethinking Racial Ideology in the United States." Presented at the Annual Meeting of the Southern Sociological Society, New Orleans, Louisiana, March 22–25, 2012.

Doane, Ashley W., and Eduardo Bonilla-Silva. *White Out: The Continuing Significance of Racism.* New York, NY: Routledge.

Ellen, Ingrid G. 2001. *Sharing America's Neighborhoods: The Prospects for Stable Racial Integration.* Cambridge: Harvard University Press.

Ellen, Ingrid G. 1998. "Stable Racial Integration in the Contemporary United States: An Empirical Overview." *Journal of Urban Affairs*, 20 (1): 27–42.

Embrick, David G. 2011. "The Diversity Ideology in the Business World: A New Oppression for a New Age." *Critical Sociology*, 37 (5): 541–556.

Goodwin, Carole. 1979. *The Oak Park Strategy.* Chicago: University of Chicago Press.

Johnson, Heather Beth and Thomas M. Shapiro. 2003. "Good Neighborhoods, Good Schools: Race and the 'Good Choices' of White Families," pp. 173–187 in Doane, Ashley W., and Eduardo Bonilla-Silva. 2003. *White Out: The Continuing Significance of Racism.* New York, NY: Routledge.

Lentin, Alana and Gavin Titley. 2011. *The Crises of Multiculturalism: Racism in a Neoliberal Age.* London: Zed Books

Lortie, Dan C. 1975. *Schoolteacher: A Sociological Study.* Chicago: The University of Chicago Press.

Maly, Michael, 2005. *Beyond Segregation: Multiracial and Multiethnic Neighborhoods in the United States.* Philadelphia, PA: Temple University Press.

Nyden, Philip, Lukehart John, Maly Michael, and William Peterman. 1998. "Neighborhood Racial and Ethnic Diversity in U.S. Cities." *Cityscape: A Journal of Policy Development and Research*, 4 (2): 1–17.

Orfield, Gary and Susan Eaton. 1996. *Dismantling Desegregation: The Quiet Reversal of Brown v. Board of Education.* New York, NY: New Press.

Randolph, Antonia. 2013. *The Wrong Kind of Different: Challenging the Meaning of Diversity in American Classrooms.* New York: Teachers College.

Rich, Meghan A. 2011. "'Socioeconomic Diversity is Overrated': White Attitudes on Race and Class in a Racially Integrated Neighborhood." *Sociological Spectrum*, 31: 525–553.

Rossell, Christine. 1990. *The Carrot of the Stick for School Desegregation Policy: Magnet Schools or Forced Busing.* Philadelphia, PA: Temple University Press.

Saito, Leland T. 2009. *The Politics of Exclusion: The Failure of Race-Neutral Policies in Urban America.* Stanford, CA: Stanford University Press.

Stoll, Laurie Cooper. 2013. *Race and Gender in the Classroom: Teachers, Privilege and Enduring Social Inequalities."* Lanham, MD: Lexington Books.

CHAPTER 12

Sympathetic Racism: Color-Blind Discourse's Liberal Flair in Three Diverse Communities

Meghan A. Burke

1 Introduction

It is well established that color-blind ideologies, which ignore the ongoing realities of racism, dominate our diversity discourse. This way of thinking and talking about race, and its associated implications, have been explored in sociology, law, psychology, education, criminal justice, medicine, and political science. However, as Malat et al. (2010) note, "there are few studies that describe examples of adapted forms of color-blind ideology" (1433). In this chapter I analyze three communities that proudly claim diversity as part of their collective identity. In particular, I demonstrate how residents in these communities who identify as liberals and progressives reproduce racism in their efforts to denounce it. They do so primarily by drawing on the same tropes of coded racism and color-blindness that are prevalent in institutional settings or in conservative political spaces, but by doing so in modified ways that are complicit with their liberal political frameworks. I term this discourse "sympathetic racism."

2 Color-Blind Ideology and Diversity Discourse

Most Americans support the concept of diversity, especially when it's discussed in universalized and abstract terms. Indeed, most diversity discourse is, as Bell and Hartmann (2007) have called it, happy. This "happy talk" glows in its positivity and its assertion that diversity is a resource, one of the benefits that can be reaped from our imagined system of equal opportunity. However, when specific institutional policies or interpersonal problems come into consideration, that positivity often dissolves into ambivalence or rejection. For example, Bell and Hartman (2007) found that "In trying to specify diversity's benefits (and before they were even asked about its challenges) a large number of interviewees found it necessary to qualify and condition their responses. Others, often unexpectedly, began talking about the problems of diversity even as they were trying to uplift its strengths" (Bell and Hartmann 2007: 900). This suggests, as do my findings in this chapter, that the principle of diversity is easy to affirm, but often difficult to realize in practice. This phenomenon is often called the "principle-implementation gap" (see Durrheim and Dixon 2004).

A related feature that also frames diversity discourse in the communities I studied is the frequent aversion to the realities of privilege and oppression documented in Anderson (1999). In these abstract, "happy," expansive ways of thinking about diversity and race, we must also imagine that we are all provided equal opportunity and that race or other identity characteristics only matter to the extent that they can make us unique or provide variety. Remarks like these tend to disavow or ignore the realities of generational inequalities that create unequal opportunities and the ongoing discrimination that still deeply impacts the socio-economic well-being of people of color and other marginalized groups. As a result, this diversity discourse perfectly aligns with color-blind racism.

That color-blind ideology permeates talk about race and diversity in the United States. While important gains were made during the 1960s Civil Rights Movement, many Americans today believe that we have attained equal opportunity. Recent Pew data from 2009 to 2014 indicates that roughly half of Americans believe that the US has made the needed changes to give blacks and whites equal rights. The same report states, "Currently, 50% say that racism is a big problem in our society today. Five years ago, just 33% of Americans identified racism as a big problem, and in January 2009, only about a quarter (26%) said this" (Pew 2015). These rates vary by race, with fewer whites than blacks holding the view that racism is a problem. Further, qualitative research like that of Bonilla-Silva (2003) and the many studies that have used his framework demonstrate a widespread belief that racial inequalities can best be explained through individual effort, and/or the associated cultural values that we imagine to differ by race. These racial attitudes have been documented and given various names since at least the 1980s. Sometimes called laissez-faire (Bobo, Kluegel, & Smith 1997) or symbolic (Kinder & Sears 1981) racism, most scholars today seem to have settled on color-blind racism, a concept made most famous by Eduardo Bonilla-Silva (2003) and psychology's Color-blind Racial Attitude (CoBRA) scale (Neville et al. 2000).

That said, there are important differences between racial attitudes, which Neville et al. (2000) and others have studied, and racial ideologies. Ideologies represent a larger framework for making sense of the world, incorporating racial attitudes but also other frameworks such as neoliberalism and political ideologies, as I will demonstrate in this chapter. In particular, Bonilla-Silva (2003) traces four specific ways of talking about race, discursive frames that represent existing ideology about the social and racial structures of inequality and segregation. These four frames are: (1) abstract liberalism – a belief in individualism and US meritocracy; (2) naturalization, a belief that segregation in public spaces and private circles is a matter of personal choice or group preference; (3) cultural racism, which favors beliefs about racial groups' differing values in explaining disparate success; and (4) minimization, which explicitly deemphasizes race or favors other explanations, such as class.

Overt racism has not disappeared. Studies confirm that many individuals still express racist sentiments in private spaces or with people whom they trust (Picca and Feagin 2007, Hill 2008, Hughey 2011). As such, instances of overt racism may have moved "back stage," expressed among trusted friends and political allies. Regardless of its stage location, social scientists continue to demonstrate the prevalence of color-blind racism, for as Zamudio and Rios (2006) note, "one aspect of the struggle against racial inequality must be to demystify this discourse, to look at how this seemingly benign discourse around race and the institutions that promote it, put their stamp on a continued racial project where whites benefit at the expense of the racialized Other" (484). There remains little doubt that this project has been successful; race scholars and critical theorists often hold up color-blindness as one of the primary tools of ongoing racial inequality.

Given this work, it now seems time for scholarship to move beyond the echo chamber that affirms the presence of color-blind ideologies, and into the nuances and contradictions that are connected to it. For example, there remains further need for situated, local studies that explore nuances or configurations of this ideology rather than those that merely demonstrate its presence. Political values are one example of associated belief systems that color-blindness can interact with in complex ways. Tracing the intersection of color-blind ideologies along with liberal or progressive political ideologies allows us to consider how or in what ways some frames are tapped over others, or modified in ways that favor white privilege or liberal politics in specific locations.

This chapter will demonstrate the specifically *liberal* flair of color-blind ideology as it was used among active members of liberal, racially diverse communities. Most importantly, it demonstrates how liberals and progressives reproduce racism in their sympathetic efforts to denounce it. They do so primarily by drawing on the same tropes of coded racism and color-blindness that are prevalent in institutional settings or conservative spaces. It is this particular turn on color-blind racism that I term "sympathetic racism." Sympathetic racism is characterized by an explicit disavowal of racism and racial inequality, but simultaneously uses familiar racist tropes. In it, the frames of color-blind racism bend, but do not break. It is liberal in its politics, benevolent in its affect, and often racist in its reliance on cultural assumptions and racial codes.

3   Methds

This research took place in Chicago, which is home to 4 of the nation's 14 communities that have maintained their racial diversity for at least ten years (see Nyden et al. 1997). Those communities are defined as "stably racially diverse" if their census tract data approximated that of the city as a whole, if the community was recognized by informants as diverse, and if it maintained that diversity for at least ten years. I focused on three of these communities that adjoin one another on Chicago's north side. Community 1 was 32% white, 30% black, 28% Latino, and 6% Asian in 2000, the most recent Census year at the time when I was conducting the interviews. Community 2 was 48% white, 17% black, 20% Latino, and 12% Asian and Community 3 was 42% white, 21% black, 20% Latino, and 13% Asian. Importantly, these communities also proudly claim diversity and their liberal and/or progressive flair as one of their defining community characteristics, making them ideal sites to explore how diversity is articulated and discussed. This chapter highlights some of those data, which were collected as part of a book (Burke 2012a) where I examined how the discourse produced by active members of these stably racially diverse communities worked to uphold a white habitus – or a white social structure and a way of experiencing the world that is informed by whiteness (see also Burke 2012b, Bonilla-Silva, Goar, and Embrick 2006). This white habitus preserves privileges for whites in that racially diverse space.

Over the span of about 12 months, immediately preceding the election of Barack Obama, I conducted interviews with 41 of the most active residents in these neighborhoods – block club presidents, activists, liaisons to the aldermen and alderwomen, directors of the major community organizations, etc. These individuals were identified using public community organization and block club lists as well as referrals, as the active members of these communities are well networked with one another, often working together on a variety of projects. Focusing on those who are in a position to have the most control in those specific community fields was crucial because of my interest not just in the content of the race talk, but specifically in how that talk translates into community action. Further, a focus on those who are most active demonstrates the influence of those racial ideologies and discourses better than a general survey or random sampling of attitudes among residents in each community.

Because I did not want to produce socially desirable answers to broad questions about "diversity," I did not ask pointed questions about race during the interviews. Instead, I concentrated questions on their involvement in the community and why they decided to move into and remain living in the communities. When residents themselves brought up race as a topic of interest or activity, as they often did, it revealed race and diversity issues as a genuine concern and, as a result, more meaningful data. Interviews lasted for about an hour, and were coded by content (housing values, beaches, transit, crime) and analytical themes (colorblindness, diversity, coded racism, etc).

It is crucial to note that while these are racially diverse communities, that racial diversity is not reflected among those who hold the most power and influence in these communities: 30 of the 41 residents who were recommended or apparent as the most powerful in these communities were white. Further, while they are not the exact same 30 individuals, 30 are also property owners; indeed, many are both white and own their own property, granting both economic power and further racial privilege in these spaces, which are so vulnerable to gentrification. Twenty-three are men, and 10 are gay or lesbian. No residents identified themselves to me as transgender or bisexual. None identified as conservative either, though there were, at the time of my research, some active and popularly-read conservative bloggers in the community. One identified as libertarian and the rest labeled themselves as moderate, liberal, or progressive. Eighteen had moved to the community within the last decade; 11 had lived there between 11–20 years, and the rest for more than 20. All but one of the interviewees discussed below are white, but with few exceptions, the voices of blacks and Latino/as in the community did not significantly differ from those of whites. This is likely a function of their social and cultural capital that grants them this political power in a white-dominated space, and strategies that some people of color use to distance themselves from their racial stereotypes, particularly in white spaces (see, e.g., McClain et al. 2006; Nopper 2010; Wellburn & Pittman 2012). It also reveals the wide reach of color-blind ideology.

4   Sympathetic Racism in Diversity Communities

The findings below reflect a simultaneous refusal of and compliance with the traditional four frames of color-blind racism in these liberal, racially diverse communities. They also reveal the deeply-seated hegemony of color-blind ideology, for those who care about issues of race and inequality in their communities and who appreciate the diversity in their neighborhood seemingly cannot escape its influence in the ways that they think and talk about race. While abstract liberalism is largely abandoned in favor of an analysis emphasizing social structures, the remaining three frames are modified to retrofit a liberal politics that is, in the end, deeply conservative in their impact on the racial status quo.

In lieu of abstract liberalism, those in these communities offered structural explanations for the problems of racial segregation and crime. This allowed them to reject the rugged individualism that is a hallmark of conservative politics. Yet this structural analysis was still complicit with the larger framework of color-blindness. Further, they used this structural framework in tandem with the other three frames. Naturalization was retained by focusing on class-driven rather than racial explanations, thus mirroring the way that the minimization of racism frame is traditionally expressed. Minimization was used to emphasize the progressive nature of either the community or the people inside of it; they emphasized that they are not the racists, that racism had been largely overcome in their communities and lives. Finally, and perhaps most harmfully, they retained cultural racism in ways that express sadness and sympathy for the assumed fact of unlearned cultural values that, they imagine, could further the success of racially marginalized groups.

4.1   *Absence of Abstract Liberalism*

Of the four frames of color-blind racism identified by Bonilla-Silva (2003), abstract liberalism was the only one that was never articulated directly. While this may seem to disprove the existence of color-blind racism in this community, the distinctive structural frame that replaced it, especially in tandem with the other three frames, is a key feature of what I am calling "sympathetic racism." Further, the emphasis on structure rather than individualism provides an important foundation for this specifically liberal turn on color-blindness, as rote individualism is often branded as conservative, especially among liberals. Further, Krysan (2002) has demonstrated that structural and social explanations for social inequality are more prevalent among those who are the most highly educated – like those active in these communities. She also demonstrates that views about racial integration are met with ambivalence despite this disavowal of overt racial bias (693). My findings echo hers, revealing the deeply ambivalent nature of pro-diversity community members.

Shannon, who is white, embodies this ambivalence in her comments about crime in the community:

> We have a high incidence of drug and gang activity. High incidence of breaking into the cars by the el tracks. I live close to [an el] stop, which

is where they just installed the blue light.... For me, one of my personal opinions about all of this that a lot of the people who are involved in any of the activity are younger, in our neighborhood at least. .... but ... the ones that I hear more about, and that's usually been young adults or young kids who are out on the street with nothing better to do. And that's a problem that we have across the United States, not just in [this community].

Notice how Shannon expresses discomfort about the reality of crime in her community. At this point in the interview she also mentioned sex offenders, and discussed how the installation of the blue safety lights and cameras in the community gave people a simultaneous feeling of security and vulnerability. But she does not blame culture or individuals for these problems; she instead hints at unemployment or a lack of social services like after-school programs to occupy the youth. Her emphasis that this is a national problem also reveals a structural perspective, by definition placing her community in a larger context that individual or cultural explanations would disavow. Later in the interview, she affirmed this stance: "Well [my] attitude is – the people aren't the problem. It's the circumstances they're put in [that] are the problem." Shannon is sympathetic to those circumstances, while the racism in the community persists.

Eric, who is also white, made similar comments about public housing in his community, which was a common point of discussion for residents' community efforts and public perceptions of the community:

The sergeant or whoever's the top cop said that there's one of the highest concentrations of people living in that area because of all the multi-unit buildings in the city. Which, you know, like, Cabrini-Green, I think at its heyday, there were, like, a million people living in a one-mile radius, on top of each other, which created horrible, horrible results. Because it was just too densely populated, you know, I mean, people were literally living on top of each other, so it just opens up crime and trash and blight and ... I mean, people can't think in that close proximity to each other. So that's one thing that – that's why that section of the neighborhood gets a lot of press... bad press for crime, gangs, drugs, because it's such a high concentration of human beings.

Though Eric's comments convey something of a psychological (and therefore individual) flair, they are also structural in that they focus on housing policy and, notice, non-racial demographics, upholding color-blind discourse. Instead, it is population density, the media, and official comments by the police that are mobilized to support his understanding of, or sympathy for, those conditions. They are, after all, "human beings."

Shannon and Eric were not the only ones to express perspectives like these. However, these kinds of comments always stepped away from the available abstract liberalism frame, which would say that problems like crime and drug use and blight are the fault of individuals. This is certainly a political move, as those tropes are characteristic of the conservative political discourse that is so readily available in the frames of color-blind racism. This reliance on a structural frame may also be a function of the residents' relatively higher education level that may have granted access to the community in the first place, especially given the large number of homeowners among those most active in these Chicago neighborhoods where even rents are expensive. As Schaefer (1996) and many others have suggested, "educated people learn acceptable responses that can be employed especially in the context of questionnaires and interviews by social scientists" (5). This, however, does not mean that there is necessarily less prejudice among an educated population, only that one has had more opportunities to learn socially acceptable responses. That prejudice is revealed in the cultural racism frame discussed later, but its structural emphasis remains strong in residents' use of naturalization. As such, I demonstrate in the next section how a structural analysis can still sit alongside the traditional color-blind frame of naturalization, upholding a "sympathetic" rather than rugged individualist framework of racism.

4.2   Naturalization

Naturalization is our second of the four frames of color-blind racism, and unlike abstract liberalism, it was present among residents of this liberal, racially diverse community. That said, unlike in most treatments of color-blind racism, especially Bonilla-Silva's (2003), it retains a structural framework and therefore liberal flare, even as it continues to deny racism and reaffirm the status quo. It is in comments like Walter's, who is white, where structural realities may be acknowledged with sympathy, but where their racial character is denounced by an emphasis on class: "And that's the one sad thing. We have essentially segregation in the school, and – and it's more economic on that. And, uh, so you have a lot of people abandoning the city, go[ing] out in the suburbs."

While economics are the front line of perpetual school segregation, they also operate through race, in dual housing markets, ongoing bias among whites, and active discrimination by real estate agents and banks. Despite that, Krysan (2002) has also demonstrated how whites tend to explain matters of segregation and integration in terms of class. She notes, "it was easy for... respondents who gave [a class-based] answer to distance themselves from holding negative racial attitudes because the forces of economics and the ways of 'society' should be blamed" (693). A later study of hers (2009) confirms that, despite this posturing, whites tend to prefer neighborhoods with few to no blacks residing in them. Of course, Walter may not feel that way, but his discourse is one that supports the idea that race and racism no longer play a central role in this segregation that he acknowledges and disavows. The acknowledgement and disavowal constitutes the sympathy; the color-blindness and its impact from positions of power, racism.

Todd, below, who is white, also acknowledges the reality of segregation inside of his racially diverse neighborhood. But rather than considering how institutional factors like racism shape property values or policing, he renders it a matter of personal choice:

> People tend to still segregate themselves by race, I think. More than they would like to think... That happens because, you know, just how Chinatown becomes Chinatown. People tend to congregate with like people.... This building becomes an African American building because, you know, an African American may own it, and it's just "Hey, I got this friend," "OK, sure." "They're – yeah, they got a job, they don't owe this that and the other thing, their credit's OK, move in!" and these things just sort of happen.

To be sure, social networks play an important role in our ability to access resources. But as became clear in a later part of our conversation, a "class not race" framework is crucial to Todd's understanding of racial segregation and inequality:

> I'm glad to see, – and its Barack who's finally started bringing up this issue in the presidential campaign now, is, you know, by and large it's become a class issue. And maybe that's been an issue longer in the history of this country than anybody ever wanted to admit and that the race issue wasn't necessarily as big a problem as it was a class issue.

Here too, Todd perfectly articulates a liberal framework that is still complicit with color-blind racism. His two comments together present the notion, as he says, that "the race issue wasn't necessarily as big a problem," which his hypothetical narrative about gaining housing would support. Friendly networks of acquaintances, not wealth gaps deeply structured by generations of racial inequality and contemporary discrimination, explain segregation in tandem with the, in his view, more fundamental issue of class. Further, the black then-candidate Obama is used as a token to validate his class-centered understanding of segregation, adding extra rhetorical power to his claim that race is not the fundamental issue. This is despite race carrying far more explanatory power in class inequality than most any other measure.

The role of these communities as explicitly liberal and proud of their diversity is crucial to bear in mind, for this site produces different dynamics than those of segregated or conservative communities. Note how Wendy, also white, connects her deep commitment to racial diversity to a discourse that ignores the racial politics of gentrification:

> Wendy: I always made a vow to myself I would want to live in a mixed community, you know. And ultimately coming [here], this was the epitome of what I had been looking for. It really was.
>
> Author: Do you worry about these neighborhoods losing this character over time?
>
> Wendy: At times I do. At times I do because of economics more than anything else. Economics. Whether people can afford to stay here or not.

This ambivalence and contradiction around the role of race in shaping her community's future, despite the commitment to racial diversity among people like her, exemplifies the ways that color-blind ideology can be so insidious in its impact. I have no doubt that Wendy does indeed care about racial diversity and does not want to see that important feature of her neighborhood lost. But if even she cannot articulate the role of race, then the community's residents, who, like her, are in positions of influence, are not equipped to challenge systemic matters of access and the racial politics of the development process.

While structurally focused, through its emphasis on class dynamics rather than personal choice, the discussion about segregation in these racially diverse neighborhoods retains a specifically liberal flair. Todd can credit Obama, who at that time was strongly perceived as a progressive, for his views, and Walter can emphasize how he finds segregation in the Chicago school system to be "sad." Wendy's commitment to living in a diverse community is clear, but her focus on racial inequality is not. They all exhibit sympathy in their comments about segregation while explicitly de-emphasizing race as a driving or central factor in explaining it. In this way they fold together color-blind ideologies with sympathy, producing the unique form of racism that is pervasive in these liberal communities.

4.3   *Minimization*

As I have discussed, most prior studies of color-blindness have not carefully traced variations in the established frames of color-blindness, such as how naturalization can rely on a class-not-race discourse that is otherwise labeled as minimization. In these communities, that discourse doesn't minimize racism, but rather emphasizes one's dismay with segregation. Racism is minimized, instead, in a juxtaposition between the tolerant progressives who are sympathetic to racism, and those who have not yet attained their (imagined) enlightened status. They are able to position themselves as one of "the good ones," minimizing the presence of racism within themselves and their community instead of broadly in the rest of society.

Patty, who is white and among those in the community that had lived there the longest, used this historical perspective to make comments not just about the "tolerance" in her community, but also within the nation as a whole:

> Fortunately, there isn't as much, I don't see as much of that now. I think race is not the issue that it was before. You know, I don't know. I mean, it was more of an issue – what are we talking about? The "70s? The – 20, 30 years ago? It was more of an issue then. For, I"m not talking about for me. It was never a big deal for us. Um, but for the people that it was a big deal for, it doesn't seem to be as big a deal for anymore.... And I always felt that one reason [this community] could manage so well, [with] diversity, is there's a mentality here that can look past things like color and language, to the person, you know, and I think there's a lot of that. And I think that's why [our community] can hold the way it does.

Patty's comments that "race is not the issue that it was before" is directly complicit with the minimization of frame. This is a near-literal example of the "past is the past" storyline that Bonilla-Silva (2003) critiques in his foundational piece on color-blindness. But her comments also celebrate her own liberal frame of mind and that of her community, despite its deep segregation within its borders and its prevalence of coded (Burke 2012a/b) and cultural racism, which I discuss below.

It is important that communities take a stand and make fighting racism one of their explicit community goals. That commitment has an impact on the culture of local communities, and can carry important political clout. But denying the fact that racism does in fact persist leaves the very communities that are so fragile – racially diverse communities chief among them – ill-equipped to preserve their diversity or to make their communities fair and just places for all. It assumes that these communities do not face serious problems of racial inequality because of their proclamation of diversity as a value or their rejection of racism in principle.

Denise, a white woman who like the others held pro-diversity beliefs that I felt to be very sincere, exemplifies this dilemma:

> Denise: I mean, we are really color-blind. We are, you know, there just – there isn't the… you don't hear about the hatred and the unfortunate remarks that are made elsewhere because it's a family here. It's a family here.
> Author: And why do you think that is?
> Denise: Because we're – we tolerate. We tolerate. Our differences are acute, but we tolerate each other. And it doesn't matter to us that you're a gay man or a black woman. It doesn't matter to us. You're a person. And that's who you have living here.

Denise's goals are noble. It is heartening to imagine that our communities really are families, where the social identities that very much shape our lived experiences (race, sexuality, gender) no longer influence differential access or treatment. But, as activists and scholars have long pointed out, tolerance is not alone a worthy goal. After all, how often do we enjoy being "tolerated"? Further, in another part of the interview, Denise also said the following when talking about her efforts around crime in the community:

> It's that kind of a thing where the hooligans are going like this [middle finger] to us. And they're also in the [park by the school].… And then I went to the beat meeting on it, and then I'm gonna go to another beat meeting on it and say, you know, they're – these hooligans– they're pelting youngsters with stones. Let's increase your patrols for an indefinite period of time. And now it's getting warm, so…

The "hooligans" that Denise refers to are a common code for black youth, who in this community like many others, are disproportionately surveilled, often thanks to the political pressure that middle class whites like Denise are able to exert on the local police force. Her "tolerance" therefore runs thin in this community that she herself has labeled as "color-blind."

4.4   Cultural Racism

Denise's comments are, then, a useful transition into the most obviously problematic of the color-blind frames used in this racially diverse community, that of cultural racism. The cultural racism frame relies on assumptions about each racial group that attribute varying success rates simply to notions about culture. In part it can rely on coded racism like that of the "hooligans" that Denise references above, and Evelyn below. But it is especially important here to see how there is an explicit statement of sympathy and an effort to underline the good people emerging from these imaginations about culture in the discourse. Evelyn, white, ties together all of these themes in her comments below:

> I mean, [we] still have a way to go on [two major thoroughfares]. And here's the issue, you know, that you get into racial and I think that the problem of – of, um, [these streets] is partially racial, but racial in the sense that the hooligans and the bad people have made an impact in the area. And there are plenty of non-whites that are very good citizens and want a safe, clean place to live just like everybody else. Um, but – but somehow or another with the four-plus-ones you got the, uh, uh, wrong element of the black community in there.

In her comments Evelyn explicitly links the problems on the streets to people of color. Her liberal and color-blind tendencies emphasize that her comments do not extend to all people of color, but they do include the notion that there is a harmful element in black culture that is explicitly racist, which reifies racial stereotypes and in that process also legitimates racial inequality.

Kurt, who is white, in his comments below, relies on tokenism, a black best friend from college, to place the blame for racial inequality squarely on black people:

> I had lunch today with one of my best friends from college, and he is a man of color who was reared by aristocratic southern black people, aunts and grandparents. And what's always been stunning about knowing this young man is that he is not one who is very big on his own race. Some people tend to use the phrase, well, they're ghetto or they behave black.
>
> Well, this kid doesn't behave in this manner at all. He loathes that. He doesn't understand why people can't work beyond the stereotype that they have brought on themselves. We've had very limited discussion of this area because he doesn't dwell on it. His opinion is he's just another person and, well, the best way to characterize him is what he once said to me about the way he views the world, and that is that he makes no apologies for having read as a child.

Kurt's comments are confusing, in that he still refers to this "best friend from college" as a "kid" and a "young man" even though Kurt appeared to be in his mid-40s. But the problems in his comments run deeper. He argues that stereotypes emerge not from a system that upholds white supremacy and privileges by mobilizing racial stereotypes, but rather that they "are brought on themselves," by faulty values and behavior.

While not especially liberal in its critique of what he imagines to be true about black culture, he does make sure to emphasize that this is a friend and that they don't dwell on race in their conversations together. This upholds the veil of color-blindness for its own sake, despite the tokenism that he deploys to engage it. Further, he is able to articulate the value that they together place on education in distancing themselves from this trope. In that sense it is also a way to assert sympathy for those choices around education – that some are allegedly punished for it and that some, he imagines, do not value it.

Education also constituted the core of Patty's remarks, which are emblematic of the sympathetic racism that I am positing in this piece. Patty and I had been talking about local schools when she said:

> One thing, and I hope this doesn't sound racist, it's not meant to be: One thing you never hear, is the schools that are struggling so much, I know a lot of the teachers in those schools, and they are giving their all to their job. But there are students coming that are not... first of all there's all kinds of nonsense goes on at home. They don't have proper meals, there might be, god knows what they do all night, the kids fall asleep in class. The news was on the other night about closing those schools and making them small schools. A freshman student from [a local public school] was interviewed, and he was black. And they said, "Well what do you think the problem is?" And this little boy said, in terms of the students that weren't doing well, he said, "It's because they families don't care."
>
> But you can't say that. And you never see it and you never hear it. He said it. But he was a student and he was black. And he could say it. But nobody else could say it... I know what some of this stuff is that happens, but nobody says it, but he said "They families don't care." And that's – that's really what it's all about.... So it's very sad.

Patty, like Kurt, also uses tokenism in repeating the comments that this young man said, which she believed she cannot say as a white woman. The bulk of her comments are devoted to "proving" that there is something inherent to black culture that does not care well for children or value education. This common racial stereotype, which empirical research always demonstrates to be untrue (see Iversen & Farber 1996; Compton-Lilly 2003; Lareau & Horvat 1999), is not however mobilized to defend white supremacy or racial inequality. Instead, Patty notes that it is "very sad." Her sympathetic racism also extends to those on the front lines of struggling schools, the teachers who work so hard to teach in underfunded and overcrowded environments.

Walter tied this sympathy to his structural understanding of housing policy in ways that still replicate racism by using the deeply problematic language of a "jungle" to refer to areas that are predominantly black:

> One of our issues here in this community [is] we have a lot of nursing homes and HUD buildings, and Section 8 buildings, which are all good and needed. The only problem is [that our alderperson] likes to attract them. We've got over-concentration. And that's the wrong thing. You would think we'd learned that lesson when we created Cabrini-Green. And you're not doing those people any favor. You're creating a-a-a jungle for them....

While the jungle language reinforces the notion of unruly black people acting like animals rather than humans, it is also deliberately liberal in his comments that public housing is "good and needed." It is also sympathetic in that he calls it "the wrong thing" and that it's not doing us "any favors."

His language of "those people," while itself loaded, also represents a distancing strategy that mirrors charity rather than justice. Indeed, sympathetic racism is explicitly not about partnering with peers or exerting empathy over shared struggle. Instead, it stands from a place atop the racial hierarchy and looks downward "with amused contempt and pity" (DuBois [1903] 2007). It is the newest form of the White Man's Burden, packaged for a color-blind social system and useful for liberals in denouncing racism and inequality while still upholding the core beliefs that sustain it.

5   Discussion

It is important to recognize what I am calling "sympathetic racism" for several reasons. The first is that it represents a particularly insidious way of thinking and talking about racism, which helps to sustain rather than challenge the status quo. It admirably rejects segregation and inequality, but still participates in the legitimation of both. It presents itself as an alternative to the color-blind mainstream, proudly embracing diversity, owning the reality of racial inequality and segregation. But it does not disrupt the notion that segregation is explicitly racialized, that race even more so than class tends to explain neighborhood preferences (Krysan 2002), and that there is ongoing and persistent racial discrimination in today's housing market (see Hanson & Hawley 2011; Ondrich et al. 2003).

It also distances the speaker or community from those "ugly racists" who are imagined to be the sole perpetrators of racism and inequality, those "intolerant" conservative bigots against whom they are more enlightened. As Bonilla-Silva (1997) argued in a paradigm-shifting piece, "[When] racism is conceived of as a belief with no real social basis, it follows that those who hold racist views must be irrational or stupid.... This view allows for a tactical distinction between individuals with the 'pathology' and social actors who are 'rational' and racism-free" (468). Crucially, it does so while using some of the very same bigoted and ignorant assumptions about racial cultural difference that legitimate conservative social policy and the same qualities that they abhor. It thus weaves together a thin veil under which the imagined good people may huddle, rather than actively and explicitly challenging the unequal social structures that they themselves acknowledge to exist.

This emphasis on liberal, "sympathetic" colorblindness is also important because it helps us to break from the assumption that color-blind ideologies are confined to conservative politics or are most prevalent among conservative voters. In some way this assumption makes sense, given color-blindness's fit with neoliberal politics and frameworks. Bonilla-Silva's (2003) frame of abstract liberalism assumes an equal playing field in order to emphasize individualism, incorporating free-market principles such as competition and a lack of regulation that are hallmarks of conservativism. But conservative politics are not the only ones affirmed through color-blind frames, as I have demonstrated elsewhere (Burke 2012a). Hughey (2012), too, has shown racism to be prevalent even among committed white antiracists, who typically sit quite far left within the political spectrum. Bonilla-Silva's (2003) later editions of *Racism Without Racists* also make his disappointment in Obama and his liberal base quite clear. Scholars must continue to study and challenge color-blind racism in liberal settings.

Sympathetic racism is further important to recognize because it reveals how deeply these color-blind ideologies are entrenched: Even those who explicitly and proudly reject the dominant framework of political conservatism, embrace racial diversity, and reject the segregation that is so often taken for granted often cannot escape its power over the ways that they talk and likely think about race. That is not to say that it is impossible, for there were indeed some community members who rejected these frameworks and expressed their frustration with those who used the frames. As Matthew, who is white, said when recalling a recent community interaction:

> I remember I had this very significant... conversation with one of the neighbors who I just assumed was this, like, sort of progressive open minded person because she was really into gardening and was really this kind of earthy person. And she just was so antagonistic towards Section 8 families and low-income families... And it was shocking to me. I couldn't even imagine that people like that existed in the neighborhood who are progressive people.

As another community member, Carla, a Latina, memorably put it, "You don't have to be in a cul-de-sac environment to have a cul-de-sac mindset, you know? [Laughs.] Okay? There's some mindsets over here that should be in Naperville."

Both of these comments reveal that it is indeed possible to pierce through these powerful frameworks of color-blindness. But Matthew and Carla were among the very few exceptions to the larger trend. Most of those who I interviewed fully embraced the frames of color-blind racism, albeit in the liberal and sympathetic fashion that I detailed above. It is crucial here to recall that I specifically interviewed those who are most powerful in these communities – those influence network with the aldermen and -women to approve the tax increment funding for businesses and work with police on their enforcement strategies in these communities, on development initiatives, and otherwise shape the community. It is these voices and perspectives that most impact community life in these racially diverse communities. And it is for this reason and others that I discuss in my book (Burke 2012a) that these communities have since the time of my study been subject to the forces of gentrification that threaten the racial diversity that they so proudly claim.

6   Conclusion

The study of color-blind racism remains an important site for studying and dismantling the racial order that provides legitimations of white privilege and supremacy and upholds the neoliberal status quo. This chapter offers an addendum to the well-established frames of color-blind racism by demonstrating a particular liberal flare that emerges in the racial discourse that takes place in racially diverse urban communities. This "sympathetic racism" is insidious, in that well-meaning folks who support liberal politics are often still making use of racial stereotypes and downplaying racism in their communities, making it then hard to challenge. These communities do indeed pride themselves on their liberal, and at times even progressive, politics. They tout ideals of diversity and social justice, but do not present a fundamentally different way of talking and thinking about segregation in their schools and or crime on their streets. Until that way of thinking and talking is changed, those who hold disproportionate social power will, despite their noble political goals, likely perpetuate racism and racial inequalities.

References

Bell, Joyce M. and Douglas Hartmann. 2007. "Diversity in Everyday Discourse: The Cultural Ambiguities and Consequences of 'Happy Talk'." *American Sociological Review*, 72 (6): 895–914.

Bobo, Lawrence, James R. Kluegel and Ryan A. Smith. 1997. "Laissez-Faire Racism: The Crystallization of a Kinder, Gentler, Antiblack Ideology." *Racial Attitudes in the 1990s: Continuity and Change*, 15: 23–25.

Bonilla-Silva, Eduardo. 1997. Rethinking Racism: Toward a Structural Interpretation. *American Sociological Review*, 62 (3): 465–480.

Bonilla-Silva, Eduardo. 2003. *Racism without Racists: Color-Blind Racism and the Persistence of Racial Inequality in the United States*. Lanham, MD: Rowman & Littlefield Publishers.

Bonilla-Silva, Eduardo, Carla Goar, and David G. Embrick. 2006. "When Whites Flock Together: The Social Psychology of White Habitus." *Critical Sociology*, 32 (2–3): 229–253.

Burke, Meghan A. 2012a. *Racial Ambivalence in Diverse Communities: Whiteness and the Power of Color-Blind Ideologies*. Lanham, MD: Lexington Books.

Burke, Meghan A. 2012b. "Discursive Fault Lines: Reproducing White Habitus in a Racially Diverse Community." *Critical Sociology*, 38 (5): 645–668.

Compton-Lilly, Catherine. 2003. *Reading Families: The Literate Lives of Urban Children*. New York, NY: Teachers College Press.

Du Bois, W.E.B. [1903] 2007. *The Souls of Black Folk*. Oxford, London: Oxford University Press.

Durrheim, Kevin, and John Dixon. 2004. "Attitudes in the Fiber of Everyday Life: The. Discourse of Racial Evaluation and the Lived Experience of Desegregation." *The American Psychologist*, 59:626–36.

Hanson, Andrew, and Zackary Hawley. 2011. "Do Landlords Discriminate in the Rental Housing market? Evidence from an Internet Field Experiment in US Cities." *Journal of Urban Economics*, 70 (2/3): 99–114.

Hill, Jane H. 2009. *The Everyday Language of White Racism*. Oxford, London: John Wiley & Sons.

Hughey, Matthew. 2012. *White Bound: Nationalists, Antiracists, and the Shared Meanings of Race*. Redwood City, CA: Stanford University Press.

Hughey, Matthew W. 2011. "Backstage Discourse and the Reproduction of White Masculinities." *The Sociological Quarterly*, 52 (1): 132–153.

Iversen, Roberta R. and Naomi B. Farber. 1996. "Transmission of Family Values, Work, and Welfare among Poor Urban Black Women." *Work and Occupations*, 23 (4): 437–460.

Kinder, Donald R. and David O. Sears. 1981. "Prejudice and Politics: Symbolic Racism Versus Racial Threats to the Good Life." *Journal of Personality and Social Psychology*, 40 (3): 414.

Krysan, Maria. 2002. "Whites Who Say They'd Flee: Who are they, and Why would they Leave?" *Demography*, 39 (4): 675–696.

Lareau, Annette and Erin M. Horvat. 1999. "Moments of Social Inclusion and Exclusion Race, Class, and Cultural Capital in Family-School Relationships." *Sociology of Education*: 37–53.

Malat, Jennifer, Rose Clark-Hitt, Diana Jill Burgess, Greta Friedemann-Sanchez and Michelle Van Ryn. 2010. "White Doctors and Nurses on Racial Inequality in Health Care in the USA: Whiteness and Colour-Blind Racial Ideology." *Ethnic and Racial Studies*, 33 (8): 1431–50.

Paula D. McClain, Niambi M. Carter, Victoria M. DeFrancesco Soto, Monique L. Lyle, Jeffrey D. Grynaviski, Shayla C. Nunnally, Thomas J. Scotto, J. Alan Kendrick, Gerald F. Lackey, and Kendra Davenport Cotton. 2006. Racial distancing in a southern city: Latino immigrants' views of black Americans. *Journal of Politics*, 68: 571–584.

Neville, Helen A., Roderick L. Lilly, Georgia Duran, Richard M. Lee and LaVonne Browne. 2000. "Construction and Initial Validation of the Color-Blind Racial Attitudes Scale (CoBRAS)." *Journal of Counseling Psychology*, 47 (1): 59.

Nopper, Tamara K. 2010. Colorblind racism and institutional actors' explanations of Korean immigrant entrepreneurship. *Critical Sociology*, 36: 65–85.

Nyden, Philip, Michael Maly and John Lukehart. 1997. "The Emergence of Stable Racially and Ethnically Diverse Urban Communities: A Case Study of Nine US Cities." *Housing Policy Debate*, 8 (2): 491–534.

Ondrich, Jan, Stephen Ross, and John Yinger. 2003. "Now You See It, Now You Don't: Why Do Real Estate Agents Withhold Available Houses from Black Customers?." *Review of Economics & Statistics*, 85 (4): 854–873.

Picca, Leslie H. and Joe R. Feagin. 2007. *Two-Faced Racism: Whites in the Backstage and Frontstage*. New York, NY: Routledge/Taylor & Francis Group.

Schaefer, Richard T. 1996. "Education and Prejudice." *The Sociological Quarterly*, 37 (1): 1–16.

Welburn, Jessica S., and Cassi L. Pittman. 2012. Stop "blaming the man": Perceptions of inequality and opportunities for success in the Obama era among middle-class African Americans. *Ethnic and Racial Studies*, 35: 523–540.

Zamudio, Margaret M. and Francisco Rios. 2006. "From Traditional to Liberal Racism: Living Racism in the Everyday." *Sociological Perspectives*, 49(4): 483–501.

PART 6

Diversity and Complex Organizations

∴

When a Lack of Diversity Matters: How Juvenile Justice Professionals See Non-White Juveniles

Paul R. Ketchum

1 Introduction

Disproportionate Minority Contact (DMC) refers to the overrepresentation of minorities at contact or decision points throughout the juvenile justice system as compared to the racial/ethnic demographics for the same area. This chapter will examine both how, and perhaps more significantly, why all significant attempts to address DMC ignore the overt, subtle and institutional racism which is the cause DMC. At the beginning of the interviews with juvenile court professionals (lawyer and judges, juvenile probation officers and police officers), participants were asked to describe, racially and ethnically, both the neighborhoods they grew up in and their current neighborhood, as well as the race/ethnicity of their closest friends. Overwhelmingly, both White and non-White professionals lived very white lives, with most describing both their current neighborhood and their closest friends as all or mostly White. This chapter will examine the impact of juvenile justice professionals living in white neighborhoods, having white friends, but working with a largely non-white youth population, on DMC.

The legal concept of *parens patriae,* which allows the state to assume control of a juvenile in place of the parent for young criminal offenders, neglected children or those deemed "incorrigible" by the state to was, and still is used to provide formal justification to intervene in the lives of non-Whites and the poor. The juvenile justice system has always been used as a tool to control "other people's children."

The system is essentially two tiered, in which non-Whites and the poor officially report to juvenile court and middle class and wealthy whites go directly to private treatment. DMC occurs in almost every jurisdiction in the country that has a significant minority population. Discrepancy in treatment of Whites and non-Whites can be seen at each step or decision point, as youth move through the system. Non-Whites are more likely to be arrested, given confinement and transferred (petitioned or waivered) to adult court. White youth, on the other hand, are more likely receive diversion, informal probation or formal probation.

There are two possible explanations for DMC, differential involvement and differential treatment. The first, differential involvement, suggest that non-White youths commit crimes at rates substantially higher than Whites. Differential treatment, on the other hand, suggest harsher treatment, throughout the system, for non-Whites. More than fifty years of research identifies the role of racialization in the justice system (Piliavin and Briar, 1964), however, none of the programs currently acknowledged by the Office of Juvenile Justice and Delinquency Prevention (OJJDP) to reduce DMC, directly address police bias and only a few address bias at later contact points though emphasizing diversion programs and/or modifying sentencing so as to emulate the treatment of White youth. The vast majority of programs are designed to reduce the amount of crime non-White youth are involved in.[1] This, of course, assumes that arrest and conviction rates for youth are an accurate indicator of crime rates. Essentially, attempts to reduce DMC revolve around *differential involvement* assuming it is the greater or even sole cause of DMC. It speaks to the power of embedded racism when the programs designed to combat racism in the juvenile justice system never actually address the racial bias which results in DMC.

Two studies,[2] recently conducted with my colleague, B. Mitch Peck, for the Oklahoma Office of Juvenile Affairs from 2012–2013, examine DMC in Oklahoma, conducted for the Oklahoma Office of Juvenile Affairs from 2012–2013, and will be used to support the conclusions reached in this chapter. The two studies reference the official police and juvenile court data used to measure DMC, self-report criminal activity from an anonymous survey given to students attending public urban, suburban and rural high schools in central Oklahoma and in-depth interviews with law enforcement, juvenile court attorneys and judges and juvenile probation officers.

2   A Brief Primer on DMC

Most of this section will focus on Black experiences. However, Blacks are not the only group significantly affected by racial (or ethnic) profiling. Hispanics are often subjected to racial/ethnic profiling however, the rate at which this happens is not easy to determine. Surprisingly, minority overrepresentation is likely *substantially underreported* in the Office of Juvenile Justice and

---

1   The OJJDP model programs guide website: http://www.ojjdp.gov/mpg/.
2   DMC in Oklahoma: Final Report, 2013 and DMC School Survey: Final Report, 2013.

Delinquency Preventions (OJJDP) data (Snyder and Sickmund 1999) and FBI reports (Steffensmeier and Demuth 2000) as not all police and court agencies separate *ethnic* groups, resulting in an often inaccurate, hodgepodge method of counting Latinos in the criminal and juvenile justice systems. Often only the race of those in the justice system, rather than ethnicity is recorded. This has led to numerous cases of Latinos being categorized as white, making it seem as if the system is less discriminatory by over-counting white arrest/conviction rates through the inclusion of Hispanics (Steffensmeier and Demuth 2000). In the Oklahoma DMC studies used here, areas with relatively small Asian populations, Asian youth were about half as likely as Whites to be arrested, charged, etc. In the one area with a fairly large Asian population in Oklahoma, Asian juveniles were equally as likely as Whites to be arrested, charged, etc.[3]

In recent decades, a number of scholars have suggested that young, angry men of color actually commit more crimes than do other individuals due to either a genetic predisposition to crime, which resurrects the long discredited theory from Lombroso, while others claim that non-White families tend to embrace a culture of violence or a culture of crime (D'Sousa 1995; Herrnstein and Murray 1994; Wilbanks 1986; Wilson and Herrnstein 1985). Overrepresentation in the justice system is perceived as a direct result of genetic or cultural failings of non-Whites which lead certain groups to be more or less likely to commit a crime. This concept assumes that each individual (a) has the ability to choose whether or not to commit a crime, (b) that social forces take a back seat to individual choice and finally (c) that arrest/conviction rates are an accurate reflection of criminal activity. The inherent problem with this perspective resides in the painting of juvenile crime/deviance as attacks against privilege, never acknowledging the need or even desirability of diversity. The "culture of violence" perspective exists only to rationalize and reinforce the *status quo*. It should be noted that while there is little current scholarly work supporting this contention, many of those interviewed for the study ascribe cultural criminalistic tendencies to minorities.

Recent research examining DMC and differential involvement tends to focus on social forces experienced more dramatically by non-Whites, resulting in higher levels of criminal behavior from the young living in poor, minority neighborhoods. These studies focus on environmental factors (Martinez 2002; Anderson 1999). This perspective suggests that issues such as poverty, disrupted home-life, relative disadvantage, limited economic and educational opportunity, disenfranchisement and limited community policing are among those factors which influence both the prevalent types of crime as well as the crime

---

3 DMC in Oklahoma: Final Report, 2013 and DMC School Survey: Final Report, 2013.

rate. From this view, minority's differential involvement in crime is due to environmental factors encouraging or otherwise rewarding criminal behavior. For instance, an earlier study of DMC in Oklahoma for the Oklahoma Office of Juvenile Affairs (Damphousse, Davis and Charish 2004) found that Black and Hispanic youths committed more crime than did white youth, however once environmental condition were controlled for, that difference disappeared.

2012 and 2013 OJJDP statistics[4] clearly show significant overrepresentation of black male youths in almost every category of juvenile court records, including arrests. This trend has been consistent over the years. However, the discrepancy in arrest and conviction rates for blacks and whites cannot be easily explained as different rates of offending between white and black juveniles (Snyder and Sickmund 1999). For example, Wordes and Bynum (1995) found, in their study of the juvenile justice system in Michigan, both through official police records and interviews with officers, that race or race-related factors, such as being in the wrong neighborhood or hanging out on the street heavily contributed to a decision by officers to initiate contact. Many of the officers interviewed also noted that boys need a father figure in their lives and that single mothers (statistically a more common living situation for Blacks) cannot adequately control delinquent behavior. Similarly, in Pennsylvania, Kemph, Leonard and Sontheimer (1995) discovered that "...offense-related, system-related, and social history factors are accorded different weight depending on race" (p. 120).

Differential involvement is ideologically grounded in blame assigned either fully (individual choice) or partially (rooted in social problems) based on arrest and conviction rates. It further assumes that arrest and conviction rates of minorities as compared to whites are reflective of actual rates of commission of delinquent and criminal acts. If minorities truly commit delinquent and criminal acts at rates well above those of whites, the only rational course is to address how to limit minorities' involvement in delinquent and criminal acts.

Differential Involvement, be it dependent or independent of social problems, is not the only potential explanation for DMC. The other major explanation is *differential treatment,* which suggests that minorities receive disproportionate punishment for crime. Potential causes of differential treatment induced DMC range from institutional racism and the effect or color-blind racism to overt racism. Color-blind racism is illustrated by juvenile justice officials focusing on factors which are strongly correlated to race, such as SES, demeanor, family structure and school status, resulting in racialized outcomes (Pope and Snyder 2003; Pope and Feyerhern 1990). Along these lines, Wordes and Bynum (1995)

---

4   http://www.ojjdp.gov/ojstatbb/ezajcs/.

found that police officers sometimes formed decisions based on expectations tinged with racial/ethnic stereotypes. Bridges and Steen (1998) found the same of court officials. In fact, a number of studies have found that while the type of current offense and prior record explain much of the observed minority over-representation in the juvenile justice system, these do not explain all of the racial differences (Austin 1995; Fagan *et al.* 1987; Krisberg *et al.* 1987). Feld (1999) argues that "A system of justice in which the most powerful explanatory legal variables-present offense and prior record-account for only about 25% of the variance in sentencing remains a highly discretionary and perhaps discriminatory one" (p. 94).

Differing rates of official placement of juvenile offenders itself creates *de facto* segregation as (1) Latino's are more likely to be placed in public facilities, (2) blacks and Latino's are more often placed in private residential care and (3) white offenders are most likely to be placed in privately run group homes and private drug and alcohol treatment centers (OJJDP Statistical Briefing Book, Kempf-Leonard and Sontheimer 1995). Another cause of *differential treatment* is what Feld (1999) refers to as "justice by geography". Feld (1999) noted that "...individualized discretion is often synonymous with racial disparities in sentencing juveniles" (p. 72). Urban and, to a lesser degree, suburban courts tend to more formalized in structure, allowing less judicial discretion. According to Feld, this is due to the larger caseloads found in urban courts, which, in turn, forces reliance upon standardized bureaucratic measures (1999).

By any measurement, minorities are over-represented in the juvenile justice system. This overrepresentation has remained fairly constant in the last decade as 1993 figures from the FBI, show that African Americans, though only 12% of the general population (about 15% of the juvenile population), accounted for 27% of all juvenile arrests, 49% of juvenile arrests for violent crime and 26% of arrests for property crime (Joseph, 1995) Significantly, the further they move through the system, the greater the disproportionate representation (Leonard *et al.* 1995). At the juvenile court level, in 1993, about 20% of all youths referred to juvenile court were detained. Of that 20%, however, judges detained about 18% of white juveniles and 26% of black juveniles (Feld 1999).

Juvenile courts are not immune from racial bias. Because minority youth are more likely to be arrested in the first place and a prior record is a major determining factor for further arrests, at each stage (initial contact, juvenile court, detention, criminal court and incarceration) the percentage of minority youth climbs as one moves through the system (Hendricks and Byers 2000).

The Office of Juvenile Justice and Delinquency Preventions (OJJDP) has concluded that "...institutional bias or racism occurs from the initial contact the juvenile makes with law enforcement up through the juvenile court system itself" (Lardiero 1997). Other evidence similarly suggests that race is frequently a factor at different points throughout the Juvenile Justice system. Bishop and Frazier (1996), using both analysis of case histories and interviews with officials at all levels of the juvenile justice system, conclude that race is the dominant factor at every stage of processing, but most important at the initial arrest stage. Free (1996) found that "African Americans were less likely than whites to be released by the police". Both the case history analysis and the interviews support the idea that race is more of a determining factor for the police than any other part of the juvenile system, likely due to a lack of public oversight as officers have significant latitude in deciding to commit to initial contact and then whether to make the contact official, such as a citation or arrest (Leonard *et al.* 1995).

The practice of racial profiling also makes African American youth more susceptible to initial contact (Jackson and Pabon 2000). The concepts of differential treatment and differential involvement collide most publicly with the issue of racial profiling. Key to the concept of mistrust of the justice system for many minorities is the concept of racial profiling or the "out-of-place" doctrine. Kathryn Russell (1998) points out that the "out-of-place" doctrine, which is number of courts have upheld as legal, gives police a legal justification for stopping and questioning blacks when they are in a predominantly white neighborhood. Studies indicate that black males are stopped and questioning by the police at a rate much higher than any other racial or ethnic group. According to Russell, this creates a problem in that black males are stopped and questioned in rate much higher than the level of Black involvement in crime. Of course racial targeting for the purpose of enhancing the efficiency of the criminal justice system (racial profiling) has effects upon the minority community well beyond the scope of the justice system. For instance, Coates (2007) explains:

> How racial non-elites respond to racial profiling may be the difference between life and death. In cities across the nation, increased levels of incarceration, fear, and even death have resulted as these nonelites have found their opportunities for freedom and security impaired ... repeated episodes of racial intimidation, profiling, and discrimination may produce increased levels of stress, hypertension, and other related health conditions.

Racial profiling targets minorities and damages their lives, yet many whites see it as, at worst, a necessary evil while programs which target the enhancement of black lives are seen negatively by whites (Bobo and Kluegel 1993).

There is evidence that suggests that many minority youth and their parents may not fully understand their options in juvenile court, or trust those representing their interests (Joseph 1995; Leonard *et al.* 1995). This may be related to research that shows that Blacks are significantly more likely to be represented by public defenders, rather than private attorney that may, in turn, play a role in the overrepresentation of minority youth in detention facilities (Hendricks and Byers 2000). However, a lack of private attorneys does not explain overrepresentation of minority juveniles at other stages of the juvenile justice system, such as initial police contact or arrest. Within the juvenile justice continuum beginning with initial police contact at the least severe end of the juvenile justice system and ending with juvenile *waivers*[5] (moving juvenile cases to criminal court to be tried as an adult) as the most severe end of the juvenile justice continuum, there is a constant growth in overrepresentation of Black youths, with the greatest level of disproportional representation in juvenile wavers to criminal court (Leonard *et al.* 1995). Interestingly, there is no rational evidence to support the disparities in sentencing or in waivers, between minority and white offenders (Hendricks and Byers 2000; Free1996; Joseph 1995; Leonard *et al.* 1995).

Bridges, Conley, Engen and Price-Spratlen (1995) found, during their interviews with juvenile court judges, a disturbing tendency for judges to decide that it was in the best interest of many minority youths to place them in a detention facility, as it was preferable to their home life, though they did not extend this same decision to white (non-Hispanic) youths (Leonard *et al.* 1995). The specter of single parent families, or more specifically of Black women raising children alone, appears to play a significant role in the juvenile justice, decision-making process. The problem with the stereotypes and assumptions, particularly those involving parental ability and involvement, is that, in an overworked system, shortcuts, in the form of decisions made using stereotypes, may be used (Feld 1999; Singer 1996).

Few juvenile court judges believe racial disparities in confinement to be racially based (Bridges and Steen 1998). Instead, most judges (Bridges and Steen 1998; Secret and Johnson 1997; Leonard *et al.* 1995) attributed the disparities to Blacks and other minorities "...substantial ethnic and racial differences in criminal behavior" (*Institutionalized Discrimination*) or the fact that youths of wealthier families have access to non-adjudicated facilities that the poor do not (*Contextual Discrimination*). Essentially, judges may use extralegal characteristics like race to create "a mental map of the accused person's underlying character" (Secret and Johnson 1997) and to predict his/her future behavior.

---

5   In OK "certification" is used in place of the term "waiver."

Alternatively, the harsher treatment of African American and Hispanic juveniles might reflect both class and race biases on the part of juvenile court
judges (Secret and Johnson 1997). In other words, "the individual's economic
and social class and the color of his skin ... determine his relationship to the
legal system" (Feld 1999).

Bridges and Steen's (1998) study of probation officers examined 233 narrative reports written by juvenile probation officers in three different counties in
the state of Washington in 1990 and 1991. Each narrative included the probation officers description of the crime and an assessment of the factors that
motivated the crime, as well as an evaluation of the youth's background assessment of his or her likelihood of recidivism. The probation officers "...tended to
attribute crimes committed by whites to negative environmental factors (poor
school performance, delinquent peers, dysfunctional family, use of drugs or
alcohol) ... [yet] ... they tended to attribute crimes committed by Black youths
to negative personality traits and 'bad attitudes' (refusal to admit guilt, lack of
remorse, failure to take offense seriously, lack of cooperation with court officials). They also found that P.O.'s (probation officers) judged Black youth to
have a significantly higher risk of reoffending than white youth" (p. 174).

3   Oklahoma Police and Court DMC Data Summary

The extent of DMC in Oklahoma is fairly ordinary, compared to other states.
Tables 14.1–14.3 give a snapshot of DMC in police contact. Utilizing police data
for 2011, we found strikingly consistent rates of minority overrepresentation
throughout the state, despite very different policing styles. In each of the tables
below, the city name was used rather than the county name, but all data is
county wide. Police data includes both police and sheriff departments for each
county.

Table 13.1 shows formal police action with juveniles by percent of citation
or arrest, the two main options for formal contact. OKC and Lawton are very
similar in their formal contact policing style in that both give citations at a 2:1
compared to arrests. Tulsa, however, is much more evenly split between the
options, with formal contact with resulting in arrest almost as likely as interactions resulting in a citation.

Table 13.2 breaks out only juvenile contact which ended in arrest and then
separates this by both city/county and race/ethnicity.

For this chapter, Table 13.3 is perhaps the most significant as it illustrates the
odds of arrest for each non-White group, when compared to Whites. For Black
youth, regardless of city/county, the odds of contact ending in arrest are twice

TABLE 13.1 Summary of police reports that ended in arrest or ticket/citation

	Arrests	Citations
Lawton (N=6,063)	32.7	67.3
Tulsa (N=20,352)	47.5	52.5
OKC (N=33,932)	32.8	67.2
Combined (N=60,347)	37.8	62.2

Note: Numbers are percentages.
Source: Ketchum, Paul, B. Mitch Peck, Patrick Polasek and Sebastian Davis. 2013. Analysis of DMC in Oklahoma, Updated with the Inclusion of Self-Report Student Surveys: Final Report. Prepared for the Office of Juvenile Affairs and the State Advisory Group on Juvenile Justice and Delinquency Prevention.

TABLE 13.2 Summary of police reports that ended in arrest by race and location

Race	Lawton N=6,063	Tulsa N=20,352	OKC N=33,932	Combined N=60,347
White	24.3	39.3	22.5	29.2
Black	42.3	57.4	38.4	46.4
Native American	54.2	57.6	42.1	49.4
Asian	25.8	26.7	7.1	14.7
Other/Don't Know	44.1	54.0	39.9	40.4

Note: Numbers are percentages.
Source: Ketchum, Paul, B. Mitch Peck, Patrick Polasek and Sebastian Davis. 2013. Analysis of DMC in Oklahoma, Updated with the Inclusion of Self-Report Student Surveys: Final Report. Prepared for the Office of Juvenile Affairs and the State Advisory Group on Juvenile Justice and Delinquency Prevention.

TABLE 13.3 Odds of arrest for race groups compared to whites by location

Race	Lawton N=6,063	Tulsa N=20,352	OKC N=33,932	Combined N=60,347
Black	2.12	1.98	2.14	2.06
Native American	3.41	2.43	2.50	2.57
Asian	1.04	0.68	0.30	0.62
Other/Don't Know	2.11	1.63	2.26	1.84

Note: Numbers are odds ratios comparing the odds of being arrested versus cited compared to Whites. Models are adjusted by gender and age.
Source: Ketchum, Paul, B. Mitch Peck, Patrick Polasek and Sebastian Davis. 2013. Analysis of DMC in Oklahoma, Updated with the Inclusion of Self-Report Student Surveys: Final Report. Prepared for the Office of Juvenile Affairs and the State Advisory Group on Juvenile Justice and Delinquency Prevention.

that of White youth. Non-Whites are slightly more than twice as likely to have police contact end in arrest, compared to Whites.

Other points of contact show similar levels of DMC. Due to limited space, we will limit the DMC data presented here to police contact.[6]

4   Differential Invovement and Student Survey Results

The growing use of citizen video recording of police actions has resulted in unprecedented evidence pointing to purposeful bias in official police records. Evidence of differential treatment by race in police stops, legal "open carry" acts and treatment of protesters have all been well documented. Claims of self-defense in the killing of unarmed Black, and though less covered by the media, Latino, men, women and children by law enforcement officers are all too often refuted by video evidence. Double standards in police and media portrayals of the 2015 riots in Baltimore and other cities compared to the mass biker gang shootout in Waco, TX in the same year add fuel to the long held suspicions of bias.

Unchallenged acceptance of police and court data has become difficult to defend. As a follow-up to our original DMC study, we conducted a small, pilot study utilizing anonymous self-report surveys of high school student from urban, suburban and rural school districts in central Oklahoma.

Though there have been relatively few studies examining self-report rates of juvenile crime, existing studies consistently show very small differences in crime rates between racial/ethnic groups (Sealock & Simpson 1998, Huizinga & Elliott 1987, Dannefer & Schutt 1982, Akers, Krohn, Radosevich, & LanzaKaduce 1981, and Voss 1963). The results of this study, consistent with the existing literature, also finds few differences in crime when controlling for race and/or ethnicity.

About 60% of the students surveyed lived attended a suburban school. The sample was evenly split in terms of male (49%) and female (51%) and race with 51% identifying as White and 49% identifying as non-White. One third of the students (33%) qualified for school lunch programs majority of the students in the sample (approximately 60%) live in a suburban area. The sample is almost evenly divided in terms of female (51%) and male (49%) participants.

---

6   The full results can be found in either "DMC in Oklahoma: Final Report" by Ketchum, Peck,
    Polasek and Davis or the 2013 and DMC School Survey: Final Report by Ketchum, Peck and
    Davis. Both are available online at the Oklahoma Office of Juvenile Affairs website and on the
    OJJDP's website.

The students are primarily aged 18 or older (63%). About a third of the students qualify for free lunch at school (33%). Most students (58%) lived with birth or adoptive parents, 25% lived with their mother only, 8% with their father only and 5% lived with another family member.

A number of differences were found based on gender, geography, and poverty (school lunch program), however, consistent with other self-report studies on juvenile crime, we found no statistical difference between White and non-White youth in amount or type of deviant or criminal activity. None. We also found no statistical difference in family structure. Intact and single parent families were represented equally for Whites and non-Whites.

Police data shows non-Whites to be more than two times as likely as Whites to be arrested, yet self-report data suggest no significant difference in crime rates. The final part of our study examined the racial attitudes of juvenile justice professionals for possible answers.

5   Interviews with Juvenile Justice Professionals

A total of 179 interviews were conducted with juvenile justice specialists including police officers, both patrol and those from specialized units focused on juveniles, intake and probation specialists, and juvenile court prosecutors, defense attorneys and juvenile court justices. These interviews were conducted by both trained college students and researchers and were coded by one senior researcher and one graduate student. Any coding differences between the two were discussed and agreed upon. Due to either equipment failure or operator error, three completed interviews were not recorded at all and six others were incomplete due to missing sections. All but one interview were race matched for interviewer and participant, to insure that minority participants would only be interviewed by minority interviewers and White participants would only be interviewed by White interviewers. The sole exception, a minority participant who requested to be interviewed by a White interviewer did not use the interview script and the data from that interview was not included in any of the tables below. Participation in the interviews was voluntary. Participants were not required by their supervisors to participate nor were incentives offered to those who participated. Identifiers are limited to jurisdiction (OKC, Tulsa or Lawton), gender, White or Non-White and professional role (Police, Court, Probation) to maintain the confidentiality of participants.

The purpose of the interviews was twofold. First, interviews with juvenile justice professionals are a valuable tool utilizing the observations and experiences of those who work closest with juvenile delinquency and crime, in order to better understand both how the juvenile justice system, as a whole, operates as well as how race/ethnicity impacts juvenile justice. Second, by examining the content of interview responses (content analysis) we are able to examine the extent of subtle (and in rare cases, overt) racial/ethnic bias among juvenile justice professionals.

Every single juvenile justice professional mentioned the role of family differences in at least partially explaining DMC. Table 70 gives a breakdown of how often, on average, different groups brought up the role of family. Professionals in careers requiring higher education (lawyers and judges) mentioned the role of families 45% more often than did police or juvenile justice specialists and White interviewees mentioned the role of family 24% more often than non-Whites. The differences between White and non-White families was the most often suggested cause of DMC in the interviews, though non-Whites were much less likely to suggest it to be a major contributor.

When asked "Pretending for a moment that you had the ability, funding and support to do so (think magic or miracle if need be), what one change would you make to minimize the need for the juvenile justice system", 31.7% suggested government or community intervention to better the lives of juveniles. Just over 20% of the participants specifically suggested that community level support and programs are necessary to minimize juvenile delinquency and crime. The percentages, however, only give part of the context. The following pages contain representative responses from juvenile justice professionals:

> *From a White, Male Police Officer*: I would increase programs available to inner city kids, to keep them busy and give them the resources that they're not getting now.
>
> *A second White, Male Police Officer*: Yeah, absolutely. I think it would just be repeating what I just said which is that we would have more – like with us we might be able to go into the schools and it would be limited. We would have to have a methodology for picking the schools that have the most need which is what we are formulating now with the police athletic league. What we are trying to do is find out which schools have the most need, go in there first. Like, they have the lowest GPA, API scores, and a graduation rate. I really believe there is direct correlation – I'm sure this will be one of the questions – but a direct correlation with "what the communities needs are and the opportunities that they have," – say like grocery stores, or parks, or community events and things like that. So, if they are given the same amount of opportunities in all the communities throughout the city – the same opportunities – then you could actually see a trend. If I were to overlay the trend of community needs, with crime, with socioeconomic status; it is all the same.

Third White, Male Police Officer: You know, here in (location deleted), I know I would – I would – there are no programs. There are – there's nothing for these kids to do, nothing. That's why – one of the reasons they get into so much trouble. There's not a lot of activities.

Interviewer: So, you'd – you'd increase the number of program sites and activities?

Third White, Male Police Officer (cont.): Sure, you know, by 10 fold. There's, you know – you know, someone has to do it and someone has to be out here doing something – they're doing something right, unless they'll be out here doing something wrong, trying to find something – getting into something, you know. In New York City, they had, you know – I've talked to them down there about – they have the PAL, Police Activity Leagues. They have, you know – Yeah. They have a lot. The police officers took time and, you know, coach baseball and coach basketball and – and got to know the kids and you know, and that are (unintelligible) with them. It doesn't happen here. It doesn't happen here.

Interviewer: Is that lack of funding or lack of interest?

Third White, Male Officer (cont.): I think it's – I think it's both. I think it's lack of funding and I think it's – it's you know, they just don't – I don't – I don't – because you know, we have a gang task force that just – you know, they're focusing on the crime instead of – instead of focusing on the kids, you know. Right, instead of being proactive, it's reactive. You know, instead of going into the schools, instead of going in – of having programs for them, taking them on trips to, you know – they used to pick us up and bus us to, you know Coney Island which would be in New York, but here we drive to Six Flags, bussing a bunch of kids. You know, we have a rapport with these kids and these kids are going to be kids that – if another kids does something wrong – you know, when they're (unintelligible), and one kid (unintelligible), you're going to have a rapport with these kids they're going to turn them over to you. You know what I mean?

However, placing the responsibility for juvenile issues on problems within the family was, by far, the most common response. 43.3% of the respondents placed family issues at the forefront of causes of juvenile delinquency and crime. A few of these responses followed up with recommendations for more mentoring or specialized programs to replace what was seen as missing from the family. For these respondents, society/community is seen as a potential resource to help minimize family issues which result in juvenile delinquency:

White, Male Police Officer 4: Short of a private prison, a boot camp type compound where kids that are at risk and on the verge, who have committed a felony crime, could be sent to where they get the discipline and the structure that I think they need to be productive. Where they could be taught right from wrong because in my opinion, that's where it starts at home. If they're not getting it at home, we should be providing it somehow. And start that type, whether it be a private or state run, but let's not get too liberal about it as far as, well you can't do this, you can't do that, you can't do this. Strict discipline along with nurturing in there together like I was raised with. You know my dad would wear me out if I messed, but he'd pat me on top of the head if I'd done good too. That's what these kids need and they're not getting it. There needs to be an alternative to the justice system. There's a completion of a three of six month live-in boot camp type environment for these kids and I think, in my opinion, it would turn them around, make them understand what's going on. These things are available, but they're not state funded that I'm aware of. A lot of the kids in trouble are financially unable to pay. The parents haven't got the money to pay for the kids to go to something like this. It would do wonders. It would do a lot of good and they wouldn't be returning to the justice system which would in turn save us money in the juvenile justice system and then in the adult system as well because they're going to end up progressing on to that. Does that make sense?

White, Female Attorney: I would have more programs for adults to mentor children. Places for kids to go. I would maybe try to educate parents – educate parents more. Oh, you said one, didn't you? I mean, I – I just think it's the – the – goes back to the fact that I think that you know, most of the juvenile offenders that I see have inappropriate parenting, or don't have supervision, don't have somebody that – that they feel like cares or takes the time. You know, maybe they do care, a lot of them probably do, but they don't – they don't care inappropriately.

Interviewer: Could you explain – I guess parent appropriate – appropriately?

White, Female Attorney (cont.): They – they don't teach them values, morals and they're not – you know, I – juveniles that show up to court and – or you know, they'll be incarcerated and they'll be in court and their parents will be there not at all, 30 minutes late. You know, they – they're not responsible. Their parents aren't responsible.

White, Male Probation Officer: Unlimited resources in the best of all worlds, probably very efficient parenting skills development for parents at birth through age 12.

Interviewer: Some type of mandatory parenting thing?

White, Male Probation Officer (cont.): Well, mandatory, even beyond that, the best of all worlds, the best teachers that could teach parenting and parenting skills to very receptive parents and very responsible parents. Those early years are the most important years, they're not the adolescent years, and too many kids get off on the wrong foot, and they may not be delinquent because they are too young to be delinquent, but when they reach adolescence then it's a mess.

More common, however, were responses placing sole responsibility for juvenile delinquency and crime on poor parenting:

White Male Attorney: (Pause). Having more responsible parents.

From a different court professional:

Second White, Female Attorney: Oh, lock up the parents. I find the biggest hurdles to these kiddos, a lot of these kids, and even the hardcore kids, it's a generalization problem. The parents have failed them in so many ways. They first of all don't make them, they have never held them accountable, they always make excuses for them. They never taught them to own it and then get over it. By the same token I don't believe we have families, parents that are instilling in these children a sense of right and wrong because the parents themselves don't have that, and like I said it's a generational thing and I'm not even sure, I can't tell you how far back it would go. Some families it might go back 2 or 3 generations. Other families not as far, but they're also not, the families aren't engaging these kids as a family. The parents are so busy doing their own thing that when a kid needs help or does something that's a cry for help, it's ignored or not acknowledged that that's what it is, kid's just labeled now, and then when you get 'em into the juvenile system, the parents are the ones' that outrage you because you give the kids a list of rules and you tell the parents, well they gotta follow these rules and you gotta help us enforce 'em, you know, and a lot of parents, the kid'll be breaking the rules all over the place and they did nothing to try to hold this kid to any sort of a standard of behavior, and I really feel like a lot of the times these kid's problems, the traumatization that these kids have, you know, especially the ones that are getting into drugs and having violent tendencies, they're being raised by parents who are gang bangers, they're being raised by grandmothers because the parents aren't on the scene to parent, so I really feel like if we started holding the parents responsible, the parents were having to pay the restitution, and the parents were having to do some time every time their kid misbehaved then maybe they would start teaching these kids from a very early point knowing that if I don't do the right thing I'm the one that's going to be held responsible, not the kid. Sorry, that's my soapbox.

While White professionals were more likely than Non-Whites to place responsibility solely on the shoulders of juveniles and/or their parents, non-Whites, especially Male, non-White police offers sometimes also did so:

> *Non-White, Male Police Officer*: Magically, make every parent accountable for their kids. Make every parent love their kids, and you know, if in a perfect world, everybody wouldn't have like, you know, twenty kids and not being able to take care of all of 'em. Where they'd have enough to take care of, and not only that, have them be, you know, good parents to their kids. I think the parents are what do the kids wrong. Because if the parents aren't disciplining their kids at the early age, or if they are disciplining them wrong, you know just yell at 'em, not giving them any consequences or anything like that, they won't know, and they'll have the attitude when they grow up that, you know, I can take whatever, I won't do anything, I won't get anything. You know, that handout, you know. When you start giving out handouts also, because if we start giving them, you know, money for whatever, you know, the parents, I'm talking about the parents, start giving them money for how many kids they have, hey you know, you got ten kids here's some money, you know to help you with that. No, if you give them nothing and let them try to support their kids by the way they do it, then they won't have that many kids. Which, I'm not saying having a lot of kids is a bad thing cause my parents had, but my dad worked hard, okay? He worked hard for what we had, okay, and there's a lot of people out there, they don't want to work hard, and they want to get a lot of stuff given to them and then they give that attitude to their kids and their kids will come out here and you know, they go rob a store or do whatever because they want that money now, you know, instead of going out there and working hard for your money, but yeah, magically, have every parent become a good parent. I'm not saying that, you know, a kid will grow up and not be bad because their parents were good or whatever, but there's a difference between, you know, love for a child and doing whatever you can to make your child be successful and to be reliable, to go out and check on them, to monitor what they are doing,

you know, instead of being lazy and just letting them run around, spoil them, do whatever they want to do. To actually go out there and be, try to make them be a productive member of this society, so that's magically. Will it ever happen? I don't think so, you know, it'll never happen.

White Male Police Officer 5: I guess if you're talking about having the money and having the resources uhm it would be parental education, and getting parents to be more involved in their kid's lives and knowing what their kids are doing and are up to. I know with social media being the way it is – Facebook, Twitter. Uhm you know, I have two kids in high school, I know their – I'm friends on their Facebook, I have their passwords to their Facebook, I can get in and see what's going on their Facebook. But, it amazes me that just for instance, one of my children's friends posted something the other day on one of their other friends sites about a rant about how stupid her mom is and this, that, and the other, and ended with something to the effect of "Yeah, well I could say the same thing about you, you stupid whore." So you know, obviously in the grand scheme of things you are talking about juvenile delinquency, you know calling your mom a whore on Facebook is small compared to committing a violent crime, but the fact is obviously this girl's mom has no idea what her daughter is doing on Facebook and to me that's just embarrassing –

Interviewer: For both.

White Male Police Officer 5 (cont.): You know as a girl, I would be embarrassed posting something like that about my mom. and as the mom I would just be absolutely totally embarrassed that my daughter is calling me a whore on Facebook. So I just – I think that would be the one place where we've got to get – we've got to educate parents to get them to pay more attention to what their kids are doing and being more you know involved in their kids' lives.

An assumption of differential involvement rooted in family differences as an explanation for DMC has long held sway in criminology. In 1965, Moynihan suggested that female headed Black households were the cause of differential involvement for Blacks. Others researchers followed suit. Wordes and Bynum (1995) and Anderson (1999) have suggested that differences between White and non-White families was key in explaining dmc by either laying the blame at the feet of domineering Black, female heads of household or Black men shirking their duties as fathers. Sarkisian refutes this explanation. Recent research, however (Sarkisian and Gerstel 2004) has found that Blacks are more likely to have an extended kin network. They live closer and see extended kin more often, which in turn increases Black men's involvement in their involvement in their children's lives. Black women also benefit from extended kin network. Contrary to many views expressed in the interviews with juvenile justice professionals, Black men's extended family structure and cultural values bring their commitment in their children's lives on a par with socially advantaged whites (Sarkisian 2007; Sarkisian and Gerstel 2004). Most significant, the National Study for Health Statistics, in a national study, found that Black fathers are actually slightly *more* involved with their children at all ages. Consistent with this, the student survey also showed no difference in family structure between White and non-White families.

Research shows that normal adolescent development results in a lessening of family attachment and a growing reliance on peers for decision making. Contrary to the expectations of most interview participants, attachment to his or her family is not the most salient factor in determining delinquency or conformity. The important factor is whether the peer group values delinquency or conformity (Childs et al. 2010). Oddly, peers were almost never mentioned in the interviews, even when participants were asked about gangs. As the following interview illustrates, even questions about peers and gangs were often redirected by the juvenile justice professional, back to the topic of the failure of non-White families.:

> *Interviewer*: Oh. Some have suggested that a culture of violence (one which accepts and even embraces violence as an acceptable means for ones' goals) exists in many barrio and ghetto neighborhoods. In your experience, does this seem to be the case?
>
> *White Female Police Officer*: Okay, no. Gangs are the kids looking for family and the violence is a pressure, peer pressure. If they had family lives then we wouldn't have the problem we're having, society wouldn't.
>
> *Interviewer*: Is that what you see a lot with your neglect cases?
>
> *White Female Police Officer (cont.)*: Mm-mm (Note: affirmative)
>
> *Interviewer*: That's interesting.
>
> *White Female Police Officer (cont.)*: Again, it's a parental issue.
>
> *Interviewer*: Yeah.
>
> *White Female Police Officer (cont.)*: Getting away from the drugs and the drinking or whatever it is.
>
> *Interviewer*: Is that what – in the majority thing you see?
>
> *White Female Police Officer (cont.)*: Mm-mm (Note: affirmative)
>
> *Interviewer*: Is just –?
>
> *White Female Police Officer (cont.)*: Yeah and some just pretty lazy.

Juvenile justice officials appear to be either unaware of or ignoring the research which shows that peers hold significantly more influence over adolescents than do parents and are then holding non-White families to a higher standard than White families. Respondents used an interesting rhetorical move when discussing the role of the family. Non-White families were referred to as making poor individual choices while White families were typically referred to as part of the collective norm:

> *Interviewer:* Okay. Let us address the issues outside of direct influence of the juvenile justice system. What effects, if any have you seen a lack of quality educational resources play in DMC?
>
> *Third White Female Attorney:* Quality educational resources. Are you talking about just an education in general, or –
>
> *Interviewer:* It's – just whatever. What effects, if any have you see n a lack of quality education and all resources play in DMC?
>
> *Third White Female Attorney (cont.):* I mean, I think that maybe through – I man I – I find that maybe from their parents, you know, maybe that they didn't – weren't educated appropriately or – and – but I – I don't really think educational resources what they caused, or the – the lack of educational resources that caused the contact.

As family structures and values are similar, we find a likely explanation for the focus on family structure in the interviews. Family appears to be code for race (Bonilla-Silva 2006, Wordes and Bynum 1995). When juvenile justice officials suggest that poor parenting and family values are to blame for DMC, what they are saying is that nonWhites have poor parenting skills and bad family values. Masked by vague notions of individualism and choice, white respondents covertly blamed minority families for not raising their children in a correct, law-abiding way (Bonilla-Silva 2006, Wordes and Bynum 1995). The blaming of the family is a justification for why minorities are overrepresented. It is a covert way to demonize nonWhite families for DMC without sounding racist (Bonilla-Silva 2006).

The overall impression from the interviews, observations and analysis is one of unspoken, choreographed actions and beliefs, most of which if taken individually would have little significance, combined to maintain the status quo, evidenced by the overwhelming overrepresentation of Blacks in the system, while paying little more than lip-service to acknowledging the racism so clearly present though the use of color blind rationalizations (Mills 1997). The vast majority of the individuals interviewed were very likable, and most gave the impression that they would abhor any overtly racist action. The racism present was subtle but understood by all. So systemic is the racial bias that many of the respondents included rhetorical moves which suggested that the interviewer understood their racialized assumptions:

> *Interviewer*: Okay. Finally, what role have you seen difficult family issues play?
> *Fourth White Female Attorney*: I mean, I think family issues play a large portion. I think – although, I – I mean, I was – I was a single mother, but a lot of the – a lot of them are single mothers. They have no father role. They have – their – their parents are just – I mean, they come in the courtroom and they – they – they argue with the kids. They're loud, they're – it's like their family is in some kind of turmoil, and – so they turn and get something – whatever they get from these other kids that they run around, or they have no – you know, their parents don't pay attention to them, pay – give them time. I think that's the big role to me. (White/Female/Lawyer)

6   Conclusions

Race permeates all aspects of American society, so it should come as no surprise that racial bias, be it institutional racism, colorblind racism and/or overt racism are significantly responsible for DMC. It is less clear as to which mechanisms, and to what extent, environmental/social problems (differential involvement of non-White youth in criminal activity) and/or direct bias from juvenile justice agencies and professionals working for those agencies (differential treatment of non-White youth by juvenile justice professionals), are the means of achieving racial inequality in the system.

There is no doubt of the overrepresentation of non-Whites in the juvenile justice system. In Oklahoma, non-White youth are almost twice as likely as White youth to be arrested, half as likely to receive informal probation, one and a half times a likely to have a petition filed, etc. In short, non-Whites are much more likely to be treated more harshly at each and every decision point in the juvenile justice system.

Multiple studies, including a pilot study addressing DMC in Oklahoma, suggest non-White youth commit crimes at rates no higher than White youth. The National Institute for Drug Abuse, reports non-Whites having lower rates of substance abuse, one of the most common reasons for juvenile arrest. According to this study, of youth between the ages of 12 and 17 with a substance abuse problem (addiction), 5 percent were black, compared to 9.2 percent for racially mixed people, 9.0 percent for whites, 7.7 percent for Hispanics and 3.5 percent for Asians and Pacific Islanders.

This leaves us with ample evidence to suggest DMC is, at least partially due to bias on the part of juvenile justice agencies and professionals. Future research needs to measure the extent of differential treatment as a cause of DMC. We need a hard number to change the national discussion on this topic, as current research is unable to give us a percent of DMC caused by differential treatment.

Conventional wisdom suggests that when you know the major, or possibly exclusive cause of a problem, mitigating the impact of that cause would be the best means of achieving success. However, in the now decades long battle to eliminate DMC, there isn't a single program designed to address police bias and those that address judicial bias do so by using a rubric for decisions or an artificial cap on punitive punishment for non-White youth. OJJDP lists no programs designed to educate or train police, court or probation professionals in overcoming racial bias. Minority youth are an easier target for addressing DMC, however their role in DMC appears to be minimal. Continuing to treat the non-problem and ignore the real cause of DMC simply assures another fifty years of the same conclusions resulting in no change.

Interviews with juvenile justice professionals suggest that factually incorrect negative characteristics, especially regarding non-White family values, are often ascribed to non-Whites, giving and excuse for greater intervention in the lives on non-White youth. The interviews suggest that the lack of diversity in the personal lives of the juvenile court professionals has led many of these folks to non-White youth and their families as culturally and morally different, leaving the professionals as the line of defense against non-White families who allow their children to run amok. Again and again we see descriptions of non-White families as not embracing the basic tenants of a civilized society. The lack of diversity in the personal lives of juvenile justice professionals results in "otherizing" non-White families where they are painted as a danger to civilized (White) society.

References

Akers, R., Krohn M., Radosevich, M., & Lanza-Kaduce, L. 1981. "Social Characteristics and Self-Reported Delinquency." *Sociology of Delinquency*, 48–62.

Anderson, Elijah. 1999. *Code of the Street: Decency, Violence, and the Moral Life of the Inner City*. New York: W.W. Norton.

Austin, James. 1995. "Racial Disparities in the Confinement of Juveniles: Effects of Crime and Community Social Structure on Punishment." In *Minorities in Juvenile*

Justice, edited by K.K. Leonard, C. Pope, and W. Feyerherm Thousand Oaks, CA: Sage Publications.

Bishop, Donna and Charles Frazier. 1996. "Race Effects in Juvenile Justice Decision-Making: Findings of a Statewide Analysis." *Journal of Criminal Law and Criminology,* 86: 392–413.

Bobo, Lawrence and James Kluegel. 1993. "Opposition to Race-Targeting: Self-Interest, Stratification Ideology or Racial Attitudes?" *American Sociological Review,* 58: 443–464.

Bonilla-Silva, Eduardo. 2006. *Racism Without Racists: Color-Blind Racism and the Persistence of Racial Inequality in the United States.* Lanham, MD: Rowman & Littlefield.

Bridges, George and Sara Steen. 1998. "Racial Disparities in Official Assessments of Juvenile Offending: Attributional Stereotypes as Mediating Mechanisms." *American Sociological Review,* 65: 554–570.

Bridges, G., D. Conley, R. Engen and T. Price-Spratlen. 1995. "Racial Disparities in the Confinement of Juveniles: Effects of Crime and Community Social Sturcture on Punishment." In *Minorities in Juvenile Justice,* edited by K.K. Leonard, C. Pope, and W. Feyerherm Thousand Oaks, CA: Sage Publications.

Chito Childs, Erica, Laudone, S., Tavernier, L. 2010. "Revisiting Black sexualities in families: Problems, puzzles, and prospects." In Battle, J., Barnes, S. L. (Eds.), Black Sexualities: Probing Powers, Passions, Practices, and Policies (pp. 138–154). New Brunswick, NJ: Rutgers University Press.

Coates, Rodney. 2007. "Covert Racism in the USA and Globally." in *Rethinking the Color Line: Readings in Race and Ethnicity* 3rd ed., edited by Charles Gallagher. New York, NY: McGraw Hill.

Damphousse, Kelly, Courtney Charish and Sebastian Davis. 2004. "Race/Ethnicity and Gender Effects on Juvenile System Processing." Oklahoma City, OK: Oklahoma Office of Juvenile Affairs.

Dannefer, D., & Schutt, R.K. 1982. "Race and Juvenile Justice Processing in Court and Police Agencies." *American Journal of Sociology,* 1113–1132.

D'Souza, Dinesh. 1995. *The End of Racism.* New York, NY: Free Press.

Fagan, J., E. Piper and M. Moore. 1987. "Violent Delinquents and Urban Youth." *Criminology,* 24: 439–471.

Feld, Barry. 1999. *Bad Kids: Race and the Transformation of the Juvenile Court.* New York, NY: Oxford University Press.

Free, M. 1996. *African Americans and the Criminal Justice System.* New York, NY: Garland Publishing.

Hendricks, J. and B. Byers (ed.). 2000. *Multicultural Perspectives in Criminal Justice and Criminology* (2nd ed.) Springfield IL: Charles C. Thomas Publisher.

Herrenstein, Richard and Charles Murray. 1994. *The Bell Curve: Intelligence and Class Structure in American Life.* New York, NY: Free Press.

Huizinga, D., & Elliott, D.S. 1987. "Juvenile Offenders: Prevalence, Offender Incidence, and Arrest Rates by Race." *Crime and Delinquency*, 33 (2): 206–223.

Jackson, R. and E. Pabon 2000. "Race and Treating Other People's Children as Adults." *Journal of Criminal Justice*, 28: 507–515.

Joseph, J. 1995. *Black Youths, Delinquency, and Juvenile Justice*. Westport, CT: Greenwood Publishing Group.

Kemph, Leonard, Kimberly and Henry Sontheimer. 1995. "Racial Disparities in the Confinement of Juveniles: Effects of Crime and Community Social Structure on Punishment." In *Minorities in Juvenile Justice*, edited by K.K. Leonard, C. Pope, and W. Feyerherm Thousand Oaks, CA: Sage Publications.

Krisberg, B., I. Schwartz, P Litsky and J. Austin. 1987. "The Incarceration of Minority Youth." *Crime and Delinquency*, 33: 173–205.

Lardiero, Carl J. 1997. "Of disproportionate minority confinement." *Corrections Today*, 59: 15–16.

Leonard, K.K., C. Pope, and W. Feyerherm (ed.). 1995. *Minorities in Juvenile Justice*. Thousand Oaks, CA: Sage Publications.

Martinez, Jr., Ramiro. 2002. *Latino Homicide: Immigration, Violence, and Community*. New York, NY: Routledge.

Mills, Charles. 1997. *The Racial Contract*. Ithaca, NY: Cornell University Press.

Moynihan, Patrick. 1965. *The Negro Family: The Case for National Action*. Washington DC: Office of Policy Planning and Research, United States Department of Labor.

Piliavin, Irving, and Scott Briar. 1964 "Police Encounters with Juveniles." *American Journal of Sociology*, Vol. 70 (2): 206–214.

Pope, Carl and William Feyerherm. 1990 (part 1& part 2). Minority Status and Juvenile Justice Processing: An Assessment of the Research Literature. *Criminal Justice Abstracts*. 22: 327–335 (part 1), 22: 527–542 (part 2).

Pope, Carl and Howard Snyder. 2003. "Race as a Factor in Juvenile Arrests." *OJJDP Juvenile Justice Bulletin*. Washington DC. U.S. Department of Justice.

Russell, Kathryn. 1998. *The Color of Crime: Racial Hoaxes, White Fear, Black Protectionism, Police Harassment, and other Macroaggressions*. New York; NY: University Press.

Sarkisian, Natalia, and Naomi Gerstel. 2004 "Explaining the Gender Gap in Help to Parents: The Importance of Employment." *Journal of Marriage and Family* 66 (2): 431–51.

Sealock, M.D., & S.S. Simpson 1998. Unraveling bias in arrest decisions: The role of juvenile offender type-scripts. *Justice Quarterly*, 15 (3): 427–457.

Secret, P.E. and J.B. Johnson 1997. "The Effect of Race on Juvenile Justice Decision Making in Nebraska: Detention, Adjudication, and Dispositon, 1988–1993." *Justice Quarterly*, 14: 445–478.

Singer, S. 1996. *Recriminalizing Delinquency: Violent Juvenile Crime and Juvenile Justice Reform*. New York, NY: Cambridge University Press.

Snyder, Howard N., and Melisssa Sickmund. 2006. *Juvenile Offenders and Victims: 2006 National Report*. Washington, DC: U.S. Department of Justice, Office of Justice Programs, Office of Juvenile Justice and Delinquency Prevention.

Steffensmeier, Darrell and Stephen Demuth. 2000. "Ethnicity and Sentencing Outcomes in U.S. Federal Courts: Who Is Punished More Harshly?" *American Sociological Review*. 65: 705–729.

Voss, Harwin L. 1963. Ethnic Differentials in Delinquency in Honolulu. *Journal of Criminal Law and Criminology*, 54 (3).

Wilbanks, William. 1986. *The Myth of a Racist Criminal Justice System*. Belmont, CA: Wadsworth.

Wilson, James Q. and Richard Herrnstein, 1985. *Crime and Human Nature*. New York, NY: Simon and Schuster.

Wordes, M., and T.S. Bynum. 1995. "Policing Juveniles: Is there Bias Against Youths of Color?" In *Minorities in Juvenile Justice*, edited by K.K. Leonard, C.E. Pope, and W.H. Feyerherm. Thousand Oaks, CA: Sage Publications.

CHAPTER 14

Critical Diversity in the U.S. Military: From Diversity to Racialized Organizations

Victor Erik Ray

1 Introduction

The u.s. military has long been considered a highly diversified organization. Since Truman's 1948 executive order ending segregation the military has pioneered "color-blind" methods of racial integration. Indeed, the military prides itself on breaking down social boundaries to create "an Army of one." According to the scholarly consensus, despite some historical resistance from the white power structure, many of these efforts have been remarkably successful relative to integration efforts in the civilian world. Moskos and Butler (1997) argue that diversity efforts in the military work because of strict non-discrimination policies and a functioning meritocracy. According to Moskos and Butler (1997), this is in contrast to civilian affirmative action programs that they charge unfairly promote underqualified people of color at the organizations' expense. Similarly, a number of scholars argue that race relations and social outcomes in the military compare favorably with the civilian labor market, with blacks in the military having higher job satisfaction and rates of intermarriage (Lundquist 2004, 2008) and lower rates of divorce (Teachman and Tedrow 2008). In general, it is unsurprising that the military lessens some types of social inequality. Indeed, many commentators have wryly claimed, the U.S military is a "socialist meritocracy" (Webb 1997) providing full employment, rank-equalized pay scales, health insurance and housing, subsidized childcare, and educational benefits—regardless of race.

However, scholars have recently challenged the reigning consensus of the military as a bastion of equality. In contrast to the view of the military as a socialist meritocracy, Burk and Espinoza (2012) note that the military has internal mechanisms that can suppress claims of discrimination, leaving soldiers with no external recourse. Similarly, time to promotion, the application of military justice, and care for injured veterans all remain unequal by race. Implicating discrimination as the cause, these scholars have called for renewed attention to the organizational mechanisms that promote racial inequality in the military (Burk and Espinoza 2012).

How can we understand the contradiction between the military's stated commitments to integration and diversity and continued racial stratification? In this chapter, I draw on fifty in-depth interviews with Iraq and Afghanistan veterans to claim that the frame of "diversity" inadequately conceptualizes the organizational and racial realities shaping the military. I begin by outlining the history and assumptions of "diversity" in the context of the military. I then introduce the concept of *punitive empathy*, arguing that the military, like many organizations, has mechanisms that suppress reports of discrimination, creating the illusion of smooth integration by creating disincentives for reporting racial harassment. Finally, I conclude with a brief sketch of my emerging perspective on racialized organizations, arguing that in a racialized social system, even organizations with an overtly integrationist perspective—like the military—will reproduce elements of the racial hierarchy.

2 Conceptalizing Diversity in the Military

At least since Moynihan's (1965) infamous *Report on the Negro Family*, scholars have argued that the military provides a haven for blacks battered by discrimination in the civilian world. This influential line of scholarship argues the military provides an experience that inculcates white norms necessary for success in the civilian world and creates an environment based upon merit (Moynihan 1965). This research tradition examines outcomes in labor markets and family processes as partly the result of black culture and claims that the military greatly lessens both maladaptive behaviors and opportunities for discrimination. Indeed, many people of color report they join the military explicitly because of the organization's reputation as an inclusive meritocracy.

In line with this explanation, blacks are greatly over-represented in the military, as they comprise about 13% of the general population but approximately 24% of the armed forces. Women account for a full 14% of military personnel, but black women "are now represented in the military at nearly double their proportion in the civilian population" (Bailey 2008, 51). However, this over-representation in numbers doesn't translate into higher status. Blacks in the military remain concentrated in the lower ranks in "support" positions and lag behind whites in both rate and time to promotion. Zweigenhaft and Domhoff (1998) point out that blacks who do move up the ranks in the military tend to do so by adopting white norms. For instance, Colin Powell cites his light skin, use of standard English, and claims that he "ain't that black" (1998, 112) to explain his mobility.

Most diversity programs focus on representation, and by this measure, the military is ahead of many civilian organizations. Yet, demographically, the military has a clear racial hierarchy. The military's claim of being one of the most integrated institutions in the United States depends upon the level of measurement. First, the number of minorities varies greatly by branch, with blacks highly concentrated in the army and less represented in the marines (Segal and Segal 2004). Second, people of color, and blacks specifically, are clustered in the lower ranks and "service" specialties. This hierarchy is long-standing, and the military recognizes that it is problematic. In response to this, the military maintains a strong affirmative action system that includes quotas. When adopting diversity policies, the military positions itself as racially neutral. That is, "diversity" is added to a military hierarchy that is considered non-racial and meritocratic. Yet, the assumption is that minorities must integrate into the military, revealing the unmarked white background on which this assumption rests.

In the military, as in the civilian sector, there is some confusion over what diversity means (Bell and Hartmann 2007). Diversity is seen as positive in the abstract—a "force multiplier," in military terminology—but highly problematic in practice. My interviews indicate that many white soldiers value a superficial diversity allowing for discussions across the taboo subject of race. However, any programmatic interventions into historical or current racial inequalities are resented. For instance, white male respondents complained that women and minorities were unfairly advantaged when it came to promotion, allegedly undermining the meritocracy. In contrast with the view of the military as a socialist meritocracy, this work sees clearly racialized constraints on for service members. For instance, the Supreme Court ruled in *Chapelle v. Wallace* that enlisted soldiers cannot sue the military for discrimination, as (according to them) adequate internal channels exist to address discrimination (Burk and Espinoza 2012). This case was brought by five Navy men who alleged "a pattern of behavior in which, [commanding officers] failed to assign them desirable duties, threatened them, gave them low performance evaluations, and imposed penalties of unusual severity" (Chappell v. Wallace 1983), because of their race. These charges were reviewed by the military justice system and revoked, despite the court finding that indeed, the constitutional rights of these black Navy men might have been violated.

Discrimination and racism in the military is still seen as the outcome of individual "racist" attitudes and not as central to organizational functioning. Like claims of discrimination in the civilian labor market (Roscigno 2007), the burden of proof for discrimination is based upon intent. Overt expressions of racism, usually including epithets, are necessary to prove racial intent. The obvious response to this is to mask intent, and a large body of experimental and qualitative research shows that whites have gotten the message and no longer express racial hostility openly (Bobo and Smith 1998; Bonilla-Silva 2006). More importantly, there may be factors in an organization that encourage or minimize discrimination. I claim two factors in the military can suppress reports of discrimination: (1), the relative level of segregation within a unit or (2) repercussions aimed at those who come forward with complaints. In the next section, I first discuss my methods, then turn to a description of the generalized racial atmosphere in the military before describing the suppression of reports of discrimination in the military.

3 Military Punitive Empathy and the Suppression of Discrimination

Military programs aimed at helping alleviate racial inequality can instead hurt soldiers who come forward with complaints. I argue that despite having affirmative action officers in every unit, mandatory diversity and sensitivity trainings, and generalized non-discrimination policies, racial harassment is still as much a part of the military as the standard-issue M16. Research indicates that "internal workplace conditions affect both workers and regulatory agents' interpretations of potentially discriminatory experiences" (Hirsh and Kornrich 2008, 1394). This is especially important in the military, as commanders have extreme discretionary power over employees who report discrimination. Further, as Joan Acker (Acker 2000) claims, organizational equity projects themselves only exist because they are countenanced by those with "long established authority" (626). These established authorities are unlikely to implement policies or procedures that fundamentally challenge hierarchies of race, class, or gender. Because complaints of discrimination can potentially challenge organizational legitimacy, there is a contradiction built into these programs. This leaves the people who have most to lose charged with the enforcement of procedures that undermine their organizational power—a classic conflict of interest. Because of this contradiction, Bielby (Bielby 2000) argues, "close examination of internal practices often shows that the company's EEO efforts to advance minorities and women through the organization contain more symbol than substance, with little impact on actual promotion policy or practice" (125). Building on this insight, I argue that military programs allow commanders and fellow soldiers to target those who make harassment claims, subjecting them to hazing, further harassment, or even expulsion from the military—ultimately reinforcing established authority. Thus, "decoupling" (Meyer and Rowan 1977) between stated organizational commitments to equality and the downplaying or denial of harassment is motivated by this contradiction.

Although the military is an officially color-blind (Bonilla-Silva 2006) organization, my research shows that the military has organizational mechanisms that allow some forms of racial and gender harassment to continue to occur and sometimes go unpunished. This is especially the case when reports of discrimination bump up against organizational needs, such as the need for bodies in battle. I call this process *punitive empathy*, an organizational mechanism through which apparently helpful programs such as equal opportunity reporting procedures exacerbate problems for soldiers by marking them as troublemakers, unfit for service or work. In Irving Goffman's (1959) classic distinction, a presentational "front stage," where individuals showcase their best selves, conceals a "back stage" where unpleasant or repressed facts are revealed. Scholars John Meyer and Brian Rowan (1997) tied this insight to organizations deriving legitimacy partly by conforming rhetorically to external "front stage" constituencies. They argue that despite front stage claims, institutions' back stage practices may be "decoupled" from publicized policy. Discretion in the application of policies allows those with organizational power to reinforce traditional hierarchies of race and gender. Apparently empathetic diversity programs become punitive when those in power punish actors who come forward to complain about inequality. Prototypically hierarchal, the military provides a case for understanding how organizations—despite perhaps good intentions—can contribute to reproducing inequalities.

The process of punitive empathy provides analytical purchase for understanding the complexities of organizational responses to external pressures for equality and compassion while maintaining old balances of power and privilege. In particular, Department of Defense antidiscrimination programs demonstrate how the military's commitment to equality can come with negative consequences. The "back stage" of these programs—where service members interact with commanders, fellow soldiers, and intricate bureaucracy—leaves them vulnerable to retribution, hazing, or worse. Punitive empathy allows organizations to essentially serve two masters—public pressure and internal goals. Spokespersons point to programs as evidence that external constituencies' issues are taken seriously while internally, service members who report problems may be punished, leading them to hide their issues or seek help elsewhere. In essence, having an anti-discrimination program *becomes* the entire program, serving a public relations function for organizations while further stigmatizing individuals.

4 Data and Methods

I draw on 50 in-depth semi-structured interviews with recently returned veterans (36 men and 14 women). Interviewees were recruited through snowball sampling and from visits to community centers, veteran job fairs, and local veterans' groups. These interviews cover many aspects of the process of reintegration, including looking for work, re-acclimating to family life, discrimination in and out of the military and mental and physical health following service. Interviews ranged from about 1 to nearly 4 hours. Interviewees were offered $25 in compensation, but many of them opted to donate the money to charity, claiming the opportunity to help another veteran was motivation enough. My respondents range in age from 24–43 and spent between 4 and 25 years in the military. They served at least one combat tour to be included in the sample, and some served as many as five tours in Iraq and Afghanistan. (The number of combat tours is separate from the number of deployments, as many soldiers are sent to international bases not directly involved in the combat mission, such as Germany, again separating them from family). Interviews were conducted in a variety of locations: college campuses, homes, coffee shops, public libraries (the latter being the best place, as they often have quiet study rooms open to the public) and even in my home. All interviews were recorded and professionally transcribed. Coding is based upon Blumer's notion of "sensitizing concepts" (Blumer 1969), using the theoretical traditions of the "racialized social system" (Bonilla-Silva 1997) to guide analysis.

From Bonilla-Silva's framework, I took the notion that much traditional sociological research examines race myopically, with unchanging measures inappropriate to new historical conditions. In response to this historically anachronistic method of understanding race relations, Bonilla-Silva argues that analysts must explicate racism in context. He claims "the form of race relations, overt or covert—depends on the pattern of radicalization that structures a particular society" (Bonilla-Silva, 1997: 468). I extend this insight, arguing that prior studies of the military analyze racial phenomena with tools inappropriate to the military environment. For instance, studies of the military often see hierarchies as legitimate (whereas they are questioned in other organizations) or downplay the effects of interpersonal racial hostility.

Analytically, following a recent advance by Mario Small (2009) on the logic of qualitative methods, the interview process allowed for theoretical "saturation" akin to that reached in experimental methods, through which repeated testing gives one greater confidence in a theoretical assertion (Tavory and Timmermans 2009). Small (2009) claims that qualitative interviewing should be seen as an iterative process during which the interviewer is revising questions and theories in light of respondents' answers. This allows researchers to reach a point of diminishing return, where additional interviews are not providing any new or relevant theoretical insights. At this point, the researcher has come to understand not only the individual cases, but how respondents think of their shared social worlds. Importantly, however, this does not mean that all respondents agree or that the narrative data is invariant. We should expect conflict between accounts, especially when discussing socially volatile issues such as race. Indeed, much of the comparative qualitative research on social understandings of race (Bonilla-Silva 2006; Lamont and Molnár 2002) shows that whites' and blacks' views of race matters consistently diverge. Similarly, survey research on racial attitudes shows disagreement across a whole host of areas, including segregation levels (Massey and Fischer 2000), responses to the criminal justice system (Alexander 2010), and many other areas of racial conflict, including social spending (Gilens, 1999). My respondents tend to conform to these large social cleavages, although they differ in some important ways. However, as a number of scholars have argued, this divergent interpretation of social life is an excellent place for theory construction and elaboration. The search for theories that reflect the empirical realities of respondents starts by showing how accounts that diverge from taken-for-granted understandings of the social world can be incorporated into a better synthetic understanding. According to Burawoy, "Objectivity is not measured by procedures that assure an accurate mapping of the world but by the growth of knowledge; that is, the imaginative and parsimonious reconstruction of theory to accommodate anomalies" (2002, 5). Following this, I argue anomalies surrounding racial interaction in the military allow us to build upon extant theory by showing how contextual variability influences the expression of discrimination.

Finally, semi-structured interviews also allow researchers to explore emergent themes and unanticipated findings (LaRossa 2005). Extant research omitted multiple aspects of service that veterans themselves indicated are important. For instance, early in my interviews, a veteran claimed he was afraid of reporting his mental health issues for fear of repercussions. In light of this insight, I began asking respondents if they experienced a similar feeling regarding racial discrimination, producing the material that motivated this chapter. Similarly, my respondents discussed the casual use of racial slurs among whites, a pattern of interpersonal communication unlikely to be picked up during a survey. Capturing these unsolicited insights from respondents is a key strength of qualitative methods and provides an excellent way to extend current theoretical understandings of racial stratification processes.

5   The Generalized Racial Atmostphere in the Military

As with any nominally diverse organization, the military is concerned with representation. My respondents acknowledge that in many cases, the military is more diverse than the jobs they held both before enlisting and after military service. However, they recognize that nominal diversity does not necessarily translate into power within the hierarchy. For instance, Peter, a black sergeant claimed that the leadership remains largely white, and opportunities for advancement are based upon implicit racial concerns. When I asked him about diversity in the military he said:

> To be honest, it's [the military] making a effort ... but it's still got a long way to come. You don't really know it until you-you on the outside looking in. I, me personally, I would say they come a long way. But – however, they still this good old boy system that's there. I would say about a generation before my generation, that's still got that, "I want to keep my boys in charge" ... as far as leadership in the Army, if you look – if you go to a unit – if you visit five to ten unit, right? You looked at that leadership, you going to see at least five to six white people before you see a black person. And let me say this, not just a black person; a minority, period. You going to see the old white dude with the grey hair before you see any minority.

Although Peter recognized that the military has attempted to move beyond racial divisions, he felt that the cosmetic diversity that the military promoted didn't necessarily extend to substantive opportunities. Nominal diversity, according to Peter, doesn't translate into organizational power within the military hierarchy. Rank—a class relationship within the military, as it apportions both economic resources and authority—is also racialized. Thus the apparently race-neutral social relationships central to the military are racial in practice. Further, although Peter partially frames the military's integration as a narrative of progress ("they come a long way") he also recognizes Steinberg's (1995) contention that the true measure of racial equality should be current parity, not comparisons to past racial inequality.

Peter's discussion of military leadership highlights the plausibly deniable racial inequality embedded in structural relationships in the military. Although this inequality is visible to anyone who observes the racial composition of a unit, it remains a naturalized and largely uncommented-upon part of the military. As Maliq points out, this racial backdrop is not fueled by overt racial animus. When asked if he ever witnessed any discrimination in the military, he claimed, "it's nothing flagrant or vulgar, it's just – you know when a person don't like you, but you don't know why a person don't like you. And we're smart–, I say" we"—the *military's* smart enough to not say why we don't like you." Maliq recognizes a central feature of how racial inequality is currently reproduced in the military. As a number of scholars have pointed out, blatant racist acts such as the use of epithets have been stigmatized in the current era (Bonilla-Silva 2006, Bobo and Smith 1998). Thus, the bar for claiming racial discrimination is operant in a given social situation has become exceedingly high, with those discriminated against needing to show racial intent. Maliq claims the "we" that the military uses to describe the relations between soldiers papers over the real racial divisions that still influence relationships in the ranks. This evasion, according to Maliq, also highlights that those who "don't like" racial minorities have recognized and adapted to the constraints—or racial etiquette—of the current racial regime.

In contrast to the claims of scholars (Moskos and Butler 1997) and the military hierarchy regarding the success of diversity in the military, my respondents point out that continued racial inequality shapes their daily career experiences in the military. Further, because these experiences are built into the hierarchy and hidden behind a non-racial veneer, service members often feel unable to confront racial inequality. In the next section, I examine how the military responds to those who come forward with complaints of racial inequality.

6   Punitive Empathy in Military Practice

Service members recognize that coming forward with complaints of discrimination can be detrimental to their careers. For instance, many of my respondents pointed to equal opportunity representatives being present in every unit as an example of efforts to quell discrimination. But when asked what happens to those that access these program representatives, they will say that the rest of the unit would ostracize them. For instance, Chuck vacillated about his understanding of race in the military. Like many of my other white respondents, he claimed that there was very little discrimination and said that equal opportunity officers were available to field complaints. However, he also explained what would happen to those who accessed this program. He said:

> I would definitely say if you're a minority, and let's say you're in a company of maybe a hundred and twenty people large and there is maybe five or six minorities, if you report it, you've got the majority against you already. Cause like let's say you're in a platoon and you're the only black

guy and you feel you're discriminated [against] and you go file the report. Right away, guys are going to be wary; they're not going to want to be around you, they are going to be wary about saying anything around you that might be offensive. So they're just going to ostracize you and you're going to be like, here's everybody – you're that guy over there.

Chuck clearly understood that those who access programs aimed at dealing with discrimination make themselves targets. This was an interesting moment in the interview, because he had just finished telling me that there was no discrimination in the military and things were "all equal." This quote also outlines the general process of punitive empathy. Chuck was aware that someone may be discriminated against and that there was a formal procedure for dealing with this. However, once that formal procedure is accessed, things get worse for the target. The individual reporting discrimination is cut off from the rest of the unit—undermining their membership in a basic unit of military life. This shows how formal reporting procedures can serve to legitimate the process while stigmatizing the individual. It also shows that the reporting process itself serves to discipline soldiers into accepting harassment, as they may know that what happens after reporting is worse.

When I asked Angela about her experiences with race and racism in the military, she had this to say:

> It was just this kind of demonizing of the brown people ... and maybe inadvertently it happens, but it didn't feel inadvertent. It felt blatant and purposeful ... you have to identify the enemy, and it wasn't just about identifying Afghans or Iraqis as enemy. It was the general classification of brown people as enemy ... you would have soldiers who would say things so offensive about blacks or Hispanics or even Iraqis or Afghans that was so racist and so offensive, but then they'd say, "you know I don't feel that way about you, we're in the same unit, we're wearing the same uniform, but those other ones that don't wear the uniform like you, they're this and they're that."

Black and brown people are demonized, according to Angela, and some soldiers considered people of color in uniform to be "exceptions." Angela went on to say that her commanding officer proudly displayed a confederate flag in his office, and that reporting this kind of thing is pointless. In contrast to the color-blind thesis that argues that the "dominant" form of racial talk in the post-civil rights era avoids direct racial reference, Angela's experiences with racial hostility were open, direct, and disturbing to her. Further, because of the rank structure of the military, she claims she had little recourse when dealing with this open hostility. Indeed, there is a backlog of equal opportunity complaints, and sufficient problems with reporting procedures exist to "keep members from filing complaints" (Burk and Espinoza 2012, 410). This is especially disturbing given that the Supreme Court ruled unanimously in 1983 (Chappell v. Wallace) that enlisted soldiers cannot sue the military for discrimination, as (according to them) adequate internal channels exist to address discrimination (Burk and Espinoza 2012). However, *the military's internal need to maintain discipline and control* meant that these possible violations were less important than control. The basic civil rights of black soldiers became a secondary concern, less important than military functioning.

Ultimately the military's claims of successful diversity are called into question by internal mechanisms that can suppress claims of racial discrimination. Two implications follow from this. First, by suppressing discrimination claims, the military can paint a picture of racial relations that may not conform to the lived reality of service members. My respondents made it clear that coming forward to report racism came at a cost—one they were not often willing to bear. Second, and relatedly, because the military justice system remains independent of civilian review, service members know that the military's decision is final. This leaves those who do pursue discrimination complaints with no recourse if they are denied. Fellow soldiers who witness this process are disciplined into conformity, as they know that their complaints are likely to be met with resistance and they may face personal repercussions.

7   Diversity in the Context of Racialized Organizations

If we take the military at its word, the organization is genuinely committed to meaningful diversification. Yet, substantial racial inequalities remain in a host of military processes (Burk and Espinoza 2012). As Embrick (2011) points out, organizational accounts of diversity tend to address superficial concerns such as numerical representation while leaving organizational power and privilege largely in the hands of white men. Thus diversity is an ideology that supports and legitimates a larger underlying racial structure (Embrick 2008, 2011). Part of this larger structure is the fundamentally racialized nature of organizations such as the military.

How can scholars move the study of diversity onto a firmer theoretical footing? First, scholars need to move beyond the idea that organizations are raceless or race-neutral. The military, many corporations, historically white colleges and universities, and many other organizations were founded on principles of racial segregation, if not outright exclusion. Repealing overt restrictions has reduced many problematic organizational practices. However, new forms of exclusion have arisen that are often more difficult to combat in practice. Second, efforts at managing diversity are based on the psychological dispositions of organizational members. Scholars should rather examine how organizational practices, such as the military's need for bodies for battle, shape organizational practices that may disadvantage racial minorities. Punitive empathy—maintaining public concern about diversity while suppressing problems associated with racial inclusion—is one mechanism through which the military manages racial inequality. Social scientists should turn their attention to other ways in which racial inequality is reproduce through seemingly neutral processes.

References

Acker, Joan. 2000. "Gendered Contradictions in Organizational Equity Projects." *Organization* 7(4): 625–632. Retrieved May 29, 2014 (http://org.sagepub.com/cgi/doi/10.1177/135050840074007).

Alexander, Michelle. 2010. "The New Jim Crow." *Ohio State Journal of Criminal Law* 9(1): 7–26. Retrieved November 5, 2014 (http://www.econ.brown.edu/fac/glenn_Loury/louryhomepage/teaching/Ec137/TheNewJimCrow-fromTheNation.pdf).

Bailey, Amy Kate. 2008. The Effect of Veteran Status on Spatial and Socioeconomic Mobility: Outcomes for Black and White Men in the Late 20th Century. Proquest/UMI 3328368.

Bell, Joyce, and Douglas Hartmann. 2007. "Diversity in Everyday Discourse: The Cultural Ambiguities and Consequences of 'Happy Talk.'" *American Sociological Review*, 72: 895–914.

Bielby, William T. 2000. "Minimizing Workplace Gender and Racial Bias." *Contemporary Sociology: A Journal of Reviews* 120–129.

Blumer, Herbert. 1969. *Symbolic Interactionism.* Englewood Cliffs, NJ. Prentice Hall.

Bobo, Lawrence D., and Ryan A. Smith. 1998. "From Jim Crow Racism to Laissez-Faire Racism: The Transformation of Racial Attitudes." Pp. 182–210 in *Beyond pluralism: The....* Retrieved June 19, 2014 (http://scholar.google.com/scholar?hl=en&btnG=Search&q=intitle:From+Jim+Crow+Racism+to+Laissez-Faire+Racism:+The+Transformation+of+Racial+Attitudes#0).

Bonilla-Silva, Eduardo. 1997. "Rethinking Racism: Toward a Structural Interpretation." *American sociological review* 62(3): 465–480. Retrieved June 4, 2014 (http://www.jstor.org/stable/2657316).

Bonilla-Silva, Eduardo. 2006. *Racism Without Racists: Color-Blind Racism and the Persistence of Racial Inequality in the United States.* Third Edit. Lanham, Boulder, New

York, Toronto, Plymouth, UK: Rownman & Littlefield. Retrieved August 29, 2014 (http://www.kilil5.com/topics/opinion?page=29).

Burk, James, and Evelyn Espinoza. 2012. "Race Relations Within the US Military." *Annual Review of Sociology* 38(1): 401–422. Retrieved May 27, 2014 (http://www.annual reviews.org/doi/abs/10.1146/annurev-soc-071811-145501).

Chappell v. Wallace, 462 U.S. 296 (1983).

Embrick, David G. 2008. "The Diversity Ideology: Keeping Major Transnational Corporations White and Male in an Era of Globalization." In *Globalization and America: Race, Human Rights & Inequality*, edited by Angela Hattery, David G. Embrick, and Earl Smith. Lanham, MD: Rowman and Littlefield.

Embrick, David G. 2011. "The Diversity Ideology in the Business World: A New Oppression for a New Age." *Critical Sociology* 37(5): 541–556. Retrieved (http://crs.sagepub .com/cgi/doi/10.1177/0896920510380076).

Gilens, Martin. 1999. *Why Americans Hate Welfare: Race, Media, and the Politics of Antipoverty Policy*. Chicago, IL: University of Chicago Press.

Goffman, Irving. 1959. "The Presentation of Self in Everyday Life." New York, NY: Doubleday.

Hirsh, C. Elizabeth, and Sabino Kornrich. 2008. "The Context of Discrimination: Workplace Conditions, Institutional Environments, and Sex and Race Discrimination Charges." *AJS; American journal of sociology* 113(5): 1394–1432. Retrieved (http:// www.ncbi.nlm.nih.gov/pubmed/18831130).

Lamont, M., and V. Molnár. 2002. "The Study of Boundaries in the Social Sciences." *Annual review of sociology* 28(2002): 167–195. Retrieved June 17, 2014 (http://www.jstor .org/stable/3069239).

LaRossa, R. 2005. "Grounded Theory Methods and Qualitative Family Research." *Journal of Marriage and Family* 67(4): 837–857. Retrieved June 4, 2014 (http://onlineli brary.wiley.com/doi/10.1111/j.1741-3737.2005.00179.x/full).

Lundquist, J.H. 2004. "When Race Makes No Difference: Marriage and the Military." *Social Forces* 83(2): 731–757. Retrieved June 10, 2014 (http://sf.oxfordjournals.org/ content/83/2/731.short).

Lundquist, J.H. 2008. "Ethnic and Gender Stratification in the Military: The Effect of a Meritocratic Institution." *American Sociological Review* 73(3): 477–496. Retrieved May 28, 2014 (http://asr.sagepub.com/content/73/3/477.short).

Massey, Douglas S., and Mary J. Fischer. 2000. "How Segregation Concentrates Poverty." *Ethnic and Racial Studies* 23(4): 670–691. Retrieved (http://www.tandfonline.com/ doi/abs/10.1080/01419870050033676).

Meyer, John W., and Brian Rowan. 1977. "Institutionalized Organizations: Formal Structure as Myth and Ceremony." *American journal of sociology* 83(2): 340–363. Retrieved June 10, 2014 (http://faculty.washington.edu/jwilker/571/571readings/MeyerRowan .pdf).

Moynihan, Daniel P. 1965. *The Negro Family: The Case for National Action*. Washington
     DC: Office of Policy Planning and Research, United States Department of Labor.

Moskos, Charles, and John Sibley Butler. 1997. *All That We Can Be: Black Leadership and
     Racial Integration The Army Way*. New York: Basic Books.

Roscigno, V.J. 2007. *The Face of Discrimination*. Plymouth: Rowman & Littlefield.

Segal, David R., and Mady Wechsler Segal. 2004. "America's Military Population." *Popu-
     lation Reference Bureau*. Washington D.C.

Small, M.L. 2009. "'How Many Cases Do I Need?': On Science and the Logic of Case
     Selection in Field-Based Research." *Ethnography* 10(1): 5–38. Retrieved May 24, 2014
     (http://eth.sagepub.com/cgi/doi/10.1177/1466138108099586).

Steinberg, Stephen. 1995. Turning Back: The Retreat from Racial Justice in American
     Thought and Policy. Boston, MA: Beacon.

Tavory, I., and S. Timmermans. 2009. "Two Cases of Ethnography: Grounded Theory
     and the Extended Case Method." *Ethnography* 10(3): 243–263. Retrieved May 28,
     2014 (http://eth.sagepub.com/cgi/doi/10.1177/1466138109339042).

Teachman, J.D., and L. Tedrow. 2008. "Divorce, Race, and Military Service: More than
     Equal Pay and Equal Opportunity." *Journal of Marriage and Family* 70 (Novem-
     ber): 1030–1044. Retrieved May 28, 2014 (http://onlinelibrary.wiley.com/doi/10.1111/j
     .1741-3737.2008.00544.x/full).

Webb, James. 1997. "The War on the Military Culture." *The Weekly Standard*, 2: 17–22.

CHAPTER 15

Undermining Prisoner Re-entry Initiatives: Neoliberalism, Race and Profits

Edward Orozco Flores

1   Introduction

On February 27th, 2014, US President Barrack Obama announced an initiative to target Black and Latino incarceration: "My Brother's Keeper" (White House 2014). Obama blamed marginal communities for their plight—as if the product of cultural pathologies—and evoked government only insofar to guide research into "what works" to create docile subjects for the state: "better husbands and fathers, and well-educated hard-working, good citizens." Obama's initiative aimed to reform the school-to-prison pipeline by building a coalition of elected officials, corporate businesses, large philanthropic foundations, and religious groups. However, as this paper will show—by examining the Chicago Mayor's 2006 Prisoner Re-entry Initiative—anti-incarceration politics may simply extend racial inequalities from the for-profit sector to the non-profit sector. Obama's anti-incarceration initiative perpetuated structural racism by enabling state reduction in social spending, supporting profit-generating activities, and drawing from racist, victim-blaming "culture of poverty" ideology.

First, Obama deflected the state's responsibility for mass incarceration, as well as racial disparities within incarceration. Obama blamed absent Black and Latino fathers, declared that "nothing keeps a young man out of trouble like a father who takes an active role in his son's life," and stated that "government cannot play... the primary role." Second, Obama deflected the state's responsibility in perpetuating racial inequalities in education. Obama claimed that he had been the product of "more forgiving" family and teachers, ignoring how mass incarceration has decreased public education funding and increased class sizes—reducing the possibility of quality, one-on-one teacher-student relationships. Third, Obama deflected the state's responsibility for racial inequalities within the private sector. Obama ignored financial deregulation and the rise of contingent labor markets, admonishing communities of color by saying "no excuses" or "it will take courage." Instead, Obama announced the "good news" that the private sector "already" knew the importance of his initiative.

Obama's initiative was symbolic of an emergent trend: the use of anti-incarceration politics to extend neoliberal economic policies and racist practices. On a national level, we were no longer having a debate about the efficacy of locking up millions more of Americans. Rather, we were drawing from a soft racial paternalism to advocate for incarceration reduction—while institutionalizing racial inequality through an apparatus of state, businesses, philanthropic foundations and religious groups. The Obama era marked a strong shift towards "violence prevention" strategies that departed from an "epidemiological approach," and focused resources on areas such as "promise zones," as if the causes of mass incarceration lay outside of mainstream institutional practices.

The politics of incarceration—the decisions that increase or decrease incarceration—have recently received more attention from scholars (i.e. Owens 2014, Goodman, Page and Phelps 2015, Schoenfeld 2011). David Dagan and Steven M. Teles (2014) argue that in recent years, policies of incarceration have spurred "negative feedback." Where public opinion polls once found that 37% of Americans ranked crime as the most important issue in 1994, only 2% did so in 2012; in addition, the rising costs of prisons are now under greater scrutiny following the recessions of the 2000s (Dagan and Teles 2014). Scholars argue that, "penal development is fueled by ongoing, low-level struggle among actors with various amounts and types of resources" (Goodman, Page and Phelps 2015, 315). The "agonistic perspective" (Goodman, Page and Phelps 2015, 318-319) highlights how local penal fields and organizations filter the large-scale forces that drive incarceration.

The large-scale politics of incarceration hinge upon neoliberalism—the offloading of risk from the state to the individual—and racial oppression. For example, many Black residents of South Los Angeles initially supported the Drug War—which disproportionately targeted Blacks—believing it to protect their children from the drug economy (Murch 2015). However, Black and Latino residents of South Los Angeles politically organized through non-profit organizations, after finding the effects of the Drug War punishment to be much more destructive to their communities than the drug economy. Activists reframed the crack crisis in terms of public health; they emphasized "structural police violence, and the development of grassroots, indigenous solutions rather than state punishment," and formulated drug war politics that were further left-of-center than Black elected officials and local clergy (Murch 2015, 172). Through the Black working class drug war politics, non-profits upstaged grassroots social movements as the site of organized dissent.

Notwithstanding the non-profit sector's role in resistance to racial oppression and incarceration, this chapter will examine how anti-incarceration efforts perpetuate structural racism through public-private partnerships and colorblind racism. Where recent research has found that the for-profit sector's celebration of diversity has masked neoliberal, colorblind racism (Embrick 2008, 2011), this chapter will draw from one example of anti-mass incarceration efforts—the Chicago Mayor's 2006 Re-entry Initiative—to argue that non-profits also perpetuate colorblind racist ideology and serve profitability.

2 The Chicago Mayor's 2006 Re-Entry Initiative

Chicago is representative of nationwide trends both in incarceration and anti-incarceration. On the one hand, Chicago has one of the highest violent crime rates in the nation, and Cook County jail is the second largest in the nation. On the other hand, Chicago was also one of the first cities to adopt progressive reforms now sweeping the nation: banning the felony conviction question from public employment applications or investing in social support services for the formerly incarcerated. In 2004, Chicago Mayor Richard Daley formed a Mayoral Policy Caucus on Prisoner Re-entry. The purpose of the caucus was to find a solution to mass incarceration's growing social and economic costs. In a publicly released statement, the mayor commented that the objective was to "break the cycle" for crime to fall, and that such a goal would require for ex-offenders to "find meaningful employment and become productive members of society." The Chicago Mayor's 2006 Re-entry Initiative emerged from this caucus, providing employment to formerly incarcerated persons; this chapter will document how such "meaningful employment" was neoliberal and racist in form.

I critically examine how the Chicago Mayor's Office used re-entry efforts to perpetuate racism. First, I examine how the Mayor's Re-entry Initiative concentrated funds into particular departments, programs and non-profits. Second, I draw from three case studies to analyze themes in the text of contracts, as well as the corporate affiliations of executive board members of contracted non-profit organizations. I find that the Mayor's Initiative subsidized arrangements between the public sector, the private non-profit sector, and the private for-profit sector, in ways that created temporary, part-time and low wage work for a population of color. Second, I find that the Mayor's Initiative articulated colorblind racism; non-profit organizations deployed racist "culture of poverty" tropes while providing substandard employment as "training."

3 Incarceration, Racism, and Marginality

Research on prison release has typically focused on the issue of social "reintegration," though this is a misnomer considering that the incarcerated are among the least integrated to begin with (Wacquant 2010). For one group today—Black men—marginality is acute: the institution of prison wields greater influence in the life course of a Black man than either college or the military (Pettit and Western 2004). Since 2001, Black men aged 20 to 34 without a high school diploma have been more likely to be incarcerated than employed in the labor market (PEW Charitable Trusts 2010, 13). In addition, projections suggest that one in six male Latinos, and one in three black males, born in 2001 will be incarcerated at some point in his life—as opposed to only one in seventeen white males (Bonczar 2003, 1, cited in Mauer 2006[1999]), 138).

Michelle Alexander (2010, 11) has termed mass incarceration the "New Jim Crow." Whereas the previous system of Jim Crow laws and racial etiquette explicitly circumscribed Blacks' political, economic, and civil rights, the post–Civil Rights era is characterized by what Eduardo Bonilla-Silva (2003, 2) terms "colorblind racism": a rationalization which explains racial inequality as "the product of market dynamics, naturally occurring phenomena, and… imputed cultural limitations." In the New Jim Crow, the rights of people of color are indirectly circumscribed through mass incarceration and the stigma of a criminal record. The formerly incarcerated are:

> …often denied the right to vote, excluded from juries, and relegated to a racially segregated and subordinated existence" … "legally denied the ability to obtain employment, housing, and public benefits—much as African Americans were once forced into a segregated second-class citizenship in the Jim Crow era."
>
> ALEXANDER 2010, 4

Longitudinal research suggests that employment is one of the most significant factors mediating the post-incarceration experience; unemployment is a risk factor for criminal activity (Fagan & Freeman 1999) while employment is associated with "pro-social" outcomes, such as success in drug treatment programs (Leukefeld, et al. 2003; Wolkstein & Spiller 1998). The formerly incarcerated gain and maintain employment at lower rates than those without records (Fagan & Freeman 1999; Holzer, Offner, & Sorenson 2005; Western 2007). Devah Pager (2003), in her audit research using testers for job applications, found that formerly incarcerated persons face labor market discrimination for their criminal records; Black job applicants with no records received fewer call-backs than whites (14% versus 34%), but call-backs were even lower when applicants of both groups had records (5% versus 17%). In contrast, a Loyola University Chicago study found that employment was associated with reductions in recidivism; persons who achieved thirty consecutive days of employment had three-year recidivism rates of 17.5%–63% lower than the Illinois statewide average (SAFER Foundation 2014). Thus, for Blacks, racism and incarceration reinforce each other as barriers to employment and social integration.

4 Neoliberalism, Racism, and Social Control

Critical sociologists and criminologists place post-1970s economic decline in advanced industrial nations at the core of their analysis of racism, marginality, and incarceration (Bauman 2003; Wacquant 2009[1999]; Young 2011). Mass incarceration is fundamentally a system of social control (Garland 2001, Simon 2009). Following the 1960s Civil Rights movements, racist backlash emerged through the coded rhetoric of "law and order" (Omi and Winant 1994 [1986]), and then, following the 1970s, the federal government began a profound shift in making domestic policy—rather than international policy—a federal priority. Criminal and penal policy, most notably the War on Drugs, moved crime from a local to a national concern. This led to a steep, decades-long rise in incarceration. Between 1970 and 1980, the U.S. incarceration rate rose from 161.4 to 220.4 per 100,000 adults.

Sociologist and law professor David Garland has argued that the post–World War II decline of Keynesian economics—the use of public spending to combat economic recession—has "challenged the legitimacy and effectiveness of welfare institutions, and placed new limits on the powers of the nation-state" (Garland 2001, 75). "The politics of post-welfarism" has helped to produce "a new set of class and race relations and a dominant political block that defined itself in opposition to old style 'welfarism.'" For example, the Manhattan Institute, a conservative think tank founded in 1978, helped rearticulate white racist hegemony through Charles Murray's Losing Ground; Murray's work critiqued the Civil Rights Movements and its big government policies, and urged social reform through social disinvestment. Furthermore, in the early 1990s, the Manhattan Institute continued to build on conservative ideas that emphasized mass arrest tactics targeting the urban—largely black and Latino—poor. The institute hosted a conference that led to a special issue in its journal, City, positing a relationship between urban disorder and crime that called for a heavy-handed policing approach to protect the interests of middle-class consumers of public space (Wacquant 2009[1999]).

Although neoliberalism has remade unequal class and race relations through fiscal austerity and crime control, dramatic prison growth now confronts public entities with a significant challenge: absorb the unsustainable costs of mass incarceration and high rates of recidivism. As of 2008, the United States was the world leader in incarceration. More than one in one hundred Americans were sitting behind bars—more people than the top 35 European countries combined (Pew Center on the States 2008). In addition, every year about 680,000 inmates are released from state and federal prisons, although it is estimated that most will return to prison within five years (Visher and Travis 2003). To this end, prominent conservatives have now been among the most vocal advocates for incarceration reductions (Dagan and Teles 2014).

The problems posed by prison costs and recidivism rates led Clinton-era attorney general Janet Reno to convene a summit of academics and practioners in 2001. From this summit, Jeremy Travis coined the term "prisoner re-entry," to refer to the goal of preventing the formerly incarcerated from returning to prison (Travis 2007). The popularization of the term "re-entry" has since shaped the discourse of incarceration. Since the summit, several executive orders and legislative acts have helped to institutionalize prisoner re-entry. In 2001, President George W. Bush signed the OFBCI act, allowing religious groups to compete for federal funding to provide social services. In 2007, the Second Chance Act authorized government agencies and non-profit organizations to provide resources to the formerly incarcerated. Most recently, in 2014, President Obama created the My Brother's Keeper Initiative, seeking to address mass incarceration by building on the successes of community groups involved with violence prevention.

Critical studies into re-entry have suggested that the rise of rehabilitation is not about providing help to ex-offenders, but about the neoliberal state offloading risk onto individuals. Social work research emphasizes the effect of religion on rehabilitation from drug use and crime (i.e. Jensen and Gibbons 2002; O'Connor and Perreyclear 2002; O'Connor, Ryan and Parkikh 1998). However, critical re-entry ethnographies have suggested rehabilitation is a political process. Halfway houses, re-entry institutions, and recovery programs regulate access to shelter, food and one's children through performances of rehabilitation (Carr 2010, Haney 2010). Ex-offenders engage with these performances of rehabilitation, reshaping their relationship with language in order to acquire access to goods. By institutionalizing "blame the victim" discourse, these settings socialize ex-offenders for contingent labor markets (Fairbanks 2009; Gowan and Whetstone 2012; Haney 2010; Kaye 2013). For example, research in Chicago has suggested that ex-offender placement services "redouble their emphasis on disciplining client behavior, on the grounds that anything short of complete compliance is tantamount to self-administered unemployability" (Peck and Theodore 2008, 273).

5   Data and Methods

The analysis in this chapter draws from the contract data I gathered on the Chicago Mayor's Re-entry Initiative through public records requests. In April 2014, I sent public records requests to the various offices linked to a press release for the Mayor of Chicago's 2006 Ex-offender/Re-entry Initiative.[1] I requested to obtain the contract numbers of the city's re-entry contracts. I sought contract number information for contracts between 2004 and 2014, by contract number, department, initiative, contract start and end date, agency, budget, and total amount expended. The Mayor's Office of Workforce Development responded by sending me a Microsoft Excel spreadsheet file that listed the information I requested. I cleaned this data by systematically cleaning entries in a way that made it suitable for statistical analysis through statistical software. The following section first presents descriptive statistics and frequency tables examining how public re-entry spending is distributed among various departments, social programs, and non-profit organizations. Second, it presents brief case studies of the three non-profit organizations—those with the largest amount of funding received from the Mayor's Initiative—and examines two elements of their contracts: the textual description of their activities and the affiliations of the members of their board of directors.

6   Findings

My findings suggest that re-entry creates an institutional apparatus in which government mitigates the risk of private sector profit-generating activity. Through the Chicago Mayor's Prisoner Re-entry Initiative, the City of Chicago subsidized public-private partnerships with private for-profit and private non-profit organizations in ways that deployed ex-offenders as contingent labor and/or to contingent labor markets. In addition, such economic arrangements rearticulated colorblind racist "culture of poverty" notions; non-profit organizations contracted to provide re-entry to ex-offenders—who were largely black and brown—portrayed them as suffering from cultural deficits. Ex-offenders were depicted as bad citizens, suggesting that the state and private firms were generous benefactors ameliorating marginality through charitable efforts.

---

1   The Mayor's Press Release was accessed on April 23, 2014 from http://nelp.org/content/up
loads/2015/03/MayorDalysPressRelease.pdf?nocdn=1.

Not only are ex-offenders deserving of contingent labor, but according to such logic they should be grateful to have such undesirable opportunities.

6.1   *The Chicago Mayoral Caucus on Re-entry's Recommendations*

The Chicago Mayoral Re-entry Caucus was chaired by two persons with strong private sector ties: Roxanne Ward, the Vice President of an investment banking firm (Ariel Capital Maganament), and Paula Wolff, a senior executive of a local policy and planning advocacy group (Chicago Metropolis 2020) founded by the Commercial Club of Chicago. The Re-entry Caucus released its report in January 24, 2006, calling for the following changes: expanded education and job opportunities, improved access to health care (specifically mentioning substance abuse and mental health treatment), family-friendly policies in the corrections system (specifically mentoring programs for the children of incarcerated persons), and stronger support in the community (specifically mentioning "resource centers" for the formerly incarcerated).

The Mayor's Press Office outlined the caucus' recommendations, and announced two new changes. First, a change in the City's personnel policy, requiring that job hiring decisions would not simply be based on the results of criminal background checks—but take into account the relationship between a job applicant's criminal background and the nature of a job. Second, the creation of two new programs for ex-offenders: a customized job training program and a social enterprise program. The City's prisoner re-entry initiatives would provide $500,000 and $400,000, respectively, to the two programs, as part of 4.3 million dollars in spending, as well as another $4 million budgeted.

The creation of the two new re-entry programs added to the long list of existing re-entry programs. The list of all existing programs, after the caucus' recommendations, were as follow:

·   Mayor's Office of Workforce Development- Customized Job Training Program
·   Mayor's Office of Workforce Development- Social Enterprise Ventures Program
·   Mayor's Office of Workforce Development- Transitional Jobs Program
·   Mayor's Office of Workforce Development- Customized Work Services Program
·   Department of Fleet Management- Automotive Repair
·   Department of Revenue- Call Center Operations and Debt Collection
·   Department of Streets and Sanitation- Neighborhood Beautification and Recycling
·   Department of Environment and Mayor's Office of Workforce Development- Collection and Recycling Center on Goose Island.

The text of the announcement of the Mayor's Initiative made explicit reference to the expendable nature of re-entry job training and employment. This included references to contracting (see Table 15.1) with staffing services, training participants to work in city services without any possibility of permanency within the public sector, or offering college credit through work done for the city.

The implied suggestion of the initiative was to treat workers as disposable commodities—available upon employer demand—just as "Just-in-Time" production provides materials upon demand. The "customized job training program" was hailed as superior to "traditional job training models" because it offered "greater flexibility and stronger ties to employer demands," as it was "specifically tailored to meet current and projected employer demand." However, the two industries targeted by the customized job training program were Shipping and Receiving, and Food Service, two growing industries in which workers have increasingly experienced struggles for union representation, better working conditions and better pay (Milkman 2006).

6.2   Using Re-entry to Outsource Public Sector Work

The Mayor's announcement of his multi-pronged re-entry initiative belied how the initiative concentrated funding streams. First, the two bodies that most contracts funded were the Mayor's Office of Workforce Development (MOWD) and the Department of Family and Support Services (DFSS), many of which pertained to "customized work services programs" and "transitional jobs programs" (see Tables 15.1 and 15.2). Other departments mentioned in the initiatives would receive support through the funding of private organizations that worked with either of these two bodies. For example, MOWD funded the CARA program, a private non-profit, under its "Customized Work Services Program," in order to do work for the Department of Streets and Sanitation.

DFSS accounted for the largest share of re-entry contracts in the sample, 82 (77.4%) (see Table 15.1). MOWD contracts accounted for only 23 (21.7%) of the contracts in the sample, and the Department of Environment held only one contract (.9%) in the sample (see Table 15.1). DFSS contracts were not only the largest share, but were also the largest in terms of the number of months contracted (1033), the amount of funds expended ($10,283,226), and the average amount of funds expended per month ($1,068,730). In fact, DFSS contracts' share of re-entry costs expended by the city (78.9%), and its share of the city's average expended costs per month (84.8%), were higher than its share of the city's contracts (77.4%) (see Table 15.1). Thus, not only did the City of Chicago contract more with DFSS than MOWD or any other department, but the amount spent in those contracts was disproportionately higher.

TABLE 15.1   Reentry contracts, by administrative department

Department	Contract		Months Funded		Expended		Exp. per Mo.	
	N	%	N	%	N	%	N	%
Department of Environment	1	0.9%	30	2.1%	$180,000	1.4%	$6,007	0.5%
Department of Family and Support Services	82	77.4%	1,033	73.4%	$10,283,226	78.9%	$1,068,730	84.8%
Mayors Office of Workforce Development	23	21.7%	345	24.5%	$2,573,758	19.7%	$184,892	14.7%
Total	106	100.0%	1,408	100.0%	$13,036,984	100.0%	$1,259,629	100.0%

SOURCE: AUTHOR ANALYSIS OF PUBLIC RECORDS REQUESTS, MAYOR'S OFFICE OF
WORKFORCE DEVELOPMENT

As Rebecca Sager (2010) noted in her study of President Bush's Office of Faith-Based and Community Initiatives (OFBCI), initiatives are often symbolic more than substantive; rather than provide new funding, initiatives often reconfigure the way in which funding is accessed through the state. Similarly, although the Mayor held a large press conference to announce his funding for re-entry initiatives through the MOWD, the amount of new funding was less significant compared to existing and new funding for DFSS. Various branches of social services had already been increasingly dealing with the issue of serving growing numbers of people being released from prison. The Mayor's Initiative was in big part symbolic, making explicit the new configuration of public spending on private non-profit contracts and their relationship with the private, for-profit sector.

The creation of the Mayor's caucus on re-entry, the report the caucus released with recommendations, and the creation of new initiatives served to help reconfigure the way that re-entry operated. The state used the re-entry initiative to trim mass incarceration costs, by aligning the interests of the private for-profit and non-profit sectors. As part of this reconfiguration, private non-profits would have to access state funding by serving the interests of private, for-profit groups: recruiting contingent labor.

TABLE 15.2 Reentry contracts, by program

Program	Contract		Months funded		Expended		Exp. per Mo.	
	N	%	N	%	N	%	N	%
Community Green Jobs	1	0.9%	30	2.1%	$180,000	1.4%	$6,007	0.5%
Customized Job Training Program	25	23.6%	288	20.5%	$3,264,081	25.0%	$284,265	22.6%
Customized Work Services Program	23	21.7%	364	25.9%	$2,550,340	19.6%	$393,556	31.2%
Social Enterprise Venture Program	7	6.6%	120	8.5%	$961,806	7.4%	$59,588	4.7%
Transitional Jobs Program	42	39.6%	510	36.2%	$5,255,313	40.3%	$447,426	35.5%
Workforce Services	8	7.5%	96	6.8%	$825,444	6.3%	$68,787	5.5%
Total	106	100.0%	1,408	100.0%	$13,036,984	100.0%	$1,259,629	100.0%

SOURCE: AUTHOR ANALYSIS OF PUBLIC RECORDS REQUESTS, MAYOR'S OFFICE OF
WORKFORCE DEVELOPMENT

6.3 *Serving Capital with Expendable Workers*

How does the Mayor's Re-entry Initiative, as a reflection of the broader movement towards re-entry, reflect the interests of capital? "Transitional jobs" have
the opposite effect of providing work for the formerly incarcerated; they undermine the job security that is necessary to remain employed, and create a
contingent labor force that serves the needs of private firms seeking expendable labor. The Mayor's Initiative blurred the provision of social services with
the fiscal austerity of neoliberal reform by contracting with non-profits to
serve city departments, as well as by contracting with non-profits to hold both
types of contracts (work services and transitional jobs). Furthermore, itera-
tions of contracts funded more than once were often listed as "ex-offender/
re-entry initiatives," "customized work services programs," or "transitional jobs
programs"—or any combination of two of these three labels.

When analyzing the different funded components of the Mayor's Initiative, it becomes clear that a great deal of funding is directed towards creating contingent labor. Table 15.2 suggests that the "Transitional Jobs Programs"

represented the largest number of contracts (42, or 39.6%), contracted months (510, or 36.2%), amount expended (40.3%, or $5,255,313), and amount expended per month (35.5%, or $447,426 per month). The program with the second biggest source of funding was the "Customized Job Training Program," which, on its face, suggests training for employment in stable, well-paying occupa-

TABLE 15.3   Reentry contracts, by contractor

Contractor	Contracts		Months funded		Expended		Exp. per Mo.	
	N	%	N	%	N	%	N	%
North Lawndale Employment Network	21	19.8%	300	21.3%	$2,305,381	17.7%	$171,536	13.6%
Safer Foundation	2	1.9%	20	1.4%	$1,218,355	9.3%	$285,551	22.7%
The Cara Program	11	10.4%	161	11.4%	$1,112,190	8.5%	$82,806	6.6%
Community Assistance Programs	7	6.6%	81	5.8%	$896,539	6.9%	$77,726	6.2%
Greater West Town Community Development	5	4.7%	60	4.3%	$844,711	6.5%	$70,393	5.6%
Career Advancement Network	5	4.7%	60	4.3%	$744,903	5.7%	$62,075	4.9%
Association House of Chicago	8	7.5%	102	7.2%	$663,252	5.1%	$66,501	5.3%
Westside Health Authority	5	4.7%	57	4.0%	$576,707	4.4%	$51,184	4.1%
Phalanx Family Center	4	3.8%	45	3.2%	$504,613	3.9%	$45,163	3.6%
Chicago Christian Industrial League	3	2.8%	36	2.6%	$480,962	3.7%	$40,080	3.2%
Salvation Army	3	2.8%	33	2.3%	$410,658	3.1%	$37,842	3.0%
Illinois Manufacturing Foundation	2	1.9%	24	1.7%	$401,889	3.1%	$33,491	2.7%
A Safe Haven Foundation-CCIL	4	3.8%	45	3.2%	$385,135	3.0%	$35,154	2.8%
St. Leonards Ministries	4	3.8%	42	3.0%	$378,183	2.9%	$38,086	3.0%
All other contractors (13)	22	20.8%	342	24.3%	$2,113,507	16.2%	$162,043	12.9%
Total	106	100.0%	1,408	100.0%	$13,036,984	100.0%	$1,259,629	100.0%

SOURCE: AUTHOR ANALYSIS OF PUBLIC RECORDS REQUESTS, MAYOR'S OFFICE OF WORKFORCE DEVELOPMENT

tions (see Table 15.3). "Customized Job Training Programs" accounted for 23.6% of contracts and 25% of expended funds (see Table 15.2). The program with the third largest source of funding was "Customized Work Services Program," with 21.7% of all contracts and 19.6% of all expended funds (see Table 15.2). The remaining three programs—"Social Enterprise Venture Program," "Workforce Services," and "Community Green Jobs"—accounted for a smaller number of contracts (15.1%) and proportion of the amount expended from the Mayor's Initiative (15.1%) (see Table 15.2).

6.4   Three Case Studies: NLEN, CARA and Safer

An analysis of data pertaining to contractors reveals that the Mayor's Initiative funded some contractors much more than others. For example, although twenty-seven contractors received contracts to do re-entry work, six contractors accounted for more than half (54.6%) of the total amount expended on the Mayor's Initiative; these contractors received a total of 51 contracts, and expended $7,122,080 (see Table 1.3). Here I examine three biggest contractors: the North Lawndale Employment Network (NLEN), the CARA program, and the Safer Foundation.

The data suggest that one contractor—the North Lawndale Employment Network (NLEN)—received many more contracts (21), and expended far more ($2,305,381), than any other single contractor. NLEN's contracts accounted for 21.3% of all contracts, and the amount they expended accounted for 17.7% of all funds that the Mayor's Initiative expended.

NLEN's board of directors reflected private sector interests. Most hailed from the private sector, and some even from the financial sector. One was a vice president for JP Morgan Chase Bank, another was a chief executive officer with a debt collection agency (Collector's Training Institute), and yet another was a managing director with a temporary staffing firm (Solomon Edward Group, LLC). Lastly, one person hailed from the office of Congressman Danny Davis, who sponsored the Second Chance Act of 2007—a major, national legislative act for prisoner re-entry.

What did NLEN's participation in the Mayor's Re-entry Initiative look like? A downloaded copy of NLEN's contract for $200,000, the largest single contract in the database under analysis, outlined a re-entry project centered on a corporation wholly owned by NLEN: Sweet Beginnings. The contract describes Sweet Beginnings as a "high quality producer of natural honey-based personal care products and estate premium honey" that invests not just in ingredients but "individuals making a new beginning."

Sweet Beginning's business model, a "social purpose business," was aimed at providing formerly incarcerated men and women viable opportunities to establish a work history, learn productive habits, and gain marketable skills as a stepping stone to further employment and career advancement so that they can... become productive members of society.[2]

In other words, they sought to provide temporary work opportunities for the formerly incarcerated, and they tied this to ideas of citizenship.

The work that NLEN provided through Sweet Beginnings was low-wage and non-standard: an hourly wage of $7.75 per hour (the Chicago minimum wage starting July 2008), for thirty hours a week, for an estimated average of twelve weeks. The reasons for non-standard employment were clear: the contract stated that health/life/dental insurance coverage would not be provided to workers.

In practice NLEN operated much like a third-party staffing firm, one of the many fueling the contingent labor market. The contract clearly stated "NLEN bears sole responsibility for provision of services." However, its contract listed Whole Foods and local farmers' markets as work sites. In addition, outreach and recruitment targeted the Illinois Department of Corrections Field Services, as well as local churches, non-profits and newsletters. The strong relationship between Whole Foods and Sweet Beginnings could be further underscored by examining the Sweet Beginnings' founder's work history—who left Whole Foods to found Sweet Beginnings only to return to Whole Foods afterwards.

NLEN's program goals clearly focused on participants' behavior modification: competitive learning, case management, job seeking skills training, on-the-job training, job placement assistance, post-employment follow up, and supportive services (i.e. transportation, uniforms, identification). Further, insofar as NELN listed services to be provided, they seemed to be services that were geared more towards serving capital (i.e. Whole Foods, or the owners of Sweet Beginnings). The provision of services listed the following: work sites; outreach and recruitment; orientation, assessment and enrollment; pre-employment training; on-the-job training; supervision and monitoring of the work site; job placement, advancement services and retention. Of particular interest was the mention of pre-employment training as a service provided. The text specifically stated "Hierarchy in the workplace: the understanding

---

2   This quote was obtained from page 28, under "Exhibit 1: Scope of Services" in a publicly-available—but unpublished—contract between the City of Chicago and the North Lawndale Employment Network: Contract Number 14792, "Social Enterprise Initiative Venture."

and acceptance of the stratification of roles and responsibilities on the job." Contrary to a form of socialization that might actually benefit workers, such as learning about labor union participation or knowing one's rights in the workplace, the "service" that NELN provided ex-offenders was to prepare them for undemocratic work relationships.

The CARA program, which held the second largest number of contracts (11, or 10.4%) and the third largest amount expended ($1,112,190, or 8.5%), provided (in part) services to the City of Chicago- Street and Sanitation Department. These services included the type of work that Streets and Sanitation typically do. However, whereas employment with Streets and Sanitation would make one a public employee—and bestow upon him/her all the benefits of public employment as outlined by a public sector labor union contract—by contracting with CARA the Department of Street and Sanitation would save money by paying for contingent labor. Thus, re-entry in this case involved the further breaking down of what used to be standard, well-paying employment with benefits.

CARA's thirteen members of the board of directors largely hailed from the private for-profit sector, and some even from the financial sector. One person was a managing director with the Goldman Sachs Group, Inc., while another was a managing director of PSF Capital Management, and yet another a retired chairman for St. Paul Federal Bank for Savings. The rest of the members of the board of directors were affiliated with healthcare groups, corporations and foundations.

The Safer Foundation received only two re-entry contracts, which comprised only 1.9% of all of the Mayor's Initiative contracts. However, Safer expended the second most amount of funds, $1,218,355, or 9.3% of all funds expended from the Mayor's Initiative. Safer also operated as a third party staffing firm, in which its employees' job was to develop long-term employer relationships that resulted in high numbers of employment placements. In fact, under the section titled "agency qualifications" in Safer's contract, the Chief Program Officer's (listed as second in charge) first listed accomplishment was the design/development of a staffing company ("Pivotal Staffing Services LLC").

Almost all of Safer's board of directors came from the private sector as well: several consultants, lawyers, and vice presidents from corporations and banks, as well as someone from the Illinois Trade Association. However, two people stood out: Roxanne M. Ward, the vice president of Ariel Capital Management, LLC, and Paula Wolff, Senior Executive from Chicago Metropolis 2020. The same two persons mentioned earlier in this chapter, who chaired the Mayoral Policy Caucus on Prisoner Re-entry which led to the Mayor's Re-entry Initiative.

7   Conclusion

The Chicago Mayor's 2006 Re-entry Initiative is an example of how the state uses neoliberal economic policy to perpetuate racism in the post-incarceration period, even in anti-incarceration efforts. The Chicago Mayor's Office articulated the idea of "habilitating" ex-offenders through contingent work, relying upon racist tropes of the formerly incarcerated—who are largely poor persons of color—as so incapable of work that they should be glad to have low-wage, unstable work. Ideologically, this is legitimated through neoliberalism—but as well through colorblind racist notions of Blacks and Latinos as possessing cultural pathologies. In practice, the Mayor's Initiative operated as a public subsidy for private firms to use non-profits for recruiting contingent labor. The large presence of private sector actors serving on the executive boards of the non-profit organizations with the largest re-entry contracts calls into question the idea that there is much distance between non-profit organizations and the for-profit sector.

White racial hegemony in the US has undergone two major rearticulations following the civil rights movement: from a pro- mass incarceration neoliberalism, to an anti- mass incarceration neoliberalism. Initially, whites and conservatives reacted against the civil rights movement by opposing desegregation and advocating for police repression, through ideas of "family values" and "law and order." These tropes, together with neoliberal economic principles, provided the ideological basis for reasserting racial hierarchies through mass incarceration. Conservative ideas of equality are cast through abstract liberalism, shifting away from big government spending on anti-poverty programs and education. Think tanks, such as the Manhattan Institute, advocated for public disinvestment by casting poor Black families as characterized by cultural pathologies and harmed by public investment.

In the era of mass incarceration, neoliberalism shifted government spending away from social welfare and public education and towards police and prisons. Several legislative measures, such as three-strikes laws and gang enhancement laws, escalated the monitoring, arrests and incarceration of low-income persons of color. The War on Drugs, and the way in which crack use was targeted much more than cocaine, is the best example of racialized state repression through growth in policing and prisons. Furthermore, the implementation of aggressive "broken windows" and "zero tolerance" policing enabled the state to gentrify urban areas and recreate them as spaces of middle-class consumption (Dickinson 2008).

However, where the state once relied upon neoliberal praxis to govern over populations of color through mass incarceration, today the state has reformulated neoliberal praxis for the purposes of anti- mass incarceration. Soaring public investments in police and prisons are no longer sustainable, and on a national and local level elected officials are seeking ways to extend the state's reach into communities of color *without* increasing incarceration rates. Elected officials now draw upon re-entry initiatives to roll back prison spending and reassert racial domination, moving ex-offenders from prisons to the civilian, contingent labor market. Re-entry initiatives serve private, for-profit firms with a large and willing contingent labor supply; contracts direct public funds towards private, non-profit firms operating as third-party staffing firms for private, for-profit firms.

Intersectionality scholars have argued that philanthropic foundations and non-profit organizations do not operate independently of the state. A conference held in 2004 titled, "The Revolution Will Not be Funded," explored the idea of non-profit social activity as embedded in a "non-profit industrial complex" (INCITE! Women of Color Against Violence 2009). Instead of accepting the current non-profit model, conference scholars questioned if there were alternatives for building social movements to dismantle white racist hegemony. Similarly, scholars interested in dismantling mass incarceration should move beyond interest in re-entry "best practices," as well as beyond deterministic, Foucauldian conceptions of neoliberalism and incarceration. How successful activist groups fare in organizing against mass incarceration, contingent labor markets and racial inequality, will depend, in significant part, upon how such groups are able to build social movements that challenge the non-profit industrial complex. In turn, an important task in challenging non-profit organizations' role in mass incarceration will be to examine how prisoner re-entry perpetuates racial inequalities through profit-generating activities.

References

Alexander, Michelle. 2010. *The New Jim Crow: Mass Incarceration in the Age of Color-blindness*. New York: New Press.

Bauman, Zygmunt. 2003. *Wasted Lives: Modernity and its Outcasts*. Cambridge: Polity Press.

Bonczar, Thomas P. 2003. "Prevalence of Imprisonment in the U.S. Population, 1974–2001." Special Report. Washington, DC: Bureau of Justice Statistics.

Bonilla-Silva, Eduardo. 2003. *Racism without Racists: Color-Blind Racism and the Persistence of Racial Inequality*. Lanham, MD: Rowman & Littlefield.

Carr, E. Summerson. 2010. *Scripting Addiction: The Politics of Therapeutic Talk and American Sobriety*. Princeton, NJ: Princeton University Press.

Dagan, David and Steven M. Teles. 2014. "Locked In? Conservative Reform and the Future of Mass Incarceration." *The Annals of the American Academy of Political and Social Sciences* 651: 266–276.

Dickinson, Maggie. 2008 "The Making of Space, Race and Place: New York City's War on Graffiti, 1970–the Present. *Critique of Anthropology* 28 (1): 27–45.

Embrick, David G. 2008. "The Diversity Ideology: Keeping Major Transnational Corporations White and Male in an Era of Globalization." In Globalization and America: Race, Human Rights & Inequality, edited by Angela Hattery, David G. Embrick, and Earl Smith. Lanham, MD: Rowman and Littlefield.

Embrick, David G. 2011. "Diversity Ideology in the Business World: A New Oppression for a New Age." Critical Sociology 37 (5): 541–556.

Fagan, Jeffery and R.B. Freeman (1999). Crime and work. *Crime and Justice*, 25, 225–290.

Fairbanks, Robert P. 2009. *How it Works: Recovering Citizens in a Post-Welfare Philadelphia*. Chicago, IL: University of Chicago Press.

Garland, David. 2001. *The Culture of Control: Crime and Social Order in Contemporary Society*. Chicago, IL: University of Chicago Press.

Goodman, Philip, Joshua Page and Michelle Phelps. 2015. The Long Struggle: An agonistic perspective on penal development. *Theoretical Criminology*, 19 (3): 315–335.

Gowan, Teresa and Sarah Whetstone. 2012. "Making the Criminal Addict: Subjectivity and Social Control in a Strong-arm Rehab." *Punishment & Society*, 14 (1): 69–93.

Haney, Lynne. 2010. *Offending Women: Power, Punishment, and the Regulation of Desire*. Berkeley, CA: University of California Press.

Holzer, Harry J., Paul Offner and Elaine Sorensen. 2005. "What Explains the Continuing Decline in Labor Force Activity among Young Black Men?" *Labor History*, 46, 37–55.

INCITE! Women of Color Against Violence. 2009. *The Revolution Will Not Be Funded: Beyond the Non-Profit Industrial Complex*. New York, NY: South End Press.

Jensen, Kenneth D., Stephen G. Gibbons. 2002. "Shame and Religion as Factors in the Rehabilitation of Serious Offenders." *Journal of Offender Rehabilitation*, 35 (3–4): 209–224.

Kaye, Kerwin. 2013. "Rehabilitating the 'Drugs Lifestyle': Criminal Justice, Social Control, and the Cultivation of Agency." *Ethnography*, 14 (2): 207–232.

Leukefeld, Carl, Hope Smiley McDonald, Michele Staton, Allison Mateyoke-Scrivner, Matthew Webster, T.K. Logan, & Tom Garrity. 2003. "An Employment Intervention for Drug Abusing Offenders." *Federal Probation*, 67: 27–32.

Milkman, Ruth. 2006. *L.A. Story: Immigrant Workers and the Future of the U.S. Labor Movement*. New York: Russell Sage Foundation.

Murch, Donna. 2015. "Crack in Los Angeles: Crisis, Militarization, and Black Response to the Late Twentieth-Century War on Drugs." *The Journal of American History*, 102 (1): 162–173.

O'Connor, Thomas, and Michael Perreyclear. 2002. "Prison Religion in Action and Its Influence on Offender Rehabilitation." *Journal of Offender Rehabilitation*, 35 (3–4): 11–33.

O'Connor, Thomas, Patricia Ryan and Crystal Parikh. 1998. "A Model Program for Churches and Ex-Offender Reintegration." *Journal of Offender Rehabilitation*, 28 (1–2): 107–126.

Omi, Michael, and Winant Howard. 1994 [1986]. *Racial Formation in the United States: From the 1960s to the 1990s*. New York: Routledge.

Owens, Michael Leo. 2014. "Ex-Felons' Organization-Based Political Work for Carceral Reforms." *The Annals of the American Academy of Political and Social Sciences*, 651: 256–265.

Pager, Devah. 2003. "The Mark of a Criminal Record." *American Journal of Sociology* 108 (5): 937–975.

Peck, Jamie and Nik Theodore. 2008. "Carceral Chicago: Making the Ex-offender Employability Crisis." *International Journal of Urban and Regional Research*, 32 (2): 251–281.

Pettit, Becky, and Bruce Western. 2004. "Mass Imprisonment and the Life Course: Race and Class Inequality in U.S. Incarceration." *American Sociological Review*, 69: 151–169.

PEW Center on the States. 2008. "One in 100: Behind Bars in America." Retrieved from http://www.pewcenteronthestates.org/uploadedFiles/One%20inpercent20100.pdf on June 1, 2010.

Pew Charitable Trusts. 2010. "Collateral Costs: Incarceration's Effect on Economic Mobility." Washington, DC: The Pew Charitable Trusts.

SAFER Foundation. 2014. "Improving Public Safety, Reducing Incarceration Rates & Costs by Lowering Recidivism in Illinois." White Paper. August 2014. Chicago, IL: SAFER Foundation. Accessed online on April 24, 2015 from http://www.saferfoundation.org/files/documents/FINAL-White-Paper---Improving-Public-Safety--Reducing-Incarceration-Rates--Costs-by-Lowering-Recidivism-in-Illinois-9-29-14.pdf.

Sager, Rebecca. 2010. *Faith, Politics, and Power: The Politics of Faith-Based Initiatives*. New York, NY: Oxford University Press.

Schoenfeld, Heather. 2011. "American Penal Overindulgence: Putting Politics in Penal Policy Reform." *Criminology and Public Policy*, 10 (3): 715–724.

Simon, Jonathan. 2009. *Governing Through Crime: How the War on Crime Transformed American Democracy and Created a Culture of Fear*. New York, NY: Oxford University Press.

Travis, Jeremy. 2007. "Reflections on the Re-entry Movement." *Federal Sentencing Reporter*, 20 (2): 84–87.

Visher, Christy and Jeremy Travis. 2003. "Transitioning from Prison to Community: Understanding Individual Pathways." *Annual Review of Sociology*, 29: 89–113.

Wacquant, Loic. 2009 [1999]. *Prisons of Poverty*. Minneapolis, MN: University of Minnesota Press.

Wacquant, Loic. 2010. "Prisoner Re-entry as Myth and Ceremony." *Dialectical Anthropology*, 34 (4): 605–620.

Western, Bruce. 2007. *Punishment and Inequality in America*. New York: Russell Sage.

White House. 2014. "Remarks by the President on 'My Brother's Keeper' Initiative." Accessed online on April 24, 2015 from https://www.whitehouse.gov/the-press-office/2014/02/27/remarks-president-my-brothers-keeper-initiative.

Wolkstein, Eileen, & Haike Spiller. (1998). "Providing vocational services to clients in substance abuse rehabilitation." *Directions in Rehabilitation Counseling*, 9, 65–97.

Young, Jock. 2011. *The Criminological Imagination*. Cambridge, UK: Polity.

PART 7

Meanings, Discourse, and Identity

∴

CHAPTER 16

On-Demand Diversity? The Meanings of Racial Diversity in Netflix Productions

Bianca Gonzalez-Sobrino, Emma González-Lesser and
Matthew W. Hughey

1   Introduction

On July 31, 2013 *the New York Times* published an article entitled, "TV Foresees Its Future, Netflix is There," in which journalist David Carr (2013) wrote:

> Beginning this year, Netflix streamed four original series—"House of Cards," "Hemlock Grove," "Arrested Development" and "Orange is the New Black." The shows earned generally good notices, kicked up a great deal of chatter, and, drum roll here, were nominated for 14 Emmys. It was the first time an Internet-only service earned a seat at the big-boy table in television.

The online, on-demand streaming provider, Netflix, broke into the world of television series production in 2012 when they released their comedy-drama *Lilyhammer*. Since then, they have released 15 television series that present a range of genres as well as an extensive listing of documentaries that include the Oscar-winning *The Square*. As television viewer trends change, Netflix has been the frontrunner in the television revolution. Within this revolution, these productions have been described as groundbreaking, diverse, and refreshing among many other accolades (Nicholson 2013, Lang 2014, Miller 2014, Rorke 2014).

While these television productions have been well received by viewers and the media writ large, there exists an important need to question the content of these shows in relation to both the legacy of film and television racial exclusion and whitewashing. It is important to consider the contemporary era in which such programming is produced—a moment of increasing racial inequality coupled with an increasing commitment to a post-racial or "color-blind" mantra. Such a background begs scholars to look closely at topics related to racial difference and diversity within Netflix productions. Racialized representations exist within larger societal structures that shape the ideological mechanisms through which meaning is attached to people. Because these racialized meanings reflect white "superiority" and the "Otherness" of people of color, they are readily absorbed into dominant, white social imaginaries. Not only are these meanings appealing to whites, but they are also used to maintain dominant structures of inequality. Since the media is one of our primary information-disseminating social institutions, studying the representations of people of color in the media helps us see how these racialized meanings are codified into "common-sense" understandings of race. This chapter sets out to critically examine issues of racial diversity and inclusion in three popular Netflix television series: *House of Cards*, *Orange is the New Black*, and *Hemlock Grove*.

2   The World of Netflix

Netflix was founded in 1997 in the United States. It was originally intended to be a mail video club, wherein users would order movies on their website and receive them via mail. With time, the company launched video-streaming services as a complimentary service to their DVD mailing enterprise. The popularity of the on-demand service grew exponentially (from 2007 to the present) and the streaming was offered as a stand-alone service in November of 2010. Netflix can be seen in North America, South America, and parts of Europe. As of 2015, the company has subscribers in 42 different countries and continues to expand their enterprise. In terms of the websites position in relation to the amount of data downloaded off of the Internet, the streaming service is the biggest source of North American downstream web traffic comprising 32.3 percent, surpassing YouTube (Sandvine 2013). In July 2014, *Forbes* magazine reported that Netflix surpassed 50 million subscribers worldwide, 36 million of them from the United States (Sharf 2014). Aside from the huge number of subscribers and services available, the Netflix library holds content from top production companies and, as of 2011, also has a large variety of original productions and continues to add to its long list of in-house productions. Netflix exclusive productions like *House of Cards*, *Orange is the New Black*, and *The Square* have been generally well received by critics and viewers (Dietz 2013).

The immense reach of Netflix and other streaming services, like Hulu and Amazon, have changed how people consume entertainment media in our society as viewers have a wide range of services available to them. They can stream television content when they want to view it from wherever they are; the digital world provides access to films and television series at the click of a button. According to one of the Nielsen Reports in 2014 "never before has the viewer had more control and more skill at navigating this evolving ecosystem of device and platforms for content discovery" (Nielsen 2014: 2). Nielsen also reported that:

> [On average] Americans spent a little more than 141 hours a month connecting with traditional television in third-quarter 2014. During the same period, the overall population also saw over an hour increase in time spent watching time-shifted content and a four-hour increase watching video on the Internet.
>
> NIELSEN 2014

As of December 2014, there has been a 3% decline in traditional television watching while on-line on-demand video is growing at a rapid rate (Steel 2014). Households with Netflix subscriptions watch significantly less network television compared to households without Netflix (Steel 2014). These numbers have an important story to tell.

Television trends are changing in the United States and across the world. The changes in the people's media consumptions and the representations and messages present in the media should be critically examined before disseminating statements about the supposed progressiveness of contemporary media and their commitment of diversity (Ryan 2015). These statements about diversity have been said in the context of media content, diversity of directors and diversity in staff. Is Netflix really that different from traditional (cable or network) television? Is the content of Netflix's series more representative of American society? Questions such as these frame our exploration of how much diversity and what kind of diversity is found in Netflix's original content.

Why choose Netflix? Netflix is the lead competitor in the on-demand industry and their original content is widely viewed. This chapter will serve as a stepping-stone in the road to understanding what media-projected messages US viewers are receiving. Netflix original series' representations of people of color and our society are not created in a vacuum.

This chapter explores the differences in representations of race, diversity and the meanings attached to them using the case of Netflix content. In other words, we explore how Netflix productions project society in terms of racial diversity and how the production team of writers and producers tackle issues of diversity. In particular, we use characters portrayed in *House of Cards*, *Orange is the New Black*, and *Hemlock Grove* to analyze diversity. While some limited research has systematically explored racial diversity in traditional television (Fuller 2010, Mastro and Behm-Morawitz 2005, Hunt, Ramon and Price 2014,

Nielsen and Turner 2014), we shift the focus to explore how racial diversity in on-demand television productions is represented and toward what end.

3 New Type of Television: Netflix Productions

We choose to analyze the first seasons of the three most popular Netflix series. These series represent the first Netflix productions and the new direction being taken by the company. All three series were nominated for Emmy's and received positive reviews from critics. Below, we briefly summarize the plots, the nominations, and the audience numbers for the three series being analyzed in this chapter.

3.1 *House of Cards*

House of Cards was the first huge success for Netflix. The first season of the political drama was released in February 2013. As of early 2015, three seasons have completed production. *House of Cards* features actor Kevin Spacey as the main character. Spacey plays a U.S. senator (and later Vice President and President) in search of revenge after being passed up for the position of Secretary of State. The first season received nine Primetime Emmy Award nominations, making *House of Cards* the first online television series to be nominated for an Emmy. The show also earned four Golden Globe nominations and won Best Actress in a Television Series Drama. Netflix does not release official audience numbers, but some estimates suggest at least 16 percent of all Netflix subscribers watched one episode of the second season of *House of Cards* in the first 24 hours after its release (Solomon 2014).

3.2 *Orange is the New Black*

The second series we analyze in this chapter is *Orange is the New Black*. Released in July 2013, the dark comedy has three seasons produced and is proclaimed Netflix's largest hit. Based on a memoir, the series tells the story of a white upper-class woman who is sent to a women's federal prison. The series has been praised for its critical portrayal of prison life and the judicial system. *Orange is the New Black* generated more views in the first day than *House of Cards* (Kafka 2013). The show earned 15 Primetime Emmy Award nominations and one Golden Globe nomination for the lead actress. Aside from the critical response, the show has also garnered a lot of attention from the media because of the diverse cast. In June 2014, the *New York Post* published an article titled "Orange is the New Black ignited a TV revolution for women." In 2013, *The Washington Post* published an article on *Orange is the New Black*, which read, "the racial breakdown's about right" (Matthews 2013), in reference to the accuracy of the television series in their representation of the racial demographics of prisons.

3.3 Hemlock Grove

The third series analyzed in this chapter is a horror thriller series titled *Hemlock Grove*. The series tells the story of a series of murders that occurring in a fictional town. *Hemlock Grove* has run for three seasons, and was first released in April 2013. Out of the three series discussed here, *Hemlock Grove* is less well known and has been less well received by critics, who've given it mixed to negative reviews. Even though it does not have the recognition and wide audience that *Orange is the New Black* and *House of Cards* have, Netflix reported that *Hemlock Grove* had more views than *House of Cards* in its initial weekend (Ludwig 2013). *Hemlock Grove* received two Primetime Emmy Award nominations in 2013.

Using these three television series produced by Netflix, we explore the following questions: How is racial diversity represented in the three Netflix television series? Is racial diversity represented through the quantity of the characters of color or through the ways in which these characters are presented? Are these series any different than traditional television series, in the quantitative way (quantity of representations) or qualitatively different (nuances and ways in which these characters are portrayed)? We explore the nuances present in these Netflix productions while critically questioning the popular discourses of racial diversity in American society.

4 Background

4.1 Critiquing Diversity

In attempts to follow the developing social "courtesy" of political correctness, large social institutions turned the idea of cultural and racial diversity into a hot-button buzzword (Demby 2015; see also Jackson et al. 2013). In this context, diversity frequently meant little more than editing promotional pamphlets and website mission statements; the social turn toward diversity scarcely altered the realities of people of color in white-dominated institutions. Academics from a range of disciplines have inquired about the problematic nature of diversity policies and their limited impact on breaking down structural inequalities. Steven Vertovec argues that diversity policies are actually strengthened by their, "[a]mbiguity, multivocality and banality" (2012: 287), which allows for dramatic, seemingly antiracist discourse without any alteration of systemic inequalities that maintain the status of whites. Sharon Collins similarly writes that, "the reality of racial, ethnic and gender inequalities within American institutions have been increasingly obscured in the name of diversity" (2011: 517). Sara Ahmed agrees that the rhetoric of diversity buttresses existing racist structures in organizations (2007: 235), and that diversity policies are used for "re-branding [organizations] as being diverse or even as being committed to diversity without, as it were, doing anything" (2007: 254). Some scholars argue that diversity policies not only fail to challenge inequality, but actually reify racist stereotypes, such as victimhood of people of color (Iverson 2007: 586).

A major theme in scholarly critiques of diversity is its problematic connection to colorblind ideologies (Bell and Hartmann 2007; Norton, Vandello, Biga and Darley 2008). In other words, diversity policies, and individuals promoting diversity, attempt to discuss racial and cultural variety without ever speaking directly about race or racism. Cedric Herring and Loren Henderson critique diversity for deviating too far from policies akin to affirmative action—which directly considers race and racism (2011: 629). Similar to Vertovec's claim that diversity policies rely on ambiguous rhetoric, Joyce Bell and Douglas Hartmann believe that the implementation of colorblindness has prevented the public from understanding any true meaning of diversity (2007: 897). Other scholars have shown that in studies replicating admissions decision processes, whites intentionally created a diverse pool of admitted applicants, but would not indicate race as a determining factor in their decision as a way to appear colorblind (Norton, Vandello, Biga and Darley 2008: 102). Amir Marvasti and Karyn McKinney assert that diversity programs rely on both colorblindness and assimilationist approaches through their emphasis on "oneness" (2011: 631).

4.2   *Sociology of the Media*

As a major source of information distribution and a paramount cultural institution, media has a profound influence on our social world. Early sociological studies of media's relationship to society discussed media as a reflection of larger social meaning and ideologies (Holz and Wright 1979). However, this research was driven by an interest in analyzing the social context of the elite subgroup of society that controlled the media. Earlier work by Marshall McLuhan (1964) described media as an extension of man; media not only depicts the world as we see it, but in turn shapes how we see and act within it.

While some scholars devoted their research on the sociology of media to understanding how violence in media affects society (Phillips 1983; Felson 1996), several scholars have sought out an explanation for how media constructs our social world *writ large*. Gamson and Latteier assert that "the special genius of [the media] is to make the whole process seem so normal and natural that the very art of social construction is invisible" (1992: 374). Deuze sees the media as so integral to contemporary social life that he argues, "life lived *in*, rather than *with*, media can and perhaps should be the ontological benchmark for a 21st-century media studies" (2011: 137). Furthermore, he writes that "media are not just types of technology and chunks of content we pick and choose from the world around us—a view that considers media as external agents affecting us in a myriad ways. If anything, today we have to recognize how the uses and appropriations of media penetrate all aspects of contemporary life" (Deuze 2011: 137). For Deuze, media has become completely enmeshed with how individuals, and groups of individuals, construct and understand themselves and their societies. Grindstaff and Turow believe that "television is a commercial institution that, in producing programing, also produces (and proscribes) social representations and ideas about the world, particularly as they relate to notions of power, place, and identity (race, class, gender, sexuality, and so forth)" (2006: 115). The claim that media affects racial (and other) identities is less typically found in sociological research. However, in broadening the disciplinary lens, we can see that many scholars see the media's role in upholding racial ideologies.

4.3 Contending with Race in the Study of Media

Building from the literature suggesting the strong social implications of media, scholars of race and ethnicity have applied the social constructionist understandings of the media to the development of racial ideologies. Littlefield argues, "[a]lthough many vehicles inform the hegemonic social structure, the media are the primary agent of socialization in which participants are seduced, educated, and transformed by ideas concerning race, gender, and class" (2008: 676). She also believes, "the media serve as a system of racialization" which have, and continue to, perpetuate dominant ideologies about race (2008: 677). Smith asserts that, "films are reflections of the times in which they are made, whereby the racial representations that audiences see will adhere to the racial order of the given moment" (2013: 780). Though Smith refers in his work only to films, rather than extending his analysis to other visual media representations, his claims can be readily applied to other forms of media that interpret and regurgitate existing paradigms of race.

Several academics have chosen to focus on non-entertainment media such as newscasting. With the increased perceptions by whites of racial threat of Muslims since 9/11, scholars have tuned in to the racialized representations of Muslims in the news. Frost questions newscasting coverage of terrorist attacks and their utilization of "race hate" of Muslims, arguing that these racist representations have real-world effects on Muslim communities (2008: 564). Saeed critiques the British press's representations of Muslims as un-British and deviant (2007). He also asserts that depictions of Muslims rely on similar racist ideologies that have been used to portray other racial minorities in the media over time (2007: 444).

Some literature on race in the media exposes the media's concern with placating a white audience ever in fear of seeming racist in a so-called post-racial society. Coover discusses the increased screening of black characters on television, and suggests that "positive portrayals of many Blacks in the media are marketable because they affirm White audience members' self- concepts as non-racist" while simultaneously supporting "many Whites' negative attitudes toward Blacks" (2001: 413). She claims that white viewers' attitudes towards black characters in television shows are unlikely to change from viewing the media, but that "racist and non-racist Whites interpret positive and negative representations of Blacks in ways that confirm their pre- existing pro- or anti-Black prejudices" (Coover 2001: 414). In other words, media reinforces whites' pre-conceived notions of blacks, depending on their interpretation of the representations. Denzin also shows how the media is used to satisfy whites' desires. Denzin discusses what he terms "hood movies," which brought "the 'real' world of the hood in front of the [white] viewer" (2003: 27). Denzin's work explains how racial stereotypes are reified through film imagery and plot, despite sometimes having progressive intentions. Some research also considers the ways in which not the white viewers, but rather the white owners and producers of media seek (self-)praise as being progressive. Amaya interrogates the ABC series *Ugly Betty*, and claims that the airing of this show not only reinforced some negative stereotypes of Latinos, but also improved ABC's reputation for having diverse programing (2010: 801).

Several other scholars of race and the media have argued that the media supports existing racist stereotypes of people of color. Fürsich demonstrates how both news and entertainment media offer limited representations of people of color that often portray them as "different, exotic, special, essentialised or even abnormal" (2010: 116). He further asserts that even when representations are more diverse, the depictions are "often linked to historically established racist imaginaries" (Fürsich 2010: 116). Fürsich claims that racial stereotypes have been stockpiled in the collective conscious of media consumers (2010: 116). One such stockpiled racial stereotype is the relationship between black and white characters. Weigel, Loomis, and Soja describe how black-white relationships depicted on prime time television "were less multifaceted and evinced less intimacy, less shared decision making, and fewer romantic implications" than white-white relationships (1980: 884). While this research showed that relationships between black and white characters were limited in depth, there are also specific forms of this relationship that recur in the media. Hughey examines the representation of the "Magical Negro"—a black character able to magically improve a broken-down white character. Hughey asserts that "while the black/white interactions may appear as harmless, or even as a marked improvement considering the legacy of overt Hollywood racism" they still reinforce the dominant racial paradigm (2009: 568). He argues that it is precisely this illusion of progress that requires further analysis (Hughey 2009: 568).

While representations of people of color in media are highly problematic, the reverse is perhaps equally as troubling; people of color still remain largely underrepresented in media. Mastro and Behm-Morawitz explain that, "the rate at which Latinos are portrayed on television remains dramatically below that of the real-world population" (2005: 110). In 2005, they analyzed 67 primetime programs—yielding 1,488 characters—in which 80.4% of characters were white, 13.8% were black, 3.9% were Latino, 1.5% were Asian, and 0.4% were Native American (Mastro and Behm-Morawitz 2005: 116). Mastro and Behm-Morawitz also noted that black characters appeared more in crime dramas and Latinos more in sitcoms (2005: 116), aligning with existing stereotypes of blacks as violent and Latinos as "the comic/buffoon" (2005: 111).

5   Data and Methods

For this chapter, we conducted a content analysis of three Netflix television series to explore the construction of racial diversity and the nuances of these representations. The television series analyzed here were chosen because they represent the most watched television series produced by Netflix and the first original series developed by Netflix. These series are also the first original productions released by the company (*Arrested Development* was the first released but it is not a Netflix original production). We analyzed the first seasons of *House of Cards*, *Orange is the New Black*, and *Hemlock Grove*. The decision to select only the episodes from the first season of each series was taken as an attempt to mitigate the role and influence of critics and calls for more diversity from the public. These seasons represent the vision and development of Netflix as a production company. The population of episodes available on Netflix is 75 ($N = 75$). Out of these 75 episodes, we chose the first season of each series for a final sample size of 39 (n = 39).

In an effort to discover the nuances present in the data, the approach to this content analysis is not only quantitative but also qualitative. The research design is comprised on the strengths of traditional content analysis while attempting to mitigate the weaknesses and adding substantive analysis of the data. After the sample size was selected, a three-tier content analysis was implemented. First, we watched the episode from the three television series as an initial sweep of the data. The scripts of the episodes were read and the episodes were watched. Second, the episodes and scripts were reviewed again and coded to determine the racial demographics of the casts, while also coding for nuanced themes of racial diversity and racialized interactions between characters in the series.

Data were coded judiciously, identifying the themes present only when it was clear that the episode contained the theme. The racial demographics of the characters of the series were quantified through visual identification and explicit remarks of the racial identities of the characters. We also explore the nuances of these representations through an in-depth examination of the character and the social position presented in the series. Our analysis is illustrative not conclusive, we do not seek to advance statistically generalizable conclusions to the entire television landscape. Rather, our intentions are to explore the new form of television being produced by Netflix and understand the representations of people of color in these productions. We question the supposed racial diversity of the characters in the television series in terms of numerical quantity and substantive nuanced representations of people of color. These Netflix representations are framed by the media as diverse and progressive compared to their traditional television counter parts, but when examining them through a critical lens, we reveal their dependence on racial stereotypes, racial ideologies, and their limited representations of people of color. The use of a quantitative approach to this content analysis gives us an insight to the number of characters that are people of color and the qualitative approach gives us an understanding of the context in which these characters were developed.

Next, we trace the results using the quantitative analysis and then by discussing the qualitative results of the study for each television series. Following the discussion of the results, we conclude with a summary of the study and future implications for research and public action.

6   Discussion

6.1   *White Political World: Diversity in House of Cards*

The first original series by Netflix, *House of Cards*, paints a homogeneous racial picture of the American political world in which only 2 people of color reside as main characters. Three other characters are people of color, but play marginal roles in the story lines and have limited screen time in the series. The majority of the main characters, which include the President of the United States, the Senate Majority Whip, journalists, and political power players, are represented as, and played by, white people. The two main characters of color in *House of Cards* play important roles in the storyline and also have important political positions in government and the political worlds.

To further understand and analyze the diversity of *House of Cards*, we will explore the two main characters of color in the series, and also briefly discuss the peripheral characters in less important roles in the storyline. The character of color with more screen time in *House of Cards* is Linda Vasquez, who appeared in 11 out of 12 episodes of the first season. Vasquez is the president's White House Chief of Staff, and plays a central role in the main storyline connected to Frank Underwood (the main character). The only explicit mention of race in relation to Linda Vasquez's character occurs in the first episode of the first season when Frank Underwood presents the main political players:

> Frank Underwood: Linda Vasquez, Walker's Chief of Staff. I got her hired. She's a woman, check, and a Latina, check. But more than that, she is as tough as a two-dollar steak.

This is the only direct expression of Vasquez's ethno-racial identity throughout the season, and the only explicit discussion of the role of gender and racial diversity in the political setting of the television series. Diversity is framed as a means to an end, where the inclusion of people of color is the politically correct action to take for the sake of inclusion. At the same time, the character Linda Vasquez, is framed as a token of diversity and progress not only in the series, as a cultural artifact but in the fictional political world of *House of Cards*. The character's ethno-racial identity is briefly discussed in the dialogue present above and obfuscated in the rest of the series. Vasquez's race simply serves the purpose of the diversification of the characters through an "add a person of color and stir" approach.

The casting of the character of Linda Vasquez also hints at the problematic assumptions tied to ethno-racial diversity. Since the early 1900s in the entertainment industry, people of color were barred from being cast in main and secondary roles. One example of this is the movie production of *West Side Story* (1961), where white actors were cast as the two main characters of color (Natalie Wood played Maria and George Chakiris was cast as Bernardo). These images are reminiscent of blackfaced whites in Hollywood. While the entertainment media has moved away from these blatant racist practices, a pan-ethnic casting occurs in which people of color are chosen for roles independent of the particular ethnicity called for by the character. While pan-ethnic casting in itself is not necessarily always negative, it demonstrates an interesting case where we can see the dynamic of race as a fluid construct. In the case of *House of Cards*, Sakina Jaffrey, a South Asian-American woman, plays Linda Vasquez, a Latina. The Latino identity of the character is represented through a pan-ethnic construction of Latino-ness, while simultaneously being constructed, through the casting of the character, as a generic person of color. The casting of Jaffrey serves as an example of the ambiguity of diversity that is not driven by actual racial diversity.

The second character of color with more screen time is Remy Danton, a black lawyer and lobbyist for a natural gas company. Danton appears in 7 episodes out of the 13 episodes of the first season. In the interactions between the characters and Danton there are no explicit references to his race, or any discussion of discrimination. This is consistent with the findings in the literature, which indicate that diversity hinges on the ability to (seemingly) remain color-blind. Mention of this character's race would, then, discredit the "progressive" and "politically correct" approach the series claims to take. The character's morals are also called into question several times during the series when he is framed as disloyal and disingenuous, thus reifying ideas of moral degradation of black and brown people. Other characters of color in *House of Cards* appear less frequently, and are labeled as guest roles. These include Terry Womack, a black congressman and the leader of the Black Caucus, appearing in 3 episodes of the first season, and Freddy Hayes, the owner of a barbeque restaurant, ex-convict, and supposed friend of Frank Underwood, who appears in 7 episodes of the first season.

House of Cards mirrors a political world where diversity is apparent yet ambiguous. This series presents the viewers with limited representations of people of color. These characters reflect dominant racial ideologies that demean and essentialize people of color as criminals and morally bankrupt. Positive portrayals of people of color in *House of Cards* (i.e. Linda Vasquez) are limited and centered on racial ambiguity. Linda Vasquez serves as a "check" in the box of supposed inclusion; a single token of "progressive imagery" of people of color in *House of Cards*. Frank Underwood's fictitious Washington D.C. maintains and reproduces what previous traditional television political dramas presented: a white-dominated political arena.

6.2   *Epitome of Diversity? Orange is the New Black and Reification of Stereotypes*

Orange is the New Black tells the story of prison life for women in the United States. At first glance, the cast and characters of the series seem very racially diverse, but when we examine the nuances and meanings attached to these representations, we see another picture. Other arguments in favor of *Orange is The New Black*'s diversity point to the number of actors of colors in the cast. Below, we explore how the series supposed diversity is more complex than the simple number of characters of colors in the story.

Quantitatively, *Orange is the New Black* lacks in racial diversity when examining the main characters. In season 1, five out of six main characters are white, while all of the characters of color are recurring characters. This translates into less screen time for the characters of color, and also less importance in relation to the storylines of the television series. Of the recurring characters, 14 out of 32 were characters of color. While *Orange is the New Black* presents a large number of characters of color in the series, it is important to consider the representations of these characters, the meanings attached to the representations, and the role and function the characters play in the storylines. A higher number of characters of color does not translate into racial diversity. The representations of these characters of color operate within power dynamics that reify the dominant racial structure and order.

Race plays an important role in the series, not only at the casting level, but also at the level of plot. Set in a prison, racial dynamics are blatant and direct in the series. While characters of color are present in all of the episodes in the first season, their roles in the plot are peripheral. The series centers on the story of a white, upper-class woman who is imprisoned for drug trafficking crimes and enters the world of penitentiary life, where there is a high population of Black women, Latinas, and lower-class white women. The characters of color serve as fillers for the plot, while the white characters receive centrality in the storyline. In other words, the representations of Black and Latina women complement the white anti-hero in her search for space in a dominantly Black and Latina space. The series mirrors a reality of prison life, where people of color are imprisoned at higher rates than whites. While this series could have served as a medium in which racial stereotypes could be broken, it represents its characters of color as lower class, uneducated, immoral criminals, and not entangled in the social positions and social structures that influence human action and order.

Stereotypes of people of color permeate every type of media and the online television series *Orange is the New Black* is not an exception. In this case 7 of the total 38 characters are Black (one of which is a main character), and 8 of 38 are Latinas (all recurring characters), in comparison to 23 white characters (five of which are main characters). The higher number of characters of color than the average television series offers extra screen time, but exposure does not necessarily equal positive, or diverse, portrayals for Black and Latina characters. The series presents a large group of black and Latina woman in a federal penitentiary. Ideas of laziness, immorality, and dependence, among other essentializing "cultural" traits are attached to the characters of color. For example, Janae Watson is a black woman who is portrayed to have a bright future as a track and field athlete and becomes involved in theft and robbery after initiating a romantic relationship with a gang member. Even this basic framework for this character is reliant on stereotypes of black people. The framing of this character's life suggests that Watson's only potential for a successful future is as an athlete, which calls upon the cultural imaginary of black people as "naturally," or essentially athletic. While there are other trajectories out of the inner city neighborhoods (limited because of structural factors), the series plays on these racial narratives of black athletic ability (framed through biological determinism) that resonate with a larger audience (Hughey and Goss 2015). Furthermore, she is unable to fulfill this potential once another black character—a male gang member—corrupts her and indoctrinates her into a life of crime, essentializing black men as inherently prone to criminal activity and to the destruction of female innocence. This character is represented as foolish and naïve. These narratives reflect racial narrative that frames people of color as gullible and unable to guide their own lives, in need of a white savior to take care of their lives (Hughey 2014).

Other stereotypical portrayals of black characters include ideas of homogeneity and singularity. In other words, the series represents a quintessential blackness, where individual black characters contain a myriad of cultural and racial stereotypes that include banal assumptions of food preferences. For example, in the episode titled "WAC Pack" elections are being held for inmate representatives. Inmates, divided into different factions by race, are campaigning for the issues they find most prevalent. When the black inmates are discussing their concerns amongst themselves, one of their primary concerns is that the dinning hall more frequently serve fried chicken—a preference racialized as being associated with black people. This racial narrative is not merely implied, but directly linked to the race of the characters:

> Taystee: In closing, let's get some motherfucking fried chicken up in here once in a while! Oh yeah! Yeah, I said it!
> Poussey: She said it.
> Taystee: I'm black
> Poussey: She's black
> Taystee: and she black
> Poussey: I'm black
> Taystee: and we like fried chicken.

This dialogue makes clear the essentialized connection between race and cultural traits. In the same scene, other matters voiced by the black inmates focus on aesthetic concerns frequently associated with black women. The same character says:

> Taystee: Furthermuch, why don't we have Ultra Sheen [hair relaxer] in the commissary? Why? You ask me, that shit is racist! Fucking racist.

While this calls attention to problematic white beauty standards and institutional disregards for the needs and interest of Black women, the Black inmates' demands are depicted as overly simplistic and trivial in contrast to the main character's concerns for improved educational programs, healthcare, and fitness opportunities voiced in the following episode, "Blood Donut." The framing of the Black characters is not only a reflection of the racial narrative present in our society but also construct the boundaries of race itself by presenting the white character as superior and entitled. This disparity between the white main character and the characters of color draws upon the ideology of white superiority, as well as what Hughey (2014) refers to as the "white savior." While the Black characters in the first season dominate the screen time, other non-white racial groups are represented with equally harmful stereotypes.

As mentioned above, all of the Latina characters are recurring and play a peripheral role to the storyline of the series. Similar to the black characters, Latina characters are constructed to fulfill racial stereotypes and expectations. Within the first season, two Latina characters, Dayanara "Daya" Diaz and Maria Ruiz, are pregnant, interpellating racist assumptions of hyper-sexuality, overpopulation of Latinos, and irresponsible sexual behavior, highlighted in Diaz's case, in which she is in an illegal relationship with a white correctional officer, John Bennet. Latina motherhood in general is also repeatedly called into question. Prior to Diaz's pregnancy, her own mother, Aleida Diaz, was imprisoned for drug-related charges. The fact that Dayanara Diaz has landed in prison following her mother's imprisonment indicates a culture-of-poverty assumption that poor decision making and criminal propensity is passed on across generations. Aleida Diaz is also known to have had five children from five different men, and currently has a boyfriend, to whom she pays far more attention than her own daughter—further "proof" of "irresponsible" mothering. In Ruiz's case, after giving birth, her daughter is taken away from her, since a child cannot be raised in prison.

Having these two pregnant Latina characters in conjunction with Aleida Diaz as an "incompetent" mother makes clear that the stereotype of poor Latina mothering is not incidentally included in the plot, but embedded in the series like many other racial assumptions. The stance that *Orange Is the New Black* takes for confronting racism is to use satire to mock racial stereotypes. For example, Piper Chapman, Alex Vause, and Nicole "Nicky" Nichols—all upper-class, cosmopolitan, white women—are mocking Lorna Morello, a working-class, white woman, for her racist outlook on Latinos:

> Morello: They live, like, 20 people to one apartment. They have more kids than even the Irish.

Though mocking racist perceptions of whites may be an improvement to the covert and overt racism of many shows, this stereotype persists beyond this scene. While the racism may have been critiqued in the dialogue above, the racist stereotypes upon which Morello was calling are reified in the "incompetent" mothering of Aleida and Dayanara Diaz and Maria Ruiz. Even if these racist ideologies are momentarily challenged, the series inevitably reinforces existing assumptions and tropes about Latinas.

Aside from the reification of stereotypes, Latino culture is also mocked and fetishized in the series. The primary source of these types of portrayals is the use of Spanish in the dialogue. Combinations of English and Spanish (commonly referred to as "Spanglish") are inserted comically into the script. For example, Maria Ruiz is bringing her concerns for the inmates to the attention of Officer Healy, and says, "Sometimes, yo necesito two pillows." This calls upon the racist perception that Latinos cannot speak "proper" English. Furthermore, it is fetishized as a marker of authenticity of Ruiz's Latina-ness, and is used as a playing chip for Netflix to claim progressive and diverse representations. Spanish is again fetishized as authentic Latina-ness among Latina characters:

> Gloria Mendoza: Esperate un momento. Dejame terminar esto [Authors' translation]:
> Wait a moment. Let me finish this]
> Dayanara Diaz: I don't speak Spanish.
> Mendoza: Great another fucking coconut. What's the matter with your mother, she don't teach you Spanish?

This draws again on the notion of "incompetent" Latina mothers; Dayanara's mother has "failed" to pass on to her daughter the positive aspects of culture while still managing to transmit her negative "cultural" propensities toward crime. Later in the episode, Dayanara Diaz's lack of authentic Latina-ness is challenged again:

> Mendoza: Hey blanca [Authors' translation: whitey], you speak Spanish?
> Piper Chapman: Un poco. Entiendo mas de lo que puedo hablar [Author's translation: A little bit. I understand more than I can speak.]
> Mendoza (to Dayanara Diaz): You see? Fucking white girl speaks Spanish.

This interaction is completely meaningless to the rest of the plot of the episode, and merely interjected to criticize Dayanara Diaz's "insufficient" Latina identity.

Overall, Latina characters are challenged for their authenticity (or lack thereof), and represented as incompetent and irresponsible mothers. Though the slightly increased representation of Latinas on screen may seduce viewers into believing *Orange is the New Black* is a progressive series, the depictions of Latina characters, like those of black characters, repeatedly reify racial tropes that reflect the dominant racial ideologies of our times.

6.3   *Hemlock Grove*

Hemlock Grove is set in a mystical alternate reality, in the world of vampires and werewolves. The series offers few representations of people of color; all 7 main characters in the first season of the series are white. Out of 9 recurring characters, there are 3 characters of color. The mystical setting of the show allows for a reconstruction of the major social divides; in the society of the series, race does not function exactly as it does in the real world. The primary social divide, then, is not race, but the divide between human and mystical creatures. All three characters of color are human, two of which are doctors of science, and the third is a former Marine. One of the doctors of science, Dr. Johann Pryce, has a relatively ambiguous racial phenotype, his race is never explicitly mentioned in the series, and his name does not indicate any non-white ethnicity.

Similar to the lack of mention of race for Dr. Johann Pryce, there is never mention of the race of the two black characters, Dr. Clementine Chasseur and Michael Chasseur (twin siblings). Both of these characters are humans, and part of "The Order of the Dragon," an organization dedicated to hunting down the werewolves and other mystical creatures. These two characters are portrayed as highly moral, professionally successful, and protective of fellow humans, which is atypical for depictions of people of color. These characters are more progressive in terms of countering racist stereotypes than, for example, the characters of color in *Orange is the New Black*, but these two characters alongside Dr. Johann Pryce do not offer sufficient diversity in the total cast of 16 characters.

The series utilizes colorblind ideology in its quiet inclusion of a few characters of color. The ambiguity of Dr. Johann Pryce's racial identity eliminates any emphasis on race relations or racial stereotypes attached to particular racial groups. Additionally, the lack of mention of race in the series due to its creation of the human/mystical divide (rather than a racial one) makes the colorblindness of the series more viable. This allows viewers to partake in an alternate world in which race has little to no significance, potentially offering a temporary escape from the guilt of racism for white viewers, and a temporary escape from a world of racist harm for viewers of color.

7   Conclusions

The problematic meanings present in the Netflix productions described in this chapter indicate that they operate on the same racialized landscape as series from more traditional media outlets. Though some series may have a more diverse cast than standard television series, the racialized meanings attached to the characters indicate that little progress is being made. Studying media can involve some challenges; what media are available to the public, and what representations the media are choosing to show, may change at any given time. Recent pressures from powerful media giants, like Hollywood studios, HBO, and Comcast, have made Netflix's continuation somewhat precarious. Some of these corporations are strategically supporting web and iPad streaming as a way to render Netflix insignificant. Though Netflix may not be a long-lasting staple for movie and series streaming, it is still relevant to analyze the meanings constructed in their productions within this given social moment. Representations and meanings in media help maintain the dominant ideologies of race. With this awareness, we can understand that every mode of media production is part of a larger system of the continuation of racial paradigms and racial inequality. Even if Netflix were to collapse, it has contributed a great deal to social understandings of race, particularly because of its (currently) extensive audience. The representations present in Netflix productions (and other media of our time) continuously construct a foundation for future media portrayals. Even though radio is now a largely outdated form of media consumption, the social ideologies that were present in radio representations lay the foundation for the representations that would later appear in television. Similarly, Netflix productions will leave their mark on how future media portrays people of color.

While media depictions of people of color affect racial ideologies, critiquing these representations is not a merely ideological exercise. The maintenance of racial ideologies is a cornerstone of racism, and the media contributes significantly to such maintenance. In other words, the racialized depictions in Netflix productions, as well as in other media, support legitimate, material inequalities separated on racial lines. Consider, for example, the supposed "insufficiency" of Latinas as mothers shown in our analysis of *Orange is the New Black*. While a Netflix series will not directly inform the racist actions taken against Latinas (such as historical and continuing sterilization efforts), it is part of upholding the larger construction of Latinas as inferior mothers in contrast to white women—the very ideology backing forced sterilization.

In the context of media's influence on not only racial ideologies but also on racism, we need to consider if "diversity" in representations actually translates to any change in social inequality. Though the argument above that media portrayals play a crucial role in the maintenance of racism could be extended to claim that merely showing a diverse cast in a series could improve opinions on diversity, it is not quite so simple. As shown in our analyses, even when a series has a diverse cast, the racial meanings made of the characters of color still reproduce inequality and racist stereotypes. For this reason, precisely, it is crucial to critique the representations in the media—particularly those that claim to be the most diverse.

References

Carr, David. 2013. "TV Foresees Its Future, Netflix is There." *New York Times*, July 31.

Collins, Sharon M. 2011. "From Affirmative Action to Diversity: Erasing Inequality from Organizational Responsibility." *Critical Sociology*, 37 (5): 517–520.

Coover, Gail E. 2001. "Television and Social Identity: Race Representation as 'White' Accommodation." *Journal of Broadcasting & Electronic Media*, 45 (3): 413–431.

Demby, Gene. 2015. "'Diversity' Criticized as an Empty Buzzword. So How Can We Make It Work?" *NPR* November 5, 2015

Denzin, Norman K. 2003. "Screening Race." *Cultural Studies: Critical Methodologies*, 3 (1): 22–43.

Deuze, Mark. 2011. "Media Life." *Media, Culture & Society*, 33 (1): 137–148.

Dietz, Jason. 2013. "House of Cards: Reviews for the Complete 1st Season." Retrieved on February 1, 2015: http://www.metacritic.com/feature/house-of-cards-netflix-full-season-1-reviews.

Felson, Richard B. 1996. "Mass Media Effects on Violent Behavior." *Annual Review of Sociology*, 22: 103–128.

Frost, Diane. 2008. "Islamophobia: Examining Causal Links Between the Media and 'Race Hate' From 'Below.'" *International Journal of Sociology and Social Policy*, 28 (11/12): 564–578.

Fuller, Jennifer. 2010. "Branding Blackness in US Cable Television." *Media, Culture and Society*, 32 (2): 285–305.

Fürsich, Elfriede. 2010. "Media and the Representation of Others." *International Social Science Journal*, 199: 113–130.

Gamson, Joshua, and Pearl Latteier. 2004. "Do Media Monsters Devour Diversity?" *Contexts*, 3 (3): 26–32.

Grindstaff, Laura, and Joseph Turrow. 2006. "Video Cultures: Television Sociology in the 'New TV' Age." *Annual Review of Sociology*, 32: 103–125.

Gutelle, Sam. 2013. "Netflix Accounts for Nearly One-Third of US Internet Traffic at Home." Retrieved February 1, 2015: http://www.tubefilter.com/2013/05/14/netflix-us-internet-traffic-percentage/.

Herring, Cedric and Loren Henderson. 2011. "From Affirmative Action to Diversity: Toward a Critical Diversity Perspective," *Critical Sociology*, 38 (5): 629–643.

Holz, Josephine R., and Charles R. Wright. 1979. "Sociology of Mass Communications." *Annual Review of Sociology*, 5 (1): 193–217.

Hughey, Matthew W. 2009. "Cinethetic Racism: White Redemption and Black Stereotypes in 'Magical Negro' Films." *Social Problems*, 56 (3): 543–577.

Hughey, Matthew W. 2014. *The White Savior Film: Content, Critics, and Consumption*. Philadelphia, PA: Temple University Press.

Hughey, Matthew W. and Devon R. Goss. 2015. "A Level Playing Field? Media Constructions of Athletics, Genetics and Race." *The ANNALs of the American Academy of Political and Social Science*, 661 (1): 182–211.

Hunt, Darnell, Ana-Christina Ramon and Zachary Price. 2014. *2014 Hollywood Diversity Report: Making Sense of the Disconnect*. Los Angeles, CA: Ralph J. Bunche Center for African American Studies at UCLA.

Iverson, Susan VanDeventer. 2007. "Camouflaging Power and Privilege: A Critical Race Analysis of University Diversity Policies." *Educational Administration Quarterly*, 43 (5): 586–611.

Jackson, Crystal, David G. Embrick, and Carol S. Walther. 2013. "The White Pages: Diversity and the Mediation of Race in Public Business Media." *Critical Sociology*, vol. 41 (3): 537–551.

Kafka, Peter. 2013. "Netflix's No-Name Show Beating 'House of Cards' and 'Arrested Development'" Retrieved February 1, 2015: http://allthingsd.com/20130723/netflixs-no-name-show-beating-house-of-cards-and-arrested-development/.

Lang, Nico. 2014. "Orange is the New Black Proves to Be the Model of Queer TV." Retrieved on February 1, 2015: http://www.advocate.com/commentary/2014/06/30/op-ed-orange-new-black-proves-be-model-queer-tv.

Littlefield, Marci Bounds. 2008. "The Media as a System of Racialization: Exploring Images of African American Women and the New Racism." *American Behavioral Scientist*, 51 (5): 675–685.

Ludwig, Sean. 2013. "Netflix Says More Members Watched 'Hemlock Grove' on First Weekend than 'House of Cards.'" Retrieved on February 1, 2015: http://venturebeat .com/2013/04/22/netflix-hemlock-grove-first-weekend/.

Marvasti, Amir B., and Karyn D. McKinney. 2011. "Does Diversity Mean Assimilation?" *Critical Sociology*, 37 (5): 631–650.

Mastro, Dana E., and Elizabeth Behm-Morawitz. 2005. "Latino Representations on Primetime Television." *Journalism and Mass Communication Quarterly*, 81 (1): 110–130.

Matthews, Dylan. 2013. "'Orange is the New Black' is the Best Show About Prison Ever Made," *The Washington Post*, July 17.

McLuhan, Marshall. 1964. *Understanding Media: The Extensions of Man*. New York, NY: McGraw-Hill.

Miller, Liz Shannon. 2014. "Review: 'Orange is the New Black' Season 2 Maintains Diversity, Dives Deeper." Retrieved on February 1, 2015: http://www.indiewire.com /article/television/review-orange-is-the-new-black-season-2-maintains-diversity -dives-deeper.

Nicholson, Rebecca. 2013. "Orange is the New Black: web TV's Breakout Moment," *The Guardian,* September 11.

Nielsen. 2014. "Content is King, But Viewing Habits Vary by Demographic." Retrieved on February 1, 2015: http://www.nielsen.com/us/en/insights/news/2014/content-is-king-but-viewing-habits-vary-by-demographic.html.

Nielsen, Sarah and Sarah E. Turner, eds. 2014. *The Colorblind Screen: Television in Post-Racial America*. New York, NY: New York University Press.

Norton, Michael I., Joseph A. Vandello, Andrew Biga, and John M. Darley. 2008. "Colorblindness and Diversity: Conflicting Goals in Decisions Influenced by Race." *Social Cognition*, 26 (1): 102–111.

Phillips, David P. 1983. "The Impact of Mass Media Violence on U.S. Homicides." *American Sociological Review*, 48 (4): 560–568.

Rorke, Robert. 2014. "'Orange is the New Black' ignites a TV revolution for women," *New York Post*, June 4.

Ryan, Maureen. 2015. "Netflix's Cindy Holland Reveals Streaming Service's 'Commitment to Diversity.'" *Variety* November 10, 2015

Saeed, Amir. 2007. "Media, Racism and Islamophobia: The Representation of Islam and Muslims in the Media." *Sociology Compass*, 1/2 (2007): 443–462.

Sandvine. 2013. "Netflix and YouTube Account for 50% of All North American Fixed Network Data." Retrieved February 1, 2015: https://www.sandvine.com/pr/2013/11/11 /sandvine-report-netflix-and-youtube-account-for-50-of-all-north-american-fixed -network-data.html.

Sharf, Samantha. 2014. "Netflix Eyes Global Streaming Domination As It Crosses 50 Million Subscriber Mark," *Forbes*, July 21.

Smith, Jason. 2013. "Between Colorblind and Colorconscious: Contemporary Holly-wood Films and Struggles Over Racial Representation." *Journal of Black Studies*, 44 (8): 779–797.

Solomon, Brian. 2014. "Netflix Binge: 'House of Cards' Season Two Viewers Surge 8x on Day One," *Forbes,* February 18.

Steel, Emily. 2014. "Research Confirms the Crowd: Netflix and Others Are Upending TV Business," *The New York Times*, December 8.

Vertovec, Steven. 2012. "'Diversity' and the Social Imaginary." *Archives of European Sociology*, 33 (3): 287–312.

Weigel, Russel H., James W. Loomis, and Matthew J. Soja. 1980. "Race Relations on Prime Time Television." *Journal of Personality and Social Psychology*, 39 (5): 884–893.

CHAPTER 17

From Capital to Credit: On the Contingent Value of Difference within Diversity Discourse

Antonia Randolph

1 Introduction

We are at an unprecedented moment in American history where it is orthodox to celebrate racial and ethnic diversity without addressing racial and ethnic inequality (Berrey 2011). In fact, our embrace of diversity is predicated upon the reproduction and resilience of the dominant racial order (Duggan 2004). I saw evidence of the newfound value that diversity has in the comments of teachers and school leaders that I studied in a large and diverse Midwestern city that I call Laketown. Teachers valued diversity when they treated interactions with and knowledge of students of color as something that benefitted themselves, the school, and/or society. This chapter sketches the market for diversity that I observed, which I describe using the metaphor of a credit lending system. Teachers create a market for diversity when they treat students of color as though their racial and ethnic minority status was valuable and reward students for that value. While scholars typically use capital to describe social value, I argue that credit is a better metaphor for understanding the contingent value that being a student of color has within the school system.

I treat race and ethnicity primarily as symbols, as identities that teachers interpret, rather than focusing on the lived experiences of racial and ethnic minority students. Teachers use a relational logic to make distinctions between people of color. Teachers understand the meaning of African-American-ness in relation to their understanding of the meaning of Korean-American-ness, for instance. I found that teachers consistently had positive perceptions of immigrant minorities (people of color who are minorities due to immigration) and negative perceptions of native-born minorities (people of color who are minorities due to slavery and conquest) (Ogbu 1995). Moreover, teachers rewarded immigrant minorities with what I call symbolic resources, or beneficial attitudes and behaviors toward students, families, and communities, because of their positive perceptions of their minority status (Randolph 2013). The fact that teachers granted students with symbolic resources meant that they saw their minority status as having symbolic currency, or as having value for legitimating racial inequality. For instance, Asian-Americans have symbolic currency when teachers invoke their characteristics as "model minorities" to reproach other minorities for not being as successful (Hsu 1996).

The chapter describes the overall model of the market for valuing diversity in schools, rather than focusing on the process for recognizing and rewarding diversity. There are three hallmarks of the credit model of valuing diversity. For one thing, teachers praised immigrant minorities for adhering to norms they associated with whites, which increased the value of white norms. Thus, a credit market is a system where the benefits minorities receive ultimately reproduce their indebtedness to white normativity. Also, the credit system disproportionately enriched teachers with benefits ranging from making their knowledge about minorities marketable to increasing their ease in diverse environments. Finally, credit is revocable: schools can withdraw value that they formerly gave to students of color. In short, schools create a credit market when they value diversity in ways that reinforce white normativity, disproportionately focus on how minority status enriches them, and treat the value of minorities as contingent.

The credit market for diversity does not just reinforce the existing racial order, it also creates a hierarchy between different minority groups. Teachers in my study treated interactions with and knowledge of African-Americans as though they were not valuable. The parallel with the credit system also applies here. Worse than having bad credit is having no credit at all. Teachers did not value African-Americans in the sense that I am using the term, nor did they reward them with benefits due to that value. Instead, they devalued African-American students, especially by viewing predominantly black schools as undesirable. Rather than rewarding black students with symbolic resources, teachers penalized African-American students by ascribing their families and communities with bad values and by having low expectations of black students (Randolph 2013). The chapter will also sketch the racial penalties African-American students face for their racialized difference from the white norm.

2   Data and Methods

My analysis is based on interviews with 100 teachers and leaders at 11 schools in Laketown. I was the primary ethnographer at one of the schools, I had access to a database containing the field notes and interviews at the other schools. The teachers were 2nd and 5th grade math, reading and science instructors.

Types of data collected for the study included classroom observations, interviews with teachers pre- and post-observation, and general teacher interviews about their background and career. We also asked questions about teacher perceptions of the students, parents, and community during post-observation interviews. The chapter analyzes pre- and post-observation interviews and general teacher interviews from the first of two years of data collection.

As in most American cities, there were more white teachers in the sample than teachers of other race and ethnicity, followed by black and then Latino teachers (Frankenberg 2006). There were only a handful of Asian teachers (see Table 17.1). Schools varied by student racial composition: seven were black, two were Latino, and two were multiracial. Multiracial schools were defined as schools where no racial/ethnic group made up more than half of the student population, while black and Latinos schools were 80–100 percent of their minority group. Schools also varied by class composition: There were three middle-class schools (including both of the multiracial schools and one of the black schools) and eight poor schools, based on the percentage of students receiving free lunch. The sample was representative of the composition of schools in the city (see Table 17.2).

TABLE 17.1   Teacher demographics

School	Black	White	Latino	Asian	Total
Bowen	3	9	0	1	13
Brantley	5	1	0	0	6
Dodge	3	18	1	3	25
Erving	1	1	0	0	2
Foster	2	1	0	0	3
Kipps	5	2	0	0	7
Martin	9	2	0	0	11
Noel	4	1	0	0	5
Putnam	0	3	3	0	6
Stanley	2	10	4	0	16
Watts	4	2	0	0	6
Total	38	50	8	4	100

SOURCE: TEACHER SELF-REPORT

The analysis draws on critical discourse analysis (CDA) to examine how teachers talk about the diversity of their students. The field of discourse analysis views language primarily as a means to achieve social goals, not as a means of communication. A premise of the analysis is that discourse is both embedded in social norms and helps to delineate them. Discourse establishes the limits of what can be thought, said or known about social phenomena by affecting our sense of what is legitimate, normal, and acceptable. Discourse analysis investigates the purposes to which individuals put language, such as categorization, justification, and attribution (Wetherell and Potter 1992).

Previous research shows that racial discourse focuses on physical or cultural differences that society uses to rank groups into hierarchies (Frankenberg 1993). In contrast, ethnic discourse emphasizes cultural aspects of minority groups as they relate to their national ancestry (Omi and Winant 1994). Informed by these distinctions, I employed a two-step process for coding interviews for racial and ethnic discourse. The first step was identifying interviews that mentioned race or ethnicity. I did this by using qualitative data management software (NUD*IST) to search the interviews for racial and ethnic *labels* such as African-American and Korean-American when talking about students and schools. Most of these comments occurred when teachers were asked about how a lesson went and about the strengths and weaknesses of the students, parents, and community.

The next step involved coding code words and narratives within the sample of interviews that used racial or ethnic labels. *Code words* are defined as phrases commonly associated with race or ethnicity, which do not explicitly use racial or ethnic labels. References to language, religion, values, customs, immigrant status and related ideas are all code words for ethnic discourse (Omi and Winant 1994). Racial code words include using phrases like "inner-city" or "welfare recipient" to invoke blackness and racial discourse (Gilens 1996). Due to pressures against being overtly racist, scholars find that Americans frequently use racial code words in interviews (Eliasoph 1999; Frankenberg 1993). *Narratives* are defined as stories that individuals tell to explain social reality. For example, a common ethnic narrative is that of the immigrant who pulls himself up by the bootstrap, while a common racial narrative is the story of the disorganized and violent black neighborhood. This more in-depth level of analysis enabled me to observe how teachers justified, legitimated and normalized their perceptions of diversity at their schools.

3   Ethnic Credits and Racial Penalties: The Market for Diversity
       in an Urban School District

The quotes below show the dynamics of valuing immigrant minorities precisely because of their supposed differences from native-born minorities and

TABLE 17.2 Student demographics

School Demographics	Black Schools							Latino Schools			Multiracial Schools	
	Brantley	Erving	Foster	Kipps	Martin	Noel	Watts	Putnam	Stanley	Bowen	Dodge
Grade Levels	K–8	K–8	K–8	preK–8	preK–8	preK–8	preK–8	preK–6	preK–8	preK–8	K–8
Enrollment	830	215	618	302	1046	1035	356	939	1363	1118	1507
% Low Income	98.7	70.2	99.4	88.4	95.4	97.6	92.4	96.3	95.3	64.0	71.6
% Black	100.0	99.5	100.0	100.0	99.7	99.5	100.0	2.8	4.3	6.1	8.2
% White	0.0	0.0	0.0	0.0	0.3	0.0	0.0	0.5	3.6	44.5	39.2
% Latino	0.0	0.5	0.0	0.0	0.0	0.5	0.0	96.4	92.0	25.3	21.6
% Asian	0.0	0.0	0.0	0.0	0.0	0.0	0.0	0.3	0.1	23.4	30.9

SOURCE: CHICAGO PUBLIC SCHOOLS WEBSITE (www.cps.edu)

rewarding them for that difference. A black teacher at a multiracial school pointed to the influx of students from a nearby housing projects when describing how her school had changed over the years. She explains that:

> I've seen a lot and you can mix cultures that are kind of on the same socioeconomic level and have at least some similar values but the problem with like some of these really really poor black kids is that they don't even share my values. Plus, they're not serviced at the rate they should be and okay call me crazy but when I can understand the Korean kid better than I can understand the black kid, don't you think you can give him some bilingual education maybe?
>
> RANDOLPH 2013: 39

Teachers and leaders throughout the study echoed her sentiments that immigrant minority students shared their pro-school values, while poor African-American students did not. While teachers were not all as explicit in the comparisons they made, their pattern was to contrast the positive characteristics they attributed to immigrant minority students with the deficits they perceived in black students.

By saying that she can understand the Korean student better than the black student, she casts the implicitly native-born black student as more "foreign" than the implicitly foreign-born Korean student. This characterization could delegitimize the black students' claim to support, that is, their need to be "serviced at the rate they should be," since black students do not have a legitimate reason to struggle with English. Yet, the next quote, which picks up where the earlier one left off, clarifies her beliefs about how race, ethnicity, and class relate to the amount of support African-American students deserve.

> This is a question that's been mulling in my mind for a long time, why are these black kids if we're taking these black kids from really low income situations, really dysfunctional families they don't get any kind of help at all outside a free lunch. So bad things happen.

The first excerpt suggests that Koreans, as immigrants, have legitimate claim to support from the school while the native-born status of blacks meant that they did not. In contrast, the second excerpt suggests that schools do not support black students enough because they do not recognize the depth of their need. This quote is more sympathetic to the needs of black students.

Still, the teacher uses the narrative of bad values to characterize black students. The narrative was typical of how the faculty talked about black poverty, but not the poverty of immigrant minority students. When asked how the "influx of some poorer students ... affected (her) job at the school," she replies:

> I spend a lot more time just trying to hunt down parents, making phone calls in the evening and getting up at 6:30 in the morning and it's real difficult because maybe you've got some parent who doesn't share your values either and the kid's only in school so that the parent can get you to sign the paper that says the kid is in school so they can get their public assistance check. It just happened to me. Begging and begging and begging with somebody to please come talk to me. No phone, so this is all being done by letter and she sends me a public assistance card.

The teacher constructs black parents as not valuing education. Instead, they use education as a means to an end- "getting their public assistance check." Across schools, teachers tied black poverty with blacks having non-mainstream values.

While the black teacher ostensibly credits Korean students with sharing her values, I contend that she is really lauding them for having values that are consistent with hegemonic whiteness. Hegemonic whiteness refers to the attitudes and behaviors that mark one as normal and moral (Hughey and Byrd 2013). Though these dispositions are rooted in the privileges that come from middle-class white identity, the dominant culture treats them as ideals to which we should all aspire. While the values seem race neutral and commonsense, they come out of a particular experience of privilege tied to white identity (Hughey and Byrd 2013). Here the commonsense expectation is that students should speak academic English and should have parents that inherently value education. The teacher reaffirmed the value of white normativity by praising Korean students for doing something that would be expected of the normative middle-class white person.

In contrast, teachers at the multiracial and the Latino schools attribute immigrant minority students with positive qualities, especially with having good values, despite their poverty. They reward the students with symbolic resources, such as giving them the benefit of the doubt about why their parents are not involved in school. When asked to describe her students' parents, a Latina teacher at a Latino school said, "They're extremely hard working. Many of them are holding down two jobs." The parents of her students wanted to support their children, even if they cannot go to events at school. They asked: "what can they do with their meager means to help their children out." She adjusted her expectations of parental involvement accordingly, saying:

Do they support their children in their studies? Insofar as they'll ask their kids, 'Is your homework done? Are you ready for school?' That's about as much as they'll do. And that's one of the reasons why I'm so demanding of my children. They have to develop responsibility. They don't have external support.

She felt that Latino parents had legitimate reasons why they could not participate at school and expected them to support their kids at home, instead. Moreover, the teacher increased her expectations of students, despite their lack of parental involvement. Rather than giving up responsibility for teaching her students due to the obstacles their parents face, she became more "demanding" of them.

Teacher perceptions construct a system of *ethnic credits* and *racial penalties*. Most teachers had positive perceptions of immigrant minorities, which they often translated into actions that could benefit some students and disadvantage others. Race of teacher affected the construction of the credit market for diversity, since white teachers were the most likely to value diversity in this way and black teachers were the least likely. Still, as we have seen, teachers across race followed the pattern of credits and penalties. Thus, teachers rewarded Asian and Latino students with *ethnic credits*, the symbolic rewards for difference granted due to positive attributions that come from a negative contrast with a disfavored racial and ethnic group (Hsu 1996; Pierre 2004).

They also heaped *racial penalties* on African-American students by not treating their difference as a source of value. Instead, they recounted stories of how they did not want to teach at the predominantly black schools in the sample and of how they were warned away from them by colleagues and family members. Further, teachers at multiracial schools tied the presence of black students to negative consequences, such as needing Special Education. The Asian-American assistant principal at a multiracial school says as much when explaining why her school focused so much on what the interviewer labels as "at-risk students," despite the school's high achievement scores:

> Assistant Principal: There was the history from Laketown in the past that so many kids are in Special Ed.
> Interviewer: Tell me about that.
> Assistant Principal: Well, it's just that it's a disproportionate number of certain minorities are place(d) in Special Ed. Yes, Blacks, and so we want to ensure that we don't want to get into that situation.

While the assistant principal does not initially say, she admits that blacks were the "certain minorities" that Laketown had placed in Special Education at "disproportionate" rates. Because they did not want to "get into that situation," the school was proactive about focusing on at-risk students. Yet, that focus ran the risk of making being an African-American student synonymous with being in Special Education. This was one of the few occasions where someone at a multiracial school explicitly used the racial label "black," though they often used ethnic labels like "Korean" and "Russian." The quote below suggests a blurring between "blackness" and needing "Special Education."

When the interviewer asked what the actual number of Special Education students were at the school, the assistant principal replies:

> Right now out of student population we have about 140 in the Special Ed department and that is a small percentage and it's just something that has been kind of neglected and they needed some kind of ... system, a framework so everyone knows [how to diagnose Special Education students]. We want to make sure we are not forgetting that population.

It is unclear which "population" she means when the assistant principal says she was afraid of "forgetting that population." Yet, the interviewer's query into why the school was focusing on "at-risk" students, the assistant principal's racialization of what at-risk meant and the relatively small numbers of black students at the school all work to equate "black" with "at-risk."

The symbolic resources that were denied to African-American students and families, but awarded to immigrant minorities, created a relative hierarchy of resources among students of color in the school district. Schools granted certain minorities credit for their difference that paid off in rewards, but shut African-American students out of the market for valuing racial and ethnic difference. Racial penalties were the counterpart to ethnic credits, due to the logic with which teachers assessed the value of diversity.

In the next section, I discuss three ways scholars have conceptualized the value of racial and ethnic diversity using capital as the root metaphor. These very different conceptualizations of minority status as valuable constructs capital as something that benefits those who possess it (Bourdieu 2002). They reflect the tendency to look at capital from the point of view of the beneficiary. In contrast, the last section of the chapter argues that credit is a better metaphor than capital to theorize the contingent value that diversity had in the eyes of teachers. Specifically, credit emphasizes the costs to people of color when teachers valued them. Moving from credit to capital from capital shifts our attention to institutions as lenders of value that can be withheld or reinvested for the benefit of the institutions. Capital is about direct benefits to the person who owns it, while credit is about the benefits that teachers and schools get from treating diversity as valuable. The analogy here is that just as credit lenders benefit disproportionately from giving credit to individuals, schools benefit disproportionately when they value diversity in ways that reinforce the normativity of whiteness.

4   Conceptualizations of Diversity as Value: Black Cultural Capital, Color Capital and Multicultural Capital

Scholars have used cultural capital to describe the benefits that individuals get from embodying, knowing about, or owning objects of high status within society (Bourdieu 2002). Research had not until recently analyzed whether racial and ethnic difference itself could function as cultural capital. Still, the advent of an ideological orthodoxy that says we should celebrate difference, but ignore racial inequality has lent new value to minority status (Berrey 2011). The valuing of diversity is orthodox in the sense that there is widespread belief in the United States and other Western democracies that the racial and ethnic differences that we might have tried to eliminate in the past should be preserved and praised. For instance, it was common at the beginning of the 20th century for American schools to insist that Eastern and Southern European immigrants speak English and remove other markers of ethnic difference (Tyack 2003). Today, many American schools strive to celebrate diversity and to support and preserve the heritage of immigrant minority students (McCarthy 1994).

Colorblind neoliberalism, or what I call colorblind multiculturalism, provides the ideological underpinning for valuing diversity (Duggan 2004). Colorblind multiculturalism combines the premium that multiculturalism places on noticing and celebrating difference with the willful ignorance about racial inequality that comes with colorblindness. Institutions value difference that puts the "American experiment" of integration in a good light and that shows that United States has an open opportunity structure for minorities (Randolph 2013). In practice, colorblind multiculturalism looks like holding Multicultural Festivals at schools, while ignoring how racial inequality contributes to the black-white achievement gap. My research shows that teachers practiced colorblind multiculturalism by only valuing the diversity they associated with immigrant minorities like Asians and Latinos, not the diversity associated with black students (Randolph 2013).

I distinguish ethnic credits from three concepts about the value of diversity that use capital as their root metaphor: black cultural capital, color capital, and multicultural capital. Black cultural capital speaks to the way blacks treat black authenticity as currency within the black community (Carter 2003). Likewise, white identity lacks currency when seen through the lens of multiculturalism. Whites make up for this loss of value by accumulating color capital, or interactions with and knowledge of the "exotic" and "soulful" culture of minorities (Hughey 2012). Finally, multicultural capital addresses the value that cosmopolitanism has for moving through the diverse social world, especially the world of work (Reay 2007). Still, the new status afforded to racial and ethnic minority status never displaces the value of middle-class whiteness. Instead, these forms of diversity-based capital reproduce the dominant racial order. Moreover, the types of value described below do not capture the contingent and costly way that teachers valued diversity in the schools I observed.

5   From Capital to Credit

Ethnic credits are different from black cultural capital, color capital, and multicultural capital. While black cultural capital is about a minority group being rewarded within non-dominant culture for their difference, ethnic credits captures the way the dominant culture rewards minority status. Color capital and multicultural capital are both about how members of the dominant group gain from valuing racial and ethnic difference. In contrast, ethnic credits examine a system where people of color benefit in the dominant culture from having their difference valued.

Multicultural capital is closer than the other conceptualizations of diversity to the system of ethnic credits and racial penalties I saw in school. In fact, the teachers at the two diverse schools in my sample sought interactions with students of color because they could gain multicultural capital. Thus, multicultural capital plays a role in why teachers value difference, but does not describe the system of value that teachers created around minority status. Specifically, the rewards minority students get for their difference are more contingent and costly than the theory of capital implies.

There are three ways that a credit market for diversity is different from a capital market for diversity. Ethnic credits are revocable; they disproportionately benefit dominant institutions (and their representatives), rather than people of color; and they reinforce the status of middle-class white norms by valuing of people of color based on how well they emulate those norms. Like capital, ethnic credits reproduce the existing social structure, but in less obvious ways. Ethnic credits reproduce the status quo of white supremacy, while appearing to reduce racial inequality. Moreover, ethnic credits create a market that penalizes people of color who do not fit into the ethnic narrative of social mobility and immigrant heritage. The credit market for diversity necessarily constructs a group of racial minorities as being outside its system of value. Thus, the credit market may be an even more intractable system of inequality than capital because ethnic credits seem to undermine racial hierarchies that they actually perpetuate.

5.1   *Revocability of Ethnic Credits*

Ethnic credits are revocable. A parallel feature of capital is that it cannot be activated unless capital is recognized by others (Devine 2009). Yet, the credit market for diversity is even more tenuous, since teachers can choose not to value characteristics they previously valued or decide that the costs of diversity outweigh its benefits. Moreover, teachers in the same institution can choose not to see diversity as valuable. In these ways, the value of diversity in a system of ethnic credits is inconstant and can decline or disappear completely. In other words, the value of diversity in a credit market is contingent.

A white bilingual education teacher at a Latino school shows the contingent value of ethnic credits. She values the diversity her Latino students bring, saying that her students gain cognitive benefits from being English language learners that monolingual students lack. Yet, she is aware that some of her of colleagues do not value the diversity of Latino students and instead view their being English language learners as a deficit. The excerpt below shows the shifting value that minority status can have within a single school. When asked whether she had a preference among the different types of English language education programs, she said:

> I have a lot of problems with the transitional program. I think there's a lot of flaws and I feel pretty adamant that [She trails off] I feel like there's an attitude that bilingual kids are stupid and a lot of people put them down. My understanding is that research shows that bilinguals are cognitively higher rated than monolinguals so in the end I mean it may take them a while, it may take them long in the beginning but in the end they're gonna come out ahead. So I feel like I fight that even at Putnam where I thought there'd be more people who were sensitive to the bilingual issue but there's a number of people that talk about how stupid the kids are. Which one I don't think any teacher should ever say that and then, too, especially just to be so insensitive to dual language.

The teacher's comment has the hallmarks of the ethnic credit process: she values the ethnic difference of an immigrant minority group and rewards them because of that difference. She rewards Latino students with the benefit of the doubt that they can overcome the current problems that being an English language learner poses. She also favorably compares immigrant minorities to another group, monolingual students, and believes that Latino students "come out ahead" due to their difference.

At the same time, she shows the variability of the ethnic credit system, namely that other teachers may not similarly value ethnic difference. This variability means that teachers can revoke the value they afford to minority status at any time. While it was orthodox across schools to see immigrant minority status as valuable, many teachers and leaders expressed negative perceptions of diversity. Often teachers who criticized diversity conceded to norms by praising it, too (Randolph 2013). Yet, even teachers who valued diversity tempered their comments by pointing out its negative consequences. In the current example, the teacher was shocked that her colleagues did not follow the norm of seeing any value in diversity. Instead, they constructed being English language learners as a sign that Latino students were "stupid." The variation in perceptions within schools is not surprising, but it does show that the value of diversity is contingent.

Likewise, the Asian-American principal at a multiracial school shows the ambivalence about diversity that makes ethnic credits a contingent form of value. Faculty laud diversity as long as it does not inconvenience them (Randolph 2013). While it is a truism that people make rational calculations based on their self-interests, the way the same teacher can value diversity then devalue it shows how fleeting the value of diversity can be (Byrne and de Tona 2014; Cucchiara 2013). The contrast with capital, which tends to hold its value, highlights the changeable value of credit.

As with many faculty in the study, the principal showed ambivalence about diversity when talking about bilingual education. In the quote below, the principal ties the need for bilingual education to the need for immigrant minority students to know their heritage. Yet, she expressed misgivings about bilingual education that reflected ambivalence about the goals of the program. The principal made these comments when describing the resistance that she received from faculty when trying to make changes to the bilingual program at school. She reports that:

> I have the fraction of bilingual teachers who were afraid of losing their job because they know that I am not a total pro-bilingual person. I'm really ... because it is a three-year transitional program. I'm strong supporter or knowing your culture, knowing your own heritage, knowing your own language. At the same time, I'm a strong proponent for learning English.

In order to survive in America, in order to get into those fields to be successful in life, you've got to know English. So I'm not a believer to put
a child in a program for five/six years and come out not knowing any
language.

She equates being a "total pro-bilingual person" with being okay with allowing a child to languish in a program where they "come out not knowing any
language." More to the point, she implies that being "pro-bilingual" means not
being "a strong proponent for learning English." This creates a false dichoto-
my between strongly supporting bilingual education and helping students
learn English. The principal expresses the kinds of suspicions about the anti-
assimilationist consequences of bilingual education that are more typical of
those who are against it (Nieto and Bode 2011).

The principal shows the contingent value of diversity in her comments
about bilingual education. She showed that she valued diversity when she says,
"I'm a strong supporter of knowing your culture, knowing your own heritage,
knowing your own language." The belief that students should know their own
culture is at the heart of valuing diversity. Nevertheless, her criticism of the
bilingual program reveals a suspicion that bilingual education produces students who are not assimilated enough.

Still, certain groups are shut out of getting credit for diversity altogether.
This was true of African-Americans in the schools I studied. Teachers penalized black students for falling short of the white ideal, but also for their perceived negative difference from immigrant minorities. The multiracial schools
treated the influx of poor black students as a sign of bad diversity. Meanwhile,
teachers at the black schools criticized students for the lack of exposure to
diversity. A white teacher at a black school obliquely refers to race when
explaining her students' discipline problems. When asked about challenges at
her school, she says:

There is no balance at the school ... I mean male, female; ethnic; racial. It
would help if there was a balance ... I know there are positive reasons for
having people of your own group teaching, for example in terms of discipline ... but the problem is that the children can't relate to others. The kids
are limited in their experiences ... they are stuck in this neighborhood.

She blames the racial isolation of her students, who go to a predominantly
black school in an all-black neighborhood, for her students' inability to "relate
to others." She follows the logic of the credit market by tying negative consequences to her students' lack of exposure to diversity. Further, she makes the

familiar assertion that poor blacks are from dysfunctional families who instill bad values in their kids. When asked about the lowest point of the previous year, the teacher explained that, "last year there was chaos" in part because "discipline was not addressed." The interviewer reports that she said:

> We need money, we need an attached social agency. Students at the school get free breakfast, some of them, free lunch and free supper, some that stay for the after school programs. For her the problem that was not being addressed was that the area had a high ratio of foster parents where the DCSF was in charge. Mrs. G [the teacher] was however sarcastic about the official 98% poverty rate at the school when [the students] were "not lacking of Super Nintendo games."

Mrs. G believes her students have misplaced values. They are poor, but they are not thrifty since they were "not lacking of Super Nintendo games." As was typical in the study, Mrs. G constructs black students as the undeserving poor. For African-American students, there was no credit for teachers to revoke. Teachers did not see value in their difference in the first place.

The contingency of ethnic credits parallels the uncertainty of the credit market. Some credit cards are not widely accepted, creating uneven access to resources even if one has credit. Additionally, lenders can change the terms on which credit is borrowed, which is akin to seeing diversity as undesirable where it was once welcomed. The racial penalty system points to another form of inequality, since some minority groups are denied credit for their difference altogether. Thus, there are more barriers from turning credit into rewards than one faces in a system based on capital. Indeed, the first barrier is having teachers value what African-Americans contribute to themselves and their schools.

5.2 Usury in the Ethnic Credit Market: Disproportionate Benefit to the Lender

Moreover, ethnic credits disproportionately benefit the lender of value, rather than the recipient of credit. Lenders earn money from credit cards by charging interest on them, often at high rates. Lenders get much richer in that exchange than credit holders do. Similarly, schools and teachers gain more in the ethnic credit system for valuing diversity than minority students do for contributing to that diversity. Teachers get to feel cosmopolitan and to practice making their curriculum relevant to diverse populations. Schools get a student population they perceive as higher achieving and better behaved. And both schools and teachers gain the ability to ignore racial inequality in explaining achievement disparities among minority groups. They can point to the success of immigrant minority groups to relieve themselves from the responsibility for helping minority groups that are underachieving.

Though immigrant minority students get some benefit from having their difference valued, the benefits that teachers and schools get from ethnic credits are even greater. Here, the Asian-American assistant principal from a multiracial school explains how valuable her training in bilingual education has become. She is responding to a request for her explain her career trajectory. Her first position was at a school in Chinatown that had a large Chinese student population. She says she began teaching:

> (W)hen bilingual education was just beginning. I majored in education and minored in history, I always liked history, and there was a position open in the bilingual program at (her first school) and they said they wanted someone to teach in history and culture as a component of their bilingual program [not] just teaching English and I said perfect because I took a lot of Chinese history in college...

The assistant principal's personal interest in history and Chinese was a "perfect" fit for the cultural approach to bilingual education at her first school. Her educational background gained added value because, in keeping with the multicultural orthodoxy, the school wanted to teach Chinese culture, not just English, to its English language learners.

The assistant principal invested even more resources in learning about Asian culture, because she knew that knowledge would pay off in the school system. She continues:

> I was hired immediately out of college and after teaching every year I figured that this is the wave of what's going on in bilingual, teaching history and culture, so I went back to [a large research university] and ... I got my Masters in Asian History from there. ...I wanted to have a firm foundation to teach it because I felt that it was important, that's why I quit teaching and got my Masters in that then I came back and there was another opening.

She got a Masters, not in education, which is typical of educators who want an advantage in their field, but in Asian History. She made this costly investment because she knew that schools would reward her for her expertise. Her first position taught her that "this is the wave of what's going on in bilingual, teaching history and culture." Her hunch that having "a firm foundation" in Asian

culture would pay off in the market bore out, since "there was another opening" waiting for when she finished her degree.

The assistant principal's experience shows the added benefits that faculty
can gain in their profession from knowledge of and interactions with immigrant minorities. Faculty also gained personal benefits. Some teachers got to
cultivate their ease and familiarity with immigrant minority cultures. They
developed their taste for being in diverse environments. A black teacher at a
multiracial school recounted how she began exploring the restaurants in the
diverse neighborhood in which her school was located. She said:

> I go to restaurants there, I find – I've eaten things I've never heard of be-
> fore and it's neat because the best thing is go down Shepherd Lane, just
> walk down Shepherd Lane and then you'll [see] a sari palace next to a
> Jewish religious store next to Tel Aviv kosher pizza, next to a Japanese
> place next to a Korean place with all Korean in the window and I shop
> there.

She developed an ease with the unfamiliar by challenging herself to go to these
ethnic restaurants.

> So I was like this is cool, this is going right down Shepherd Lane. This is
> the experience for a long time and I was brave, I'd go ahead. If you do this
> you will go in places and many of those places no English will be spoken
> so it's like being in a foreign country and that changes from building to
> building.

By teaching at a multiracial school in a diverse neighborhood, the teacher
had the chance to immerse herself in difference, so much so that she felt like
she was "in a foreign country." This "cool" experience allowed her to become
"brave" about going into places where "no English is spoken." She increased her
skills for navigating diversity. Thus, teachers got a return on their investment in
ethnic credits at both multiracial schools that paid off in their everyday lives,
not just in school.

Finally, teachers also expressed their identification with groups that were different from themselves through interacting with diverse students. In this case,
teachers gained from diversity in a more personally meaningful way. They felt
personally enriched by their interactions with immigrant minority students.
These personal gains were no less significant than their professional ones, even
if they did not translate into advantages within the dominant culture.

A black teacher at the other Latino school also identified across ethnic lines. She believed that she could better identify with the plight of her students than her white colleagues because she was also racial/ethnic minority. She is explaining why her views of the school or more positive than some of her colleagues. The interviewer notes that the school is predominantly Hispanic and asks:

> Interviewer: So have you found that to be challenging to deal with the...?
> Teacher: Well actually it has been um, it's been very positive for me. Because I'm Spanish speaking...
> Interviewer: Really?
> Teacher: ...and I've studied Spanish language and culture. So it's been really...
> Interviewer: More familiar to you.
> Teacher: More familiar to me.

Like the assistant principal at the multiracial school, she gained professionally because her educational background is useful at a school that values diversity. Yet, she was not a bilingual education teacher. This teacher's personal interest in "Spanish language and culture" pays an extra dividend within the market for diversity at her school because she was better able to get along with her students than her colleagues.

She then goes on to talk about more personally meaningful ways that she benefits from teaching at a Latino school. She says:

> Teacher: Yes. And um, it really has been a positive experience.
> Interviewer: So it's not as big of a challenge as it might seem or...?
> Teacher: No. Or as it is for some of my colleagues.
> Interviewer: Right.
> Teacher: You know, especially with the language barrier and...
> Interviewer: Right, cultural barriers too.
> Teacher: ...the struggle, yeah. Because I understand the cultural barriers. I know all about them.

The interviewer and teacher are talking about race without explicitly naming it. The white interviewer does not ask what the teacher means when she says that she "know(s) all about" "cultural barriers," because she understands that they are talking about racial inequality. The teacher feels a kinship with her Latino students, as a fellow person of color, which her white colleagues do not have. She may have learned about Latino students out of academic interests, but she "understands" culture barriers from personal experience.

In contrast, teachers rarely talked about the personal and professional benefits they got from knowledge of and interactions with African-American students. When they did, it was African-American teachers talking about how they identified with the disadvantages that black students faced. Even then, black teachers' pleasure in teaching black students was tempered by the class distance they felt from their predominantly poor students (Randolph 2013). Rarest of all was a non-black teacher talking about what they gained from teaching black students. The quote below is an exception that proves the rule.

The Latina assistant principal at a Latino school thought Latinos could learn from the racial pride that she ascribed to African-Americans. She was confronting a clique of Latino girls in a class that had defaced lockers and bathrooms with racist messages about blacks. The class was predominantly Latino, but had about seven African-American girls. The assistant principal tells the class:

> We, as Latinas ... we need to have more pride in ourselves. As African-Americans, you need to show it because you've got it. Number two ... you are NOT Low Down Girls [the name of the clique]. By saying that, you are degrading yourselves.

She says that the Latina students who misbehaved could learn something from the "pride" that African-American students have. This crediting of African-Americans with values from which non-blacks could learn was singular. Black faculty expressed pride in their blackness, but this teacher was the only one to say that non-blacks could gain something from being more like blacks. African-Americans faced another racial penalty because only other blacks saw something to admire about or learn from blackness.

Teachers gained, personally and professionally, from their interactions with and knowledge of immigrant minority students. In one sense, these excerpts show that faculty gained multicultural capital from working with immigrant minority students. Yet, I contend that the benefits that teachers gained were over and above the benefits that students got from the transaction. This is due to the fact that the students' benefits were contingent, as I said in the previous section. Moreover, as I argue in the next section, the benefits were costly to the students. For these reasons, the benefits that teachers got from their multicultural capital amounted to interest, a disproportionate benefit that teachers got from capitalizing on ethnic credits that students did not get.

5.3   *Increased Indebtedness: Ethnic Credits Reify the Value of White Normativity*

Finally, the ethnic credit system is like the credit market because it puts people further in debt. Lenders prefer individuals who are not able to pay off all of their debt and who lengthen the term of their indebtedness. They make more interest that way. In a similar fashion, white normativity increases in value as teachers affirm diversity. This is because teachers are often lauding characteristics they associate with hegemonic whiteness when they praise immigrant minorities. The system of ethnic credits strengthens the position of hegemonic whiteness within the market for valuing identity. Thus, the ethnic credit system is costly to its recipients, just as credit is costly to credit card holders over time.

For instance, a white teacher at a multiracial school praised a Vietnamese-American girl for becoming more easy-going in class, like her normative white counterparts. The teacher was explaining what he meant by students who had "pulled themselves up" in class and was using this student as an example. The student was already high achieving, but the teacher felt her fear of being made fun of made it hard for to interact with other students. He launched a campaign to loosen her up, saying, "And uh, I just tried to encourage her, because she's really smart, and she thought that the language would make kids laugh at her" (Randolph 2013, 115). Yet, the teacher did not just want the student to get along better with the other students, he wanted her to engage in harmless mischief like they did. Thus, he said:

> There's a couple of others like that I'm working on. I always say at the beginning, 'Down the road, Suzy, I'm gonna have yous throwing spitballs across the room.' I said 'You watch, you watch. You're gonna be running around throwing spitballs and I'm gonna have to say Suzy, I'm gonna call your mother!'

The teacher appreciated the progress Suzy had made in becoming more comfortable with her classmates, but would be happiest if she acted out more. This seemingly strange hope had to do with making Suzy more like her white American counterparts. Thus, she would succeed in his eyes socially when her behavior was more normative, even to the point of encouraging her to make harmless mischief of "throwing spitballs" in class.

Teachers also reinforced the value of middle-class white normativity by judging immigrant minorities against that metric when they behaved ways that made them seem too strange. A white teacher at a multiracial school argued that immigrant minority parents do not take their kids on field trips like normative white middle-class parents did. The teacher explains that she prepares students to write fluently by exposing them to experiences that they might write about. She says:

> And I schlep them all over Laketown. Well, a lot of them don't get places because of their cultures. Family field trips are not something that they do, it's not on a Sunday – there are some kids who do a lot, there are some families extremely involved but most of the ones where the kids were not born in this country the moms haven't become fluent in the language and they don't drive, they don't leave the neighborhood many times the first time a child has seen [a famous local landmark] is when they've been on a bus with me going downtown for something or they'll go the whole summer without seeing the lake and never go to museums. And that's more the norm than the exception in the group of kids that have.

According to the teacher, it is not the "norm" for immigrant minority families to take "family field trips ... on a Sunday," as is typical for the normative middle-class white family. Her comments invoke both race and class, since the ability to drive downtown on a Sunday to see city landmarks is a function of class privilege. While she does not explicitly mention race, her belief that the families do not take field trips because "of their cultures" and because they have not "become fluent in the language and they don't drive" suggest that she is thinking in racial terms. As much as faculty value ethnic difference, they still judge immigrant minorities by middle-class white norms and note when they fall short of them.

In this way, ethnic credits add value to hegemonic whiteness. Immigrant minorities will never catch up to the value that schools and teachers place on whiteness. In fact, the process of crediting immigrant minorities for being like whites reinforces the distinction between whites and people of color. Idealized white behaviors and attitudes become more valuable in this exchange. Ethnic credits increase the indebtedness of immigrant minorities to white middle-class norms, since the value of their difference depends on how closely they mirror hegemonic whiteness.

6   Discussion

Due to its revocability, high interest rate, and tendency to increase indebtedness, a credit market better describes the value that teachers and leaders ascribed to diversity than capital does. Specifically, the type of value that teachers ascribed to diversity was contingent and costly in a way that the value of capital is not. The value was contingent in its revocability- teachers could decide at any moment that diversity was not actually valuable. The value was costly in the way teachers and schools got disproportionate benefits from valuing immigrant minorities. Teachers increased their skill teaching diverse populations, cultivated their multicultural capital, and further socialized themselves into a taste for navigating diversity through their decision to value diversity. Teachers also valued diversity in a way that only strengthened the value of normative whiteness. This meant that immigrant minorities would be perpetually reliant on the dominant culture to credit their form of difference as desirable, rather than changing the standard by which schools judge the value of racial and ethnic identity.

The system of ethnic credits (and racial penalties) raises important issues for the field of critical diversity studies. A critical issue is whether fields besides education have a credit market for difference that privileges immigrant minorities over native-born minorities in a way that perpetuates white supremacy. Research showing that employers in the service economy prefer immigrant minorities to African-Americans suggests that this might be the case in the field of work. Employers credit immigrant minorities with having a demeanor that is good for service work, such as not challenging authority, and prefer them over African-Americans in certain sectors of the service economy for that reason (Waldinger and Lichter 2003). Immigrant minorities such as Latinos gain status from this negative comparison with African-Americans, but do so at the cost of employers seeing them as having subordinate personalities.

Future research should also examine under what conditions fields create a credit market for diversity. So far, research on the value of diversity has focused on select countries, especially the United Kingdom and the United States. Scholars should examine whether other countries that have increasingly diverse populations develop a credit market for diversity. Likewise, scholars should study the response to diversity within schools in cities across the United States. My research examined a large, diverse, Midwestern city with a history of struggles over black-white segregation. That backdrop of extreme segregation is part of what lent value to multiracial schools, since they proved that integration could work. In the future, scholars should study how different histories of racial and ethnic struggle shape the way that schools responds to diversity (Devine 2013).

The switch from capital to credit extends our understanding of how diversity functions in modern times. It shows that the value that schools place on diversity creates relative benefits for immigrant minorities that

African-Americans do not get. Not only does the credit market of diversity reproduce the inequality between white and black students, it creates a hierarchy among students of color. Still, the credit metaphor shows that the benefits
that immigrant minorities get are contingent and costly, and are themselves
a form of debt. In this way, the racial order is able to turn the recognition of
diversity into another way to reproduce white supremacy.

References

Berrey, Ellen. 2011. "Why Diversity Became Orthodox in Higher Education, and How It
Changed the Meaning of Race on Campus." *Critical Sociology*, 37 (5): 573–96.

Bourdieu, Pierre. 2002. "The Forms of Capital." Pp. 280–291 in *Readings in Economic
Sociology*, edited by Nicole Woolsey Biggart. Blackwell Publishers Ltd, 2002. Retrieve
from: http://onlinelibrary.wiley.com/doi/10.1002/9780470755679.ch15/summary.

Byrne, Bridget, and Carla de Tona. "Multicultural Desires? Parental Negotiation of Mul-
ticulture and Difference in Choosing Secondary Schools for Their Children." *The
Sociological Review*, 62 (3). Retrieved August 2014 from: http://o-search.proquest
.com.read.cnu.edu/socabs/docview/1561478330/abstract/46757C66404C46C9PQ/7
?accountid=10100.

Carter, P.L. 2003. "'Black' Cultural Capital, Status Positioning, and Schooling Conflicts
for Low-Income African American Youth." *Social Problems*, 50 (1): 136–155.

Cucchiara, Maia. 2013. "'Are We Doing Damage?' Choosing an Urban Public School in an
Era of Parental Anxiety." *Anthropology and Education Quarterly*, 44 (1). Retrieve from:
http://o-search.proquest.com.read.cnu.edu/socabs/docview/1313253716/abstract/
46757C66404C46C9PQ/13?accountid=10100.

Devine, Dympna. 2009. "Mobilising Capitals? Migrant Children's Negotiation of Their
Everyday Lives in School." *British Journal of Sociology of Education*, 30 (5): 521–535.
doi:http://o-dx.doi.org.read.cnu.edu/10.1080/01425690903101023.

Devine, Dympna. 2013. "Practicing Leadership in Newly Multi-Ethnic Schools: Tensions in the Field?" *British Journal of Sociology of Education*, 34 (3). Retrieved from:
http://o-search.proquest.com.read.cnu.edu/socabs/docview/1346911067/abstract
/6E81A543FEC45B2PQ/6?accountid=10100.

Duggan, Lisa. 2004. *The Twilight of Equality?: Neoliberalism, Cultural Politics, and the
Attack on Democracy*. Boston: Beacon Press.

Eliasoph, Nina. 1999. "Everyday Racism in a Culture of Political Avoidance: Civil Society, Speech, and Taboo." *Social Problems*, 46 (4): 479–502.

Frankenberg, Ericka. 2006. "The Segregation of American Teachers." Cambridge, MA:
The Civil Rights Project at Harvard University.

Frankenberg, Ruth. 1993. *White Women, Race Matters: The Social Construction of Whiteness*. Minneapolis, MN: University of Minnesota, 1993.

Gilens, Martin. 1996. "'Race Coding' and White Opposition to Welfare." *American Political Science Review* 90 (3): 593–604.

Hsu, Ruth Y. 1996. "'Will the Model Minority Please Identify Itself?' American Ethnic Identity and Its Discontents." *Diaspora: A Journal of Transnational Studies*, 5 (1): 37–64.

Hughey, Matthew W. 2012. "Color Capital, White Debt, and the Paradox of Strong White Racial Identities." *Du Bois Review* 9 (1): 169–200. doi:http://o-dx.doi.org.read.cnu .edu/10.1017/S1742058X11000506.

Hughey, Matthew W., and W. Carson Byrd. 2013. "The Souls of White Folk beyond Formation and Structure: Bound to Identity." *Ethnic and Racial Studies*, 36 (6): 974–981. doi:10.1080/01419870.2013.753153.

McCarthy, Cameron. 1994. "Multicultural Discourses and Curriculum Reform: A Critical Perspective." *Educational Theory*, 44 (1): 81–98. doi:10.1111/j.1741-5446.1994.00081.x.

Nieto, Sonia, and Patty Bode. 2011. *Affirming Diversity: The Sociopolitical Context of Multicultural Education, 6th ed.* Boston, MA: Pearson.

Ogbu, John. 1995. "Cultural Problems in Minority Education: Their Interpretations and Consequences- Part One: Theoretical Background." *The Urban Review*, 27 (3): 189–205.

Omi, Michael, and Howard Winant. 1994. *Racial Formation in the United States: From the 1960's to the 1990's*, 2nd ed. New York, NY: Routledge.

Pierre, Jemima. 2004. "Black Immigrants in the United States and the 'Cultural Narratives' of Ethnicity." *Identities*, 11 (2): 141–70.

Randolph, Antonia. 2013. *The Wrong Kind of Different: Challenging the Meaning of Diversity in American Classrooms.* New York, NY: Teachers College Press.

Reay, Diane, Sumi Hollingworth, Katya Williams, Gill Crozier, Fiona Jamieson, David James, and Phoebe Beedell. 2007. "'A Darker Shade of Pale?' Whiteness, the Middle Classes and Multi-Ethnic Inner City Schooling." *Sociology*, 41 (6): 1041–1060. doi:10.1177/0038038507082314.

Theodorou, Eleni, and Loizos Symeou. 2013. "Experiencing the Same but Differently: Indigenous Minority and Immigrant Children's Experiences in Cyprus." *British Journal of Sociology of Education*, 34 (3). Retrieved from: http://o-search.proquest.com .read.cnu.edu/socabs/docview/1346910986/abstract/6E81A543FEC45B2PQ/5 ?accountid=10100.

Tyack, David. 2003. *Seeking Common Ground: Public Schools in a Diverse Society.* Cambridge, MA: Harvard University Press.

Waldinger, Roger, and Michæl I. Lichter. 2003. *How the Other Half Works: Immigration and the Social Organization of Labor.* Berkeley, CA: University of California Press.

Wetherell, Margaret, and Jonathan Potter. 1992. *Mapping the Language of Racism: Discourse and the Legitimation of Exploitation.* New York, NY: Columbia University Press.

CHAPTER 18

The Spectacle of Volunteerism: Aid, Africa, and the Western Helper

Michele C. Deramo

1   Introduction

Higher education makes the case for preparing students to live and work in a globalized world. Its methods for achieving this outcome include internationalizing the content of the curriculum, increasing opportunities for undergraduates to travel abroad for academic study, immersing students in cultural diversity, and engaging students in community service. According to strategic planning documents at a land grant university in the southeastern United States, the institution has as its 2013–2018 goal that it "prepare students for global leadership and service by increasing opportunities to engage in study, research, internships, and participation in service-learning projects that involve international issues" (Envisioning Virginia Tech, 18). This essay focuses on the rise of service abroad experiences for college students, for the purpose of interrogating the assumptions of intercultural competence and global awareness that are its presumed learning outcomes. Specifically, I am interested in programs that target African nations as sites for global learning and recipients of Western globalization. What do students learn through these encounters constructed around themes of service? Is the learning reciprocated by any measureable benefit to the host sites? Or is volunteerism a spectacle that furthers a Western agenda through positive public relations? The answers to these questions give insight into both the limits of these programs in achieving their desired learning outcomes, as well as the inadequacy of how these outcomes are defined.

I begin the chapter with an autoethnographic framing of my inquiry, followed by an analysis of the visual discourse surrounding international volunteering from a Western perspective. I proceed with an overview of volunteerism in African nations that includes long-term opportunities of six months in-country or longer, as well as short-term experiences, some of which are less than ten days in length. I examine how the discourse of the "Western helper," a term I use to describe a relation of power evident in particular representations of volunteerism, is manifest in program design and delivery. I conclude by suggesting an alternative model that shifts the discourse toward a cosmopolitan response that is rooted in curiosity, intelligence, and global citizenship.

1.1   *Framing the Inquiry*

I approach this inquiry with a particular bias, one that is seeded and nurtured by a Roman Catholic childhood. Some of the earliest messaging I received came from the Maryknoll magazines that covered my grandmother's kitchen table along with her rosary beads and prayer cards. The covers of this pocket-sized magazine featured scenes from the missionary fields: nuns, priests, and lay people working with the world's poorest people in places like Taiwan, Peru, and Sudan. The magazine was as plain as the religious sisters it followed, yet it served as a threshold to a world beyond my own, a world that was exotic and primitive and needful.

Maryknoll magazine served to powerfully imprint in my consciousness both a disposition toward charitable work as an element of faith, as well as visual representations of who was a helper and who was helped. As a child, I did not question the presence of mostly white religious missionaries among the darker skinned peoples of the world. Nor was this visual relationship deeply considered once I began my professional career in higher education as a director of community service-learning. The association of social need with communities of color had been ingrained and naturalized in my consciousness.

Over time this association became explicit when reading students' reflections and seeing that the learning emerging from the service encounters perpetuated the status quo: instead of questioning the inequities, students professed gratitude for their privileged place in society. Even after designing better reflection prompts and engaging more vigorously with students' reflection processes, the results fell short of the lofty outcomes we espoused. By the time I left the service-learning field after twenty years, I had grown skeptical of service-learning's capacity to reach the level of critical awareness that prompted systematic change. The amount of effort needed to produce critical results was not feasible through an institutional structure that measured success through hours of service and numbers of students.

The commodification of community service scales up when service is linked to concepts like global, globalized, and globalization that are insufficiently analyzed for meaning and subsequently conflated with market-driven outcomes. Ivan Illich's speech to North American volunteers illuminates this point: "Next to money and guns, the third largest North American export is the U.S. idealist, who turns up in every theater of the world: the teacher, the volunteer, the missionary, the community organizer, the economic developer, and the vacationing do-gooders." (1968) Illich's speech was made at a time of rising global industrial development and the emergence of the Peace Corps. It is from this context that he critiques the efforts of international volunteers as emissaries of a capitalist society. Nevertheless, his biting commentary stands the test of time. Educators and organizations engaged in social justice and development work continue to use Illich's speech to prompt critical reflection.

More recently, critics use social media to amplify their message and counter the spectacle of Western helpfulness. Nigerian-American author and photographer Teju Cole responded to the viral success of the Kony 2012 campaign[1] with a seven-part Twitter response that began "From Sachs to Kristof to Invisible Children to TED, the fastest growth industry in the US is the White Savior Industrial Complex." (2012) And, the Africa for Norway campaign[2] and its Rusty Radiator Awards (http://www.rustyradiator.com),[3] founded by the Norwegian Students' and Academics' International Assistance Fund (SAIH), creates humorous videos such as "Who Wants to Be a Volunteer?" to raise awareness of the harmful effects of communications and fundraising campaigns that rely upon stereotypes of hunger, crime, and poverty in Africa.

2   Representations of Volunteerism

The specter of imperialism resides in the person of the unreflective idealist—from the United States and elsewhere in the Global North—whose exercise of national power and ideology is cloaked in helpfulness. This specter is evident in the representations of volunteers and beneficiaries. At my institution, there is a poster series for the Division of Student Affairs Aspirations for Student

---

1 Kony 2012 was a film produced by *Invisible Children, Inc.* for the purpose of raising global awareness of the war crimes enacted by Joseph Kony, a central African warlord notorious for recruiting child soldiers, in order to have Kony arrested by the end of the year. The film went viral, garnering over 100 million views to date. The film was coupled with a publicity campaign that included hanging posters and wearing wrist bands bearing the words: Kony 2012. While the film and campaign had high-level supporters such as Human Rights Watch, it also had critics, many from Ugandans and Ugandan organizations that questioned the legitimacy of the campaign and its oversimplification of events in the country.

2 The Africa for Norway campaign spoofed celebrity-driven efforts like Band Aid by featuring young Africans wearing Radi-Aid t-shirts collecting radiators for the freezing people in Norway and African musicians singing, "Now the tables have turned ... Now it's Africa for Norway." Published on YouTube November 16, 2012.

3 The Rusty Radiator Awards, launched in 2013, is an anti-award that goes to fundraising videos with the worst use of stereotypes. The organization also has a Golden Radiator award for those videos that use creativity and engagement to further understanding of complex issues.

Learning. One of these aspirations, Courageous Leadership, has a poster featuring a white female on a project somewhere in Africa. The student is glancing over her shoulder, a smile on her face while walking down a long road, accompanied by four barefoot children. The poster situates this student as the courageous leader who, according to the aspirations, is "willing to challenge the status quo in pursuit of a more humane and just world" and "speak up when they witness an injustice and reach out to those who are vulnerable, marginalized, or in need of assistance." (Division of Student Affairs, "Our Aspirations for Student Learning"). The positionality of the courageous leader is marked by the volunteer's nationality, race, and dress: the white sneakers and hoodie, the North Face backpack, the neatly pinned hair. She is a clean, bright contrast to the dusty children in ragged clothes who hold tightly on her hands. The poster includes the quote from Ralph Waldo Emerson: "Do not follow where the path may lead. Go instead where there is no path and leave a trail." Even though the volunteer is clearly some place, the quote suggests that she, the courageous leader, is the one who signifies the location.

Representations of volunteers working in Africa have contributed to a discourse reifying Africa as a place of need, and the Western Helper as its resolution. The poster described above is not unique in this regard. I enter the words "volunteering Africa" in an Internet search engine. Over half of the 50 images on the first page show photographs of young, predominantly White women with dark-skinned children. In their midst, the volunteer stands out like a beacon. As a whole, the images construct a view of an undifferentiated Africa as the naïve child, and the volunteer, in a retreat from the privilege of her ordinary life, as the parent. Typically, the volunteers are not shown doing any particular kind of work. The images are staged with the children as props around the volunteer. The purposes of the photographs are not to convey information about development or relief work, but rather to recruit participants from a particular segment of the Western population to buy an experience that is at once exotic, adventurous, and altruistic. And, while altruism may indeed be a motivating factor for the volunteers who join the experience, the question remains about the value of their presence.

The persistent use of children in visual communications is not limited to volunteer appeals. According to historian Emily Baughan, depictions of women and children in humanitarian appeals dates back to the mid-eighteenth century when new print medias began publicizing stories about the sufferings of people in far off lands. In these appeals, the "distant stranger" was never equal to the benefactor whose giving was invested with righteousness, as evident in the supplicant posturing of the stranger. Women and children in particular were considered to be blameless and helpless, thereby obscuring the complexity of politics and creating instead an illusion of innocence that positions the distant stranger as devoid of political ideals and agency. (Baughan 2015)

The images of fair-haired helpers with their arms wrapped around smiling black children mask the deeper and more difficult entanglements of Western nations and their former colonies. Indeed, volunteers deliver more than their talents, skills, and care to the environments where they are placed. They also embody and transport a system of values that are inserted into the culture through the act of helping. While the premise is to do good and alleviate suffering, the intervention of a particular set of visitors from advanced capitalist nations into villages with underdeveloped infrastructures and higher rates of illiteracy, food insecurity, disease, and poverty reinforces the inequality and exploitation of one nation over another.

In his book, *The Uncertain Business of Doing Good: Outsiders in Africa*, documentarian Larry Krotz explores the varieties of encounters occurring between individuals engaged in extended humanitarian and medical work in Africa and those with whom they work. He raises a series of important questions about the attitudes and motivations of those who are genuinely desirous of affecting positive change, yet perplexed by the realities they find. Despite their perplexity, they remain determined to forge ahead with their mission. What are the impacts of their dedication? Often, the work yields good results—the outsiders he follows are all experts in their fields. However, the results are limited. The structural change imagined for these efforts never actually happens. Further, the outside experts unwittingly assume the position of the powerful upon whom the "African" is dependent. Consequently, the need for the continuous stream of volunteers remains, whether the volunteers are professionals engaged in public health, civil engineering, and agricultural projects, or helpful visitors playing with children at orphanages.

3   Overview of Volunteerism in Africa

A survey of organizations sending volunteers to Africa presents an array of options ranging from voluntourism and mission work to collaborative educational ventures mediated by third-party providers and placements with non-governmental and charitable organizations through the United Nations Volunteer (UNV) program or governmental programs such as the Peace Corps. A conservative estimate of 2008 figures provided by Brookings Institution analysts suggests that over one million Americans are reported volunteering abroad. This figure includes the Peace Corps, as well as smaller programs categorized as generalist, professional, corporate, and faith-based. The faith-based category does not include volunteerism that is linked to proselytizing.

Opportunities through large scale organizations such as the UNV and Peace Corps require placements of one year or longer and expect their applicants to complete a rigorous vetting process, followed by an equally rigorous training period that includes language immersion. These organizations have bureaucratic structures that develop placements in concert with nationally and internationally articulated priorities, and systematically track volunteer placement and project outputs. According to its 2013 Annual Report, the UNV placed 6,301 volunteers in 152 countries, with 80% of the volunteers coming from the global south. Recognizing the role that volunteers can play in advancing peace and development worldwide, the United Nations promotes volunteerism not only as an intervention, but also as a means for building civil society within countries where conflict, natural disaster, or underdevelopment weakens the social fabric. The UNV is unique in its emphasis on promoting national volunteerism in developing countries. In addition to its careful documentation of numbers of volunteers sent to, sent from, and working within their own country, there is also a strong rhetorical weight given to stories of people, often young professionals, who are engaged in civic projects in their own country. A visual comparison is worth noting as well. All of the photographs in the annual report show the volunteers doing something specific—teaching a class, conducting a meeting, conferring with elders on a plot of land, and so forth. While the UNV does place volunteers from Europe, Australia, and the United States in developing countries, these volunteers tend to not be highlighted in the report.

The Peace Corps, an extension of the United States' diplomatic efforts, uses "soft power"[4] to promote democracy and address key areas such as education, youth and community development, health, business and information & communication technology, agriculture, environment, and food security. Notably, the Peace Corps has mandated that all volunteers serving throughout Africa and the Caribbean be trained to address the HIV/AIDS crisis, regardless of their primary assignment objectives. Currently, the Peace Corps sends 45% of its 6,818 volunteers to countries in Africa. (Peace Corps Fast Facts, retrieved November 3, 2015)

The UNV and Peace Corps represent two large-scale volunteer programs responsible for placing significant numbers of volunteers across the global south. However, they are representative of only a portion of the volunteers traveling to Africa. It is far more difficult to capture comprehensive data on the total

---

4 A policy brief from The Brookings Institution identifies international volunteering as the most important of the "soft power" programs of the United States government for improving international relations and contributing directly and indirectly to national security.

number of volunteers that go to various parts of Africa.[5] According to a brief prepared by the Center for Social Development, only 15% of international volunteers are in-country for six months or more, with 45% spending two weeks or less. Most volunteers are very young—between 15–24 years (26.8%), White (87%), and affluent (48% from households earning over $100,000). Many lack the language proficiency needed to communicate directly and effectively with the very people they have gone to help.

Two of the more reputable organizations specializing in short term international volunteerism are Cross Cultural Solutions and Global Volunteers. Both were granted Special Consultative Status by the United Nations. Special consultative status is granted to nongovernmental organizations that have a special competence in, and are concerned specifically with, only a few of the fields of activity covered by the United Nations Department of Economic and Social Affairs. These organizations tend to be smaller and more recently established. Their work aligns with United Nations priorities and deliberations.

Cross Cultural Solutions, founded in 1995, offers volunteer stints ranging from one to twelve weeks in length, with destinations in Morocco, Ghana, and Tanzania. Its clientele range from teens traveling independently, to families and corporate groups wanting unique bonding experiences. Its website makes the claim that "the change we all wish to see won't be realized through big, sweeping acts—not by governments, or armies, or the UN" but through "small, personal acts of kindness and selflessness, and through the spreading of tolerance and understanding between people and cultures."

Global Volunteers, founded in 1984, a decade before the rise of "volunteer vacations," likewise conducts programs in Ghana, Tanzania, and South Africa for a broad clientele. Branding its work as "Travel that feeds the soul" the organization provides short-term experiences of one–three weeks, and extended experiences of up to 24 weeks. Its website includes a list of endorsements from news agencies and travel magazines extolling the organization as a standard bearer in the field of voluntourism.

3.1   *Interrogating Volunteerism Abroad*
Is it possible for a continuous cycle of untrained, short-term volunteers to make a difference? Global Volunteers asserts that while the impact of any single

---

5 Volunteer programs in Africa tends to be based in Ghana, Tanzania, Uganda, and South Africa. Global Volunteers also has a program in Kenya and with the Masai. Volunteer 4 Africa also works in Ethiopia, Senegal, and Togo. Madibas, a "Responsible Travel company" that invites its clients to be more than a tourist—"to be a traveler, a conservationist and a humanitarian" is based in South Africa with offices in the U.S. and the U.K. It has the broadest range of options, including Lesotho, Namibia, Botswana, Zimbabwe, Mozambique, Zambia, Madagascar, Malawi, and Swaziland.

volunteer is small, the long-term organizational relationships do add up to some significant results. Its website dedicates significant space to defining Global Volunteers' organizational philosophy of service, which emphasizes collaboration with local and grassroots leadership and the willingness to learn from and share in the life of others. The statement also discusses the role of the outsider as someone who "can provide some catalytic assistance to empower others toward self-reliance" but whose position is "vital, albeit precarious."[6] Global Volunteers offers this critical reflection on the power inequities inherent in volunteerism:

> We have found that people everywhere need and want to share their personal gifts and talents. However, it is not always easy for individuals to discern how to best make this type of contribution. Global Volunteers affords such an opportunity. A contemporary theologian observed that the poor of the world are enslaved; they are shackled by their struggle for daily subsistence. He also observed that the affluent of the world are likewise enslaved; they are chained to their material possessions. We are both enslaved, and thus, neither the economically poor nor the economically affluent can fully appreciate the full value of life.
>
> Global Volunteers offers the possibility to shatter those chains. Many of our service programs are in rural communities in developing countries, emerging democracies and economically impoverished villages and small towns in developed countries. By working with and learning from economically struggling people, the materially affluent volunteers can learn first-hand that the mere acquisition of possessions is not a very satisfying route to happiness and that love and friendship, stable families and vibrant communities can be reality, even amidst enormous hardship. At the same time, the economically poor can acquire new skills and catalytic assistance from the volunteers, thus creating new possibilities for self-reliance as they continue to enjoy the richness of their culture, communities and simplicity of life.

Philbrook's bid for reciprocity across the gulf of economic difference tends to spiritualize the potential for change, keeping it personal—at least for the volunteer, and to romanticize the poor as happy despite their privation. The interrogation of power relations and distribution of wealth is absent from this framing of reciprocity. Hence, Philbrook constructs an abstraction whereby

---

6   Strategy for Development A PHILOSOPHY OF SERVICE by Global Volunteers Co-founder and President Burnham J. Philbrook, Copyright 2006. Retrieved July 7, 2011 from http://www .globalvolunteers.org.

the communal alienation affecting some wealthy nations is equivalent to grinding material poverty and civil instability. The relations of poor and rich nations remains unexamined. It is unlikely that a two-week immersion of the affluent Western helper in undeveloped communities will prompt the level of critical reflection that can lead to transformative change that extends beyond the personal to the social and political.

Cross Cultural Solutions also has an international infrastructure that works with 250 in-country staff members. Its mission and core values are based in the concepts of shared humanity, respect, and integrity, as well as the belief that cultural difference can be an asset rather than a barrier to solving social problems. Volunteer impact surveys conducted with Cross Cultural Solutions' in-country partners use satisfaction ratings and anecdotes to provide evidence of social impact. Feedback suggests that the presence of volunteers enhances the work of organization, in part because the volunteers are culturally different.

A supervisor from a primary school in South Africa wrote: "The children are very happy! The volunteers have contributed to improving the attendance of the school. The children don't want to miss a day. Parents say their children insist on coming rain or shine. Volunteers have also helped us meet our government's social service evaluation standards." Another supervisor with an orphanage in Ghana indicated that the volunteers' work influenced local action: "Some of the children in public schools will now visit us to interact with the orphans and learn songs, rhymes, poems, and games that they've learned from the volunteers. To us, this is a huge impact—other children now realize that orphans have something to share, too.... Also, people in the community have begun volunteering to help at the orphanage."[7]

Both anecdotes point to meaningful positive impacts—increased school attendance, the achievement of national metrics, the acceptance and inclusion of marginalized populations into the community. Most interesting is the point of how the helpfulness of Western volunteers inspires locals to be helpful as well. Volunteerism is celebrated as a value in itself—the coming together of diverse peoples and groups, the enthusiasm of a common project, the pleasure of doing good work.

But is good will good enough? Neither of the organizations address, for example, why there are so many orphans in the first place. Nor do they state why the Western helper is needed to travel far distances to improve the life circumstances of these orphans. Or why an orphanage system is the best way to manage all of these children who are not being cared for by relatives. And, by the way, where are the relatives—are they deceased? Incapacitated? Are they

---

7   From the Cross Cultural Solutions website: http://www.crossculturalsolutions.org/. See *Volunteer Impact Ensuring our Volunteer's Impact on the Community Remains Positive.*

unable to provide? Were the children removed from their families, brought to the orphanages by neighbors, or found wandering alone and given shelter? Thus, volunteers see only the need and not the complex historical and cultural circumstances underlying the need.

And then there is the question of return on investment. It costs a minimum of $3,251 (without airfare, visa, and immunization fees) for someone to travel from the United States to Ghana (as an example) for a two-week experience through Cross Cultural Solutions.[8] The program fee alone insures that only those people with sufficient disposable income can consider a foray of this kind. Is the work accomplished and the relationships formed during that brief period worth the cost and effort taken to get there and get established? Would the money raised to purchase an experience that is transformative primarily for the Western visitor be spent more effectively in other ways? Would the talents and energy expended by local hosts and administrators in the receiving countries be better directed to other ends? Esther Wanjiku Chege, teacher and educator in Kenya, believes that the cost-benefit ratio of hosting volunteers largely depends on their professional output, particularly the skills and abilities the volunteers bring. "Those with specializations tend to benefit the organizations more than the cost incurred. However, if there is no specialization, the cost and the benefit tend to balance" (Facebook correspondence, March 14, 2011). In other words, any gains for the recipients are ephemeral, lasting only as long as the volunteer's visit. For some indigenous grassroots organizations, even these ephemeral gains have value. Alfred Onyango who works with the Angira Development Community said that Western volunteers are "handy" because African organizations "lack adequate funds to pay workers at the community level" (Email correspondence, March 12, 2011). Yet, the provision of free labor inhibits local entrepreneurship and other initiatives that could reverse an economy built upon unreliable revenue.

An assessment of the value of volunteerism is not limited to short-term experiences. In 2008, Robert Strauss, a former Peace Corps volunteer, recruiter, and country director, raised critical questions about the evolution of sending what he calls "too many innocents abroad." His New York Times Opinion piece made the claim that the agencies' need to keep its numbers robust trumped the quality of work accomplished, "perhaps because the agency fears that an objective assessment of its impact would reveal that while volunteers generate good will for the United States, they do little or nothing to actually aid

---

8   "Ghana—Meet the Family You Never Knew You Had" on Cross Cultural Solutions website, http://www.crossculturalsolutions.org/destinations/volunteer-ghana, accessed November 18, 2015.

development in poor countries" (January 9, 2008). Strauss, who is now a management consultant, even went so far as to charge that the agency was neglecting its customers (the communities hosting volunteers) when it relied solely on personal anecdote and volunteer satisfaction polls rather than systematic evaluations of projects and project communities. Perhaps the most compelling point in Strauss' argument was the arrogance of sending inexperienced volunteers to poor countries under the assumption that their privilege and status as Americans qualified them to propose solutions in places where they had no experience:

> In Cameroon, we had many volunteers sent to serve in the agriculture program whose only experience was puttering around in their mom and dad's backyard during high school. I wrote to our headquarters in Washington to ask if anyone had considered how an American farmer would feel if a fresh-out-of-college Cameroonian with a liberal arts degree who had occasionally visited Grandma's cassava plot were sent to Iowa to consult on pig-raising techniques learned in a three-month crash course. I'm pretty sure the American farmer would see it as a publicity stunt and a bunch of hooey, but I never heard back from headquarters.

Needless to say, Strauss' opinions generated significant response, including a statement from the National Peace Corps Association president, Kevin Quigley, who defended the agency as having a three-fold mission that included cross-cultural and diplomatic objectives, as well as development goals. Overall, the responses, whether they were in agreement with Strauss or not, agreed that the Peace Corps' greatest value was its impact on the volunteers.

If this critique is leveled against Peace Corps volunteers who are vetted and trained prior to placement and then committed to a 27-month stay, what can be said about the volunteers who simply drop in to developing countries for short-term placements? Even if the volunteers conscientiously observe the mission of their service providers, are they prepared to negotiate the cultural, social, and political complexities they are bound to face? What tools do they bring with them to mediate these challenges? Or, do they enact through their naïveté yet another form of neo-colonialism where they unwittingly advance a Western globalization agenda in otherwise independent states? Indeed, has volunteerism become the grand narrative of powerful countries (specifically, the United States)?

Mabel Erasmus (2011), a professor of Higher Education Studies at the University of Free State, has observed helpful visitors coming to her country "for the purpose of 'doing good' and 'helping' 'poor' South Africans," bringing with them gifts of toys, boxes of crayons, and clothes—items that are fun for children to receive, but not vital to their well-being or particularly meaningful contributions to the community. She has also observed students whose faculty-led visits were part of international service-learning experiences, and noted that these volunteers had an entirely different approach—one that was grounded in academic content and thoughtful pedagogy. Initially, Erasmus had misgivings about importing a United States educational approach based on the actions of the United States in the world. However, because she had cultivated collegial relationships with her colleagues in the United States, and trusted the individuals who engaged in service-learning praxis, Erasmus determined that a closer inquiry was needed:

> In view of the persistence of the wide gap between what is stipulated by the South African constitution, on the one hand, and the harsh realities of the lives of the majority of people in the country, on the other, we ... realize that we need to work closely with colleagues in the United States and other countries in our efforts to find more effective ways to prepare students for their future roles as responsible citizens and leaders of their countries and the world.
>
> ERASMUS, 349

Thus, international service-learning held promise insofar as it presented new opportunities for South Africans who would be authors of their own future rather than recipients of externally delivered aid.

4   Is International Service-learning a Solution?

International service-learning represents the intersection of three distinct educational domains: service-learning, study abroad, and international education. ISL draws strengths from each of these educational strategies, however it is the principles of mutual benefit and reciprocity that define best practices in service-learning that transforms the ISL exchange. Service-learning researchers, Robert Bringle and Julie Hatcher, provide an operative definition:

> ISL is a structured academic experience in another country in which students (a) participate in an organized service activity that addresses identified community needs; (b) learn from direct interaction and cross-cultural dialogue with others; and (c) reflect on the experience in

such a way as to gain further understanding of course content, a deeper understanding of global and intercultural issues, a broader appreciation of the host country and the discipline, and an enhanced sense of their own responsibilities as citizens, locally and globally.

BRINGLE, *HATCHER*, 19, 2011

Among the assumptions underpinning international service-learning is the notion of humility on the part of the volunteers whose decision to travel and serve abroad is embedded in the larger objective of purposeful learning. The context for learning is critical reflection, where actions are followed by dialogue and self-interrogation, which presumably leads to new action, in an ever-deepening cycle of discovery. The engagement is dynamic and the volunteers are prepared to be challenged and, ultimately, to be changed by their encounters. At the same time, the volunteers, who are first and foremost learners, are prepared to do work that draws upon their own skill sets and contributes something worthwhile to the communities they are visiting.

The notion of humility, described in the literature as "listening to the community," counters the spectacle of an increasingly commercialized volunteerism industry. Whereas most purveyors of international experiences claim that their activities are developed in concert with local partners, not all incorporate a means for critically examining the relationships of helper and helped through a lens of sociopolitical theory. In fact, power relations often remain unchanged, so that the presence of need becomes in itself an economic engine that brings external support to under-resourced areas. Conversely, well-designed international service-learning initiatives can act to unveil these relations and give voice to multiple narratives.

At Swarthmore College, an undergraduate who participated in a course on Democracy in Action developed a community service-learning project as an exchange student at the University of Western Cape, Cape Town, whereby he involved youth at a newly integrated high school, Zonnebloem, in learning the skills of active citizenship. The development of an active citizenry is a priority in post-apartheid South Africa, and the project was designed to impart skills such as community needs assessment to youngsters who would then enact them in their community. In this example, the Zonnebloem youngsters learned something that would enable them to have structural impact on the emerging democracy in their nation. Yet, the Swarthmore student experienced deeper insights about democracy as well. While he began his project well-informed about the democratic traditions in the United States, he realized through his service-learning that he could not merely transpose this tradition to South

Africa. What made the exchange successful was his uncovering and raising up of the indigenous democratic traditions articulated by Steven Biko, Nelson Mandela, Sol Plaatjes, and Mohandas Gandhi. (Mendel-Reyes and Weinstein 1996) The Zonnebloem youth responded more readily to the homegrown theories than to ideas transplanted from the United States, and therefore could situate their own action within a South African democratic tradition. If the Swarthmore student had not been mindful of this fact when he tried to teach democratic action through a North American lens, the project may have unfolded as an interesting activity that concluded when the student left, instead of becoming an integral component of the school's curriculum in line with national objectives.

Another feature of the Swarthmore student's experience that is worth noting here is the fact that his service-learning occurred as part of an international exchange with a South African university. The significance of this detail is that the student entered the country as a learner, rather than as a helper. He participated in coursework in classrooms led by South African educators. He studied alongside South Africans who shared concerns about democracy and citizen action. Presumably, he was immersed in local culture, living in student housing with South African students, eating in the dining halls, and socializing in the local taverns. Consequently, the student's capacity to receive from the experience was enlarged beyond the personal or spiritual. His total experience served to link local concerns with national, international and intellectual affairs, thereby redrawing the parameters of citizenship beyond the borders of nations to the global.

The Swarthmore example demonstrates what Longo and Saltmarsh propose when they advocate for a reframing of language from international to global service-learning. According to Longo and Saltmarsh, the international coinage tends to place greater emphasis on the location of the service, whereas a global framing points toward outcomes that transcend the issues particular to bordered nations. These outcomes include the kinds of competencies typically associated with study abroad programs—language skills, knowledge of the host country, and intercultural sensitivity, as well as the knowledge and dispositions to navigate and act within contexts where "there is no script." (Longo, Saltmarsh, 73, 2011) This engagement calls forth reflective inquiry "on the origins and intent of the projects in which [students] participate, the relationship of the projects to the social and power structures of the host community and country, and the degree to which their projects and activities might either perpetuate or liberate political, social, and economic structures." (Longo, Saltmarsh, 77, 2011) Within this framework, volunteerism is global citizenship, which is an expression of cosmopolitanism.

In general, universities are invested in international/global service-learning initiatives as extensions of their broader internationalization goals. Rhetorically, these goals include the value of preparing graduates to be culturally competent and civically engaged. Pragmatically, however, cultural and civic objectives are secondary to the demands of globalization, and the commodification of higher education in an increasingly competitive global market (Plater 2011, 38). Nevertheless, a growing contingent of educators and researchers (Bringle, R. & Hatcher, J. 2011; Hartman, E. 2014; Hartman, E. & Kiely, R. 2014; Talwalker, C., 2012) are invested in models of internationalization that counter Western hegemony and advance global citizenship, and regard international / global service-learning as a means for achieving this. By design, these initiatives prompt a level of critical, systemic reflection that would otherwise remain buried in the myth of American exceptionalism:

> If proponents of international education are really to foster global civil society and citizenship, the task is twofold. First, students (and their teachers) must get out of the United States for a significant part of their education. Second, and no less important, *the United States must get out of the students* (and their teachers). In other words, faculty and higher education administrators should be working against the "relentless commodification" of everything ... to help students understand the manner in which the consumerist sensibilities to which they have been socialized distorts their understanding of other cultures and peoples.
>
> KARN, *SKELLEY,* 2004

Likewise:

> Those learning through service must share their gazes and shift their eyes away from the "others" with whom they are working, to themselves. They will then become members of the casts they analyze, alongside the communities where service is provided. They will become objects of their gazes and that of others.
>
> KAHN, 115, 2011

Thus, global / international service-learning requires extensive preparation prior to the experience that includes an examination of the United States' role in the world and the interconnectedness of Western military and colonial interventions and conditions in developing nations. Issues of reentry must also be factored into the design, in order to direct students to how they might enact their burgeoning global consciousness in their home environments. In addition to a robust program design, international service-learning initiatives must be sustained by a long-term institutional commitment that is not contingent on the leadership of a single faculty member.

Of course, as with any initiative, there are thick and thin models. Not all service-learning abroad is conducted with the level of rigor and intentionality described here. In fact, as universities promote internationalization among undergraduates and establish metrics for increasing students' travel abroad, there is likely to be a rise in short-term opportunities that accommodate academic calendars and student demand. Third party providers like Cross Cultural Solutions will continue to flourish in order to meet this growing market. The presence of a pedagogical design that is grounded in cosmopolitanism can somewhat stem the tide of volunteer spectacle by setting standards of practice that influence the work of third party providers, or works in close partnership with them—so that the provider is responsible for the logistical details while educators integrate content work with preparation, education, and reflection. Even more powerful is the prospect of conducting exchanges with universities abroad, so that Westerners can host students from Ghana or South Africa or other developing nations as helpful visitors in our own country.[9]

Hilary Kahn writes that "Neocolonialism need not be limited to situations where so-called independent states are directed by or dependent on more powerful nations; it also lurks within imperialistic attitudes that seep into ways of defining, observing, and practicing development and educational programs in international contexts" (Kahn, 115, 2011). Indeed, how institutions construct their interactions with African nations can serve to either perpetuate inequitable relations, or can establish a new ground for engagement. Language of globalization, laden as it is with the freight of consumer capitalism, should perhaps be replaced with that of global citizenship, a term based in cosmopolitan theory.

Cosmopolitanism is a philosophy based on the twin concepts of a common humanity that transcends the particularities of social and political boundaries, and a deep respect for those very particularities that distinguish groups across communities of humans. Cosmopolitanism is morally challenging insofar as it requires that we hold in tension our obligations to the world, with

---

9 For several years, I supervised a service-learning exchange that aimed to realize this purpose of reciprocal learning through civic action. Unfortunately, the requirements of the bi-lateral exchange format made it difficult to sustain.

the rights and self-determination that each group claims for itself. If we follow the critique of the Western helper to its end point, we are then left with the question of whether it is ever appropriate for the people of one nation to intervene in the circumstances of another. This problem is followed by the question of what should be done when the crises of the other produces such enormous suffering that non-response is unethical? Kwame Appiah grapples with this very problem when he addresses the question of our basic obligations to strangers in the world. He advises "the exercise of reason, not just explosions of feeling" (Appiah, 170, 2006). This means coupling engagement with intelligence and curiosity—an authentic cosmopolitan response that seeks to understand *why* before imposing a course of action that may not be in line with systemic realities. Thus, cosmopolitanism provides a way between the two poles of intrusion and inaction that presents new possibilities for transnational relationships. Specifically, global citizenship as an expression of cosmopolitanism can begin to lift the spectacle of volunteerism in order to uncover more authentic interactions that are transformative for everyone involved.

5   Conclusion

The cultivation of cosmopolitan sensibilities is now more critical than ever. I conclude this chapter in the aftermath of the November 13th ISIL attacks on Paris. My social media newsfeed is flush with posts in solidarity with Paris— news stories, photographs, memes and the ubiquitous Parisian flag filter that so many have adopted for their profile picture. As I scroll through the feed, I read a post from a young man who came to the United States as a child as a part of the mass resettlement of Somali Bantu refugees:

> I guess African lives don't matter. #more people die of poverty, violence, hunger and terrorist attacks in my continent, half of the kakuma refugee camp had been flooded with water. People have nowhere to sleep. But no body made a flag for kenya to show support. But I still prey [sic] for Paris and to those who lost their lives may Allah keep their souls at peace.

This young man, once a beneficiary of service whose introduction to this country occurred through the bodies of white volunteers, aptly observed the selective empathy of the country that is now his home, and did so by adapting the language of the Black Lives Matter movement in the United States. Which lives matter? Which lives are grievable?[10] The outpouring of emotion for Paris, compared to the dearth of awareness or recognition of conflicts occurring throughout the Global South is a harsh reminder of how unevenly human life is valued. The spectacle of public mourning for Paris occurs because they—White Europeans—are like us. The insecurity and imminent danger of terrorism is incompatible with our ideas about iconic places like Paris. However, for places like Beirut, Baghdad, and Yola, Nigeria, each struck by terrorism within the same span of time, violence and upheaval are regarded as natural occurrences in places that are always already unstable and, thus, unliveable.[11]

America's public mourning for Paris occurs within a climate of creeping xenophobia targeting in particular Muslims, dark-skinned immigrants, Syrian refugees, and anyone who phenotypically resembles them. Westerners who have historically circulated freely across the globe as soldiers, travelers, volunteers, and purveyors of both ideas and capital now exercise their right of refusal, calling instead to build walls and institute surveillance in order to protect against Brown and Black bodies that are perceived as threats. But the rhetoricians of fear are not the only voices raised in protest. On college campuses and in communities of color across the nation, a movement is growing among minoritized groups demanding recognition—that their lives *do* matter, that their lives are grievable.

It is a privilege to travel elsewhere and expect that we will be welcomed—indeed, to assume that our presence is desired. But how well do we receive those to whom we travel to help when they arrive on our territories? Indeed, how well do we live with our fellow citizens whose experiences of America are tied to histories of oppression? A global citizenship rooted in cosmopolitanism requires that we problematize our desire to help distant strangers abroad, that we interrogate the meaning of our helpfulness and situate our small acts of kindness within the larger, complex histories of intervention, occupation, and colonization. It is then, after we have engaged in deep, dialogical reflection about our positionality in the world and its relations to others—both here and abroad—that we might ask the question: How can I help?

---

10   "Grievable lives" is the central concept of Judith Butler's book, *Frames of War: When is Life Grievable?*

11   An estimated 44 terrorist attacks occurred during the month of November 2015. The attack on Paris claimed the highest number of deaths (137) and injuries (368). However, in late October a bombing in Sinai, Egypt claimed 224 lives. Earlier in the month, a suicide bombing in Ankara, Turkey resulted in 102 deaths and 538 injuries. The incidents in Sinai and Ankara did not generate a similar response from Western countries event though the number of deaths and injuries were greater. Source: "List of Terrorist Incidents, 2015" at Wikipedia, retrieved 11/30/15.

References

Appiah, Kwame Anthony. 2006. *Cosmopolitanism, Ethics in a World of Strangers*. New York: W.W. Norton & Company, Inc.

Baughan, Emily. 2015. "The Emergence of Humanitarian Appeals" in *The Radiator Report Challenging a Single Story*. Retrieved from: http://www.rustyradiator.com/africa-is-a-country/a-short-history-of-helping-far-off-peoples.

Bringle, Robert G., Julie A Hatcher. 2011. "International Service-Learning." In *International Service-Learning, Conceptual-Frameworks and Research*, IUPUI Series on Service-Learning Research, Volume I edited by Robert G. Bringle, Julie A. Hatcher, and Steven G Jones, 3–28. Sterling, Virginia: Stylus.

Erasmus, Mable. 2011. "A South African Perspective on North American International Service-Learning." In *International Service-Learning, Conceptual Frameworks and Research*, IUPUI Series on Service-Learning Research, Volume I, edited by Robert G. Bringle, Julie A. Hatcher, Steven G Jones, 347–371. Sterling, Virginia: Stylus.

Hartman, E. 2014. "Educating for Global Citizenship: A Theoretical Account and Quantitative Analysis." *eJournal of Public Affairs*, March.

Hartman, E. & R. Kiely 2014. "A Critical Global Citizenship." In *Crossing Boundaries: Tension and Transformation in International Service-Learning*, edited by M. Johnson and P.M. Green. Sterling, Virginia: Stylus Publishing.

Illich, Ivan. 1968. "To Hell with Good Intentions." Speech given at the Conference on InterAmerican Student Projects (CIASP) at St. Mary's Lake of the Woods Seminary, Chicago, April 20, 1968.

Jenkins, Karen and James Skelly. 2004. "Education Abroad is Not Enough." *International Educator*, Winter.

Kahn, Hilary E. 2011. "Overcoming the Challenges of International Service Learning, A Visual Approach to Sharing Authority, Community Development, and Global Learning." In *International Service-Learning, Conceptual Frameworks and Research*, IUPUI Series on Service-Learning Research, Volume I edited by Robert G. Bringle, Julie A. Hatcher, Steven G. Jones, 113–124. Sterling, Virginia: Stylus.

Longo, Nicholas V. and John Saltmarsh. 2011. "New Lines of Inquiry in Reframing International Service Learning into Global Service Learning." In *International Service-Learning, Conceptual Frameworks and Research*, IUPUI Series on Service-Learning Research, Volume I edited by Robert G. Bringle, Julie A Hatcher, Steven G. Jones, 69–85. Sterling, Virginia: Stylus.

Mendel-Reyes, Meta and Jeremy Weinstein. Fall 1996. "Community Service Learning as Democratic Education in South Africa and the United States." *Michigan Journal of Community Service Learning*, 3: 103–112.

Plater, William M. 2011. "The Context for International Service-Learning, An Invisible Revolution is Underway." In *International Service-Learning, Conceptual Frameworks and Research*, IUPUI Series on Service-Learning Research, Volume I edited by Robert G. Bringle, Julie A. Hatcher, Steven G Jones, 29–56. Sterling, Virginia: Stylus.

Talwalker, Clare. 2012. "What Kind of Global Citizen is the Student Volunteer?" *Journal of Global Citizenship and Equity Education*, 2 (2): 21–40.

Index

www.ingramcontent.com/pod-product-compliance
Lightning Source LLC
Chambersburg PA
CBHW062107040426
42336CB00042B/2261